DAY HIKING

The San Juans and Gulf Islands

Cypress Lake, Cypress Island

Previous Page: Iceberg Point, San Juan Islands
National Monument, Lopez Island

Fawn lilies at Whistle Lake, Fidalgo Island

Sandhill crane at Reifel Migratory Bird Sanctuary, Westham Island

Sinclair Island county dock with Cypress Island in the background

Enjoying the view from Sunset Beach on Vendovi Island

Mount Baker from Patos Island

Rainbow at Pass Lake, Deception Pass State Park, Fidalgo Island

Midden Beach on Gray Peninsula, Montague Harbour Marine Provincial Park, Galiano Island

Wide sandy beach at the top of Sidney Spit

Burgoyne Bay and Sansum Narrows from Mount Maxwell

DAY HIKING

The **San Juans** and **Gulf Islands**

saanich peninsula · anacortes · victoria

by Craig Romano

MOUNTAINEERS
BOOKS

Mountaineers Books is the nonprofit publishing division of The Mountaineers, an organization founded in 1906 and dedicated to the exploration, preservation, and enjoyment of outdoor and wilderness areas.

MOUNTAINEERS BOOKS

1001 SW Klickitat Way, Suite 201 • Seattle, WA 98134
800.553.4453 • www.mountaineersbooks.org

First edition, 2014
Printed in the United States of America
Distributed in the United Kingdom by Cordee, www.cordee.co.uk

Copy Editor: Julie Van Pelt
Book Design: Mountaineers Books
Additional Design and Layout: Jen Grable
Cartographer: Pease Press Cartography
All photographs by author unless otherwise noted.

Cover photograph: *Taylor Bay near the Malaspina Galleries, Gabriola Island*
Frontispiece: *Finlayson Arm from Jocelyn Hill, Gowlland Tod Provincial Park*

Library of Congress Cataloging-in-Publication Data
Romano, Craig.
 Day hiking : the San Juans and Gulf Islands / by Craig Romano.
  pages cm.
 ISBN 978-1-59485-758-4 (pbk.) — ISBN 978-1-59485-759-1 (ebook)
1. Hiking—Washington (State)—San Juan Islands—Guidebooks. 2. Hiking—British Columbia—Gulf Islands—Guidebooks. 3. San Juan Islands (Wash.)—Guidebooks. 4. Gulf Islands (B.C.)—Guidebooks. I. Title.
 GV199.42.W22S37 2014
 796.5109797—dc23
                          2013048310

♻ Printed on recycled paper

ISBN (paperback): 978-1-59485-758-4
ISBN (ebook): 978-1-59485-759-1

Table of Contents

Tsawwassen and Point Roberts

Gulf Islands

Victoria and Saanich Peninsula

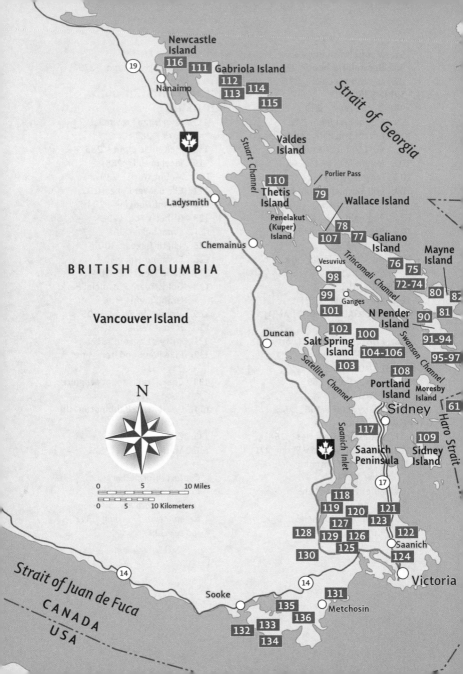

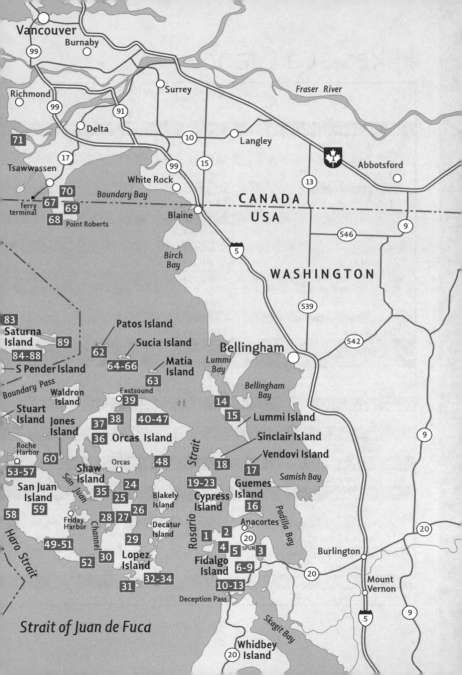

Hikes at a Glance

HIKE	DISTANCE (ROUND-TRIP)	RATING	DIFFICULTY	KID-FRIENDLY
ANACORTES AND FIDALGO ISLAND				
1. Washington Park	2.2 miles (3.5 km)	3	2	•
2. Guemes Channel and Ship Harbor	1.6 miles (2.6 km)	3	1	•
3. Tommy Thompson Trail	3.8 miles (6.1 km)	3	1	•
4. Little Cranberry Lake	1.9 miles (3.1 km)	3	2	•
5. Big Beaver Pond	2.7 miles (4.3 km)	1	1	•
6. Heart Lake	3 miles (4.8 km)	2	2	•
7. Sugarloaf	2.5 miles (4 km)	3	3	•
8. Mount Erie	5.2 miles (8.4 km)	3	3	
9. Whistle Lake	4.3 miles (6.9 km)	3	2	•
10. Sharpe Park and Montgomery-Duban Headlands	2.6 miles (4.2 km)	3	3	
11. Rosario Head	1.7 miles (2.7 km)	4	2	•
12. Lighthouse and Lottie Points	2.6 miles (4.2 km)	4	2	•
13. Pass Lake	2.8 miles (4.5 km)	2	2	•
SAN JUAN ISLANDS				
Lummi Island				
14. Otto Preserve	1.2 miles (1.9 km)	2	1	•
15. Baker Preserve	3.6 miles (5.8 km)	3	3	
Guemes Island				
16. Guemes Mountain	2.4 miles (3.9 km)	3	2	•
Vendovi Island				
17. Vendovi Island	3.2 miles (5.1 km)	5	2	•
Sinclair Island				
18. Mary Leach Natural Area	2.6 miles (4.2 km)	2	2	•
Cypress Island				
19. Eagle Cliff	2.8 miles (4.5 km)	5	3	•
20. Duck Lake and Smugglers Cove	5.1 miles (8.2 km)	3	2	•
21. Reed and Cypress Lakes	4.6 miles (7.4 km)	3	3	•
22. Strawberry Bay and Reef Point	10 miles (16.1 km)	4	5	
23. Bradberry Lake	4.8 miles (7.7 km)	3	4	
Lopez Island				
24. Upright Head Preserve	1.2 miles (1.9 km)	2	1	•

DOG-FRIENDLY	WILD-FLOWERS	BEACH WALKING	WHALE-WATCHING	OLD GROWTH	BIRD-WATCHING	HISTORICAL	CAR CAMP NEARBY	WALK-IN/BOAT ACCESSIBLE CAMPING	WHEELCHAIR ACCESS
•		•				•	•		•
•		•			•	•	•		•
•					•	•	•		•
•					•		•		
•							•		
•				•			•		
•	•			•			•		
•				•			•		
•	•			•			•		partial
				•		•	•		
		•			•	•	•	•	
•		•		•	•	•	•	•	
•				•			•		
•									
	•				•				
•	•								
•	•	•			•				
•						•			
	•			•	•			•	
•		•		•			•	•	
	•				•	•		•	
•	•	•				•		•	
•					•	•		•	
•				•			•		

HIKE	DISTANCE (ROUND-TRIP)	RATING	DIFFICULTY	KID-FRIENDLY
25. Upright Channel	3.4 miles (5.5 km)	3	1	•
26. Spencer Spit	1.2 miles (1.9 km)	3	1	•
27. Hummel Lake	2 miles (3.2 km)	2	1	•
28. Fisherman Bay Preserve: The Spit	1 mile (1.6 km)	3	1	•
29. Lopez Hill	3.1 miles (5 km)	2	2	•
30. Shark Reef Sanctuary	1 mile (1.6 km)	3	1	•
31. Iceberg Point	3.8 miles (6.1 km)	5	2	•
32. Chadwick Hill	3 miles (4.8 km)	4	3	•
33. Watmough Bay	1.3 miles (2.1 km)	3	1	•
34. Point Colville	2.2 miles (3.5 km)	4	2	•
Shaw Island				
35. Indian Cove	5.6 miles (9 km)	4	2	•
Orcas Island				
36. Turtleback Mountain Preserve: Ship Peak Loop	2.9 miles (4.7 km)	4	3	•
37. Turtleback Mountain Preserve: Turtlehead Summit	5.7 miles (9.2 km)	5	3	•
38. Judd Cove Preserve	0.6 mile (1 km)	2	1	•
39. Crescent Beach Preserve	1.5 miles (2.4 km)	1	1	•
40. Cascade Lake	2.9 miles (4.7 km)	3	2	•
41. Sunrise Rock	1.4 miles (2.3km)	2	2	
42. Cascade Falls	3.1 miles (5 km)	2	2	•
43. Mountain Lake	3.9 miles (6.3 km)	3	2	•
44. Twin Lakes and Mount Pickett	7.6 miles (12.2 km)	3	3	
45. Mount Constitution	7.1 miles (11.4 km)	5	4	
46. Cold Springs and North Trail Loop	11.4 miles (18.3 km)	5	5	
47. Southeast Boundary Trail	8.7 miles (14 km)	3	4	
48. Obstruction Pass State Park	1.9 miles (3.1 km)	3	2	•
San Juan Island				
49. American Camp and South Beach	2.8 miles (4.5 km)	5	2	•
50. Frazer Homestead Preserve	2.6 miles (4.2 km)	2	1	•
51. Mount Finlayson	3.5 miles (5.6 km)	5	2	•
52. Cattle Point	1.4 miles (2.3 km)	3	1	•
53. Bell Point and English Camp	1.7 miles (2.7 km)	3	1	•
54. Young Hill	2.2 miles (3.5 km)	4	3	•
55. Mitchell Hill	2.9 miles (4.7 km)	2	3	

DOG-FRIENDLY	WILD-FLOWERS	BEACH WALK-ING	WHALE-WATCH-ING	OLD GROWTH	BIRD-WATCH-ING	HIS-TORICAL	CAR CAMP NEARBY	WALK-IN/ BOAT ACCESSIBLE CAMPING	WHEEL-CHAIR ACCESS
•		•					•	•	
•		•			•	•	•	•	
•							•		partial
		•			•	•			partial
•	•								
•					•				
•	•		•		•				
•	•								
•		•			•				partial
•	•		•	•	•				
•		•			•		•		
•	•								
•	•								
•						•			partial
•		•							
•				•		•	•		
				•			•		
•				•		•	•		
•				•			•		
•				•					
	•					•	•		
•				•		•	•		
•				•			•		
•	•	•						•	
•	•	•				•			partial
•	•								
•		•				•			
•		•				•			
•		•				•	•		
•	•					•	•		
•				•		•	•		

HIKE	DISTANCE (ROUND-TRIP)	RATING	DIFFICULTY	KID-FRIENDLY
56. Briggs Lake	4 miles (6.4 km)	3	2	•
57. Roche Harbor: Wetlands Loop	0.8 mile (1.3 km)	2	1	•
58. Lime Kiln Point	2.2 miles (3.5 km)	4	2	•
59. King Sisters Preserve	1.4 miles (2.3 km)	2	1	•
Jones Island				
60. Jones Island	2.4 miles (3.9 km)	4	2	•
Stuart Island				
61. Turn Point	6 miles (9.7 km)	4	3	•
Outer San Juan Islands				
62. Patos Island	2.2 miles (3.5 km)	5	1	•
63. Matia Island	1.8 miles (2.9 km)	4	2	•
64. Ev Henry Finger and Johnson Point	4.7 miles (7.6 km)	5	3	•
65. Shallow Bay and Lawson Bluff	4.1 miles (6.6 km)	5	2	•
66. Ewing Cove	6 miles (9.7 km)	5	2	•
TSAWWASSEN AND POINT ROBERTS				
67. Monument Park	1.6 miles (2.6 km)	2	2	•
68. Lighthouse Marine Park	0.8 mile (1.3 km)	2	1	•
69. Lily Point	1.6 miles (2.6 km)	3	2	•
70. Boundary Bay Regional Park	2 miles (3.2 km)	3	1	•
71. George C. Reifel Migratory Bird Sanctuary	1.5 miles (2.4 km)	3	1	•
GULF ISLANDS				
Galiano Island				
72. Bellhouse Provincial Park	0.4 mile (0.6 km)	3	1	•
73. Bluffs Park	1.4 miles (2.2 km)	3	2	•
74. Mount Galiano	3.8 miles (6.1 km)	5	3	•
75. Galiano Island Heritage Forest	1.7 miles (2.8 km)	1	2	•
76. Gray Peninsula	1.5 miles (2.4 km)	4	1	•
77. Pebble Beach Reserve	2.1 miles (3.4 km)	3	2	•
78. Bodega Ridge Provincial Park	2.8 miles (4.6 km)	5	3	
79. Dionisio Point Provincial Park	3.3 miles (5.3 km)	4	2	•
Mayne Island				
80. Mount Parke	2.6 miles (4.2 km)	3	3	•
81. Henderson Community Park	0.8 mile (1.3 km)	2	2	
82. Campbell Point	1 mile (1.6 km)	4	1	•

DOG-FRIENDLY	WILD-FLOWERS	BEACH WALK-ING	WHALE-WATCH-ING	OLD GROWTH	BIRD-WATCH-ING	HIS-TORICAL	CAR CAMP NEARBY	WALK-IN/BOAT ACCESSIBLE CAMPING	WHEEL-CHAIR ACCESS
•					•				
•					•				
•			•			•	•		partial
•	•								
		•	•	•	•			•	partial
•	•		•			•		•	
•			•	•		•		•	partial
			•		•	•		•	
		•	•		•	•		•	
		•			•	•		•	
		•			•	•		•	
•		•	•		•	•	•		
•		•	•		•	•	•		•
•		•	•		•	•	•		partial
•		•	•		•	•			partial
					•				partial
•	•					•			
•	•			•					
•	•								
•									
•		•			•	•	•		
•		•				•			
	•								
•	•	•			•			•	
•	•			•					
•	•								
•		•			•				

HIKE	DISTANCE (ROUND-TRIP)	RATING	DIFFICULTY	KID-FRIENDLY
Saturna Island				
83. Winter Cove	0.9 mile (1.5 km)	2	1	•
84. Taylor Point	5.6 miles (9 km)	4	4	
85. Mount Warburton Pike	3.4 miles (5.5 km)	5	3	•
86. Lyall Creek	1.4 miles (2.3 km)	2	2	•
87. Narvaez Bay	1.8 miles (2.9 km)	3	2	•
88. Monarch Head	1.5 miles (2.4 km)	3	2	•
89. East Point	0.5 mile (0.8 km)	4	1	•
Pender Island				
90. George Hill	1.2 miles (2 km)	3	3	•
91. Clam Bay	1.4 miles (2.3 km)	2	2	•
92. Mount Menzies	0.8 mile (1.3 km)	1	2	
93. Roe Islet	0.8 mile (1.3 km)	4	1	•
94. Roe Lake	1.6 miles (2.6 km)	2	2	•
95. Mount Norman	1.8 miles (2.9 km)	3	3	•
96. Bedwell Harbour	3 miles (4.8 km)	4	3	
97. Greenburn Lake	1.4 miles (2.3 km)	2	1	•
Salt Spring Island				
98. Duck Creek	1.2 miles (1.9 km)	2	1	•
99. Mount Erskine	3.4 miles (5.5 km)	5	3	
100. Bryant Hill Park and Andreas Vogt Nature Reserve	2.9 miles (4.7 km)	2	2	•
101. Mount Maxwell	4.9 miles (7.9 km)	5	3	
102. Burgoyne Bay	1.6 miles (2.6 km)	3	1	•
103. Mill Farm and Mount Bruce	7.6 miles (12.2 km)	3	4	•
104. Reginald Hill	1.8 miles (2.9 km)	4	3	
105. Beaver Point and Ruckle Farm	1.8 miles (2.9 km)	4	1	•
106. Ruckle Provincial Park: Yeo Point	5.7 miles (9.2 km)	5	3	•
Wallace Island				
107. Chivers Point	4 miles (6.4 km)	4	2	•
Princess Margaret (Portland) Island				
108. Princes Margaret (Portland) Island	4.3 miles (6.9 km)	5	2	•
Sidney Island				
109. Sidney Spit	3.9 miles (6.3 km)	5	1	•
Thetis Island				
110. Pilkey Point	9.4 miles (15.1 km)	3	3	

DOG-FRIENDLY	WILD-FLOWERS	BEACH WALK-ING	WHALE-WATCH-ING	OLD GROWTH	BIRD-WATCH-ING	HIS-TORICAL	CAR CAMP NEARBY	WALK-IN/BOAT ACCESSIBLE CAMPING	WHEEL-CHAIR ACCESS
•		•			•				partial
		•		•		•			
•	•								
•				•					
•		•			•			•	
•									
•	•	•	•		•	•			partial
•	•								
•		•		•					
•				•					
•		•			•	•			
•						•			
•							•		
•	•	•		•	•			•	
•					•				
•				•					
	•			•					
•	•								
	•				•				
•	•				•	•			
•					•		•		
•	•								
	•	•			•	•	•		
	•				•	•	•		
•	•				•	•		•	
•		•	•		•	•		•	
•		•			•	•		•	
•					•				

HIKE	DISTANCE (ROUND-TRIP)	RATING	DIFFICULTY	KID-FRIENDLY
Gabriola Island				
111. Malaspina Galleries	1.6 miles (2.6 km)	4	2	•
112. Sandwell Provincial Park	1.4 miles (2.3 km)	3	2	•
113. 707-Acre Community Park	4.8 miles (7.7 km)	2	2	•
114. Elder Cedar Nature Reserve	1.1 miles (1.8 km)	3	2	•
115. Drumbeg Provincial Park	1.2 miles (1.9 km)	4	1	•
Newcastle Island				
116. Newcastle Island	6.4 miles (10.3 km)	5	2	•
VICTORIA AND SAANICH PENINSULA				
117. John Dean Provincial Park	2.9 miles (4.7 km)	3	3	•
118. McKenzie Bight	3.2 miles (5.1 km)	3	3	•
119. Jocelyn Hill	8.3 miles (13.4 km)	5	4	
120. Mount Work	4 miles (6.4 km)	4	4	
121. Elk/Beaver Lake	6.7 miles (10.8 km)	2	2	•
122. Mount Douglas	2.6 miles (4.2 km)	4	3	•
123. Rithet's Bog	1.9 miles (3 km)	2	1	•
124. Swan Lake	1.7 miles (2.7 km)	2	1	•
125. Thetis Lakes	3.2 miles (5.1 km)	3	2	•
126. Seymour Hill	2 miles (3.2 km)	3	3	•
127. Lone Tree Hill	1.5 miles (2.4 km)	4	3	•
128. Goldstream Provincial Park: Grand Loop	5.6 miles (9 km)	3	3	
129. Mount Finlayson	2.6 miles (4.2 km)	5	5	
130. Mount Wells	2 miles (3.2 km)	5	4	
131. Witty's Lagoon	1.6 miles (2.6 km)	3	2	•
132. Pike Point and Iron Mine Bay	2.8 miles (4.5 km)	3	1	•
133. Coast Trail: Mount Maguire Loop	10.2 mi. (16.4 km)	4	5	
134. Coast Trail: Babbington Hill Loop	7 miles (11.3 km)	5	5	
135. Cedar Grove	2.9 miles (4.7 km)	2	2	•
136. Matheson Lake	2.4 miles (3.9 km)	3	2	•

DOG-FRIENDLY	WILD-FLOWERS	BEACH WALKING	WHALE-WATCHING	OLD GROWTH	BIRD-WATCHING	HISTORICAL	CAR CAMP NEARBY	WALK-IN/BOAT ACCESSIBLE CAMPING	WHEELCHAIR ACCESS
		•			•		•		
•		•			•				
•									
•				•					
•		•			•				
•		•		•		•		•	
•	•			•		•	•		
•		•			•				
•	•				•				
•	•								
•						•			
	•			•		•			
•					•				
					•	•			
•	•								
•	•			•					
•	•								
•	•				•		•	•	
	•			•			•		
	•				•	•	•		
•	•	•			•				
•		•			•	•			•
			•		•	•			
		•	•		•	•			
•				•	•				
•					•				

Acknowledgments

Researching and writing *Day Hiking: The San Juans and Gulf Islands* was fun, exciting, and a lot of hard work. I could not have finished this project without the help and support of many people.

A huge thank you to all of the great people at Mountaineers Books, especially publisher Helen Cherullo, project manager Mary Metz, and editor in chief Kate Rogers, who was patient with all my challenges in putting this book together.

I want to especially acknowledge, once again, my editor Julie Van Pelt. I have worked with her on all of my Day Hiking books, and I feel that we have hiked the state together. Julie's professionalism and attention to detail (and dealing with all of my dangling modifiers) have greatly contributed to making this book a finer volume.

I could not have hopped twenty-eight islands and researched so many great places without the help of Barbara Marrett of the San Juan Islands Visitors Bureau,

Cathy Ray and Tessa Humphries of Tourism Victoria, Lana King and Nadine Chodl of Tourism Vancouver Island, Eric Kalnins of BC Ferries, Jesse Keefer, and Bill Eisenhauer. Thank you all.

A big *grazie* too to the following people for welcoming me aboard their vessels: Beau Brandow, Alan Hobbes Buchanan, Jake Dey, Dick Hobbis, Kurt Irwin, Walter Pfahl, Rey Rubalcava, and Chris and Toi Wright.

Thanks go out to Jack Hartt with Washington State Parks and a huge thank you to Kathleen Foley with the San Juan Preservation Trust for providing me with so much useful background information.

I want to also once again thank God for watching over me while on the trail. And lastly, but most importantly, I want to thank my loving wife, Heather, for supporting me while I worked on yet another guidebook. Thanks for hiking with me too, to some of the special places in this book, and for providing me with more precious memories.

A NOTE ABOUT SAFETY

Safety is an important concern in all outdoor activities. No guidebook can alert you to every hazard or anticipate the limitations of every reader. Therefore, the descriptions of roads, trails, routes, and natural features in this book are not representations that a particular place or excursion will be safe for your party. When you follow any of the routes described in this book, you assume responsibility for your own safety. Under normal conditions, such excursions require the usual attention to traffic, road and trail conditions, weather, terrain, the capabilities of your party, and other factors. Because many of the lands in this book are subject to development and/or change of ownership, conditions may have changed since this book was written that make your use of some of these routes unwise. Always check for current conditions, obey posted private property signs, and avoid confrontations with property owners or managers. Keeping informed on current conditions and exercising common sense are the keys to a safe, enjoyable outing.

—*Mountaineers Books*

Introduction

It was the mountains that lured me to the Pacific Northwest in the summer of 1989, and the mountains have kept me firmly planted here ever since. And while there's no shortage of excellent hiking in the Cascades, Olympics, Coast Ranges, Blues, and Selkirk Mountains, the San Juan and Gulf Islands of the region's Salish Sea should not be overlooked when it comes to fine trails. I've been hooked on hiking in these islands ever since I first took to the trails of Orcas Island's Moran State Park in the autumn of 1989.

The San Juan and Gulf Islands are a one-of-a-kind natural landmark, an archipelago of hundreds of islands, large and small, located within a vast network of coastal waterways that straddle the Washington and British Columbia border. These islands take up residence in two countries yet share a common human, cultural, and natural history. Each island also retains its own identity—its own distinct atmosphere.

This book celebrates the beauty and the natural and human history of these Salish Sea islands, along with a bit of the mainland, treating this region divided by an international border as one. You'll find 136 hikes in this guide, split roughly 50-50 between Washington and British Columbia, encompassing all of the ferry-accessible islands as well as many of the islands that are state and provincial marine parks—twenty-eight islands in all. Also included are Anacortes and Fidalgo Island, Tsawwassen and Point Roberts, and Victoria and the Saanich Peninsula—gateways to the islands that share the region's cultural, historical, and natural features.

While you may think the islands are primarily for motor- and sailboaters, kayakers and canoeists, this book aims to convince you that they are prime day-hiking destinations as well. Most hikes in this book are accessible by ferry and roads—no boat needed. And of the few islands in this book that don't have ferry access, almost all can be reached by reliable water taxi services. Some of the islands, depending on where you live, are conducive to day trips; many warrant a weekend getaway or three-day holiday excursion. Getting to them is half the fun and part of the adventure. Settle on an island for a couple of days and day hike to your heart's content.

In this book you'll find trails to secluded beaches, bays, and coves; trails on rugged coastal ledges and bluffs; trails through magnificent old-growth forests that were old even when George Vancouver sailed into the Salish Sea. You'll find trails to nature preserves, historical sites, old homesteads, lighthouses, hilltops, and open bluffs that burst with wildflowers. Choose from hikes that are perfect for children, friendly to dogs, or great for observing wildlife. Another draw of this region is its mild weather. Located directly within the rain shadow cast by the Olympics and Vancouver Island mountains, the hikes in this region are accessible (and almost always snow-free) all year round. I'm excited to share these hikes with you!

And with that, it's time once again for my "battle cry" from my previous titles in the Day Hiking series. As our world continues to urbanize—its denizens growing more sedentary, materialistic, and disconnected from the natural world each day—life for many has lost its real meaning. Nature may need us to protect it from becoming paved over—but we need nature to protect us from the encroachments of vacuous consumption and shallow pursuits. So, shun the mall, turn off the TV, ditch the smart phone, and hit the trail! Yes, you! Go take a hike! Celebrate life and return from the natural world a better and more content person.

If I'm preaching to the choir, help me then to introduce new disciples to our sacred creed. For while we sometimes relish our solitude on the trail, we need more like-minded souls to help us preserve what little wildlands remain. Help nature by introducing family members, coworkers, neighbors, children, and government officials to our wonderful trails. I'm convinced that a society that hikes is good not only for our wild and natural places (people will be willing to protect them) but also for us (we will live healthy and connected lives).

USING THIS BOOK

The Day Hiking series strikes a fine balance. The guidebooks are designed to be as easy to use as possible while still providing enough detail to help you explore a region. As a result, these books include all the information you need to find and enjoy the hikes but leave enough room for you to make your own discoveries. I have hiked every mile of these trails, so you can follow my directions with confidence. Conditions do change, however. More on that below.

What the Ratings Mean

Each hike starts with detailed trail facts. The **overall rating** of 1 to 5 stars is based on a hike's overall appeal, and the numerical **difficulty score** of 1 to 5 measures how challenging the hike is. These ratings are purely subjective, based on my impressions of each route, but they do follow a formula of sorts.

The overall **rating** is based on scenic beauty, natural wonder, and other unique qualities, such as the potential for solitude and wildlife-viewing opportunities.

***** Unmatched hiking adventure. A bucket list hike!

**** Excellent experience that ranks among the best hikes

*** A great hike that is sure to impress and inspire

** May lack exceptional scenery or unique trail experience, but offers little moments to enjoy

* Worth doing as a refreshing walk, especially if you're in the neighborhood

The **difficulty** score is based on trail length, cumulative elevation gain, steepness, and trail conditions. Generally, trails that are rated more difficult (4 or 5) are longer and steeper than average. But it's not a simple equation. A short, steep trail over uneven surfaces and ledges may be rated 5, while a long, smooth trail with little elevation gain may be rated 2.

5 Extremely difficult: excessive elevation gain and/or more than 5 miles one-way

4 Difficult: Some steep sections, possibly rough trail or poorly maintained trail

3 Moderate: A good workout but no real problems

2 Moderately easy: Relatively flat or short route with good trail

1 Easy: A relaxing stroll in the woods

Roundtrip distance is given in miles and kilometers. While I have measured most of the hikes using GPS and have consulted maps and land management agencies for all the hikes, the distance stated may not always be exact, but it'll be pretty close. Kilometers are rounded up in the hike descriptions, and the cumulative total is the proper mile equivalent.

Many of the islands' trails are kid and family friendly.

Elevation gain is given in feet and meters. It represents the *cumulative* elevation gain on a route, that is, the total amount that you'll go up on a hike. Meters are rounded up in the hike descriptions, and the cumulative total in meters is pretty close to its equivalent in feet.

A hike's **high point** is the highest elevation you'll encounter, given in feet and meters. It's worth noting that not all high points are at the end of the trail—a route may run over a ridge before dropping to the coast, for instance.

The **maps** listed for each hike are the relevant topographic maps: in the United States, US Geological Survey (USGS) or Green Trails maps; in Canada, the Centre for Topographic Information's National Topographic System (NTS) maps. When the land management agency or oversee-

ing land steward has a map available, it is referenced as well. For an excellent overview map of the San Juan Islands, complete with parks and preserves, consult Square One Maps (squareonemaps.com).

The **contact** listed for each hike is the area's land management agency or land steward. Appendix I: Contact Information contains the specific phone numbers and websites for all agencies, listed alphabetically. Always check with the governing agency before you set out, to get current information about trail conditions and any permit or fee requirements.

Notes for each trip detail things like permits required, possible hazards, and seasonal closures.

Trailhead **GPS coordinates** are provided to help get you to the trail—and back to your car if you wander off-trail.

Icons at the start of each hike give a quick overview of each trail's offerings:

Kid-friendly

Dog-friendly

Exceptional wildflowers in season

Beach-walking opportunities

Whale-watching

Exceptional old-growth forest

Exceptional bird-watching

Historical relevance

The route descriptions tell you what you might find on a hike, including geographic features, scenic potential, flora and fauna, and

A heron looks for dinner in Wittys Lagoon.

Certain restrictions apply in regard to crossing the border. Due to heightened concern over child abduction, children traveling with one parent, grandparents, or guardian(s) should carry proof of custody or a letter authorizing travel from the non-accompanying parent(s). This is in addition to proof of the child's citizenship. Anyone with a criminal record (including a drunk-driving conviction) may be barred entry into Canada. There are also limits and restrictions on what you can take over the border (foods, weapons, etc.). Consult US Customs and Border Protection (www.cbp.gov/travel), the Canada Border Services Agency (www.cbsa-asfc.gc.ca/menu-eng.html), and the US Embassy (for information for Canadians: http://canada.usembassy.gov/visas/information-for-canadians.html).

more. Driving directions from the nearest large town or ferry terminal (for the islands) will get you to the trailhead. Options for Extending Your Trip round out many hikes so that, if you like, you can add miles to your hike or visit nearby trails and places of interest.

Of course, you'll need some information long before you leave home. So, as you plan your trips, consider the following.

BORDER CROSSINGS

All Americans traveling to Canada and Canadians traveling to the United States must have either a valid passport or an enhanced driver's license (issued by Washington, Michigan, New York, Vermont, British Columbia, Manitoba, Ontario, and Quebec) for clearing customs. This is required for all land crossings, air crossings, and international ferry crossings.

PETS

Americans wanting to take their dog with them to Canada must have a certificate to show that the animal has been vaccinated against rabies within the last three years. The certificate has to be dated and signed by a veterinarian, and it must identify the animal by breed, age, sex, coloring, and any distinguishing marks. For a dog less than three months old or a guide dog, you do not need a certificate, but the animal has to be in good health when it arrives.

Canadian dogs heading to the United States must be vaccinated against rabies at least thirty days before entering the United States. This requirement does not apply to puppies less than three months old.

CURRENCY

Americans and Canadians traveling outside their countries should carry at least a small amount of local currency. Exchange rates for the American dollar and Canadian dollar (called a *loonie*, after the one-dollar coin that pictures a loon), have been close to parity for several years. Some merchants will accept foreign currency at par. Most merchants readily accept major credit cards (Master-Card and Visa work best). Using credit cards avoids exchange worries (although most cards charge an exchange fee).

CELL PHONES

There is cell phone coverage throughout most of the islands, depending on your carrier. It is not uncommon for American providers to cover Canadian soil and vice versa. However, if you don't have an international calling plan, you will incur costly roaming charges. Most cell phone providers offer reasonable plans that cover both the United States and Canada,

Penny can't wait to start hiking on Sinclair Island.

and you may want to consider such a plan if you'll be crossing the border frequently. Otherwise, consider a phone card—but finding a pay phone (what's that?) may be a challenge.

FERRIES

For many hikes in this guidebook, you'll need to navigate a ferry system or two, ranging from near ocean liners to small, open-deck, county-operated ferries. With a little advance planning, you shouldn't have too much trouble setting sail for your destination.

Washington State Ferries

Washington State Ferries (WSF) (www.wsdot .wa.gov/ferries) serves the four main San Juan Islands from its terminal at Anacortes on Fidalgo Island (reached via State Route 20 from Burlington on Interstate 5, about halfway between Seattle and Vancouver, British Columbia). The WSF also provides interisland ferry service and seasonal sailings to Sidney on Vancouver Island.

The WSF does not accept reservations, except on the Sidney run, for which car reservations are mandatory (because this is an international sailing, proper documentation is required). Summer traffic (especially on weekends) can be heavy, requiring that you queue up well ahead of your sailing time. Winter service to the islands is less frequent, but getting a space (except on holiday weekends) is generally not an issue.

Walk-on and bicycle passengers can board the sailing of their choice without worrying about a long wait. There are plenty of parking spaces (for a fee) at the Anacortes ferry terminal to accommodate these travelers.

On board, you'll find viewing lounges, newspapers, a cafeteria, and Wi-Fi (for a fee), as well as travel brochures.

BC Ferries

BC Ferries (www.bcferries.com) operates one of the largest ferry fleets in the world. Its main terminal for travel from the lower British Columbia mainland (aka the Lower Mainland) is in Tsawwassen, about 20 miles (32 km)

Water taxis are available to shuttle you to islands not serviced by ferries.

south of Vancouver and 25 miles (40 km) west of the Peace Arch border crossing. From Tsawwassen there are frequent crossings to Swartz Bay on Vancouver Island (about 20 miles [32 km] north of Victoria) as well as direct and inter-island service for Galiano, Mayne, Pender, Saturna, and Salt Spring islands. Of note: service to these islands is more frequent from Swartz Bay, sometimes making a through-trip (sailing from Tsawwassen to Swartz Bay and then onward to one of the islands) a better choice.

BC Ferries offers car reservations (for a fee) for sailings from Tsawwassen to Vancouver Island and the Gulf Islands. Reservations are highly recommended. For Gabriola and Thetis islands, which can only be reached by ferry from Vancouver Island, you first must sail to Departure Bay or Duke Point (near Nanaimo) on Vancouver Island. These Nanaimo-area terminals can be reached by ferry from either Tsawwassen (convenient for people traveling from the United States) or from Horseshoe Bay north of Vancouver. Reservations are available on these sailings.

Walk-on and bicycle passengers can board the sailing of their choice without worrying about a long wait. There is plenty of parking (for a fee) at both the Tsawwassen and Swartz Bay terminals to accommodate these travelers. There is also bus service to Tsawwassen from Vancouver (via Pacific Coach, www.pacificcoach.com, or Translink, www.translink.ca).

The BC Ferries vessels that connect to Vancouver Island are quite luxurious compared to those of Washington State Ferries. They have huge carrying capacities, multiple levels, solariums, restaurant service, work stations, TVs, a nursery, bookstore and gift shop, travel information, Wi-Fi (for a fee), and quiet lounges.

Black Ball Ferry

The Black Ball Ferry (https://cohoferry .com) is a private line that offers (almost) year-round service between Port Angeles on Washington's Olympic Peninsula and Victoria on Vancouver Island. Its ferry, the MV *Coho*, has a classic retro feel and is equipped with food service, viewing lounges, duty-free shop, and gift shop. Reservations are required for cars but not for walk-on passengers and bicyclists. There are private pay-parking lots near the terminals in Port Angeles and Victoria. Because this is an international sailing, proper documentation is required.

County Ferries

Skagit County operates the ferry to Guemes Island (www.skagitcounty.net) and Whatcom County operates the ferry to Lummi Island (www.co.whatcom.wa.us). Both runs generally see light traffic except for commuting hours, weekends, and holidays. Multiple sailings usually mean short wait times—and no waits for bicyclists and foot passengers.

GOING CAR-FREE

The islands are excellent destinations for car-free travel. The advantages of taking your bike or walking on the ferry are much cheaper ferry fees, no reservations necessary, no need to arrive early for the ferry—and leaving a lighter carbon footprint. Many of the islands, with their lightly traveled roads, are bike-friendly. The islands do tend to be hilly, so bicycling them may be challenging.

Many island accommodations are also bike-friendly, with secure bicycle storage. Many of the public campgrounds offer biker/hiker campsites that don't require reservations. On Vancouver Island, it's possible to

Bicycling is a popular means of transportation on the islands.

bike from both the Swartz Bay and Sidney ferry terminals all the way to Victoria entirely on bike paths. In this book, I have noted trailheads that provide bike racks, which will make it easier to secure your bike (which you should always do) when setting off for a hike.

While I don't encourage hitchhiking, it's quite common on the islands. It's also a common occurrence to be walking on an island road and have someone drive up to you and offer you a ride. On most of the Gulf Islands, there are designated passenger pickup stops (like bus stops), where you can wait for passing drivers to give you a ride (if they choose). Some of these designated stops are close to or at parks and trailheads too. While the islands tend to be very safe places, use discretion and sound judgment in deciding whether to solicit or offer a ride.

Buses

Many of the parks and trails, as well as the ferry terminals, in the Victoria area can be reached by public transit. Consult the Victoria Regional Transit System (www.transitbc .com/regions/vic) for schedules and routes. Summer bus service is also available on Orcas and San Juan islands (www.sanjuan transit.com), and year-round bus service is available on Salt Spring Island (www .transitbc.com/regions/ssi). A community bus line is also operated on Gabriola Island (gabriolacommunitybus.com).

CAMPING AND LODGING

The islands offer a wide variety of lodging options. Securing a room or campsite can be a challenge in the summer months as well as on certain holiday weekends (e.g., Victoria

Day in British Columbia and Memorial Day in the United States).

In each area introduction in this book I list public and some private campgrounds where available. It's especially important to make reservations before traveling to the smaller islands, as accommodations are extremely limited. Friday Harbor on San Juan Island and Ganges on Salt Spring Island offer many lodging options, but they too will fill up during busy travel periods.

PERMITS, REGULATIONS, AND FEES
In this book you'll find properties managed by land trusts, which are usually open to the public without fees; the US National Park Service (San Juan Island National Historical Park) and Parks Canada (Gulf Islands National Park Reserve), which charge no day-use fees for areas listed in this book; the US Bureau of Land Management which charges no day-use fee for San Juan Islands National Monument; provincial parks which charge no day-use fee; and county and regional parks, some of which charge a seasonal day-use fee.

Destinations managed by Washington State Parks require a day-use fee in the form of the Discover Pass (www.discoverpass .wa.gov) for vehicle access. A Discover Pass costs US$10 per vehicle per day or US$30 for up to two vehicles annually. You can purchase the pass online, at many retail outlets, or better yet, from a state park office to avoid the US$5 handling fee. Each hike description in this book clearly states if a fee is charged or a pass is required.

WEATHER
The San Juan and Gulf Islands share a Mediterranean climate, with generally mild winters and warm, dry summers. The thermometer rarely tops 80°F (27°C) or dips below 32°F (0°C) here. Furthermore, the area lies within a rainshadow, thanks to the Olympics and Vancouver Island mountains that catch and trap storm systems. Victoria, for example, receives on average only 23.9 inches (61 cm) of annual precipitation, making it one of the driest locations on Canada's west coast. Friday Harbor on San Juan Island gets about 28 inches (71 cm) of precipitation annually, likewise for Anacortes on Fidalgo Island. November through April tend to be the wettest months, August and September the driest. Except for the highest reaches of Salt Spring and Orcas islands, snowfall is extremely rare in the region. The San Juan and Gulf Islands offer excellent hiking opportunities year-round.

That said, you should always pack raingear. Being caught in a sudden rain and wind storm without adequate clothing can lead to hypothermia (loss of body temperature), which is deadly if not immediately treated. Most hikers who die of exposure (hypothermia) do so not in winter, but during the milder months when a sudden change of temperature, accompanied by winds and rain, sneaks up on them. Always carry extra clothing layers, including rain and wind protection.

Lightning is extremely rare in the islands, but if you hear thunder, waste no time getting off of open ridges and away from water. Take shelter, but not under big trees or rock ledges. If caught in an electrical storm, crouch down, making minimal contact with the ground, and wait for the boomer to pass.

Strong winds can be a concern in the islands, especially in late fall and winter. Avoid hiking during high winds, which carry with them the hazards of falling trees and branches.

Always check the National Weather Service (www.noaa.gov) or Environment Canada (weather.gc.ca) weather forecast for the region before you go, and plan accordingly.

ROAD AND TRAIL CONDITIONS

In general, trails change little year to year. But change can and does occur. A heavy storm can cause a river to jump its channel, washing out sections of trail or access road. Windstorms can blow down trees across trails, making paths unhikable. With this in mind, each hike in this book lists the land manager to contact prior to your trip to ensure that your chosen road and trail are open and safe.

On the topic of trail conditions, it is vital that we thank the countless volunteers who donate tens of thousands of hours to trail maintenance each year. The Washington Trails Association (www.wta.org) alone coordinates upward of one hundred thousand hours of volunteer trail maintenance annually. Consider getting involved. A list of conservation and trail organizations and advocates is located at the back of this book.

WATER

Treat all backcountry water sources to prevent exposure to *Giardia* (a waterborne parasite) and other aquatic nasties. Treating water is as simple as boiling it, chemically purifying it (adding iodine tablets), or pumping it through a water filter and purifier.

BEARS

Except perhaps in a few of the larger regional and provincial parks outside of Victoria, encountering bears is not an issue for the hikes in this book. But if you do encounter one, the following tips should help keep you (and the bear) safe:

- **Make a wide detour** around the bear, or if that's not possible, leave the area.
- **Do not run**, as this may trigger a predatory/prey reaction from the bear.
- **Talk in a low, calm voice** to the bear to help identify yourself as a human, and **don't stare directly** at the bear.
- **If you surprise a bear and it charges** from close range, lie down and play dead. A surprised bear will leave you once the perceived threat is neutralized. However, if it still attacks, fight back. Kick, stab, punch at the bear. If it knows you will fight back, it may leave you and search for easier prey.

COUGARS

As with bears, the only hikes in the book where you risk encountering a cougar (and a very rare possibility at that) are in one of the large regional and provincial parks outside of Victoria. If you do encounter one, remember that cougars rely on prey that can't, or won't, fight back. So, as soon as you see the cat, heed the following:

- **Do not run!** Running may trigger a cougar's attack instinct. Back away slowly if you can safely do so, not taking your eyes off of the animal.
- **Stand up and face the cougar.** If you seem like another aggressive predator rather than prey, the cougar will back down.
- **Pick up children and small dogs.**
- **Try to appear large.** Wave your arms or a jacket over your head.
- **Maintain eye contact** with the animal. The cougar will interpret this as a show of dominance on your part.
- **If the cougar attacks**, fight back aggressively. Shout loudly. Throw things. Wave your trekking poles, and if the cat gets close enough, whack it hard with your poles.

WANT TO PROTECT IT? BUY IT!

What's the fastest, most surefire, and often least controversial way to protect land? Buy it yourself! And that's exactly what land trusts across the United States and Canada do. A concept that began in Massachusetts in the late 1800s, land trusts today number in the thousands from coast to coast, nearly all of them nonprofit organizations whose primary purpose is to buy land and secure development rights in order to protect natural areas, farmland, shorelines, wildlife habitat, and recreational land. Once the land is secured, trusts then usually transfer it with legally bound stipulations to government agencies to be managed for the public. Many trusts, however, also maintain their own preserves, and most of these are open to the public.

These are some of the many land trusts operating in the islands:

The San Juan Preservation Trust (www.sjpt.org), founded in 1979, has protected more than 260 properties, 37 miles (60 km) of shoreline and 15,000 acres (6000 ha) on twenty islands. The trust ranks in the top 2 percent of land trusts nationally (of more than seventeen hundred) in number of properties protected.

Gabriola Land and Trails Trust (www.galtt.ca), established in 2004, has been instrumental in developing Gabriola Island's trail system and in establishing new parks.

Galiano Conservancy Association (galianoconservancy.ca), established in 1989, has protected more than 1000 acres (400 ha).

Lummi Island Heritage Trust (www.liht.org), established in 1998, has protected more than 850 acres (340 ha).

Salt Spring Island Conservancy (www.saltspringconservancy.ca), established in 1995, has protected more than 3000 acres (1200 ha).

Skagit Land Trust (www.skagitlandtrust.org), established in 1992, has protected more than 6400 acres (2600 ha).

AN OUTDOORS ETHIC

A strong, positive outdoors ethic includes making sure you leave the trail (and park) as good as (or even better than) when you found it. But a sound outdoors ethic goes deeper than simply picking up after ourselves (and others) when we go for a hike. The same ethic must carry over into our daily lives. We need to ensure that our elected officials and public-land managers recognize and respond to our wilderness needs and desires. Get involved with groups and organizations that safeguard, watchdog, and advocate for land protection. And get on the phone and keyboard and let land managers and public officials know how important protecting lands and trails is to you.

TRAIL ETIQUETTE

We need to be sensitive not only to the environment surrounding our trails but to other trail users as well. Some of the trails in this book are also open to mountain bikers and equestrians. When you encounter other trail users, whether they are hikers, runners, bicyclists, or horse riders, the only hard-and-fast rule is to follow common sense and

Feral goats on Saturna Island

exercise simple courtesy. With this Golden Rule of Trail Etiquette firmly in mind, here are other things you can do to make everyone's trip more enjoyable:

- **Right-of-way.** When meeting other hikers, the uphill group has the right-of-way. There are two reasons for this. First, on steep ascents, hikers may be watching the trail and may not notice the approach of descending hikers until they are face-to-face. More importantly, it is easier for descending hikers to break their stride and step off the trail than it is for those who have gotten into a good, climbing rhythm.

- **Moving off-trail.** When meeting other user groups (like bicyclists and horseback riders), the hiker should move off the trail. This is because hikers are more mobile and flexible than other users.

- **Encountering horses.** When meeting horseback riders, the hiker should step off the downhill side of the trail unless the terrain makes this difficult or dangerous. In that case, move to the uphill side of the trail, but crouch down a bit so you don't tower over the horses' heads. Also, make yourself visible so as not to spook the big beastie, and talk in a normal voice to the riders. This calms the horses. If hiking with a dog, keep your buddy under control.

- **Stay on trails.** Don't cut switchbacks, take shortcuts, or make new trails.

- **Obey the rules** specific to the trail you're visiting. Many trails are closed to certain types of use, including mountain biking and hiking with dogs.

- **Hiking with dogs.** Hikers who take dogs on the trails should have their dog on a leash or under very strict voice command at all times. And if leashes are required, then this *does* apply to you. Too many dog owners flagrantly disregard this regulation, setting themselves up for tickets, hostile words from fellow hikers, and the possibility of losing the right to bring Fido out on that trail in the future. Dog waste should be properly disposed of too. Far too many hikers (this author included, who happens to love dogs) have had very negative encounters with dogs (actually, the dog owners) on the trail. Many hikers are not fond of dogs on the trail, and some are actually afraid. Respect their right to not be approached by your pooch. A well-behaved leashed dog, however, can help warm up these hikers to your buddy.

- **Avoid disturbing wildlife.** Observe wildlife from a distance, resisting the urge to move closer (use your telephoto lens). This not only keeps you safer, but it prevents the animal from having to exert itself unnecessarily in fleeing from you.
- **Never roll rocks off trails or cliffs.** You risk endangering lives below you.
- **Use privies, or bury your waste.** An important Leave No Trace principle involves the business of taking care of business. The first rule of backcountry bathroom etiquette says that if an outhouse exists, use it. Otherwise, choose a site at least 200 feet from water, campsites, and trails. Dig a cat hole. Once you're done, bury your waste with organic duff and a "Microbes at Work" sign (just kidding).
- **Pack it in, pack it out.** This includes even biodegradable items like orange peels and pistachio shells.
- **Take only photographs.** Leave all natural things, features, and historical artifacts as you found them for others to enjoy. "Leave only footprints, take only pictures," is a slogan to live by.

GEAR

While a full description of all suitable gear is beyond the scope of this book (which is about where to hike not how to hike), it's worth noting a few pointers here. No hiker should venture far up a trail without being properly equipped.

Let's start with your feet: A good pair of boots can make all the difference between a wonderful hike and a blistering affair. For socks, synthetic ones work best for me. Wearing liners worn with wool socks is also a good choice.

For clothing, wear whatever is most comfortable, unless it's cotton. When cotton gets wet, it stays wet and lacks any insulation value. In fact, wet cotton sucks away body heat, leaving you susceptible to hypothermia. Think synthetics and layering.

Every hiker who ventures into the woods should also pack the Ten Essentials, as well as a few other items that aren't necessarily essential but that are good to have on hand in an emergency.

The Ten Essentials

1. **Navigation (map and compass):** Carry a topographic map of the area you plan to be in and knowledge of how to read it. Likewise a compass. A GPS unit can be useful too.
2. **Sun protection (sunglasses and sunscreen):** Even on wet and cloudy days, carry sunscreen and sunglasses. You never know when the clouds will lift. You can easily burn near water.
3. **Insulation (extra clothing):** Storms can and do blow in rapidly. Be sure to carry rain and wind gear and extra layers.
4. **Illumination (flashlight/headlamp):** If caught after dark, you'll need a headlamp or flashlight to be able to follow the trail. If forced to spend the night, you'll need light to set up an emergency camp, gather wood, and so on. Carry extra batteries too.

Look closely to see a bald eagle perched in a lone fir on an islet off Gabriola Island.

5. **First-aid supplies:** At the very least your kit should include bandages, gauze, scissors, tape, tweezers, pain relievers, antiseptics, and perhaps a small manual. Consider first-aid training through a program such as MOFA (Mountaineering Oriented First Aid).

6. **Fire (firestarter and matches):** If you're forced to spend the night, an emergency campfire will provide warmth. Be sure you keep your matches dry. Sealable plastic bags do the trick. A candle can come in handy too.

7. **Repair kit and tools (including a knife):** A knife is helpful; a multitool is better. A basic repair kit should include such things as nylon cord, a small roll of duct tape, some 1-inch webbing and extra webbing buckles (to fix broken pack straps), and a small tube of superglue. A handful of safety pins can do wonders too.

8. **Nutrition (extra food):** Always pack more food than what you need for your hike. If you're forced to spend the night, you'll be prepared. Pack energy bars for emergency pick-me-ups.

9. **Hydration (extra water):** Carry at least one 32-ounce (1-liter) water bottle. Bring iodine tablets or a filter in case you're forced to draw water from a natural source.

10. **Emergency shelter:** This can be as simple as a garbage bag or something more efficient, such as a reflective space blanket. A poncho can double as an emergency tarp.

TRAILHEAD CONCERNS

Sadly, the topic of trailhead and trail crime must be addressed. While violent crime is extremely rare on the trail (practically absent, thankfully), it's a grim reminder that we are never truly free from the worst elements of society.

By and large our hiking trails are safe places, far safer than many city streets. Common sense and vigilance, however, are still in order. This is true for all hikers, but particularly for solo hikers. Be aware of your surrounding at all times. Leave your itinerary with someone back home. If something doesn't feel right, it probably isn't. Take action by leaving the place or situation immediately. But remember, most hikers are friendly, decent people. Some may be a little introverted, but that's no cause for worry.

By far your biggest concern should be with trailhead theft. Car break-ins are a far too common occurrence at some of our trailheads, especially in British Columbia's Lower Mainland and Victoria area. Do not—absolutely under no circumstances—leave anything of

One of Moran State Park's rustic signposts

value in your vehicle while you're hiking. Take your wallet, cell phone, and listening devices with you. Or better yet, don't bring them along in the first place. Don't leave anything in your car that might look valuable. A duffle bag on the back seat may contain dirty T-shirts, but a thief might think there's a laptop in it. Save yourself the hassle of returning to a busted window by not giving criminals a reason to clout your car.

If you arrive at a trailhead and someone looks suspicious, don't discount your intuition. Take notes on the person and his or her vehicle. Record the license plate and report the behavior to the authorities. Do not confront the person. Leave and go to another trail.

While most car break-ins are crimes of opportunity by drug addicts looking for loot to support their fix, organized gangs intent on stealing IDs have also been known to target parked cars at trailheads. While some trailheads are regularly targeted, and others rarely if at all, there's no sure way of preventing this from happening to you other than being dropped off at the trailhead or taking the bus. But you can make your car less of a target by not leaving anything of value in it.

ENJOY THE TRAILS

Most importantly, be safe and enjoy the thrill of discovery and exercise on the trails in this book. They exist for our enjoyment and for the enjoyment of future generations of hikers. Happy hiking!

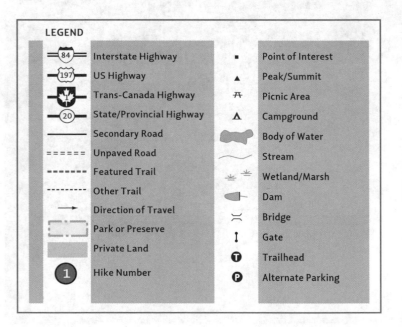

LEGEND

84	Interstate Highway
197	US Highway
(maple leaf)	Trans-Canada Highway
20	State/Provincial Highway
——	Secondary Road
======	Unpaved Road
- - - - -	Featured Trail
· · · · ·	Other Trail
→	Direction of Travel
(dashed box)	Park or Preserve
(gray box)	Private Land
1	Hike Number
■	Point of Interest
▲	Peak/Summit
⊼	Picnic Area
▲	Campground
(shape)	Body of Water
∿	Stream
☼ ☼	Wetland/Marsh
◁—	Dam
≍	Bridge
I	Gate
T	Trailhead
P	Alternate Parking

anacortes and
fidalgo island

View south of Campbell Lake and Skagit Bay from Mount Erie

Named after the Spanish explorer Salvador Fidalgo, Fidalgo Island is connected to the mainland by State Route 20's twin bridges and to Whidbey Island by the Deception Pass Bridge. Home to Anacortes—a bustling city of about sixteen thousand, with two oil refineries, seafood and ship-building industries, and a historical commercial district—Fidalgo also contains several thousand acres of parks and forests and an extensive trail system.

Skagit County operates a small ferry to nearby Guemes Island and Washington State Ferries operates a large ferry with service to the main San Juan Islands and to Sidney, British Columbia, on Vancouver Island. While Anacortes and Fidalgo Island are gateways to the San Juan Islands, they host plenty of maritime delights themselves.

Camping is available at Deception Pass State Park, Anacortes' Washington Park (www.cityofanacortes.org/parks/WAPark /wa_park.htm), the Fidalgo Bay Resort (www.fidalgobay.com), and Pioneer Trails RV Park (www.pioneertrails.com).

firs around a rocky headland rife with beaches, coves, bluffs, and jaw-dropping maritime views in a beloved Anacortes park.

GETTING THERE

From exit 230 on Interstate 5 in Burlington, follow State Route 20 west for 11.7 miles (18.8 km) to the junction with SR 20-Spur. Continue right on SR 20-Spur to Anacortes, passing the traffic circle and coming to a traffic light at a junction with 12th Street in 4 miles (6.4 km). Turn left and continue on SR 20-Spur for 3.1 miles (5 km) to the junction with the ferry access road. Continue straight on Sunset Avenue for 0.9 mile (1.4 km) to day-use parking (elev. 60 ft/18 m) near the ranger residence in

A pair of hikers admire Mount Erie across Burrows Bay.

① Washington Park

RATING/ DIFFICULTY	LOOP	ELEV GAIN/ HIGH POINT
***/2	2.2 miles (3.5 km)	280 feet (85 m)/ 250 feet (76 m)

Map: Green Trails Deception Pass/Anacortes Community Forest Lands No. 41S; **Contact:** City of Anacortes Parks and Recreation, Washington Park; **Notes:** Route is open to vehicles after 10:00 AM; **GPS:** N 48 29.926, W 122 41.570

Walk beneath a canopy of salty Douglas

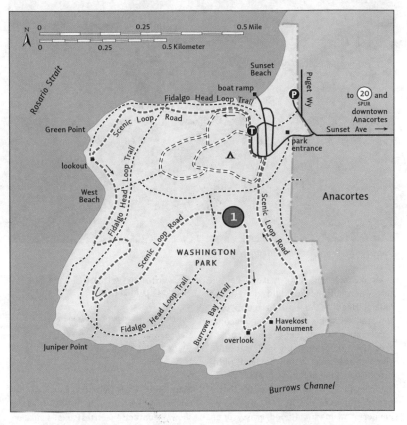

Washington Park. If the small day-use parking area is full, find more parking near playfields east of the boat launch.

ON THE TRAIL

Several miles of trails crisscross this gorgeous 220-acre (89-ha) park on Fidalgo Head, which juts into Rosario Strait. Some are brushy. Some are well maintained. They're all worth checking out. However, this loop along the park's narrow paved loop road is a classic. The road is open to automobiles (one-way,

10 mph speed limit) after 10:00 AM, but don't let that discourage you. This is one of the most popular walking routes in the area and pedestrians outnumber other users.

From the day-use parking area, walk north (counterclockwise), passing the park's popular campground on the left and Sunset Beach on the right. Enjoy level walking to Green Point (elev. 30 ft/9 m), with its gorgeous San Juan Islands view, before starting to climb high bluffs above the crashing surf.

The boardwalk on the Ship Harbor Interpretive Trail

At 0.8 mile (1.3 km), make a hairpin turn where a trail leads right to the tip of Fidalgo Head. At the third sharp turn, pass the trail to Juniper Point. After reaching an elevation of 250 feet (76 m), drop 80 feet (24 m), passing big cedars before climbing again. Pass a trail that leads right, dropping steeply to Burrows Pass. Then at 1.6 miles (2.6 km), reach one of the loop's best overlooks (elev. 230 ft/70 m). On this juniper- and madrona-lined grassy open bluff, savor views to Mount Erie and across Burrows Pass to bulky Burrows Island. A short trail diverts right for more viewing.

The road then descends, passing the Havekost Monument that honors the pioneer who, in 1911, donated the first parcel of what would become this beautiful park. Keep descending, passing through thick second-growth forest interspersed with big old stumps, closing the loop at 2.2 miles (3.5 km). Consider camping at the park and hiking this loop at sunset.

② Guemes Channel and Ship Harbor

RATING/ DIFFICULTY	ROUNDTRIP	ELEV GAIN/ HIGH POINT
***/1	1.6 miles (2.6 km)	Minimal/10 feet (3 m)

Map: Green Trails Deception Pass/Anacortes Community Forest Lands No. 41S (trail not shown); **Contact:** Anacortes Parks Foundation; **Notes:** Wheelchair-accessible. Dogs permitted on-leash; **GPS:** N 48 30.230, W 122 40.210

Explore two fun, family-friendly trails not far from the Washington State Ferries terminal in Anacortes. One is a paved path along Guemes Channel, providing excellent views of Guemes and Cypress islands. The other follows a boardwalk through rich wetlands bordering a beautiful sandy beach.

GETTING THERE

From exit 230 on Interstate 5 in Burlington, follow State Route 20 west for 11.7 miles (18.8 km) to the junction with SR 20-Spur. Continue right on SR 20-Spur to Anacortes, passing the traffic circle and coming to a traffic light at a junction with 12th Street in 4 miles (6.4 km). Turn left and continue on SR 20-Spur for 2.7 miles (4.3 km). Turn right onto Ship Harbor Boulevard and reach a junction in 0.1 mile (0.15 km). Turn left onto Edwards Way and follow it 0.2 mile (0.3 km) to the trailhead at the road's end.

ON THE TRAIL

Two trails diverge from this cul-de-sac. Both are new, popular with locals, in the process of expanding, and destination-worthy if you're visiting from outside the area. Hike the Guemes Channel Trail first, heading east on a nearly level paved path. Enjoy exceptional views of Cypress and Guemes islands across the channel and glimpses of Blakely and Lummi islands and even Entrance Mountain on Orcas Island. Stop at interpretive signs and admire the stately trees that shade the path with their overhanging branches.

The path ends at 0.45 mile (0.7 km). Locals, community leaders, and trail advocates are working hard to extend this trail all the way to downtown Anacortes, connecting it with the Tommy Thompson Trail (Hike 3). It will become an amazing asset when completed. For now, however, head back to the trailhead.

Then hike west on the Ship Harbor Interpretive Trail, following a wide and smooth path through a wetland and along a gorgeous sandy beach. The trail meanders through thick vegetation, passing splendid

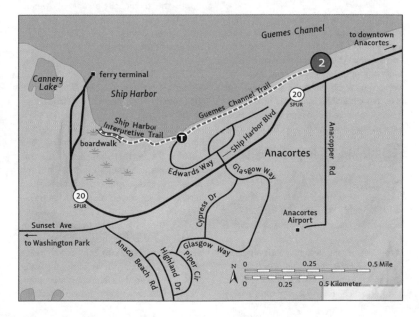

The Tommy Thompson Trail follows a long trestle across Fidalgo Bay.

viewpoints of the harbor and nearby ferry terminal. Several points allow beach access, which makes for some fine walking when tides are low. The trail continues on a boardwalk through an ecologically important wetland (stay on the trail), ending at 0.35 mile (0.6 km). When funding is secured, the trail will continue to the ferry terminal. Head back the way you came.

3 Tommy Thompson Trail

RATING/ DIFFICULTY	ROUNDTRIP	ELEV GAIN/ HIGH POINT
***/1	3.8 miles (6.1 km)	Minimal/10 feet (3 m)

Map: Green Trails Deception Pass/Anacortes Community Forest Lands No. 41S (trail partially shown); **Contact:** City of Anacortes Parks and Recreation, Tommy Thompson Parkway;

Notes: Open to bicycles. Dogs permitted on-leash; **GPS:** N 48 29.676, W 122 36.163

Stroll for 1 mile (1.6 km) across Fidalgo Bay on a causeway and old railroad trestle on this popular paved rail trail. Look for herons, loons, grebes, otters, and seals in the bay's sparkling waters and glistening mudflats. Enjoy views of Mount Baker, Cap Sante, Guemes Island, and Hat Island. There are also interpretive signs, a totem pole, and an otter sculpture to admire.

GETTING THERE
From exit 230 on Interstate 5 in Burlington, follow State Route 20 west for 11.7 miles (18.8 km) to the junction with SR 20-Spur. Continue right on SR 20-Spur for 2.6 miles (4.2 km) to Anacortes, and turn right (just before the traffic circle) onto R Avenue. After 0.1 mile (0.15 km), turn right onto 34th Street. Drive 0.3 mile (0.5 km) to the trailhead at the road's end.

ON THE TRAIL
Named after a local railroad enthusiast, the Tommy Thompson Trail follows an abandoned rail line for 3.3 miles (5.3 km) from March Point to Old Town Anacortes. Popular with bicyclists, runners, and walkers, the northern reaches of the trail travel primarily through industrial lots and shipyards. The southern section described here, however, travels along Fidalgo Bay— and then crosses it.

From the 34th Street trailhead, one of several access points, begin walking south. Within 0.15 mile (0.2 km), come to a shoreline picnic area. Soak up views across the water of Mount Baker, the Chuckanut Mountains, Anderson Mountain, and Lyman Mountain, and of the big oil refinery at March Point. But don't rest yet, as the trail only gets better. Soon come to the first of several interpretive signs and a beautiful otter sculpture.

Then pass a large private residence and cross the grassy lawns of the Fidalgo Bay Resort, a camping area owned by the Samish Tribe. At 1 mile (1.6 km), come to a totem pole, resort access road, and another trailhead (limited parking, privy available). Continue on the trail to its best part—a nearly 1-mile (1.6-km) causeway and trestle across Fidalgo Bay.

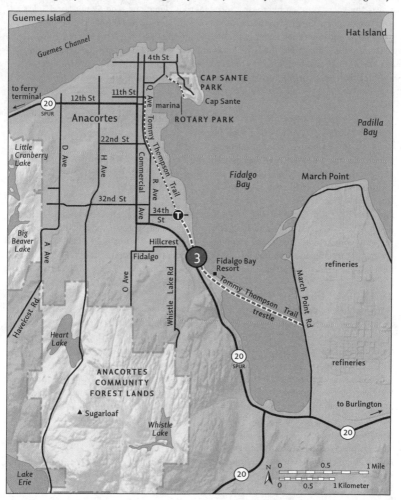

SEEING THE FOREST THROUGH THE STREETS

Managed by the City of Anacortes, Anacortes Community Forest Lands (ACFL) contain more than 2800 acres (1130 ha) of forest, wetlands, lakes, and small peaks, all within minutes of Skagit County's second-largest community. Originally consisting of parcels once used to protect the city's water supply, the ACFL has increased in size over the years through purchases and generous donations. The Skagit Land Trust (www.skagitlandtrust.org) owns the conservation rights on much of the ACFL, assuring that this ecological and recreational gem, with its 50-plus miles (80-plus km) of trails, remains in a natural state. Managed by the city's Parks and Recreation Department and an advisory board, the ACFL is also monitored by an active citizen's group, the Friends of the Forest (www.friendsoftheacfl.org), which promotes education, outreach, and stewardship.

Wildlife viewing is excellent here. Watch for otters and eagles. At low tide, look for birds on the extensive mudflats. During the winter months, loons can be spotted in the bay. At 1.6 miles (2.6 km), reach the restored wooden trestle, the highlight of this hike. Wander across it for 0.4 mile (0.6 km), reaching trail's end at March Point Road. Then turn around and languidly retrace your steps, perhaps stopping for quiet contemplation at one of those benches you passed by earlier.

EXTENDING YOUR TRIP

Want more exercise? From the 34th Street access, head north on the Tommy Thompson Trail. In 0.25 mile (0.4 km), pass the Soroptomist Station trailhead, complete with privies. Reach the trail's end at the Cap Sante Marina 1.1 miles (1.8 km) farther. Walk through the marina for another 0.4 mile (0.6 km) to the Rotary Park and trails to Cap Sante Park; or walk 0.7 mile (1.1 km) along 6th Street and Cap Sante Drive and take in spectacular views of Fidalgo Bay, March Point, and Mount Baker from the Cap Sante headland (approx. elev. 200 ft/60 m).

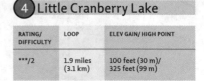

4 Little Cranberry Lake

RATING/ DIFFICULTY	LOOP	ELEV GAIN/ HIGH POINT
***/2	1.9 miles (3.1 km)	100 feet (30 m)/ 325 feet (99 m)

Map: Green Trails Deception Pass/Anacortes Community Forest Lands No. 41S; **Contact:** City of Anacortes Parks and Recreation, Community Forest Lands; **Notes:** Partly open to bicycles. Dogs permitted on-leash; **GPS:** N 48 30.266, W 122 38.699

Stroll around a tranquil lake through groves of handsome firs and thick patches of salal and over sunny shoreline ledges. Surrounded by big trees and cradling two boggy islands harboring, yes, cranberries, Little Cranberry Lake is an attractive body of water with plenty of wildlife—watch for eagles, beavers, and otters.

GETTING THERE

From exit 230 on Interstate 5 in Burlington, follow State Route 20 west for 11.7 miles (18.8 km) to the junction with SR 20-Spur.

Continue right on SR 20-Spur to Anacortes, passing the traffic circle and coming to a traffic light at a junction with 12th Street in 4 miles (6.4 km). Turn left and continue on SR 20-Spur for 1.6 miles (2.6 km), turning left on Georgia Avenue. Continue for 0.2 mile (0.3 km) and turn right onto a gravel road signed for Anacortes Community Forest Lands (ACFL). Drive 0.3 mile (5 km) to the trailhead (elev. 290 ft/88 m).

ON THE TRAIL

This loop around Little Cranberry Lake is almost entirely on hiker-only trails. Young children and focused naturalists need not worry about having to dodge mountain bikers, which are ubiquitous on adjacent Anacortes Community Forest Lands trails.

Starting from the kiosk, hike east on Trail No. 100. Cross an earthen dam built in the early 1900s, which transformed this wetland depression into a shallow lake. The way hugs the lakeshore beneath mature Douglas firs and through a thick understory of ferns and salal. Stay right at a junction and come to an observation deck. Pause to look or keep hiking.

At 0.2 mile (0.3 km), head right onto Trail No. 102 and continue hugging the shoreline. While the copious junctions can be confusing (carry a map), they are mostly well-signed. From this point forward, it's hikers only. Soon come to two more junctions—stay to the right. Actually, stay to the right at all junctions on this route, keeping the lakeshore always in view.

Mosey through jumbled boulders, beneath ledges, and right along the water's edge. Admire madronas among the cedars and firs. Watch kingfishers fish. Scan the boggy islands, one on each end of the lake, for avian and small-mammal activity.

At 0.8 mile (1.3 km), reach a junction. Head right, crossing a bridge over an inlet stream, and immediately come to another junction. Yep—go right. Now on Trail No. 132, negotiate a short rocky section beneath ledges, and then resume easier walking. At 1.1 miles (1.8 km), at the lake's southwest corner, bear right at a junction onto Trail No. 105. Cross a creek and come to another junction.

Take Trail No. 101 to the right along the lake's western shoreline. Climb up and over some sunny ledges, which invite napping

Stately trees line Little Cranberry Lake's shoreline.

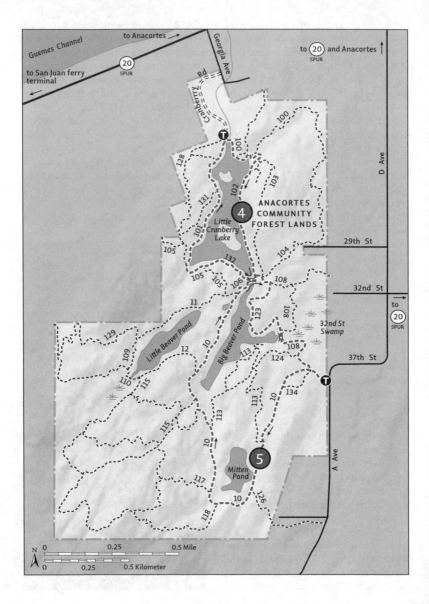

Guemes Channel

to Anacortes →

← to San Juan ferry terminal

20 SPUR

to **20** and Anacortes ↑ SPUR

Georgia Ave

Cranberry Rd

T

128

131

101

105

105

105

100

102

103

4

ANACORTES
COMMUNITY
FOREST LANDS

D Ave

29th St

Little
Cranberry
Lake

132

106

104

108

32nd St

to **20** SPUR

11

129

109

110 115

Little Beaver Pond

12

10

Big Beaver Pond

123

108

108

32nd St
Swamp

37th St

T

113

124

134

115

113

113

10

A Ave

10

117

118

Mitten
Pond

5

10

126

N

0   0.25   0.5 Mile

0   0.25   0.5 Kilometer

on warm sunny days. Just before closing the loop, come to a ledge overlooking the lake and granting a good view. At 1.9 miles (3.1 km), arrive back at the trailhead.

EXTENDING YOUR TRIP

Get a map and set out on radiating trails. You can easily combine this hike with a trip around Big Beaver Pond (Hike 5).

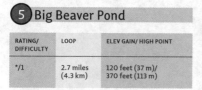

5 Big Beaver Pond

RATING/ DIFFICULTY	LOOP	ELEV GAIN/ HIGH POINT
*/1	2.7 miles (4.3 km)	120 feet (37 m)/ 370 feet (113 m)

Map: Green Trails Deception Pass/Anacortes Community Forest Lands No. 41S; **Contact:** City of Anacortes Parks and Recreation, Community Forest Lands; **Notes:** Some trails open to bicycles, horses (and motorcycles Apr 1–Oct 31). Dogs permitted on-leash; **GPS:** N 48 29.492, W 122 38.193

Wander aimlessly and easily on a network of trails through a network of wetlands. Come in spring for woodland blossoms or in fall for yellow-brushed shrubbery streaking the enveloping dark-green forest. Look for beavers, coyotes, ducks, and eagles in this wildlife haven.

GETTING THERE

From exit 230 on Interstate 5 in Burlington, follow State Route 20 west for 11.7 miles (18.8 km) to the junction with SR 20-Spur. Continue right on SR 20-Spur for 2.7 miles (4.3 km) to Anacortes, turning right at the traffic circle onto Commercial Avenue (still SR 20-Spur). In 0.2 mile (0.3 km), turn left at the traffic light onto 32nd Street. Continue 0.8 mile (1.3 km) to D Avenue and turn left. Follow this arterial (which becomes 37th Street and then A Avenue) for 0.5 mile (0.8 km) to the trailhead (elev. 300 ft/91 m).

ON THE TRAIL

Start on Trail No. 10, an old woods road, coming to a junction with Trail Nos. 108 and 134 in 0.1 mile (0.15 km). Most of the trails on this loop are multiuse, favored by mountain bikers, dog walkers, and trail runners. The trails can get busy but they are rarely crowded. Winter weekdays especially are fairly quiet.

Trail No. 134 makes a small loop back to Trail No. 10, and you'll be returning on Trail No. 108. So stay on Trail No. 10, passing an old dump (currently being reclaimed), and gently climb through a mature forest of Douglas fir, grand fir, and western red cedar. At 0.4 mile (0.6 km), come to a junction with Trail No. 113 (elev. 370 ft/113 m), which heads right for 0.4 mile (0.6 km) to Big Beaver Pond. Continue straight, soon coming upon Mitten Pond, appropriately named for its shape. Trail No. 126 comes in from the left—it's part of the Pacific Northwest Trail (PNT), a long-distance national scenic trail connecting the Olympic coast to Glacier National Park.

Continue on Trail No. 10, now part of the PNT, crossing Mitten Pond's outlet stream (elev. 320 ft/98 m). Ignore Trail Nos. 118 and 117 on the left. At 1.1 miles (1.8 km), reach Trail No. 113, which offers a shorter loop back. Continue straight on Trail No. 10, ignoring two more trails taking off left. At 1.4 miles (2.3 km), come to Trail No. 12 (elev. 350 ft/107 m), which leads to Little Beaver Pond (see Extending Your Trip). The recommended loop continues right on Trail

The trail leading to an observation deck at Big Beaver Pond

No. 10. Soon, marshy tree- and snag-filled Big Beaver Pond (more like a swamp) comes into view as the trail drops closer to its shore.

At 1.7 miles (2.7 km), reach another junction. The old road continues as Trail No. 11, leading to Little Beaver Pond. Take single-track Trail No. 106 right, reaching an arm of Big Beaver Pond at the water's level. At 1.8 miles (2.9 km), come to a junction at Little Cranberry Lake. Head right on Trail No. 104, crossing a creek connecting Cranberry to Big Beaver, and climb a small rise, ignoring Trail No. 102. At 1.9 miles (3.1 km), come to a junction with Trail Nos. 103 and 108. Head right on Trail No. 108 and then, soon after, right onto Trail No. 123.

Pass through a stile and enjoy this hiker-only path along the shores of Big Beaver Pond. Take your time, as the bird-watching is good on this 0.4-mile (0.6-km) path. Return to Trail No. 108 and turn right, crossing a bridge. Skirt the 32nd Street Swamp and continue along a row of big firs and cedars, passing Trail Nos. 124 and 114 and reaching Trail No. 10 at 2.6 miles (4.2 km). The trailhead is 0.1 mile (0.15 km) to the left.

EXTENDING YOUR TRIP

A myriad of interconnecting trails leads to innumerable hiking opportunities. Consider Trail No. 113 along Big Beaver Pond's south shore and to a boardwalk observation deck. Loop around Little Beaver Pond by following Trail Nos. 12, 115, 109, and 11. A map comes in handy!

6 Heart Lake

RATING/ DIFFICULTY	LOOP	ELEV GAIN/ HIGH POINT
**/2	3 miles (4.8 km)	160 feet (49 m)/ 500 feet (152 m)

Map: Green Trails Deception Pass/Anacortes Community Forest Lands No. 41S; **Contact:** City of Anacortes Parks and Recreation, Community Forest Lands; **Notes:** Some trails open to bicycles, horses. Dogs permitted on-leash; **GPS:** N 48 28.534, W 122 37.691

Grandest of the bodies of water within the Anacortes Community Forest Lands (ACFL), Heart Lake has its paddling and fishing admirers. But hikers take heart, for this heart-shaped lake's finest feature isn't its size; it's its enveloping old-growth forest— one of the finest in the Puget Lowlands.

GETTING THERE

From exit 230 on Interstate 5 in Burlington, follow State Route 20 west for 11.7 miles (18.8 km) to the junction with SR 20-Spur. Continue left on SR 20 and after 1.8 miles (2.9 km), turn right onto Campbell Lake Road. Drive 1.5 miles (2.4 km) and bear right onto Heart Lake Road. Continue 2 miles (3.2 km) to the trailhead at the boat launch on the left (elev. 340 feet/104 m). Privy available.

ON THE TRAIL

Trails nearly encircle quiet Heart Lake, making for a nice loop—or feel free to wander aimlessly on the myriad of trails radiating from this suggested route. Start by following Trail No. 210 north, passing several large Douglas firs along the lakeshore. At 0.2 mile (0.3 km), reach the first of many junctions.

Bear left and shortly afterward turn left onto Trail No. 210, an old woods road.

Cross Heart's outlet creek, enjoying good views across the lake to the Sugarloaf summit. Bear left, leaving the old road but continuing on Trail No. 210, and stay left again at the next junction, continuing to the lake's marshy southwestern cove.

At 1.1 miles (1.8 km), bear left again (still on Trail No. 210), traversing magnificent ancient groves of giant cedars and firs. At 1.8 miles (2.9 km), reach Trail No. 212 (elev. 420 ft/128 m). Turn left, following it 0.3 mile (0.5 km) to Heart Lake Road. Now either walk the road (use caution) for 0.7 mile (1.1 km)

One of the finest stands of old-growth forest in the Puget Lowlands can be found at Heart Lake.

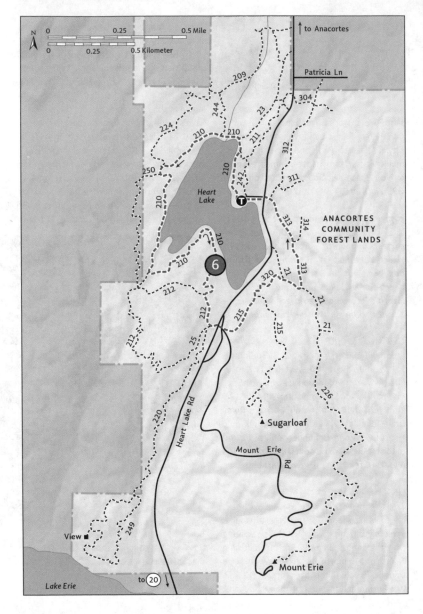

N

0   0.25   0.5 Mile

0   0.25   0.5 Kilometer

to Anacortes

Patricia Ln

209

304

23

244

224

210

210

211

312

250

210

210

242

311

Heart
Lake

T

210

313

314

ANACORTES
COMMUNITY
FOREST LANDS

210

210

6

320

21

313

210

212

212

215

21

212

215

21

25

226

212

Heart Lake Rd

Sugarloaf

Mount   Erie

Rd

220

249

View

Mount Erie

Lake Erie

to 20

back to the trailhead; or, better yet, cross the road and proceed to the Sugarloaf trailhead, picking up Trail No. 215. After 0.2 mile (0.3 km), bear left onto Trail No. 320 and start climbing. Bear right onto Trail No. 21, climb some more, and then turn left onto Trail No. 313 (elev. 500 ft/152 m). Follow it downhill back to the trailhead at 3 miles (4.8 km).

EXTENDING YOUR TRIP
From near the road crossing, Trail No. 220 takes off south. Follow this quiet path 0.8 mile (1.3 km) to Trail No. 249, which loops around in 1.1 miles (1.8 km), passing an open ledge providing a nice view of Mount Erie and a sunny lunch spot.

7 Sugarloaf

RATING/ DIFFICULTY	LOOP	ELEV GAIN/ HIGH POINT
***/3	2.5 miles (4 km)	650 feet (198 m)/ 1044 feet (318 m)

Map: Green Trails Deception Pass/Anacortes Community Forest Lands No. 41S; **Contact:** City of Anacortes Parks and Recreation, Community Forest Lands; **Notes:** Some trails open to bicycles, horses. Dogs permitted on-leash; **GPS:** N 48 28.069, W 122 37.776

The hike up Sugarloaf—the second highest summit on Fidalgo Island—is short and sweet. A delectable destination indeed, with its big trees, sunny and open south-facing slopes, and sweeping views of the San Juan Islands, Olympic Mountains, Whidbey Island, and nearby Fidalgo high point, Mount Erie. Sugarloaf may play second fiddle to Mount Erie in height, but its summit sans road and crowds makes it a first-rate destination for hikers.

GETTING THERE
From exit 230 on Interstate 5 in Burlington, take State Route 20 west for 11.7 miles (18.8 km)

Sugarloaf's open summit provides excellent views of Burrows and Allan islands.

to the junction with SR 20-Spur. Continue left on SR 20 and after 1.8 miles (2.9 km), turn right onto Campbell Lake Road. Drive 1.5 miles (2.4 km) and bear right onto Heart Lake Road. Continue 1.5 miles (2.4 km) and turn right at a sign indicating "Mt Erie Viewpoint." Proceed a couple of hundred feet (do not turn right up Mount Erie Road) to the trailhead (elev. 390 ft/119 m). Privy available.

ON THE TRAIL

It's easy to get lost (intentionally or uninten-tionally) in this Anacortes Community Forest Lands parcel, with its spaghetti heap of trails. Carry a map and pay attention to junctions, which thankfully are almost always well marked. This hike to Sugarloaf doesn't require too many twists and turns!

Beginning on Trail No. 215, head through a swampy draw graced with a few big Douglas firs and cedars. In a 0.2 mile (0.3 km), come to a junction with Trail No. 320. Bear right, continuing on Trail No. 215, and start climb-ing—steeply at times. Ferns, moss, and salal line the way. At 0.5 mile (0.8 km), come to a junction with Trail No. 225. Stay right on Trail No. 215 and continue climbing under a canopy of mature Doug firs, working your way up and around a series of mossy ledges.

At 1 mile (1.6 km), encounter another trail junction. Trail No. 215 continues straight, descending Sugarloaf's south face and reach-ing the Mount Erie Road in 0.3 mile (0.5 km). Go left through a stile and follow hiker-only Trail No. 227 for about 0.1 mile (0.15 km) to another junction. Turn right onto Trail No. 238, soon arriving on the blocky summit of 1044-foot (318-m) Sugarloaf. Pass Trail No. 228 (which connects back to Trail No. 215) and shortly afterward come to a spur trail branch-ing right. Follow it to sunny ledges and some sweet viewing of Whidbey, Burrows, Allan, and

Lopez islands. The big blob in front of you is Mount Erie, highest point on Fidalgo Island.

EXTENDING YOUR TRIP

Do some *sugarloafing* and just enjoy the sun and views—or consider exploring some of the peak's radiating trails. You can follow Trail No. 238 around the summit to views east to the Cascades, and then follow Trail No. 226 to Trail No. 225 and then back to Trail No. 215 for a slightly longer return. Or follow Trail No. 215 through a nice meadow to the Mount Erie Road. Then walk a short distance east on the road to Trail No. 26, where in 0.3 mile (0.5 km) you can connect with Trail No. 216 to Mount Erie (Hike 8).

8 Mount Erie

RATING/ DIFFICULTY	LOOP	ELEV GAIN/ HIGH POINT
***/3	5.2 miles (8.4 km)	910 feet (277 m)/ 1273 feet (388 m)

Map: Green Trails Deception Pass/Ana-cortes Community Forest Lands No. 41S; **Contact:** City of Anacortes Parks and Rec-reation, Community Forest Lands; **Notes:** Some trails open to bicycles, horses. Dogs permitted on-leash; **GPS:** N 48 28.069, W 122 37.776

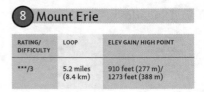 *Stand above abrupt cliffs on the highest peak on Fidalgo Island and behold some of the finest views in the islands. Admire the glacially carved bumpy hills surrounding Deception Pass and the active glaciers on Mount Baker and other North Cascades summits. Watch falcons and paragliders ride thermals above spar-kling Campbell Lake, the largest body of water on Fidalgo Island.*

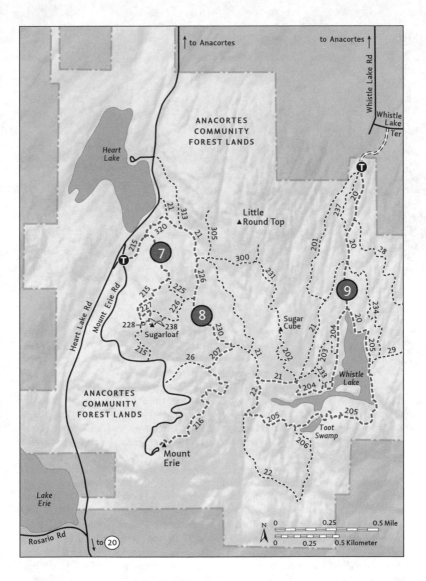

The view from Mount Erie of Campbell Lake and Skagit Bay is breathtaking.

GETTING THERE

See directions to Hike 7.

ON THE TRAIL

Yes, you can drive to the summit of Mount Erie—but why, when there's a trail that'll take you there? This hike would no doubt be five stars if the road didn't exist. On sunny weekends, throngs of visitors crowd summit viewing posts. Try a weekday—especially in winter, when ice may close the road.

Begin on Trail No. 215, the way to Sugarloaf. In 0.2 mile (0.3 km), come to a junction. Head left on Trail No. 320, traversing an impressive grove of old-growth cedar above Heart Lake. After crossing a creek, at 0.4 mile (0.6 km) come to Trail No. 21 near a monster Douglas fir. Turn right and follow this old fire road (ignoring a left-hand trail in a few hundred feet) on a steady ascent, coming to a junction at 0.8 mile

(1.3 km). Bear right onto Trail No. 226 and hike through a low gap (elev. 650 ft/198 m). Stay left at the next junction, where Trail No. 226 heads up to Sugarloaf. Now on Trail No. 230, enjoy easy walking, descending into a ravine above a bubbling creek and reaching a junction (elev. 570 ft/174 m) at 1.4 miles (2.3 km).

Turn right onto Trail No. 207 and switchback upward, reaching a junction (elev. 720 ft/219 m) at 1.6 miles (2.6 km). Here, Trail No. 26 heads right 0.3 mile (0.5 km) to the Mount Erie Road, offering a much shorter and easier approach to this hike. Continue left through a stile onto hiker-only Trail No. 216 and start winding your way up Fidalgo Island's highest summit. The way is rough in sections, having you hobbling over roots and scampering up ledges at times. You'll pass several confusing unmarked trails within the first 0.5 mile (0.8 km)—stay left at all of these junctions.

At 2.1 miles (3.4 km), the trail brushes up along the road before making its final pitch over ledges and through thick forest. Bear left at a junction just below the summit, reaching the road at the summit at 2.5 miles (4 km). Now turn left and hit the pavement, walking a short distance to several developed viewpoints. The one overlooking March Point and Fidalgo Bay is becoming overgrown. Spend your time instead at the busy overlook south, near the communications towers. Find a quiet nook and savor the scenery.

The view is excellent over Whidbey Island to Glacier Peak, Three Fingers, and Mount Rainier. Also in view are Skagit Bay, with Kiket, Skagit, and Hope islands, and Campbell Lake directly below the mountain's north face. That lake's little island happens to be the largest island in a lake on an island in Washington State. Rock climbers can often be seen clambering up the cliffs below, where peregrine falcons also nest. Other big birds thunder from the Whidbey Island Naval Air Station to the south.

EXTENDING YOUR TRIP

You can easily combine this hike with a Sugarloaf trip (Hike 7) by following Trails No. 26 and 215. Or vary your return on interconnecting trails. You may want to have a map, however, to help you negotiate them.

9 Whistle Lake

RATING/ DIFFICULTY	LOOP	ELEV GAIN/ HIGH POINT
***/2	4.3 miles (6.9 km)	400 feet (122 m)/580 feet (170 m)

Map: Green Trails Deception Pass/Anacortes Community Forest Lands No. 41S; **Contact:** City of Anacortes Parks and Recreation, Community Forest Lands; **Notes:** Some trails open to bicycles, horses (and motorcycles Apr 1–Oct 31). Dogs permitted on-leash; **GPS:** N 48 28.419, W 122 36.338

This is a nice woodland romp to a good-sized lake flanked with towering timber and mossy ledges that bleed wildflower blossoms in the spring. Whistle Lake is a popular place for summer splashing and casting and in spring for busy birdsong and bountiful bouquets—come in winter for the misty solace. Eagles, woodpeckers, and owls hang around all year, adding excitement to the primeval surroundings.

Looking out across Whistle Lake to Mount Erie

GETTING THERE

From exit 230 on Interstate 5 in Burlington, follow State Route 20 west for 11.7 miles (18.8 km) to the junction with SR 20-Spur. Continue right on SR 20-Spur for 2.7 miles (4.3 km) to Anacortes, turning left at the traffic circle onto Commercial Avenue. After 0.4 mile (0.6 km), turn left onto Fidalgo Avenue and drive 0.2 mile (0.3 km). Turn left onto Saint Marys Drive, which soon becomes Hillcrest Drive, and continue for 0.3 mile (0.5 km). Turn right onto Whistle Lake Road and follow it for 0.9 mile (1.4 km), turning left onto Whistle Lake Terrace. Immediately turn right onto a dirt road and reach the trailhead (elev. 380 ft/116 m) at the road's end in 0.3 mile (0.5 km). Privy available.

ON THE TRAIL

The second largest lake within the Anacortes Community Forest Lands, Whistle Lake once provided Anacortes with its drinking water. Today it's a popular local swimming and fishing hole. Steep ledges and beautiful tracts of old-growth forest surround it. And a nice trail system allows you to circumnavigate it.

Follow Trail No. 20, a wide service road, beneath a thick forest canopy, passing by a few giant Douglas firs. Ignore the various side trails radiating from this well-trodden path—unless your intention is to hike some of the forested side trails. At 0.6 mile (1 km), come to a major junction complete with a privy. Continue on Trail No. 20 another 0.1 mile (0.15 km), coming to a junction with Trail No. 204 (Kenny Oakes Trail) at a cove on Whistle Lake (elev. 435 ft/133 m).

You'll be returning from the right, so keep hiking straight. At 0.8 mile (1.3 km) from the trailhead, come to the end of the old service road at a pleasant swimming area on the lake, a good destination for a short

hike. To continue around the lake, pick up Trail No. 205 and follow it along the rugged shoreline, ignoring radiating side trails. Pass a few lakeside ledges that grant good views of Mount Erie before crossing a creek and steeply climbing a ledge (elev. 560 ft/171 m) shrouded with trout lilies.

Drop off the ridge (ignoring an unmarked side trail heading right) and cross a small earthen dam (elev. 435 ft/133 m) beside a huge leaning fir. Skirt the Toot Swamp on your left, coming to a junction with Trail No. 206 at 2.2 miles (3.5 km). Head right, staying on Trail No. 205. Steeply climb 60 feet (18 m) to reach a junction at 2.5 miles (4 km).

Turn right onto Trail No. 22, dropping to a swampy cove (elev. 440 ft/134 m) before steeply climbing alongside a creek to reach another junction shortly afterward, complete with kiosk. Turn right onto wide Trail No. 21 and, after passing Trail no. 202, reach a junction with Trail No. 204 (elev. 580 ft/177 m) at 2.8 miles (4.5 km). Head right onto Trail No. 204, losing elevation and soon coming to a large ledge overlooking the lake. Be careful here while you admire springtime flowers and nearby nesting eagles.

After enjoying the view, continue on Trail No. 204, traveling lakeside and up and over some ledges sporting showy flowers in spring and good views any time. At 3.6 miles (5.8 km), return to Trail No. 20. Turn left and head 0.7 mile (1.1 km) back to the trailhead.

10 Sharpe Park and Montgomery-Duban Headlands

RATING/ DIFFICULTY	LOOP	ELEV GAIN/ HIGH POINT
***/3	2.6 miles (4.2 km)	535 feet (163 m)/ 435 feet (133 m)

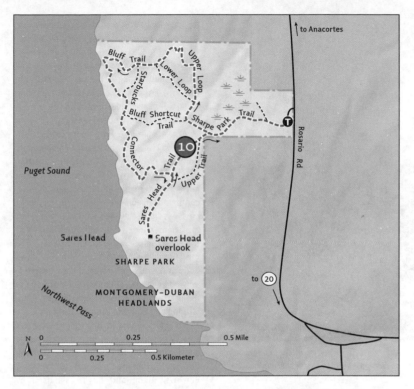

Map: Green Trails Deception Pass/Anacortes Community Forest Lands No. 41S (not all trails shown); **Contact:** Skagit County Parks and Recreation, Sharpe Park and Montgomery-Duban Headlands; **Notes:** Dogs permitted on-leash. Steep drop-offs—keep children close; **GPS:** N 48 25.837, W 122 39.890

Hike a rough-and-tumble loop on a ruggedly beautiful and surprisingly quiet stretch of coastline just north of busy Deception Pass, one of the largest stretches of undeveloped shoreline on Fidalgo Island. Drop to a rocky hidden cove before climbing to a spectacular rocky headland rising more than 400 feet (120 m) above the sea. Admire big firs, majestic madronas, and breathtaking views of Lopez, Allan, Burrows, and Whidbey islands. Sunsets here are stunning.

GETTING THERE

From exit 230 on Interstate 5 in Burlington, follow State Route 20 west for 11.7 miles (18.8 km) to the junction with SR 20-Spur. Continue left on SR 20 for 5.1 miles (8.2 km) and turn right onto Rosario Road. Drive 1.7 miles (2.7 km) to the trailhead (elev. 320 ft/98 m). Privy available.

Montgomery-Duban Headlands contain some of Fidalgo Island's wildest shoreline.

ON THE TRAIL

This 112-acre (45-ha) Skagit County Park is comprised of two parcels: Sharpe Park and the Montgomery-Duban Headlands. The latter parcel was acquired in 2003 thanks to the San Juan Preservation Trust and a generous donation from the Montgomery-Duban family. The loop described travels over rough terrain—it's possible to hike just to Sares Head, however, a much easier trip.

Starting from an oft-damp picnic area, follow the trail past the Rachel Carlson Memorial into thick woods. Soon come to a large wetland complex, compliments of the resident beavers. A short spur heads right for

a closer look. The main trail continues left, skirting the wetlands and reaching a junction in 0.3 mile (0.5 km). If you're interested in just visiting Sares Head, follow the trail left (it splits—take either one) for 0.4 mile (0.6 km). Otherwise, continue right, passing cedars, firs, and Sitka spruce on your way to the Montgomery-Duban Headlands.

At 0.4 mile (0.6 km), come to the Bluff Shortcut Trail, offering a shorter loop option. Continue right, coming to another junction at 0.5 mile (0.8 km). Opt for the Lower Loop left if you want the easier route; otherwise, continue right on the Upper Loop, climbing mossy ledges (elev. 435 ft/133 m) that sport madronas, shore pines, and window views of the Salish Sea. Then switchback down off of the ledge, meeting back up with the Lower Loop at 0.8 mile (1.3 km). Continue descending and in another 0.1 mile (0.15 km) come to the Starbucks Connector (elev. 260 ft/79 m), offering an "espresso" lane to the bluffs.

Go right instead for the longer loop, and steeply descend to spectacular coastal cliffs and ledges with breathtaking views of the dramatic shoreline and out to Whidbey, Burrows, Allen, and Lopez islands. Now exercising caution, follow the trail along the shoreline, rounding rocky coves and passing by lone junipers and through tunnels of madronas. Come to a flat-topped ledge (elev. 35 ft/11 m) that calls out for a lunch break. Watch for eagles and seals while you munch away.

When you're ready, continue hiking, steeply climbing to the Starbucks Connector at 1.3 miles (2.1 km). Stay right and reach the Bluff Shortcut Trail (elev. 190 ft/58 m) and a memorial bench at 1.4 miles (2.3 km). Continue right, dropping 30 feet (10m) to cross a creek. Then follow a rolling course over grassy and mossy ledges and through open forest, coming to the Lower Sares Head Trail (elev. 285 ft/87 m) at 1.7 miles (2.7 km). Stay right and soon come to the Upper Sares Head Trail. You'll be returning left to reach the trailhead—but first head right, climbing on mossy ledges through big firs to reach wide-open Sares Head (elev. 420 ft/128 m) at 1.9 miles (3.1 km).

Savor the outstanding views to Lopez Island and the Olympic Peninsula. Watch for soaring and roosting eagles and listen for pelagic birds and marine mammals in the surf hundreds of feet below. Enjoy good views too of Northwest Island, Deception Island, Rosario Head, and Lighthouse Point in Deception Pass State Park. When it's time to head home, follow the Sares Head Trail (Upper or Lower) 0.4 mile (0.6 km) back to the main trail and turn right, reaching the trailhead in another 0.3 mile (0.5 km).

EXTENDING YOUR TRIP
Consider checking out the newly built (2014) primitive 0.7 mile loop trail on Sares Head.

⑪ Rosario Head

RATING/ DIFFICULTY	ROUNDTRIP	ELEV GAIN/HIGH POINT
****/2	1.7 miles (2.7 km)	210 feet (64 m)/ 90 feet (27 m)

Map: Green Trails Deception Pass/Anacortes Community Forest Lands No. 41S; **Contact:** Washington State Parks, Deception Pass State Park; **Notes:** Discover Pass required. Dogs permitted on-leash. Steep drop-offs—keep children close; **GPS:** N 48 24.997, W 122 39.072

👪 ✈ 🥾 🏠   *A spectacular rocky headland, Rosario*

Head is rife in natural beauty and human history. Hike high above Bowman Bay on a trail built by President Franklin D. Roosevelt's Tree Army to a point revered by the Coast Salish peoples. Then scan the waters for a myriad of marine life. Sunsets are spectacular here.

GETTING THERE
From exit 230 on Interstate 5 in Burlington, follow State Route 20 west for 11.7 miles (18.8 km) to the junction with SR 20-Spur. Continue left on SR 20 for 5.1 miles (8.2 km) and turn right onto Rosario Road and then immediately turn left onto Bowman Bay Road. After 0.3 mile (0.5 km), turn left and drive 0.1 mile (0.15 km) to a large parking area, boat launch, and trailhead (elev. 10 ft/3 m). Restrooms and water available.

ON THE TRAIL
Hikers will find much to their liking at Washington's most visited state park. Deception Pass State Park occupies more than 4100 acres (1659 ha) on Fidalgo and Whidbey islands and contains more than 40 miles (64 km) of trails. This hike from Bowman Bay to Rosario Head touches on only a small section. But what a section!

From the boat launch parking area, head right (west) across grassy lawns, coming to the CCC (Civilian Conservation Corps) Interpretive Center (open in summer). Stop in to learn about what this Great Depression–era federal program, often referred to as Roosevelt's Tree Army, did for America.

Deception Pass State Park consisted of two CCC camps: one made up of young men from Oregon and Washington, the other of young men from the East Coast. They were segregated due to perceived cultural differences. They all worked hard, transforming

Crashing surf at Rosario Head

this corner of Washington into a prime state park by building trails, roads, campgrounds, and sturdy structures.

Enjoy their legacy by hiking the trail west. After skirting a campground in tall timber, climb high above Bowman Bay on trail blasted in ledges. Enjoy excellent views of the Gull Rocks below and Lighthouse Point across the bay. Under a canopy of stately firs, spruce, and madronas, descend 80 feet (24 m) to a trail junction (elev. 10 ft/3 m) at a picnic area at 0.7 mile (1.1 km). Right leads to Rosario Beach and a trailhead (alternative start). You want to head left.

Pass a dock on Sharpe Cove and come to the Maiden of Deception Pass. In 1983, the Samish Tribe placed this 23-foot (7-m) carved cedar story pole here at one of their traditional tribal campsites. Walk around it, reading interpretive panels that tell the story

of the maiden and of the Samish people's relationship with the Salish Sea.

Then follow the 0.3-mile (0.5-km) loop up and around 60-foot (18-m) Rosario Head. Keep children and dogs close as you walk along cliffs that drop straight to Rosario Strait. Savor spectacular views of Sares Head, Whidbey Island, the San Juans, and the Olympic Mountains. Scan Deception Island, Northwest Island, and the Urchin Rocks for marine mammals and birds. Return the way you came once fully content.

EXTENDING YOUR TRIP
Combine with Lighthouse Point (Hike 12) and/or Pass Lake (Hike 13)

12 Lighthouse and Lottie Points

RATING/ DIFFICULTY	ROUNDTRIP	ELEV GAIN/HIGH POINT
****/2	2.6 miles (4.2 km)	400 feet (122 m)/ 100 feet (30 m)

Map: Green Trails Deception Pass/Anacortes Community Forest Lands No. 41S; **Contact:** Washington State Parks, Deception Pass State Park; **Notes:** Discover Pass required. Dogs permitted on-leash; **GPS:** N 48 24.997, W 122 39.072

Rugged coastal headlands, placid coves, tidal pools teeming with crusty critters, towering ancient evergreens, and breathtaking views—this short hike in Deception Pass State Park packs it in. Plus, admire Deception Pass itself, with its treacherous waters and historical bridge connecting Fidalgo and Whidbey islands.

GETTING THERE
See directions to Hike 11.

ON THE TRAIL
Start by walking south along the rose- and salal-lined sandy beaches of Bowman Bay, passing the boat launch and pier. Climb over a bluff that offers good views of the bay, reaching a junction (elev. 40 ft/12 m) at 0.3 mile (0.5 km). The way left climbs 120 feet (37 m) to SR 20 and intersects the Pacific Northwest Trail. Continue right instead and soon reach another junction.

Left goes to Lottie Point. Right goes to Lighthouse Point. Head right first, dropping to near sea level and walking along a tombolo—a spit connecting an island or offshore rock with the mainland shore, formed by wave-carried sedimentation. Clamber up some ledges, entering old-growth Douglas fir forest and reaching a junction at 0.6 mile (1 km). You'll be returning right, so continue left, passing ledges and grassy bluffs that grant excellent views of Deception Pass and North Beach on Whidbey Island.

The way rounds the cliffy headland just east of Lighthouse Point, reaching an excellent viewpoint of Rosario Strait and Lopez Island. At 1.1 miles (1.8 km), a side trail (elev. 80 ft/24 m) leads 0.2 mile (0.3 km) left to Vista Point, which overlooks Bowman Bay, if you're interested (but don't follow the trail beyond Vista Point, as it's rough and overgrown). The main trail continues west through gorgeous old growth, reaching a familiar junction at 1.3 miles (2.1 km).

Turn left, retracing your steps over the tombolo to the Canoe Pass Trail to Lottie Point at 1.6 miles (2.6 km). Take the trail through big firs along Lottie Bay, reaching another junction at 1.8 miles (2.9 km). The trail loops here. Continue right, steeply switchbacking up and over the 100-foot (30-m) point and reaching a spur at 2 miles (3.2 km). Take the 0.1-mile (0.15-km) return spur to a bluff at water's edge, which grants exceptional views of the 1935-built Deception Pass Bridge and the treacherous waters of Canoe and Deception passes.

Then continue the loop, climbing 50 feet (15 m) before dropping back to a familiar junction in 0.2 mile (0.3 km). Turn right and hike 0.3 mile (0.5 km) (bearing left at a junction) back to your vehicle.

Deception Pass Bridge from Lottie Point

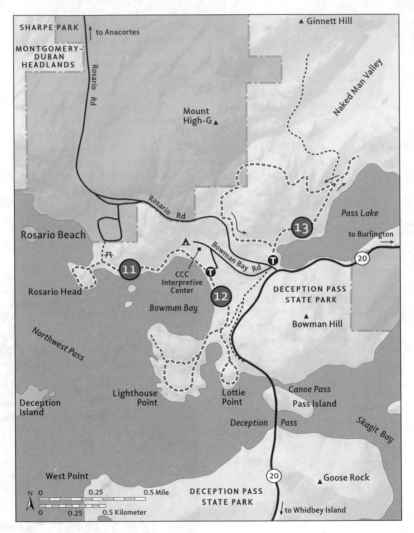

EXTENDING YOUR TRIP

Follow the connector trail to the Pacific Northwest Trail, where you can hike right 0.5 mile (0.8 km) to the Deception Pass Bridge, or left 0.5 mile (0.8 km) through gorgeous old growth to Pass Lake (Hike 13).

13 Pass Lake

RATING/ DIFFICULTY	LOOP	ELEV GAIN/HIGH POINT
**/2	2.8 miles (4.5 km)	470 feet (143 m)/ 480 feet (146 m)

Map: Green Trails Deception Pass/Anacortes Community Forest Lands No. 41S; **Contact:** Washington State Parks, Deception Pass State Park; **Notes:** Discover Pass required. Dogs permitted on-leash; **GPS:** N 48 25.028, W 122 38.647

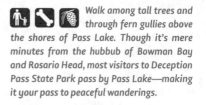

Walk among tall trees and through fern gullies above the shores of Pass Lake. Though it's mere minutes from the hubbub of Bowman Bay and Rosario Head, most visitors to Deception Pass State Park pass by Pass Lake—making it your pass to peaceful wanderings.

GETTING THERE

From exit 230 on Interstate 5 in Burlington, follow State Route 20 west for 11.7 miles (18.8 km) to the junction with SR 20-Spur. Turn left, and continue on SR 20 for 5.1 miles

Placid Pass Lake on an overcast day

(8.2 km) and turn right onto Rosario Road. Then immediately turn right to the Pass Lake boat launch and trailhead (elev. 130 feet/40 m). Privy available.

ON THE TRAIL

Except for the constant highway buzz and the roar of Whidbey Island Naval Air Station jets overhead, Pass Lake is a peaceful place. Start on the Pass Lake Trail (part of the Pacific Northwest Trail, or PNT, that runs from the Olympic coast to Glacier National Park in Montana), heading north and ascending a bench above the lake. Despite the trail's proximity to the shoreline, big trees limit lake viewing to just glimpses. At 0.1 mile (0.15 km), bear right at a junction. You'll be returning from the left. Lined with ferns and salal, the trail traverses a mature forest of Douglas fir, grand fir, and a few Sitka spruces. Except for a short climb of 70 feet (21 m) to skirt a rocky knoll, the way is pleasant and pretty level.

At 0.7 mile (1.1 km), come to a junction. The Ginnett Hill Trail (part of the PNT) continues straight. Your loop carries on left. But first take the 0.3-mile (0.5-km) trail to the right to old pastures and orchards near the ranger's residence on the north end of the lake. You should have the place to yourself, but for some deer. Retrace your steps back to the junction and continue on the loop, now an old fire road.

Wind through thick forest, climbing to about 480 feet (146 m) before gradually descending. Briefly leave the park, passing through a recent timber harvest, and then follow the skid road toward Rosario Road. At 2.4 miles (3.9 km), turn left back onto trail, climbing 50 feet (15 m) over a mossy knoll. Drop back into handsome old-growth forest, coming to a familiar junction in 0.3 mile (0.5 km). Turn right to return to your vehicle.

EXTENDING YOUR TRIP

Follow the up-down-up Ginnett Hill Trail 1 mile (1.6 km) to an old homesite with a decent view of Pass Lake and Bowman Hill. En route you'll skirt Naked Man Valley, which may be too much to bare!

AN ISLAND COMES FULL CIRCLE

Traditional land of the Swinomish Tribe, 96-acre (39-ha) Kiket Island was once considered for a nuclear power plant before becoming a private retreat for a local vintner. In 2010 the island, along with nearby Flagstaff Island, was purchased, for US$14.3 million, by Washington State Parks with the help of the Trust for Public Land, becoming the Kukutali (meaning "cattail" or "cattail mat") Preserve. As part of the purchase negotiations, the new preserve is co-owned and co-managed with the Swinomish Tribe, in essence bringing Kiket Island full circle.

Located in Similk Bay and connected to Fidalgo Island by a tombolo, Kiket contains more than 2 miles (3 km) of prime shoreline and a wildlife-rich lagoon. Currently, access to the preserve is available only through guided tours held Saturdays at 9:00 and 11:00 AM. Call (360) 661-0682 for a reservation. The tour includes a 2-mile (3-km) out-and-back hike to the tip of the island.

san juan islands

Cattle Point, San Juan Islands National Monument, San Juan Island

Lummi Island

Lummi Island is the northeastern-most island within the San Juans archipelago. The 5923-acre (2397-ha) island is part of Whatcom County and is serviced by a small county ferry from Gooseberry Point. The island is named for the Lummi Tribe (whose reservation includes nearby Portage Island but not Lummi Island itself), and about 850 people live there year-round.

The northern half of Lummi contains farms and is pastoral, while the island's southern half is mountainous and thickly forested. The Washington Department of Fish and Wildlife manages a large tract on the island, and the Lummi Island Heritage Trust manages three preserves open to the public.

Lummi's proximity to Bellingham and its short ferry crossing makes it conducive for day trips. Except for primitive boat-in-only campsites, there is no camping on the island.

14 Otto Preserve

RATING/ DIFFICULTY	LOOP	ELEV GAIN/HIGH POINT
**/1	1.2 miles (1.9 km)	130 feet (40 m)/ 250 feet (76 m)

Maps: USGS Lummi Island, heritage trust map online; **Contact:** Lummi Island Heritage Trust, Otto Preserve; **Notes:** Dogs permitted on-leash; **GPS:** N4 8 41.885, W 122 40.472

Wander through quiet woods and old farmland in the heart of Lummi Island. The Lummi Island Heritage Trust's first protected property, the Otto Preserve now totals more than 100

acres (40 ha) and includes the island's largest wetland complex.

GETTING THERE

From exit 260 on Interstate 5, follow Slater Road west 3.7 miles (6 km) and turn left onto Haxton Way. Continue 6.6 miles (10.6 km) to the Lummi Island ferry. From the ferry landing on island, head left on South Nugent Road for 1.6 miles (2.6 km). Turn left onto Sunrise Road and drive 0.3 mile (0.5 km) to the preserve and trailhead (elev. 120 ft/37 m).

ON THE TRAIL

Once a farm used for raising Scottish highland cattle, the preserve still sports many old buildings, including one now used for housing the Lummi Island Heritage Trust's office. This hike starts by a kiosk northeast of the office.

Follow the old woods road-turned-trail and immediately come to a junction near a dedication rock. You'll be returning from left, so carry on to the right through a forest of big firs. At 0.1 mile (0.15 km), the 0.2-mile (0.3-km) Walden Walk veers right, passing by a window view of Lummi Peak before rejoining the main trail.

Continue straight, at first steeply, coming to the Walden Walk (elev. 200 ft/61 m) again at 0.2 mile (0.3 km). Now enjoy fairly easy walking, cresting a 250-foot (76-m) hillside before descending. At just over 0.5 mile (0.8 km) come to a junction with the 0.4-mile (0.6-km) Baumgart Woods Trail, which loops through a parcel added to the original preserve.

Continue straight, reaching the other end of the Baumgart Woods Trail at 0.6 mile (1 km). If you want an easy return to the trailhead, continue left for 0.3 mile (0.5 km) on the Main Loop. Otherwise, make a more interesting return by hiking straight a short

Lummi's Otto Preserve allows for quiet walks in the woods.

distance to another junction, and then take the Betty's Shortcut Trail left. This new trail (built in 2013) skirts a large wetland complex graced with big cedars and birches.

Return to the Main Loop at 1.1 miles (1.8 km). Turn right and immediately come to the Hay Barn Loop. Continue straight 0.1 mile (0.15 km) to complete your loop, or extend it by 0.1 mile (0.15 km) by going right and passing a cedar grove, an old barn, and a pasture before returning to the trailhead.

EXTENDING YOUR TRIP

Combine with a visit to the trust's nearby Baker Preserve (Hike 15) or the small Curry Preserve, with its nice fields and Mount Baker views.

15 Baker Preserve

RATING/ DIFFICULTY	ROUNDTRIP	ELEV GAIN/HIGH POINT
***/3	3.6 miles (5.8 km)	1030 feet (314 m)/ 1100 feet (335 m)

Maps: USGS Lummi Island, heritage trust map online; **Contact:** Lummi Island Heritage Trust, Baker Preserve; **Notes:** Open daylight hours only. All visitors must sign register. Group size limited to six. Dogs prohibited; **GPS:** N 48 41.670, W 122 39.698

Wind up steep slopes beneath a cloak of greenery to flowered ledges high on Lummi Peak, at more than

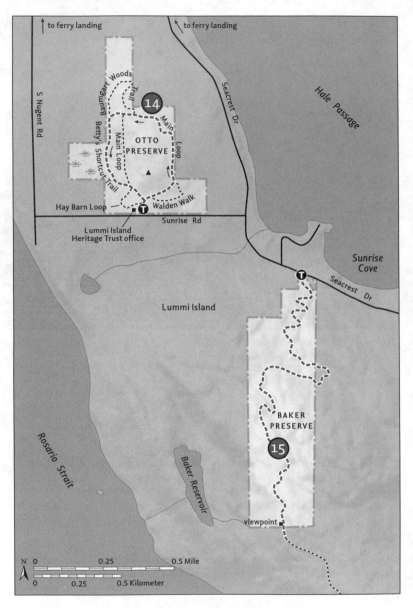

to ferry landing

to ferry landing

S Nugent Rd

Hale Passage

Seacrest Dr

Bangert Woods Trail

14

OTTO PRESERVE

Main Loop

Main Loop

Betty's Shortcut Trail

Hay Barn Loop

Walden Walk

Lummi Island Heritage Trust office

Sunrise Rd

Sunrise Cove

Seacrest Dr

Lummi Island

Rosario Strait

Baker Reservoir

BAKER PRESERVE

15

viewpoint

N

0   0.25   0.5 Mile

0   0.25   0.5 Kilometer

1600 feet (488 m) one of the highest summits in the San Juans and until recently off-limits to visitors due to private ownership. Thanks to the Lummi Island Heritage Trust, hikers can now explore a part of this prominent landmark. Watch eagles, hawks, and vultures ride thermals above. And enjoy eagle's-eye viewing of the islands and the Salish Sea sparkling below.

GETTING THERE

From exit 260 on Interstate 5, follow Slater Road west 3.7 miles (6 km) and turn left onto Haxton Way. Continue 6.6 miles (10.6 km) to the Lummi Island ferry. From ferry landing on island, head left on South Nugent Road for 0.6 mile (1 km). Turn left onto Seacrest Drive and drive 1.7 miles (2.7 km) to the preserve and trailhead (elev. 70 ft/21 m).

ON THE TRAIL

The 129-acre (52-ha) Baker Preserve abuts the 355-acre (144-ha) Baker Ranch to the north and the 700-acre (283-ha) Washington Department of Fish and Wildlife (WDFW) Lummi Unit to the south, forming a large protected swath on Lummi Peak. The ranch is currently closed to the public, but the WDFW unit can be accessed via this hike.

Following an old skid road, the way starts off steeply up ferny slopes, paralleling a small creek-cradling ravine. Through a uniform forest of maturing second growth, pass big stumps of what once grew here. The grade eventually eases. At 1 mile (1.6 km), the trail bends left onto an old logging road. The walking is fairly pleasant now, as the old track winds up the north shoulder of the peak.

After passing a small swampy pool, begin to catch window views of the islands through the trees. At 1.8 miles (2.9 km), just after leav-

You can see Sinclair and Cypress islands from Lummi Peak's lofty ledges.

ing the preserve and entering WDFW land, turn right at a signed junction to a ledge-top viewpoint (elev. 1100 ft/335 m), complete with interpretive signs and wooden railings. The latter protect not only you from wandering off the ledge but also rare flowers from being trampled.

Enjoy views of Sinclair, Cypress, Orcas, Clark, Matia, Sucia, Patos, and Saturna islands. Frosty Canadian North Shore summits can also be seen. Check snags for eagles and look for peregrine falcons—they nest in Lummi Peak's precipitous cliffs.

EXTENDING YOUR TRIP

You can continue walking the old road south for another 1 mile (1.6 km) on WDFW land, through attractive forest and by wetlands close to cliff tops. Lummi Peak's summit is thickly wooded and offers no views—so don't bother bagging it.

Guemes Island

Across the Guemes Channel a mere 0.5 mile (0.8 km) from Anacortes, Guemes Island is easily accessible via a Skagit County ferry. Named for the viceroy of Mexico by the Spanish explorer José María Narváez in 1791, Guemes is also known locally as Dog Island for the large population of Salish wool dogs that once lived here. Pastoral and with a population of about six hundred year-round residents, Guemes is an excellent island for cycling. The Skagit Land Trust has two courtesy bikes available for checkout for a few hours on the island. Get the bikes at Anderson's General Store (www.guemesislandstore.com; US$50 deposit) located next to the ferry landing. There are no campgrounds on Guemes.

16 Guemes Mountain

RATING/ DIFFICULTY	ROUNDTRIP	ELEV GAIN/HIGH POINT
***/2	2.4 miles (3.9 km)	600 feet (183 m)/ 688 feet (210 m)

Map: USGS Anacortes North; **Contact:** Skagit Land Trust, Guemes Mountain; **Notes:** Dogs permitted on-leash; **GPS:** N 48 32.594, W 122 35.758

Gentle Guemes Mountain is the centerpiece to 534 acres (216 ha) of public and private protected land, thanks to the Skagit Land Trust, San Juan Preservation Trust, island residents, and hundreds of conservation-minded citizens. Follow a hiker-only path, thanks to the Washington Trails Association, weaving through attractive

Guemes Mountain offers good views of Guemes' farmlands and Cypress Island.

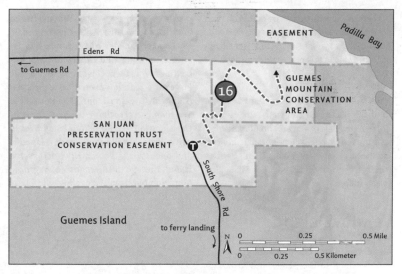

forest to the broad prairie summit that bursts with wildflowers in the spring and rewards with sublime views of rolling pasture, emerald islands, and snow-capped peaks.

GETTING THERE

From exit 230 on Interstate 5 In Burlington, follow State Route 20 west for 11.7 miles (18.8 km) to the junction with SR 20-Spur. Continue right on SR 20-Spur for 2.7 miles (4.3 km) to Anacortes, turning right at the traffic circle onto Commercial Avenue (which is still the SR 20-Spur). After 1.3 miles (2.1 km), turn left onto 12th Street (still the SR 20-Spur) and continue for 0.5 mile (0.8 km). Turn right on I Avenue and reach the Guemes Island ferry in 0.4 mile (0.6 km). From the ferry landing on the island, turn right onto South Shore Road and follow it 2.1 miles (3.4 km) (bearing left at 1.7 mi/2.7 km) to the trailhead (elev. 90 ft/27 m). Bike rack available.

ON THE TRAIL

Follow the trail through a maturing forest of fir and madrona and across a forest floor of ferns and salal. At 0.5 mile (0.8 km), wind through a cedar grove before entering a stretch of alders that provide teaser views. After crossing a small creek, the way follows an old skid road through a formerly logged area.

Crest the small mountain's ridge and angle left, ignoring a path right that leads to private property. At 1.2 miles (1.9 km), reach the 688-foot (210-m) summit and views! East it's Samish Island, the Chuckanut Mountains, and frosty Mount Baker. North it's little Jack Island, Vendovi Island, Eliza Island, Lummi Island, and a slew of Canadian peaks, with the distinguished Golden Ears calling the most attention. To the west it's Orcas's Mount Constitution, Fidalgo's Mount Erie, Burrows Island, a swath of pasture across Guemes, and wild Cypress Island behind it.

There are several good viewpoints on the mountain, but keep your travels on established paths so as not to disturb sensitive plants growing in this prairie environment.

EXTENDING YOUR TRIP

From Young's County Park on the northern tip of the island, you can walk 2 miles (3.2 km) of nice public beach around Clark Point. Near the ferry landing is more public beach and the San Juan Preservation Trust's Peach Preserve, with beautiful sandy beach and upland trails.

Vendovi Island

Skagit County's 217-acre (88-ha) Vendovi Island had long been privately owned and off-limits to the public. But in 2012, the San Juan Preservation Trust acquired the island in one of its largest purchases, opening it to public visitation and assuring that it remains in a natural state in perpetuity. There is no camping or moorage on the island.

RATING/ DIFFICULTY	ROUNDTRIP	ELEV GAIN/HIGH POINT
*****/2	3.2 miles (5.1 km)	400 feet (122 m)/ 260 feet (79 m)

Maps: USGS Anacortes North, preservation trust map online; **Contact:** San Juan Preservation Trust, Vendovi Island Preserve; **Notes:** Open 10:00 AM–6:00 PM, May–Sept. All visitors must sign in at kiosk at head of dock. Dogs must be on-leash and pet waste packed out. Obey all posted rules and regulations; **GPS:** N 48 36.860, W 122 36.769

Vendovi Island was named in 1841 by Commander Wilkes for an imprisoned Fijian chief who killed and cannibalized a whaling crew. It was once one of the largest privately owned undeveloped islands in the San Juans. Thanks to the San Juan Preservation Trust's purchase of the island in 2012, for half of its appraised value, Vendovi will remain undeveloped—and open to the public. Hike across the island through lush woods to a grassy bluff that bursts with dazzling wildflower

A young hiker surveys the Salish Sea from Jack's Back Overlook.

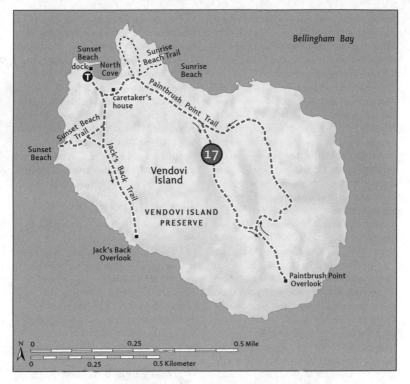

N

0   0.25   0.5 Mile

0   0.25   0.5 Kilometer

blossoms. *Walk along a midden beach that sparkles in the evening light. And watch pigeon guillemots nesting in North Cove. Vendovi is a magical and ecologically important island.*

GETTING THERE

You need a private boat or to arrange for a water taxi to access Vendovi Island. Island Express Water Taxi in Anacortes (www.islandexpresscharters.com) and Leap Frog Water Taxi in Bellingham (www.leapfrogwatertaxi.com) both offer reliable service. The trailhead is at the North Cove dock. Privy available. No water.

ON THE TRAIL

Upon arrival at North Cove, look for pigeon guillemots nesting in the breakwater and sign in at the kiosk. Be sure to adhere to all rules and regulations when visiting this ecologically important island. Head 0.1 mile (0.15 km) up to what was once a private residence, now the caretaker's home. Then continue hiking at 0.2 mile (0.3 km) to a junction (elev. 60 ft/18 m) at the cemetery plot of the former owner of the island.

The trail left goes to a bluff overlooking North Cove and looping back to this junction in 0.2 mile (0.3 km). Another trail from this spot veers 0.1 mile (0.15 km) to beautiful

Sunrise Beach, with its weathered logs for sitting on and admiring the view of Eliza Island, the Chuckanut Mountains, and perhaps a seal or two plying the waters. Both trails are worthy side trips.

Follow the Paintbrush Point Trail, an old woods road, up the center of the island. Notice the thick understory along the way, attesting to the lack of deer on the island. Douglas squirrels are the main terrestrial mammal here. At 0.4 mile (0.6 km), come to a trail split (elev. 125 ft/38 m). Go right here and return later on the trail from the left.

Traversing ferny forest, ascend between the island's two high points, cresting a 260-foot (79-m) hill before descending and coming to a junction (elev. 220 ft/67 m) at 0.8 mile (1.3 km). You'll be continuing to the left, but first head right for 0.2 mile (0.3 km) to Paintbrush Point (elev. 250 ft/76 m), which is carpeted in springtime with paintbrush and other showy flowers. And what a view! Check out Samish Island, little San Juan Preservation Trust–protected Jack Island, Guemes Island, and Cypress Island. You can see Anacortes and Burrows Island, too, and often oil tankers coming and going to March Point. Perish the thought of the effects of an oil spill on this pristine island.

Now return, veering right at the first junction for a slightly longer trip back to the caretaker's house at 1 mile (1.6 km). You're not done hiking yet, though—you have two more destinations to visit. Head left on Jack's Back Trail, passing the old shop and coming to a junction at 0.1 mile (0.15 km) with the Sunset Beach Trail (elev. 50 ft/15 m). Continue straight, first passing another trail to Sunset Beach and, after a short climb and descent, come to Jack's Back Overlook in 0.3 mile (0.5 km). Enjoy good views of Jack, Cypress, and Sinclair islands.

Then retrace your steps 0.3 mile (0.5 km) to the last junction and turn left, enjoying some nice tread work thanks to the Washington Trails Association. In 0.15 mile (0.2 km), come to gorgeous Sunset Beach, with its white-shelled midden shoreline. Enjoy the sweeping view of Lummi and Sinclair islands. You'll have to enjoy the sunset from the water, however, as you need to head back before 6:00 PM—so hike 0.35 mile (0.6 km) back to the dock, content that this gorgeous island will remain a wild and spectacular place for your return trip.

Sinclair Island

Once known as Cottonwood Island by early pioneers, Skagit County's 1015-acre (411-ha) Sinclair Island boasts a year-round population of about three. It was once home to a schoolhouse, post office, and a community called Urban. Now the island consists primarily of seasonal residences. Sinclair Island is nearly all privately owned, but two county dirt roads make for peaceful wandering.

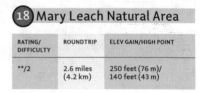

18 Mary Leach Natural Area

RATING/ DIFFICULTY	ROUNDTRIP	ELEV GAIN/HIGH POINT
**/2	2.6 miles (4.2 km)	250 feet (76 m)/ 140 feet (43 m)

Map: USGS Cypress Island; **Contact:** Washington Department of Fish and Wildlife, Mary Leach Natural Area; **Notes:** Dogs permitted on-leash. The county dock is closed due to 2011 storm damage. You can moor boats south of the dock and walk public tidelands during low tides to reach the public road. Adjacent uplands are privately owned. No potable water; **GPS:** N 48 37.005, W 122 41.584

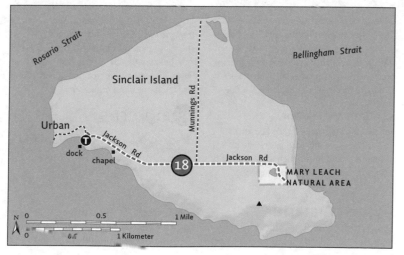

Hike across thickly forested, lightly settled Sinclair Island on a county road that's pretty much a wide trail. Then visit an old farm and the site of the island's first post office, now a wildlife preserve and rapidly reverting back to a presettlement state.

GETTING THERE

You need a private boat or to arrange for a water taxi to access Sinclair Island. Island Express Water Taxi in Anacortes (www.islandexpresscharters.com) and Leap Frog Water Taxi in Bellingham (www.leapfrogwatertaxi.com) both offer reliable service.

ON THE TRAIL

Start from the county dock that protrudes from a grassy and rocky bluff on the island's southwest shore, but pause for some nice views of nearby Cypress Island before taking to the trail. Then walk up a thickly vegetated path, soon reaching a junction with Jackson Road, a county roadway that's not much more than a wide trail.

Left leads to the old settlement of Urban, which isn't urban at all—just seasonal homes. Head right, passing a few homes and a cute little chapel in the woods. Most of the way is through thick jungle-like forest, owing to there being few, if any, deer (foraging) on the island. After gently climbing to about 140 feet (43 m), start a long gentle descent.

At 0.7 mile (1.1 km), come to a junction with another "trail," county-owned Munnings Road, which heads north across the island in a near straight line. Continue straight, coming to another junction at 1.2 miles (1.9 km). The way left is a private drive. Continue straight, the way soon transitioning into a grassy path as it enters the 35-acre (14-ha) Mary Leach Natural Area. Wander around the property, noting old apple trees among the growing-in pasture. Near an old dilapidated homestead surrounded by head-high nettles, find an interpretive sign and memorial to Mary Leach, a first lieutenant in the US Army during World War II. Upon her death she willed this peaceful property to the

The Mary Leach Natural Area apple orchard

state. If you don't mind crashing through some brush, you can reach adjacent public tidelands that make for nice exploring during low tide.

EXTENDING YOUR TRIP
Follow Munnings Road 1 mile (1.6 km) to its end at the shoreline, with an excellent view of Lummi Island. The beach left and right is private, so just admire it from this spot.

Cypress Island

Cypress Island is the largest relatively undeveloped island in the San Juan archipelago—more than 5100 acres (2064 ha) of this 5500-acre (2226-ha) Skagit County island are protected from development, and only a handful of people live here. The Skagit Land Trust owns some conservation easements on the island, but the majority of Cypress is managed as a natural resources conservation area (NRCA) by the Washington Department of Natural Resources (DNR). In the 1980s, Spokane industrialist Raymond Hanson proposed a huge resort and golf course on the island. Organized opposition from residents and conservationists led to Hanson instead selling to the state and many trails now utilize old roads built in preparation for the development. The DNR is currently working on a management plan for the Secret Harbor property it acquired in 2009.

The island is mountainous and heavily forested, with several small lakes. You won't find any cypress trees: Captain George Vancouver mistook the island's junipers for cypress (which grow in the American southeast) when he mapped the area in 1792. There is no backcountry camping in the island's interior, but Cypress has two shoreline campgrounds—at Cypress Head and Pelican Beach. Check with the DNR (www.dnr.wa.gov) for camping and island visitation rules and regulations.

19 Eagle Cliff

RATING/ DIFFICULTY	ROUNDTRIP	ELEV GAIN/HIGH POINT
*****/3	2.8 miles (4.5 km)	752 feet (229 m)/ 752 feet (229 m)

Maps: USGS Cypress Island, DNR map online; **Contact:** Washington Department of Natural Resources (DNR), Northwest

District; **Notes:** Trail closed Feb 1–July 15 to protect threatened, endangered, and sensitive species. Dogs prohibited on Eagle Cliff Trail; **GPS:** N 48 36.181, W 122 42.223

👨‍👧 ⚙️ 🌰 🦅 *Stand upon a high grassy, rocky knob that rises abruptly above Rosario Strait, and gaze out to majestic Mount Constitution and Lummi Peak, the loftiest summits in the San Juan Islands. Admire the deep unbroken forests and unscathed hills of Cypress Island before you—a view Captain Vancouver would recognize.*

GETTING THERE
You need a private boat or to arrange for a water taxi to access Cypress Island. Island Express Water Taxi in Anacortes (www.island expresscharters.com) and Leap Frog Water Taxi in Bellingham (www.leapfrogwatertaxi .com) both offer reliable service. The hike begins from Pelican Beach (moorage, no dock). Privy available.

ON THE TRAIL
Starting from Pelican Beach (named not for the bird, but for the Pelican class of sailboats belonging to a local group that meets here), pass prime shorefront campsites and come to a kiosk. Read about the island and then start up a boardwalk to the trail. Steadily climb through a mature forest of Douglas firs and cedars.

At 0.4 mile (0.6 km), reach a junction (elev. 190 ft/58 m). The Pelican Beach Trail continues straight 0.2 mile (0.3 km) to the Duck Lake Loop (Hike 20). Head right instead, ascending through open forest and across grassy balds and mossy ledges. Views emerge as you wind up and around grassy ledges. Some steps help you negotiate one of the steeper ones.

At 1.4 miles (2.3 km), reach the open, rocky 752-foot (229-m) summit graced with a few "cypresses" (junipers). The view is breathtaking: north to Lummi Island and British Columbia's Golden Ears Mountains and company; west to Blakely, Obstruction, and Orcas islands, with Peavine and Obstruction passes separating them. Look east for a Baker glimpse and south to Lopez Island's Chadwick Hill and the emerald-cloaked hilly backbone of Cypress. Look in the air too for this cliff's namesake and for peregrine falcons, which nest on this stunning outcropping.

Looking south down Rosario Strait from Eagle Cliff

EXTENDING YOUR TRIP

Combine with a hike to Duck Lake and/or Smugglers Cove (Hike 20). Eagle Cliff can also be accessed from Eagle Harbor.

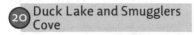

20 Duck Lake and Smugglers Cove

RATING/ DIFFICULTY	ROUNDTRIP	ELEV GAIN/HIGH POINT
***/2	5.1 miles (8.2 km)	720 feet (219 m)/ 310 feet (94 m)

Maps: USGS Cypress Island, DNR map online; **Contact:** Washington Department of Natural Resources (DNR), Northwest Dis-trict; **Notes:** Dogs permitted on-leash; **GPS:** N 48 35.204, W 122 41.723

Follow a gently graded old log-ging road to a large wetland matted in lily pads and flanked with bulrushes hiding songbirds and waterfowl. Then hike a lit-tle-used trail to a small cove beneath the sheer east face of Eagle Cliff once favored by bootleggers and homesteaded by a reclusive, tenacious woman.

GETTING THERE

You need a private boat or to arrange for a water taxi to access Cypress Island. Island

Eagle Cliff hovers over Smugglers Cove.

Express Water Taxi in Anacortes (www.island expresscharters.com) and Leap Frog Water Taxi in Bellingham (www.leapfrogwatertaxi. com) both offer reliable service. The hike begins from Eagle Harbor (moorage, no dock). Privy available.

ON THE TRAIL

At the Eagle Harbor landing, take a moment to read the excellent interpretive kiosk. There are a lot of informative trail signs and good trail markings throughout the island. From the landing, the Cypress Mainline leads left (south). Head right instead, coming to a junction (elev. 100 ft/30 m) in 0.1 mile (0.15 km). The grassy path left leads back to the mainline, and the wide path right is your return route. For now, stay straight on the Duck Lake Loop.

Gently ascend on an old logging road. Much of Cypress was logged in the 1930s, but small pockets of old growth remain. At 0.7 mile (1.1 km), stay left at a junction; the trail right returns steeply to Eagle Harbor. The way ahead levels out, reaching Duck Lake. More of a large wetland, Duck Lake is surrounded with thick vegetation and provides excellent wildlife habitat. Look for ducks among the cattails and newts crossing the path.

At 1 mile (1.6 km), come to a junction (elev. 310 ft/94 m). The loop continues right, but first a trip to the left, to Smugglers Cove, is warranted. Soon pass an old homesteader's cabin rapidly being reclaimed by nature. Then skirt Duck Lake, enjoying nice views from forest openings. After crossing the lake's outlet stream on a good bridge, begin descending, passing through pockets of big Douglas firs. At 2.2 miles (3.5 km), come to Smugglers Cove, nestled beneath the stark face of Eagle Cliff.

Enjoy good views across Rosario Strait to Orcas Island. When the tide is low, wander the cobblestone beach. A remote location, it was chosen in the 1930s by rugged and reclusive homesteader Zoe Hardy to eke out her farm. Around 1940, Ms. Hardy found out she had cancer, causing her to cut off all contact with others before disappearing.

Retrace your steps 1.2 miles (1.9 km), climbing back to the junction at Duck Lake. Then head left and once again descend, coming to a junction at 3.6 miles (5.8 km) from your start at Eagle Harbor. The way left leads 0.2 mile (0.3 km) to the Eagle Cliff Trail and continues 0.4 mile (0.6 km) to Pelican Beach (an alternative start for this hike). You want to veer right, following the Duck Lake Loop, passing some big maples and cedars as you descend to Eagle Harbor. At low tide, feel free to do some beach exploring.

At 4.7 miles (7.6 km), pass the shortcut trail back toward Duck Lake. Then continue along Eagle Harbor, enjoying excellent views out to the Cone Islands and snowcapped Mount Baker in the distance and climbing back to your first junction at 5 miles (8 km). Your boat or water taxi pickup awaits you 0.1 mile (0.15 km) to the left.

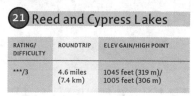

21 Reed and Cypress Lakes

RATING/ DIFFICULTY	ROUNDTRIP	ELEV GAIN/HIGH POINT
***/3	4.6 miles (7.4 km)	1045 feet (319 m)/ 1005 feet (306 m)

Maps: USGS Cypress Island, DNR map online; **Contact:** Washington Department of Natural Resources (DNR), Northwest District; **Notes:** Dogs permitted on-leash at Reed Lake. Dogs prohibited on Cypress Lake Trail; **GPS:** N 48 35.202, W 122 41.729

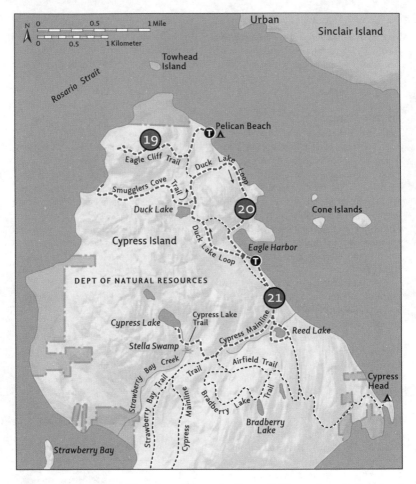

Hike to two of the handful of lakes that dot Cypress Island. One was once slated to provide water to a megadevelopment—now it sits quiet except when mating and migrating birds fill the air with song and chatter. The other lake, the largest on the island, sits snuggly along the mountainous backbone of this nearly undeveloped and wild island.

GETTING THERE

You need a private boat to access Cypress Island, or arrange a water taxi. Island Express Water Taxi in Anacortes (www.islandexpress charters.com) and Leap Frog Water Taxi in

Bellingham (www.leapfrogwatertaxi.com) both offer reliable service. The hike begins from Eagle Harbor (moorage, no dock). Privy available.

ON THE TRAIL

From Eagle Harbor, head left on the Cypress Mainline, a wide old road that Department of Natural Resources staff still occasionally drive for administrative purposes. Steadily climb on the old haul road, coming to a junction in 0.3 mile (0.5 km). The grassy way right leads back to Eagle Harbor. Continue straight, coming to another junction (elev. 390 ft/119 m) at 0.7 mile (1.1 km).

Go left here, passing an old DNR compound, and soon come to an interpretive display about Reed Lake near a junction. You'll be returning from the right, so stay left, coming to the earthen dam at the lake's outlet (elev. 350 ft/107 m). Reed Lake is natural but was altered to supply water to a huge development that thankfully never materialized. Look among the bulrushes and lily pads for equally appreciative amphibians and waterfowl.

Cross the dam and bear right at another junction. The trail left leads 0.6 mile (1 km) to the Cypress Head Trail (Hike 23). Circle the pine- and rhododendron-lined lake, wandering past some madronas and big firs too. Soon after rock-hopping across the lake's inlet stream, close the loop at 1.3 miles (2.1 km). Turn left and hike 0.1 mile (0.15 km) back to the Cypress Mainline. Then head left, steadily climbing through open dry forest and paralleling a tumbling creek. Shortly after crossing the creek, reach a junction at 2.1 miles (3.4 km). The way left leads to the old airstrip and Bradberry Lake (Hike 23). Stay on the mainline and at 2.2 miles (3.5 km), near a gap in the mountainous back-

bone of the island, come to a junction (elev. 880 ft/268 m), complete with privy.

Take the old road right, noting that dogs are not allowed on this trail due to sensitive wetlands. Round huge Stella Swamp, catching glimpses of this sprawling wetland through the open forest. After crossing Strawberry Bay Creek on a bridge, veer left at a sign and come to Cypress Lake (elev. 1005 feet/306 m) at 2.7 miles (4.3 km). The trail continues a short distance left. Find a nice spot to sit and savor the serenity of this special place.

Cypress Lake

When it's time to head home, retrace your steps 0.5 mile (0.8 km) back to the junction in the gap, and follow the Cypress Mainline 1.4 miles (2.3 km) back to Eagle Harbor.

EXTENDING YOUR TRIP

Instead of returning via the Cypress Mainline, follow the Airfield Trail 1.1 miles (1.7 km) to the connector trail back to Reed Lake.

22 Strawberry Bay and Reef Point

RATING/ DIFFICULTY	ROUNDTRIP	ELEV GAIN/HIGH POINT
****/5	10 miles (16.1 km)	2180 feet (664 m)/ 960 feet (293 m)

Maps: USGS Cypress Island, DNR map online; **Contact:** Washington Department of Natural Resources (DNR), Northwest District; **Notes:** Dogs permitted on-leash; **GPS:** N 48 35.202, W 122 41.729

Hike up and over the mountainous spine of Cypress Island to a remote beach and a spectacular point that grants sweeping views of an island-dotted sea. Visit an abandoned mine and site of an old reef-fishing operation, letting sea breezes and voices from the past lull you.

GETTING THERE

You need a private boat or to arrange for a water taxi to access Cypress Island. Island Express Water Taxi in Anacortes (www.islandexpresscharters.com) and Leap Frog Water Taxi in Bellingham (www.leapfrogwatertaxi.com) both offer reliable service. The hike begins from Eagle Harbor (moorage, no dock). Privy available.

ON THE TRAIL

From Eagle Harbor, head left on the Cypress Mainline, a wide haul road turned trail, still used occasionally by Department of Natural Resources vehicles. Steadily climbing, stay left at a junction at 0.3 mile (0.5 km) and right at another trail that leads to Reed Lake (Hike 21) at 0.7 mile (1.1 km). Stay right at yet another junction, soon coming to a trail intersection, complete with privy, at 1.4 miles (2.3 km). Cypress Lake (Hike 21) is to the right.

Continue left on the Cypress Mainline, skirting Stella Swamp and going through a broad gap on Cypress's hilly backbone. Ignore a trail to the right that leads to private property on Strawberry Bay. At 1.8 miles (2.9 km), come to a signed junction (elev. 950 ft/290 m). You'll be returning from the left, so go right on the Strawberry Bay Trail, on lightly used but discernible tread that steeply descends through open dry forest.

The way eventually utilizes an old road bed, traveling through pine and rhododendron groves and crossing seeps that make the trail muddy in spots. At 3.3 miles (5.3 km), reach a junction (elev. 260 ft/79 m) with the Reef Point Trail. First, an out-and-back 1.2-mile (1.9-km) trip to the right is in order, dropping down to Strawberry Bay. Named in 1792 by Lieutenant William Broughton for its abundant strawberries, this bay, with its wide tidal flats, is a pure joy to walk and explore. Respect private property to the north.

Return to the previous junction and then hike south along a high bluff that grants occasional views out to little Strawberry Island and big Orcas Island. After some easy going, come to a junction at 5.5 miles (8.9 km). You'll be continuing left, but head right first for 0.1 mile (0.15 km) to gorgeous Reef Point.

From this grassy wildflower-blotched bluff, enjoy sweeping views of Rosario Strait dividing Blakely, James, Decatur, Fidalgo, and Burrows islands. Watch for ferries, orcas, and seals. There's quite a bit of history here too, from scattered mining debris once used to extract olivine from the 1920s to 1973, to the reef-net fishing operations that once flourished north of here in the late 1800s, capturing migrating Fraser River salmon.

After soaking up sun, scenery, and serenity, begin hiking back to your start. Retrace your steps 0.1 mile (0.15 km) back to the last junction and head right, through a nettle-lined alder tunnel (keep your hands close-by). Reach a junction at 6.1 miles (9.8 km). Right leads to the old Secret Harbor Residential Treatment Center, now being rehabilitated into a natural state.

Head left on the Cypress Mainline on a gentle but long climb across dry, open forested slopes beneath the island's highest point. Pass some junipers and an old gravel pit before topping out at 960 feet (293 m). Shortly afterward, come to a familiar junction at 8.2 miles (13.2 km). Keep right on the mainline, reaching your starting point in 1.8 miles. It's all downhill.

Rugged Reef Point was once the site of a mining operation.

23 Bradberry Lake

RATING/ DIFFICULTY	ROUNDTRIP	ELEV GAIN/HIGH POINT
***/4	4.8 miles (7.7 km)	1125 feet (343 m)/ 1125 feet (343 m)

Maps: USGS Cypress Island, DNR map online; **Contact:** Washington Department of Natural Resources (DNR), Northwest District; **Notes:** Dogs permitted on-leash; **GPS:** N 48 34.108, W 122 40.260

Hike to a remote lake hidden in the lofty lonely interior of the San Juans' largest (nearly) undeveloped island. Pass a view-granting ridgeline airstrip, remnant of thankfully abandoned plans for a large golf resort.

GETTING THERE

You need a private boat or to arrange for a water taxi to access Cypress Island. Island Express Water Taxi in Anacortes (www .islandexpresscharters.com) and Leap Frog Water Taxi in Bellingham (www .leapfrogwatertaxi.com) both offer reliable service. The hike begins from the Cypress Head Campground (moorage, no dock). Privy available.

ON THE TRAIL

Cypress Head is a beautiful headland connected to the rest of Cypress Island by a tombolo. Gorgeous camp and picnic sites tempt you to spend some time here, perhaps on your return. To start your hike, locate the Cypress Head Trail leading right and immediately begin climbing steeply. This trail is much rougher than the others on the island.

The way winds around parcels of private property and crosses a couple of private drives. Stay on the trail and respect the landowners' privacy. Traverse steep slopes and angle upward; occasional stone steps aid your ascent. At 1.6 miles (2.6 km), come to a junction (elev. 740 feet/226 m). The trail right travels 0.6 mile (1 km) to Reed Lake. Continue left instead, emerging onto an old airstrip (elev. 925 ft/282 m) and reaching a trail junction at 1.9 miles (3.1 km). The airstrip was part of a mega-resort development scheme that would have ravaged this

Once slated to be surrounded by homes, Bradberry Lake instead remains a peaceful and isolated place.

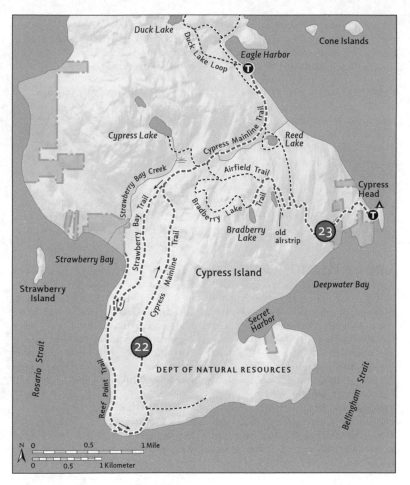

remarkable island. In 2010, the Department of Natural Resources planted saplings on the strip, but shallow soil and low rainfall has resulted in slow forest regeneration. Feel free to walk to both ends of the 0.75-mile (1.2-km) airstrip for limited views north and south. A small pond borders the airstrip on the south extension.

For Bradberry Lake, turn right on the airstrip, walking a short distance before turning left and reaching a junction at 2.1 miles (3.4 km). To the right, the old road, now Airfield Trail, leads 0.7 mile (1.1 km) to the Cypress Mainline. You want to go left instead, climbing steeply 0.3 mile (0.5 km) to the small forest-ringed lake (elev. 1125 feet/343 m). Signs indicate that you can swim here. It's pretty murky though, and you'll no doubt be sharing these waters with some critters. Settle for a lakeside picnic instead before heading back.

EXTENDING YOUR TRIP

You can continue beyond the lake on a very lightly used trail that utilizes a winding road built for the megaresort that never came. The trail climbs a little more, traveling near the island's 1525-foot (465-m) high point and returning to the Airfield Trail in 1 mile (1.6 km). You can then make a lollipop loop back by hiking left 0.3 mile (0.5 km) to the Cypress Mainline and then turning right to return via Reed Lake.

Lopez Island

Third-largest of the San Juans, Lopez Island is 29.8 square miles (77.2 sq. km) and has gentler topography than its neighbors. This makes it a favorite destination for bicyclists, but hikers will find much to like too, including a couple of units of the newly established San Juan Islands National Monument.

Home to about 2300 residents, the island is known for its rural charm and friendliness, including the ritual of drivers greeting everyone with a wave (be sure to respond in kind). The island is named for Gonzalo López de Haro, a Spanish naval officer and the first European to "discover" the San Juan Islands archipelago.

Washington State Ferries offers year-round service from Anacortes to Lopez Island, and the short sailing makes the island a good choice for day trips from the mainland. Services include a grocery store at Lopez Village near Fisherman Bay, an easy bike ride from the ferry landing.

Camping options include Spencer Spit State Park (www.parks.wa.gov), Odlin County Park (www.co.san-juan.wa.us/parks), and Lopez Farm Cottages and Tent Camping (www.lopezfarmcottages.com).

24 Upright Head Preserve

RATING/ DIFFICULTY	ROUNDTRIP	ELEV GAIN/HIGH POINT
**/1	1.2 miles (1.9 km)	300 feet (91 m)/ 160 feet (49 m)

Maps: USGS Shaw Island, land bank map online; **Contact:** San Juan County Land Bank, Upright Head Preserve; **Notes:** Dogs permitted on-leash; **GPS:** N 48 34.131, W 122 53.076

Once slated for a housing development, this small preserve on the rocky northern tip of Lopez Island was protected in 1998 by the San Juan County Land Bank. Occupying a rugged headland jutting into Harney and Upright channels, it's a wonderful place to watch ferries pass by or to enjoy a short hike while waiting for a ferry.

GETTING THERE

From Anacortes, take a Washington State ferry to Lopez Island. Follow Ferry Road for 0.1 mile (0.15 km) and turn left into the ferry parking area. The trail (elev. 60 ft/18 m) starts on west side of road, on a gated road signed "Penny Lane."

ON THE TRAIL

Perhaps with a Beatles tune in your head, start walking up Penny Lane. In about 250 feet (76 m), the pavement ends, but the utilities line keeps going—thirteen homes were slated to be built on this cliffy tip of

Lopez Island. The planned subdivision road is now a wide and well-groomed trail. Climb about 100 feet (30 m) through a thick forest understory and then begin gently descending. Ignore unmarked trails that lead to private property.

At 0.3 mile (0.5 km), reach a junction (elev. 110 ft/34 m) marked by a small cairn. Head left—you'll be returning from the right. Now on real trail, climb to the forested edge of the headland, coming to an observation deck (elev. 140 ft/43 m) at 0.4 mile (0.6 km). The view here of Orcas and Shaw islands

is somewhat obscured by vegetation—the next outlook is much better.

Head north and steeply descend, coming to a bench and viewpoint (elev. 20 ft/6 m) just above the water's edge at 0.5 mile (0.8 km). Here take in a nice view of Entrance Mountain and Buck Bay on Orcas Island—and of several busy channels plied by ferries and pleasure craft.

Continue hiking, climbing back up to the subdivision road-trail (elev. 80 ft/24 m). At 0.6 mile (1 km), come to a junction. You'll be returning to the right, but first head left 0.1

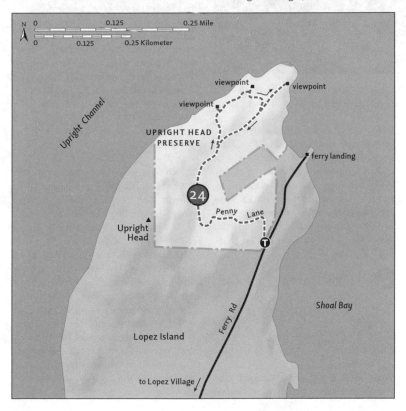

Mount Woolard and Entrance Mountain on Orcas Island seen from Upright Head

mile (0.15 km) to another viewpoint at the tip of Upright Head (elev. 50 ft/15 m). Here among madronas, junipers, and, in spring, wildflowers, take in a good view of Blakely Island and Eagle Cliff on Cypress Island. Watch ferries, too, and if you notice the one you're waiting for pull into the terminal, you'd best make your way back to your vehicle. Just follow the road-trail 0.5 mile (0.8 km) back to the trailhead.

25 Upright Channel

RATING/ DIFFICULTY	ROUNDTRIP	ELEV GAIN/HIGH POINT
***/1	3.4 miles (5.5 km)	Minimal/25 feet (8 m)

Map: USGS Shaw Island; **Contact:** San Juan County Parks, Lopez Island; **Notes:**

Dogs permitted on-leash; **GPS:** N 48 33.390, W 122 53.415

One of the longest beach hikes in the San Juan Islands, this walk along busy Upright Channel to appropriately named Flat Point skirts beneath bluffs of big trees. Admire roosting eagles, bobbing buffleheads, and darting kingfishers along the way. Look for otters and raccoons in the tidal flats. And watch ferries plying the channel, one of the key transportation routes through the San Juans.

GETTING THERE
From Anacortes, take a Washington State ferry to Lopez Island. Follow Ferry Road for 1.1 miles (1.8 km) and turn right into Odlin County Park. Proceed 0.2 mile (0.3 km) to the day-use parking area. Privy and bike rack available.

ON THE TRAIL
With its campsites, old-growth forest, boat launch, and wide sandy beach, 80-acre (32-ha) Odlin County Park is one of Lopez Island's most popular places. Situated along Upright Channel just to the west of Upright Point, Odlin provides access to more than 1.5 miles (2.4 km) of public tidelands. While it's possible to do this hike at both high and low tides, plan it for a low tide to avoid scrambling over and under downed trees.

From the day-use area walk 0.1 mile (0.15 km) to the boat launch. Then hit the sand and walk west across a wide, inviting beach. Pass shoreline campsites, soon coming to coastal bluffs topped with big trees. Look for eagles nesting in them and kingfishers surveying from overhanging limbs.

At about 0.5 mile (0.8 km), round the bluffs and come to another wide sandy beach area. Flat Point can be seen in the distance. Across Upright Channel is a good view to Canoe Island guarding Shaw Island's Indian Cove. Continue walking, coming to rocky and cobble-strewn sections of beach. Pass some big glacial erratics and staircases, which lead to a handful of homes hidden in the trees (do not trespass).

Pass an old boathouse and a couple more homes before coming to a stretch of smooth sandy beach. At 1.4 miles (2.3 km), reach the small Upright Channel State Park, with its Cascade Marine Trail campsites (for boaters) and a short trail that climbs steeply

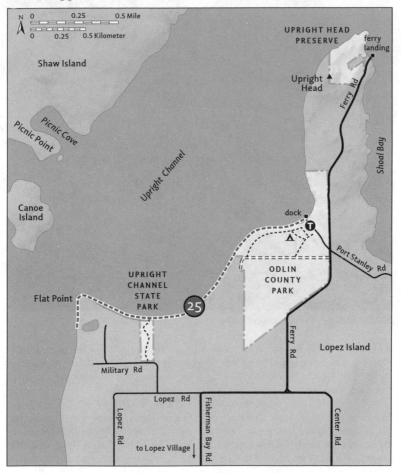

Inviting sandy beach along Upright Channel

to Military Road (alternative access, Discover Pass required). Continue walking on a glorious stretch of sandy beach, soon passing homes crowding Flat Point.

At 1.7 miles (2.7 km), round the sandy point and take in excellent views across the San Juan Channel to San Juan Island's Mount Finlayson and the Olympic Mountains beyond. The tidelands become private a short distance south of the point, so turn around and languidly walk back to your start, savoring this sweet saltwater sojourn.

EXTENDING YOUR TRIP

Explore Odlin County Park's short but delightful trails. From the walk-in camping area, follow the Sunset Trail along the bluffs, returning on Long Lane. Then take

Fawn's Way to the Big Tree Loop through a stately grove of old growth gracing a seasonal creek.

26 Spencer Spit

RATING/DIFFICULTY	ROUNDTRIP	ELEV GAIN/HIGH POINT
***/1	1.2 miles (1.9 km)	60 feet (18 m)/ 60 feet (18 m)

Map: USGS Blakely Island; **Contact:** Washington State Parks, Spencer Spit State Park; **Notes:** Discover Pass required. Dogs permitted on-leash. Facilities closed late autumn to early spring. If road is gated, park on shoulder and walk 0.4 mile (0.6 km) on park road to trailhead, or take trail that heads right from gate 0.4 mile (0.6 km) to spit; **GPS:** N 48 32.181, W 122 51.569

Walk along a spit teeming with birdlife. Check out historical structures and admire saltwater views south across Lopez Sound and north across Swifts Bay. This hike is short, but you'll want to linger long on some of the finest beach in the San Juans.

GETTING THERE
From Anacortes, take a Washington State ferry to Lopez Island. Follow Ferry Road for 1.1 miles (1.8 km) and turn left onto Port Stanley Road. Proceed 2.5 miles (4 km) and turn left onto Bakerview Road to the state

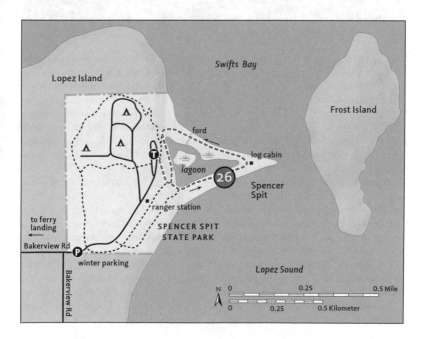

Spencer Spit reaches out to Frost Island.

park entrance in 0.5 mile (0.8 km). Drive another 0.4 mile (0.6 km) to the day-use area and trailhead (elev. 60 feet/18 m). Privy and bike rack available.

ON THE TRAIL

Start on your short downhill journey to the spit and immediately come to a junction. Left heads to a picnic shelter—go right instead. Soon come to another junction. Left heads to walk-in shoreline campsites (consider spending the night)—continue straight instead, soon coming to a picnic area at the base of the spit at 0.1 mile (0.15 km). The spit was homesteaded in the 1880s by the Spencer and Troxell families. Fruit trees, structures, and other remnants of their tenure grace the environs. So, too, do scores of passive rabbits.

Ready to explore the spit? If the tide is high, stick to the wide trail running its length.

Otherwise, scamper over beached logs to the beach. It's 0.4 mile (0.6 km) to the tip of the spit, where Frost Island teasingly tempts you to touch it. If the spit ever extends enough to Frost, a land formation known as a tombolo will be created. The channel separating these two landforms, however, is deep and swift moving, so the likelihood of this happening is not great.

Check out the log cabin at the tip of the spit. Constructed of driftwood logs, it's a 1978-built replica of a 1913 structure. When it's time to move on, either retrace your steps or if you don't mind getting your feet wet, return via the spit's north shore. Walking on sandy beach, watch for playful harbor seals and plying ferries. Hone your binoculars on little Flower Island for avian activity and admire Orcas Island's Mount Constitution rising in the background.

At 0.2 mile (0.3 km) from the cabin, come to a creek draining the spit's interior lagoon. You'll need to get your feet wet crossing it, but do not enter the lagoon. It's a sanctuary for breeding, nesting, and feeding birds. Continue along the beach another 0.2 mile (0.3 km), coming to the walk-in campground. Then turn south, following a lagoon-hugging trail 0.2 mile (0.3 km) back to the picnic area. En route, look for muck-darting herons and shrub-scratching towhees as well as scores of other species. From the picnic area it's 0.1 mile (0.15 km) back to the trailhead.

EXTENDING YOUR TRIP

A pleasant 1.6-mile (2.6-km) trail travels the park's periphery. Pick up the trail from the spit picnic area and follow it counterclockwise, crossing the park road near the entrance, and then continue around the appealing campground, terminating near the walk-in sites along the shore.

27 Hummel Lake

RATING/ DIFFICULTY	ROUNDTRIP	ELEV GAIN/HIGH POINT
**/1	2 miles (3.2 km)	145 feet (44 m)/ 220 feet (67 m)

Maps: USGS Shaw Island, land bank map online; **Contact:** San Juan County Land Bank, Hummel Lake Preserve; **Notes:** Dogs permitted on-leash; **GPS:** N 48 31.021, W 122 53.521

A peaceful 80-acre (32-ha) preserve within the heart of Lopez Island; enjoy quiet woodland roaming where you're more apt to run into deer than fellow hikers. Then saunter across a meadow to a small floating dock and let the resident birds and frogs of the island's largest freshwater lake serenade you.

GETTING THERE

From Anacortes, take a Washington State ferry to Lopez Island. Follow Ferry Road for 2.1 miles (3.4 km) and bear left onto Center Road. Continue for 2.2 miles (3.5 km) and turn left into Hummel Lake Preserve (0.3 mi/0.5 km after the Hummel Lake Road junction) to reach the trailhead (elev. 140 ft/43 m). Privy and bike rack available.

ON THE TRAIL

Forest walk or lakeshore lounge—which do you prefer first? How about the walk?

Reeds and bulrushes along Hummel Lake provide excellent habitat for birds and small mammals.

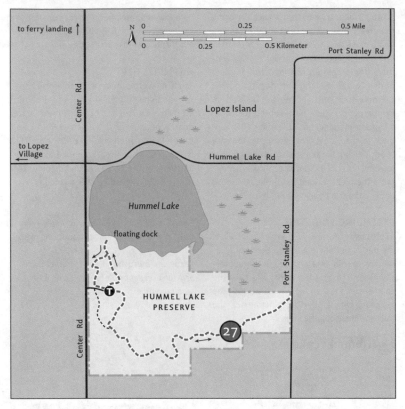

Locate the trail at the east end of the parking lot and immediately enter a cedar grove. The way climbs, traversing an increasingly dark and mossy forest. Pass a trail on the right, which circles back to the parking lot, before reaching a bench at the trail's high point (elev. 220 ft/67 m). Then in mature Douglas fir forest, begin descending, coming to an old pasture near some wetlands. The way continues on an old woods road, terminating at 0.8 mile (1.3 km) at Port Stanley Road (elev. 180 ft/55 m).

Retrace your steps back to the trailhead and then pick up the 0.4-mile (0.6-km) lake loop at the west end of the parking lot. Follow the wheelchair-accessible trail through a cedar grove and past picnic tables, coming to a delightful meadow. The loop angles back to the access road, but first head over to the floating dock that slices through cattails, allowing you a good look of Hummel Lake. Stay for a while for soothing views and a blackbird symphony. Then follow the west side of the loop back to your vehicle.

28 Fisherman Bay Preserve: The Spit

RATING/ DIFFICULTY	ROUNDTRIP	ELEV GAIN/HIGH POINT
***/1	1 mile (1.6 km)	Minimal/20 feet (6 m)

Maps: USGS Shaw Island, land bank map online; **Contact:** San Juan County Land Bank, Fisherman Bay Preserve; **Notes:** Dogs permitted on-leash. Stay on trail through dunes to avoid disturbing rare plants; **GPS:** N 48 31.019, W 122 55.356

Hike across fields, an old orchard, and coastal dunes to a beautiful sandy beach. Then wander along the shore to the tip of a spit at the mouth of Fisherman Bay. Enjoy charming views of Lopez Village on the bay and of Turtleback Mountain rising behind Shaw Island.

GETTING THERE

From Anacortes, take a Washington State ferry to Lopez Island. Follow Ferry Road 2.1 miles (3.4 km) and bear right onto Fisherman Bay Road. Drive 3.9 miles (6.3 km), passing

Lopez Village across Fisherman Bay

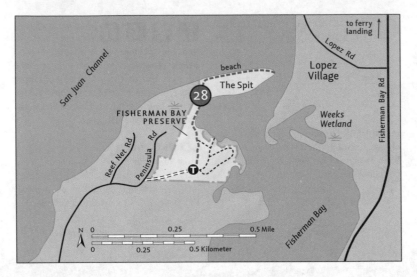

Lopez Village, and turn right onto Bayshore Road. Proceed 1.4 miles (2.3 km) and turn left onto Peninsula Road. Continue for 0.5 mile (0.8 km) to the end of the county road. Then drive 0.2 mile (0.3 km) on dirt road, turning right in 0.1 mile (0.2 km) (signed for the preserve) to reach the trailhead. Privy and bike rack available.

ON THE TRAIL

At an old homestead on a grassy upland, three trails diverge from the trailhead. They all interconnect and loop around, traversing field and orchard and affording splendid views of the spit and across Fisherman Bay. Plan on tacking on an extra 0.2 mile (0.3 km) if you care to explore them after your return from the spit.

The most direct path to the spit is the trail heading left. Take it, skirting field and wetlands before dropping down to the spit. Now follow a wide path across low dunes. Do not stray off the path, as the surrounding dune

complex—uncommon in the San Juans—harbors fragile and rare plants and provides nesting grounds for a handful of birds.

Reach the beach and turn right, walking the driftwood-lined wide and sandy shoreline. Look for waterfowl and pelagic birds offshore, and watch for passing ferries. Admire views of Shaw Island, with Orcas's Turtleback Mountain rising behind it. At 0.5 mile (0.8 km), come to the tip of the spit and a boat graveyard. Wave to passing boats still in service and to folks over in the village. Stay for a while before retracing your steps back to the trailhead.

EXTENDING YOUR TRIP

On your drive back to the ferry landing, stop at Otis Perkins County Park and walk 0.6 mile (1 km) on the tombolo, also part of the Fisherman Bay Preserve. At Lopez Village is a third unit of the preserve, the Weeks Wetland, with a short interpretive trail to an observation deck.

29 Lopez Hill

RATING/ DIFFICULTY	LOOP	ELEV GAIN/HIGH POINT
**/2	3.1 miles (5 km)	300 feet (91 m)/ 535 feet (163 m)

Maps: USGS Richardson, USGS Lopez Pass, Friends of Lopez Hill map online; **Contact:** Friends of Lopez Hill; **Notes:** Open to mountain bikes, horses, hunting (check seasons). Dogs permitted on-leash; **GPS:** N 48 28.896, W 122 52.217

Wander aimlessly (or with a purpose) on miles of quiet forested trails on Lopez Island's highest point. There are no sweeping views here, but you'll find plenty of solitude, attractive forest groves, mossy flowered ledges, amphibian- and bird-bellowing wetlands, and plenty of surprises—like delightful signposts and a Buddha.

GETTING THERE

From Anacortes, take a Washington State ferry to Lopez Island. Follow Ferry Road 2.1 miles (3.4 km) and bear left onto Center Road. Continue south for 4 miles (6.4 km) and turn left onto School Road. After 1 mile (1.6 km), bear right onto Lopez Sound Road. Then drive 1.1 miles (1.8 km) (pavement ends after 0.8 mi/1.3 km), turning right onto a dirt road. Continue 0.2 mile (0.3 km) to the trailhead (elev. 270 ft/82 m).

ON THE TRAIL

Lopez Hill consists of a 400-acre (162-ha) tract owned by the Department of Natural Resources and managed through a fifty-year lease (signed in 2009) by San Juan County. A very active citizens group, the Friends of Lopez Hill, formed to permanently protect this large undeveloped tract and to develop and promote recreational opportunities on it. The group has built a network of trails, with colorful names and signposts sporting unique pictographs that capture each trail's name. You'll enjoy scouting the signposts.

For an introductory loop , follow the Burnt Stump Trail through wetlands and big trees, coming to a junction with the Hook-up Trail in 0.4 mile (0.6 km). You'll be returning from the left, so continue straight, dropping into a lush creek-cradling ravine after a short climb. Continue through more wetlands and big trees and begin climbing, traversing moss-carpeted ledges to reach the 3 Cedars Trail (elev. 470 ft/143 m) at 1 mile (1.6 km).

One of Lopez Hill's colorful trail signs

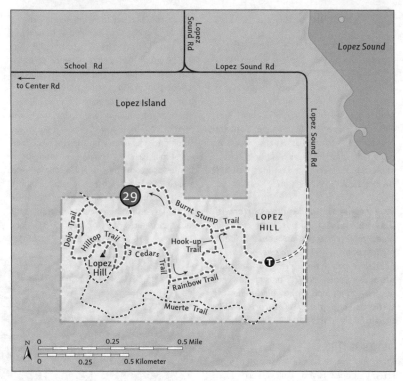

Head right, slightly descending and soon reaching the Dojo Trail. Right heads to private property, so head left, walking along mossy ledges to a junction with the Hilltop Trail (elev. 480 ft/146 m) at 1.3 miles (2.1 km). Continue left to ascend Lopez's rooftop, coming to the short summit spur at 1.5 miles (2.4 km). Take its roundtrip 0.1 mi (0.15 km) to Lopez Hill's 535-foot (163-m) open and grassy but viewless summit. A Buddha and hammock were in place last time I hiked here, and the lovely summit is indeed ideal for meditating and vegetating. Raucous ravens and eagles may disturb the silence.

Return to the Hilltop Trail and turn right. After 0.1 mile (0.15 km), reach a junction. Go left and in another 0.1 mile (0.15 km), reach the 3 Cedars Trail once again. Take this trail right, gradually descending and eventually coming to a creek, the three cedars (actually, there are a few more), and a junction at 2.2 miles (3.5 km). Bear left onto the Rainbow Trail, descending through mossy dark forest to reach a junction with the Hook-up Trail at 2.5 miles (4 km). Follow this trail left, crossing a creek and soon reaching the Burnt Stump Trail at 2.7 miles (4.3 km). The trailhead and your vehicle await you 0.4 mile (0.6 km) to the right.

EXTENDING YOUR TRIP

Hike some of the other Lopez Hill trails and venture if you dare along the Muerte Trail (just the name is ominous). Check out an old log cabin at the eastern end of the Rainbow Trail.

30 Shark Reef Sanctuary

RATING/ DIFFICULTY	ROUNDTRIP	ELEV GAIN/HIGH POINT
***/1	1 mile (1.6 km)	40 feet (12 m)/ 60 feet (18 m)

Map: USGS Richardson; **Contact:** San Juan County Parks, Lopez Island; **Notes:** Dogs permitted on-leash; **GPS:** N 48 27.760, W 122 56.240

Mount Finlayson across Middle Channel

Wander through shoulder-high salal and tall timber to a tight rocky channel teeming with bird and marine life. Watch eagles, cormorants, kingfishers, and oystercatchers dine on seafood. And observe seals basking on channel rocks and swimming in the strong currents. Shark Reef Sanctuary is an excellent destination for children (and adults) seeking outdoor discovery.

GETTING THERE

From Anacortes, take a Washington State ferry to Lopez Island. Follow Ferry Road 2.1 miles (3.4 km) and bear right onto Fisherman Bay Road. Continue for 5 miles (8 km), passing Lopez Village and turning right onto

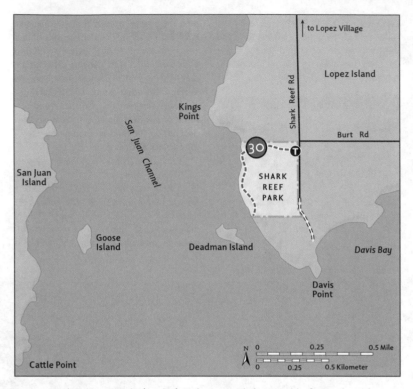

Airport Road. Drive 0.4 mile (0.6 km) and turn left onto Shark Reef Road. Continue for 1.8 miles (2.9 km) to the trailhead, 0.1 mile (0.2 km) beyond the Burt Road junction. Privy and bike rack available.

ON THE TRAIL

Originally a military post, then a Department of Natural Resources tract, the 39-acre (16-ha) Shark Reef Sanctuary was eventually transferred to San Juan County Parks and has become one of Lopez Island's most popular hiking destinations.

On good trail, set out through thick forest carpeted in salal. Pass a handful of old firs spared the ax and after a short descent, reach the rocky shoreline (elev. 20 feet/6 m). Turn south and walk on ledges along Cattle Pass, its strong currents separating Lopez from San Juan Island.

At 0.5 mile (0.8 km), the trail ends at a rocky and grassy bluff framed by windblown shore pines. Seek a sunny sitting spot and enjoy the scenery. Across the channel, Mount Finlayson rises above the golden lawns of Cattle Point. Dallas Mountain, highest point on San Juan Island, peeks out just to the northwest. Look south to the Olympics, hovering above the Strait of Juan de Fuca, and east to Iceberg Point. Directly in front of you in the channel are Deadman Island and a series of reefs and offshore rocks. At low tide, these areas teem with seals. Shark Reef itself is actually to the north and not visible from this point.

31 Iceberg Point

RATING/ DIFFICULTY	ROUNDTRIP	ELEV GAIN/HIGH POINT
*****/2	3.8 miles (6.1 km)	380 feet (116 m)/ 135 feet (41 m)

Map: USGS Richardson; **Contact:** San Juan Islands National Monument; **Notes:** Dogs permitted on-leash. Do not park beyond Agate Beach County Park. Landowners have generously granted access via their private property—stay on trail and do not trespass; **GPS:** N 48 25.738, W 122 52.623

Take in stunning views of the Olympic Mountains across the sparkling waters of the Strait of Juan de Fuca as you hike through prairie grasses atop coastal bluffs. One of the most breathtaking spots in the San Juans, Iceberg Point will leave you frozen in astonishment.

GETTING THERE

From Anacortes, take a Washington State ferry to Lopez Island. Follow Ferry Road 2.1 miles (3.4 km) and bear left onto Center Road. Continue for 5.6 miles (9 km) and bear left onto Mud Bay Road. Follow it for 2.8 miles

Boundary reference monument at Iceberg Point

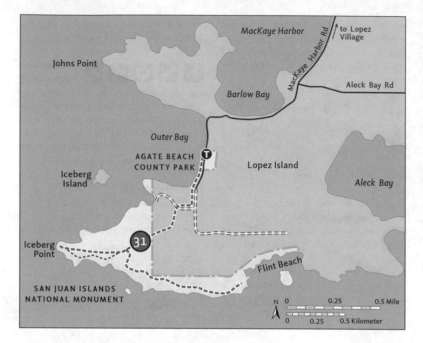

(4.5 km), turning right onto MacKaye Harbor Road. Drive 1.8 miles (2.9 km) to Agate Beach County Park. Park here. Privy available.

ON THE TRAIL

Located at the southern tip of Lopez Island, 76-acre (31-ha) Iceberg Point is one of many small properties in the San Juans administered by the Bureau of Land Management. In 2013, these areas—many containing rare plants and important cultural sites— became protected as a national monument (see "A Monumental Achievement" sidebar). Iceberg Point is one of the larger parcels, and it harbors native fescue grasses, prickly pear cactus, old-growth junipers, and several rare flowers, including a yellow population of chocolate lilies.

Start by hiking south on the county road, soon coming to unpaved private Flint Road. Continue uphill on Flint and at 0.3 mile (0.5 km), turn right at a gated private road with an old saw as a sign, pegged high on a post marking the way to the point. At 0.4 mile (0.6 km), bear left at a green gate (do not trespass onto private property on the right), continuing through mature forest on old road that eventually dwindles into trail.

At 0.6 mile (1 km), reach the national monument (elev. 130 feet/40 m) and a bike rack (no bikes permitted beyond). Keep hiking, passing some big trees, and reach a trail junction at prairie's edge (elev. 100 feet/31 m) at 0.8 mile (1.3 km). Let the explorations begin. First, continue right, across one of the finest remaining prairies in the San Juans.

Soon, reach another junction. Stay right on the main path, skirting wind-contorted firs and pines; or take the path left, running closer to water's edge and rounding high banks and rocky bluffs. Either way leads 0.4 mile (0.6 km) to Iceberg Point (elev. 20 ft/6 km), a cliffy promontory housing a navigational beacon. You're a long way from the North Atlantic, so you won't see any icebergs here. The point was named in 1854 by George Davidson of the US Coast Survey for the copious striations left in the ledges by Ice Age glaciers.

For present-day glaciers, look northeast across Outer Bay to Mount Baker and south across the strait to glacier-covered Mount Rainier and the snowy Olympics. Directly west are the golden slopes of Mount Finlayson and Cattle Point on San Juan Island. The views are mesmerizing.

Next, retrace your steps 0.4 mile (0.6 km) to the junction and head right 0.2 mile (0.3 km), reaching a high rocky knoll (elev. 135 ft/41 m) that sports a large white boundary monument. The view is sweeping. Scan the striated shoreline all the way to Iceberg Point and beyond. Notice the glacial erratics littering the terraced ledges. Notice the birds too—raptors and eagles are prolific here.

Continue 0.5 mile (0.8 km) on a rough-at-times trail, heading east across a landscape reminiscent of Ireland or Scotland. Ignore a side trail leading left to private property, and after passing through a grove of windblown firs, reach the trail's end at a rocky point, with good views to the islands offshore and of Point Colville. From here, it's 1.5 miles (2.4 km) back to your vehicle.

EXTENDING YOUR TRIP
Skip the 0.2-mile (0.3-km) trail at Agate Beach, but do take the stairway down to the beach at Outer Bay. The birding, especially in winter, is excellent.

A MONUMENTAL ACHIEVEMENT: SAN JUAN ISLANDS NATIONAL MONUMENT
On March 25, 2013, President Barack Obama signed a proclamation designating approximately 1000 acres (405 ha) of Bureau of Land Management (BLM) properties within the San Juan Islands as the San Juan Islands National Monument. This was made possible by the Antiquities Act of 1906, which authorizes the president to set aside public land as parks or conservation areas by executive order; this powerful instrument has been used many times before, by presidents from Theodore Roosevelt (who established the first national monument) to George W. Bush (who established the largest national monument).

While this new national monument in the San Juans is comparatively small, it is historically, culturally, and ecologically significant and had long been sought by many islanders and conservationists. About sixty separate sites make up the monument. Many of the properties are small islets and former lighthouse sites. But several parcels are sizeable, offering excellent hiking. These include Iceberg Point (Hike 31), Chadwick Hill (Hike 32), Watmough Bay (Hike 33), and Point Colville (Hike 34) on Lopez Island; Cattle Point (Hike 52) on San Juan Island; Turn Point (Hike 61) on Stuart Island; and the whole of Patos Island (Hike 62). Aside from protecting beautiful scenery, these parcels also include historical structures, old-growth forest, and several rare and endangered species.

32 Chadwick Hill

RATING/ DIFFICULTY	ROUNDTRIP	ELEV GAIN/HIGH POINT
****/3	3 mile (4.8 km)	380 feet (116 m)/ 460 feet (140 m)

Maps: USGS Lopez Pass, San Juan County Land Bank Watmough Bay Preserve map online; **Contact:** San Juan Islands National Monument; **Notes:** Dogs permitted on-leash; **GPS:** N 48 25.891, W 122 49.714

Stand atop this 470-foot (143-m) hill on the southern tip of Lopez Island and behold one of the most dramatic views in the San Juans. From Chadwick's dizzying clifftops, stare straight down to sparkling Watmough Bay wedged between sheer rock faces and steep emerald slopes. Then cast your attention outward to the snowy sentinel, Mount Baker, hovering above shimmering waters.

GETTING THERE

From Anacortes, take a Washington State ferry to Lopez Island. Follow Ferry Road 2.1 miles (3.4 km) and bear left onto Center Road. Continue for 5.6 miles (9 km) and bear left onto Mud Bay Road. Follow it for 4.2 miles (6.8 k), turning right onto Aleck Bay Road. Drive 0.5 mile (0.8 km) and continue straight onto Watmough Head Road. Continue for 0.5 mile (0.8 km) to the unmarked trailhead (elev. 160 ft/49 m) at a gate at the end of a field. There is limited parking on the roadside—do not block adjacent drive.

Watmough Bay from Chadwick Hill

ON THE TRAIL

Start by walking along the field edge on an old tractor track. At 0.2 mile (0.3 km), come to a gate and enter the largest parcel of the new San Juan Islands National Monument (see "A Monumental Achievement" sidebar). Encompassing Chadwick Hill, Watmough Bay, and Point Colville, this Bureau of Land Management–administered tract, along with adjacent San Juan County Land Bank property, protects more than 400 acres (160 ha) of one of the most stunning landscapes in the San Juans.

Now in cool forest, follow the old track, soon coming to an unmarked junction. The way left leads 0.3 mile (0.5 km) to grassy wetlands teeming with birds. Continue straight instead, and at 0.4 mile (0.6 km) come to another unmarked junction. You'll be returning from the left, so head right, gradually ascending under a cool canopy of cedars, firs, alders, and madronas. The trail splits in another 0.1 mile (0.15 km)—go either way, as they soon meet up again.

At 1 mile (1.6 km), crest a ridge (elev. 420 feet/128 m) and start descending in thick salal, passing several wetland pools cradled in ledge pockets. After losing 80 feet (24 m) of elevation, start climbing again. Ignore a path to the left at a small knoll, but take note of the trail heading left shortly afterward at 1.3 miles (2.1 km). This will be your return route after hiking to the hilltop and back.

Stay right and climb, crossing mossy ledges. At 1.6 miles (2.6 km), crest Chadwick's summit ridge (the actual summit is to the north), where open grassy ledges (elev. 460 ft/140 m) greet you. The view over Watmough Bay and out across Rosario Strait is stunning. The drop is downright frightening; keep children and dogs nearby and don't venture too close to the cliff edge.

Find yourself a nice sunny spot and take in the maritime views and the eagles that frequently soar above Chadwick's craggy south face.

When it's time to return, retrace your steps 0.3 mile (0.5 km) to the last junction and then head to the right through a grove of mature Douglas firs, coming to the edge of a pasture. The way then turns left on a fairly level grade, reaching the main trail in 0.7 mile (1.1 km). Your vehicle awaits you 0.4 mile (0.6 km) away.

EXTENDING YOUR TRIP

From Chadwick's summit, do not follow the trails that descend the south face, as one path traverses private property and the other is a dangerous route along ledges and cliffs. Instead, consider the 0.3-mile (0.5-km) side trail near the hike's beginning, which leads to wetland pools where you can delight in a little bird-watching.

33 Watmough Bay

RATING/ DIFFICULTY	ROUNDTRIP	ELEV GAIN/HIGH POINT
***/1	1.3 miles (2.1 km)	190 feet (58 m)/ 150 feet (46 m)

Maps: USGS Lopez Pass, land bank map online; **Contact:** San Juan County Land Bank, Watmough Bay Preserve; **Notes:** Dogs permitted on-leash; **GPS:** N 48 25.747, W 122 49.053

This short and easy hike leads to a wedge of a bay beneath steep, stark, towering cliffs. Sit on a polished driftwood log and stare at Mount Baker across Rosario Strait. Then hike up a tall-timbered slope of

Watmough Head before finishing up with a stroll around a quiet bird-loving marsh.

GETTING THERE

From Anacortes, take a Washington State ferry to Lopez Island. Follow Ferry Road 2.1 miles (3.4 km) and bear left onto Center Road. Continue for 5.6 miles (9 km) and bear left onto Mud Bay Road. Follow it for 4.2 miles 6.8 km), turning right onto Aleck Bay Road. Drive 0.5 mile (0.8 km) and continue straight onto Watmough Head Road. In 0.9 mile (1.4 km), turn left into Watmough Bay Preserve and drive 0.1 mile (0.15 km) to the trailhead. Privy and bike rack available.

ON THE TRAIL

Watmough Bay sits in the heart of 400-plus acres (160-plus ha) managed by the Bureau of Land Management and the San Juan County Land Bank. This rocky and heavily forested landscape is quite different from the island's signature pastoral countryside.

Head east on a wide and well-groomed trail down a hollow that's well shaded thanks to tall trees and steep surrounding slopes. At 0.2 mile (0.3 km), reach gorgeous Watmough Bay, tightly hemmed in by cliffy 470-foot (143-m) Chadwick Hill to the north and thickly timbered 242-foot (74-m) Watmough Head to the south. A cobblestone beach lined with driftwood entices you to the shore. Walk along the surf, enjoying a wonderful view of Mount Baker hovering over Burrows and Fidalgo islands, perfectly framed between Watmough's sentinel summits.

You can easily spend hours here, but if you want more exercise, that can be arranged too. From the bay follow a trail to the right, steeply climbing 150 feet (46 m) above the surf. Traverse old-growth forest, passing big fire-scarred firs and eventually

coming to the trail's end at 0.3 mile (0.5 km), at a dirt road.

Retrace your steps back to the bay and then walk north along the beach 0.1 mile (0.15 km), picking up trail once again. Now hike west along a quiet marsh, past big cedars and beneath the towering rocky southern façade of Chadwick Hill. Pass a steep and unmarked trail to Chadwick's summit. It's a dangerous exposed scramble route that should be ignored. Continue hiking around the marsh, returning to the access road above the trailhead at 0.4 mile (0.6 km) from the beach.

Mount Baker hovers in the distance above Burrows, Allan, and Fidalgo islands.

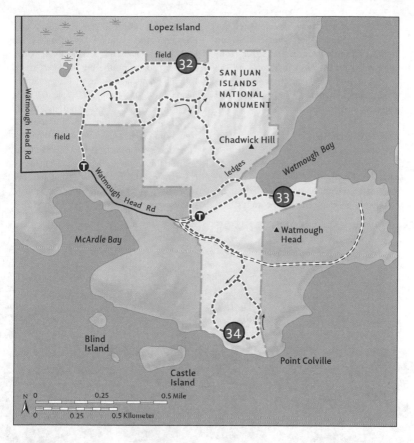

34 Point Colville

RATING/ DIFFICULTY	ROUNDTRIP	ELEV GAIN/HIGH POINT
★★★★/2	2.2 miles (3.5 km)	180 feet (55 m)/ 130 feet (40 m)

Maps: USGS Lopez Pass, land bank map online; **Contact:** San Juan Islands National Monument and San Juan County Land Bank, Watmough Bay Preserve; **Notes:** Dogs permitted on-leash. Coastal cliffs—keep children nearby; **GPS:** N 48 25.747, W 122 49.053

A spectacular promontory of coastal cliffs, native prairie grasses, and old-growth forest rivaling Iceberg Point in beauty—but not in crowds. On this short hike long on maritime views, watch for marine mammals and pelagic birds on nearby offshore islands. And savor stunning views across Rosario Strait and the Strait of Juan de Fuca to snowy backdrops compliments of the Cascade and Olympic mountains.

GETTING THERE
See directions to Hike 33.

ON THE TRAIL
The road to Point Colville's trailhead can be rough and parking can be tight, so it's best to start this hike from the Watmough Bay Preserve parking area. Walk 0.1 mile (0.15 km) back to Watmough Head Road. Then turn left, following the primitive dirt track through primeval forest to an unsigned trailhead (elev. 130 ft/40 m) at 0.5 mile (0.8 km), in a grove of giant fire-scarred Douglas firs.

Pass a bike rack and a lot of impressive trees, coming to a junction at 0.7 mile (1.1 km). You'll be returning from the left, so keep right, soon breaking out of forest cover to coastal bluff prairie that harbors rare prickly pear cacti and abundant showy wildflowers come spring. Pass a rough side

Castle Island guards the rocky headlands of Point Colville.

spur (elev. 40 ft/12 m) that leads to the right to the water, and using caution start angling east across high clifftops around the point.

Stop frequently to marvel at blocky Castle Island just offshore and Colville Island a little farther out. Binoculars will allow you to see seabird colonies, perhaps even tufted puffins. Take in good views too of Burrows Island, Mount Baker, and Fidalgo's Mount Erie. Pass a side spur that steeply drops to a secluded beach. Then, after passing near a lone house, traverse a Sitka spruce grove before closing the loop at 1.5 miles (2.4 km). Continue straight to return 0.7 mile (1.1 km) to your vehicle.

EXTENDING YOUR TRIP
Combine with a trip to Watmough Bay (Hike 33).

Shaw Island

At 7.7 square miles (20 sq. km), Shaw Island is the smallest of the San Juans serviced by the Washington State Ferries. Shaw is quiet and relatively undeveloped, with a year-round population of about 250. Named by the Wilkes Expedition in 1841 for Captain John D. Shaw, an American hero of the War of 1812, the island is home to two monasteries and one of the last one-room schoolhouses in the state.

While there is very little public land on the island, the University of Washington and the San Juan Preservation Trust own large tracts that permit hiking. The island's lightly traveled roads are also ideal for walking. Overnight accommodations are limited to vacation rentals, Our Lady of the Rock Monastery (http://olrmonastery.org), and the 11 campsites at the Shaw Island County Park (www.co.san-juan.wa.us/parks).

35 Indian Cove

RATING/ DIFFICULTY	ROUNDTRIP	ELEV GAIN/HIGH POINT
****/2	5.6 miles (9 km)	330 feet (101 m)/ 150 feet (46 m)

Map: USGS Shaw Island; **Contact:** San Juan Preservation Trust, Graham Preserve; **Notes:** Road walk with very little traffic; **GPS:** N 48 35.056, W 122 55.795

Hike quiet country roads along pictur-esque Blind Bay to the gorgeous white sandy beach of Indian Cove. Then explore a little peninsula in Squaw Bay before hiking on a peaceful forested trail through a San Juan Preservation Trust preserve.

GETTING THERE
Leave your car at the Anacortes ferry terminal and take a Washington State ferry to Shaw Island. The hike begins at the ferry dock.

ON THE TRAIL
Walk off the ferry and immediately come to the Shaw General Store, in business since 1898 and a great place to grab a snack for the hike. Now walk along Blind Bay Road, one of the quietest stretches of pavement you'll ever travel. Orchards and sheep farms line the roadway on the left, while boat-bobbing and bird-bustling Blind Bay hugs it on the right. Turtleback Mountain hovers in the background. The way is level with a few little dips and rises.

At 1.3 miles (2.1 km), come to a junction with Squaw Bay Road at the Shaw Community Center. You'll be returning on a trail to this point. Turn left and walk the road, coming to the 60-acre (24-ha) Shaw

Island County Park at 2 miles (3.2 km). Walk down the park access road through the campground and tall timber, reaching the beach at 2.2 miles (3.5 km). A picnic, nap, or walk on this white sandy beach in Indian Cove—one of the prettiest beaches in the San Juan Islands—is a must. Share views of Canoe, Lopez, and San Juan

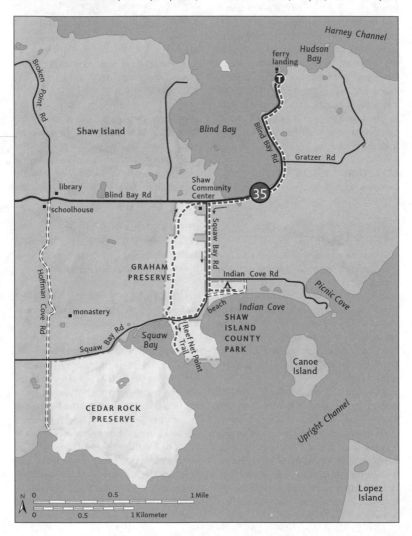

The author admires Indian Cove's sandy South Beach.

islands against an Olympic Mountains backdrop with kingfishers, eagles, and oystercatchers.

Sated, return 0.2 mile (0.3 km) to Squaw Bay Road and turn left, walking a bluff along a split-rail fence that encloses an old orchard of the 99-acre (40-ha) Graham Preserve, bequeathed to the San Juan Preservation Trust by Ernest and Beverly Graham in 2009. At 2.7 miles (4.3 km), come to the Reef Net Point Trail on your left. Follow it through forest along Squaw Bay, passing an old cabin that once served as the island's first schoolhouse, and coming to a grassy point at 3 miles (4.8 km). Enjoy the view of the wildlife-rich small bay.

Return 0.3 mile (0.5 km) to Squaw Bay Road, locating a trail across the pavement. Follow this 2013-built trail through the Graham Preserve's peaceful forest, climbing a small hillside (elev. 150 ft/46 m). Then gently descend to the Shaw Community Center at

4.3 miles (6.9 km). Return to the ferry landing by retracing your steps 1.3 miles (2.1 km) along Blind Bay Road.

EXTENDING YOUR TRIP

From the Reef Net Point Trail continue west on Squaw Bay Road 0.9 mile (1.4 km), turning left on graveled Hoffman Cove Road and walking 0.4 mile (0.6 km) to its end. Then head left on a grassy road-trail (dogs prohibited) to the beautiful 370-acre (150-ha) Cedar Rock Preserve, managed by the University of Washington. One of several properties on Shaw and Lopez islands protecting more than 1400 acres (566 ha) donated by the late Dr. Frederick Ellis and family, this preserve contains 2.3 miles (3.7 km) of stunning undeveloped coastline. Feel free to explore, but stay on established trails.

Consider returning to Blind Bay Road via Hoffman Cove Road, passing Our Lady of

…astery and climbing a steep,
…) hill to Shaw's red one-room
…nd library at 1.6 miles (2.6
…e it's 2.3 miles (3.7 km) to the
ferry landing.

Orcas Island

Named not for killer whales (*Orcinus orca*) that live in the surrounding waters but for a Spanish viceroy who sent an exploring expedition here in 1791, Orcas Island is the largest of the San Juans, at 57.3 square miles (148.4 sq. km). With a population of around 5500, Orcas has two huge tracts of public land including Washington's fourth-largest state park that has some of the best hiking in the islands.

Washington State Ferries offers year-round service from Anacortes to Orcas Landing on Orcas Island. Bicyclists will find good roads and some hilly terrain, especially in the eastern reaches of the island. Eastsound is the island's commercial center and largest community, offering a wide array of services, including a large grocery store. Moran State Park has 151 campsites. Obstruction Pass State Park has 9 backcountry and paddle-accessible sites (no water). West Beach Resort (www .westbeachresort.com) and Doe Bay Resort (doebay.com) also offer camping.

36 Turtleback Mountain Preserve: Ship Peak Loop

RATING/ DIFFICULTY	LOOP	ELEV GAIN/HIGH POINT
****/3	2.9 miles (4.7 km)	860 feet (262 m)/ 931 feet (284 m)

Maps: USGS Eastsound, land bank map online; **Contact:** San Juan County Land Bank, Turtleback Mountain Preserve; **Notes:** Dogs permitted on-leash; **GPS:** N 48 38.495, W 122 58.624

From this open summit of Turtleback Mountain, stand starboard and set your sail to the sights of a maritime mélange of islands, harbors, and headlands. There are good terrestrial views too, out across the rolling pastures of the Crow Valley to the emerald hulk of Mount Constitution. In spring and early summer, Ship Peak is decked with quite a floral arrangement.

GETTING THERE

From Anacortes, take a Washington State ferry to Orcas Island. Head north on Orcas Road (Horseshoe Highway) for 2.5 miles (4 km) and turn left onto Deer Harbor Road. Continue for 2.2 miles (3.5 km), passing West Sound, and turn right onto dirt Wild-rose Lane. Drive 0.1 mile (0.15 km) to the trailhead (elev. 120 ft/37 m). Privy and bike rack available.

ON THE TRAIL

Turtleback Mountain Preserve is one of the largest conservation success stories in the San Juans (see "Saving the Turtle" sidebar), at 1578 acres (639 ha) and growing. Thanks to the folks managing the preserve, the trail system continues to expand. The Lost Oak and Morning Ridge trails are some of the newer paths, allowing for nice loop trips to Ship Peak.

This is a short hike, but it's steep. You don't need to be shipshape, but your anchor may drag a little along the way. Start near an old foundation and horse-chestnut tree, following the South Trail into a small ravine and across a creek. Reach an old road in 0.2

SAVING THE TURTLE

In the 1920s prominent ship builder and former Seattle mayor Robert Moran donated more than 3500 acres (1416 ha) of spectacular Orcas Island property to the state to be established as a park. Today, Moran State Park protects more than 5000 acres (2023 ha) of old-growth forest, pristine lakeshore, and scenic mountaintop in one of Washington's priciest and most-threatened-with-development scenic corners. Fortunately, Moran's legacy was not the last grand initiative to protect Orcas Island's rural charm and natural heritage.

In 2006, 1578 acres (638 ha) of Turtleback Mountain were permanently taken off the real-estate listings and added to the public trust, protecting one of the last large undeveloped tracts in the San Juan Islands. And what a tract! But perhaps more impressive than Turtleback's spectacular vistas is how rapidly concerned citizens mobilized to protect it.

The property was put up for sale in the summer of 2005 by a private foundation. It was immediately eyed by residential and resort developers. To many island residents and visitors alike, the thought of this familiar landmark being marred by homes was unbearable. A partnership of conservation organizations immediately mobilized to raise the funds necessary to purchase the property. Spearheaded by the San Juan Preservation Trust, the Trust for Public Land, and the San Juan County Land Bank, the partnership raised US$18.5 million in just six months. It was the largest fund-raising campaign ever undertaken in San Juan County.

In January 2007 the Turtleback Mountain Conservation Area was officially opened to the public. The San Juan County Land Bank now owns it, while the San Juan Preservation Trust retains a conservation easement on it, ensuring that it remains in a natural state and open to the public in perpetuity. The land bank (www.sjclandbank.org), established in 1990 and funded primarily by a 1 percent real-estate excise tax, continues to protect prime island properties.

The San Juan Preservation Trust (www.sjpt.org), a nationally accredited nonprofit organization established in 1979, continues to protect outstanding island properties too, including the recent acquisition of the Turtleneck Preserve (Hike 37) and Vendovi Island (Hike 17). The trust has permanently protected more than 260 properties, 37 miles of shoreline, and 15,000 acres on twenty islands. Many of these properties are open to hiking and several are highlighted in this book.

mile (0.3 km). Turn right and soon come to a junction with the Lost Oak Trail, on the left. You'll be returning on that path, so continue full-steam ahead. Under a canopy of Douglas firs, madronas, and Garry oaks, follow the winding woods road upward. At 0.7 mile (1.1 km), reach a bench at a viewpoint down to West Sound. Camas, larkspur, and other blossoms brighten this spot in early season.

Continue climbing on the South Trail (or opt for the new, slightly longer, parallel Morning Ridge Trail that traverses open shrubby slopes reminiscent of a Southern Appalachian bald). The way steepens,

Ship Peak affords territorial views of West Sound.

slowing you to a turtle's crawl, giving you more time to enjoy expanding views to Salt Spring, Saturna, Lopez, and San Juan islands—and the Olympic Mountains in the distance. At 1.2 miles (1.9 km), reach the West Overlook (elev. 820 ft/250 m), once the site of a home and now sporting a bench where you can sit among camas lilies and look out across the Salish Sea. Sunsets from this spot are spectacular.

Continue on single-track trail, dropping about 50 feet (15m) before ascending open mossy ledges adorned with oaks to reach a junction at 1.5 miles (2.4 km). Take the short spur trail right, to the Ship Peak overlook

(elev. 931 ft/283 m), and cast your eyes to the horizons. What a view! East Sound, West Sound, and Mount Constitution rising over the rolling pastures of Crow Valley.

Once visually satisfied, retrace your steps to the last junction and hike to the right 0.4 mile (0.6 km), gradually descending (and bearing right at an unmarked junction) to a signed junction (elev. 825 ft/251 m) with the Lost Oak Trail. Here, in mature open forest, head left and continue descending. Pass an old fence line and several wolf trees (large individual trees with spreading crowns, the result of growing in open areas), evidence that this was once pasture. Pass some sunny ledges and locate the lost oak. Then steeply descend into thick dark forest, reaching the South Trail at 2.6 miles (4.2 km) at a familiar junction. Turn right and reach the trailhead in 0.3 mile (0.5 km).

EXTENDING YOUR TRIP

Combine with trails in the northern half of Turtleback Mountain Preserve (Hike 37). From the Lost Oak Trail junction, head right on the Ridge Trail 0.4 mile (0.6 km) to the Center Loop Trail. An old skid road through selectively cut forest, the Center Loop Trail lacks views but makes for good trail running.

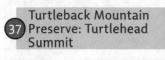

37 Turtleback Mountain Preserve: Turtlehead Summit

RATING/ DIFFICULTY	ROUNDTRIP	ELEV GAIN/HIGH POINT
*****/3	5.7 miles (9.2 km)	1295 feet (395 m)/ 1025 feet (312 m)

Maps: USGS Eastsound, land bank map online; **Contact:** San Juan County Land Bank, Turtleback Mountain Preserve; **Notes:** Partly open to bicycles (even days) and horses (odd days). Dogs permitted on-leash; **GPS:** N 48 40.036, W 122 56.811

Stand atop Turtleback Mountain's head for one shell of a view—one of the best in the San Juans. Thanks to a recent land acquisition, the prominent and well-recognized Turtlehead peak is now connected to its namesake preserve and open to hikers. En route, be sure to stop at the Waldron Overlook for a look at that reclusive island's impressive cliffs, with golden-faced Saturna Island in the distance.

GETTING THERE

From Anacortes, take a Washington State ferry to Orcas Island. Head north on Orcas Road (Horseshoe Highway) for 3.5 miles (5.6 km), turning left onto Nordstrom Lane. Continue for 0.6 mile (1 km) to Crow Valley Road and turn right. Drive 1.6 miles (2.6 km) to the trailhead (elev. 260 ft/79 m). Privy available.

ON THE TRAIL

Follow an old skid road, now multiuse trail, that almost became a private drive to showy ridgetop homes. Thanks to conservation groups and individuals, this road to 1519-ft (463-m) Turtleback Mountain and the 1719 acres (696 ha) surrounding it have become one of the largest protected parcels in the San Juan Islands (see "Saving the Turtle" sidebar).

Follow what is now officially the North Trail. After 0.5 mile (8 km) of gentle climbing, come to a junction. The short spur right leads 0.15 mile (0.25 km) to the camas-blossoming, madrona-fringed North Valley Overlook (elev. 550 ft/168 m). Consider the detour for a nice view of Orcas's Mount Constitution, Entrance Mountain, and Mount Woolard.

The North Trail steadily climbs, winding through mature timber and passing a huge Douglas fir. The grade eases as the trail brushes up along a grassy wetland, fragranced with skunk cabbage. At 1.6 miles (2.6 km), come to a junction (elev. 1025 feet/312 m) with a spur to the Waldron Overlook. Follow it right a short distance (0.1 mi/0.15 km roundtrip) to a clifftop promontory with a stunning view of Waldron Island's impressive Point Disney cliffs across President Channel. Keep children and dogs close-by, as it's a sheer drop behind the split-rail fence. Containing one of the largest intact Garry oak forests in the San Juans, Point Disney was protected from development by

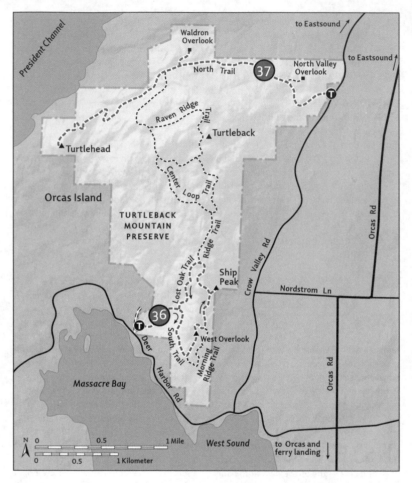

the Nature Conservancy and the San Juan Preservation Trust.

When done viewing, return to the junction and head out on the Turtlehead Trail. Opened in 2013 and built by a consortium of folks, including the Washington Trail Association, Washington Conservation Corps, and Orcas Island Youth Conservation Corp, the trail tra-verses the recently acquired 111-acre (45-ha) Turtleneck Preserve to the 30-acre (12-ha) Turtlehead (aka Orcas Knob) property.

Follow the well-graded trail through a cedar grove, gently descending to a 750-ft (229-m) gap. Then regain lost ele-vation, winding around ledges and through attractive forest to emerge on the grassy, rocky 1005-foot (306-m) bald at 2.9 miles (4.7 km). The views from this prominent landmark are simply sublime. Stare out at San Juan, Shaw, Jones, Spieden, and Stuart islands. Salt Spring, Moresby, Sidney and Vancouver islands too! Don't forget to look back at the Turtleback. Return the way you came, and come back in spring when wildflowers make this a painted turtle.

EXTENDING YOUR TRIP
You can easily spend all day hiking on Turtleback Mountain, though many of its trails are old roads, which may be more appealing for mountain biking or trail run-

ning. From the Turtlehead Trail junction, follow the North Trail 0.7 mile (1.1 km) to a wetland and the Raven Ridge Trail (double-track), which leads to a 1.6-mile (2.6-km) loop over Turtleback's 1519-foot (463-m) summit—no views, but plenty of quiet forest and a small grassy bald. Want more? Continue right at the Raven Ridge junction and hike 0.2 mile (0.3 km) to the Center Loop Trail. Take it 1 mile (1.6 km) to a junction. Continue on the loop left for 0.6 mile (1 km) to the Raven Ridge Trail, or hike 0.4 mile (0.6 km) right on the Ridge Trail to access trails leading to Ship Peak and the southern trailhead (Hike 36).

The Turtlehead offers sweeping views of the San Juan Islands.

38 Judd Cove Preserve

RATING/ DIFFICULTY	LOOP	ELEV GAIN/HIGH POINT
**/1	0.6 mile (1 km)	125 feet (38 m)/ 125 feet (38 m)

Maps: USGS Eastsound, land bank map online; **Contact:** San Juan County Land Bank, Judd Cove Preserve; **Notes:** Dogs permitted on-leash. Do not disturb marine life. Do not trespass onto adjacent private property; **GPS:** N 48 41.086, W 122 55.613

Amble down a peaceful country path to a beautifully restored nineteenth-century limekiln overlooking a secluded bay on East Sound. Scout the stony shoreline for shorebirds, waterfowl, and small mammals, while a small cascade provides background water music. Then take a trail traversing the old limestone quarry, now put to rest beneath a quilt of greenery.

GETTING THERE

From Anacortes, take a Washington State ferry to Orcas Island. Head north on Orcas Road (Horseshoe Highway) for 6.9 miles (11.1 km) to a junction with Crow Valley Road. Bear right and immediately turn right onto graveled Fowlers Way. Drive 400 feet (120 m) to the trailhead (elev. 80 ft/24 m).

ON THE TRAIL

A small preserve managed by the San Juan County Land Bank, Judd Cove packs quite of bit of history and scenery within its 14.5 acres (6 ha). Opened to the public in 2009, it remains one of Orcas Island's best-kept secrets.

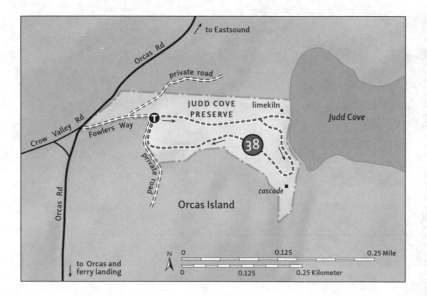

Greggs limekiln at Judd Cove was built in the 1880s.

Start on an old road and descend to the cove. Pass by a monstrous maple tree before coming to a trail junction (your return) at 0.15 mile (0.25 km). Continue straight to the Greggs limekiln on the edge of a pasture, above Judd Cove. Built in the 1880s, this kiln was one of many that fueled the San Juan Islands' economy in the early twentieth century.

Next, stroll down to the cove. Admire the view across East Sound to Mount Constitution. Imagine one hundred years ago the ships coming to port here to haul away barrels of refined lime, a key ingredient in concrete. Except for raucous gulls and a small cascade hidden by big trees, the cove is a quiet place these days.

Return up the bluff on the 0.4-mile (0.6-km) trail, above the cove and rounding some big boulders, stumps, and standing firs and cedars. After skirting an old limestone quarry and private residence, reach Fowlers Way just south of the trailhead and your start.

39 Crescent Beach Preserve

RATING/ DIFFICULTY	ROUNDTRIP	ELEV GAIN/HIGH POINT
*/1	1.5 miles (2.4 km)	40 feet (12 m)/ 60 feet (18 m)

Maps: USGS Eastsound, land bank map online; **Contact:** San Juan County Land Bank, Crescent Beach Preserve; **Notes:** Open to bicycles. Dogs permitted on-leash; **GPS:** N 48 41.757, W 122 53.494

Enjoy a quiet woodland walk just upland from Crescent Beach's oyster-spawning waters and outside of bustling Eastsound, the cultural and commercial hub of Orcas Island. This preserve's draw is the beach, leaving the trail a lightly used byway favored mainly by locals and resident deer.

GETTING THERE
From Anacortes, take a Washington State ferry to Orcas Island. Head north on Orcas Road (Horseshoe Highway) for 8.1 miles (13 km), turning right onto Main Street. Proceed through Eastsound on Main Street (which becomes Crescent Beach Drive), driving 0.9 mile (1.4 km) to a parking lot on the left and the trailhead.

ON THE TRAIL
Acquired by the San Juan County Land Bank around the turn of the recent century, the beautiful and ecologically important Crescent Beach area is finally open to the public.

From a bluff above the beach, follow the Woodland Trail through forest, wetland, and an old orchard.

The way heads north through a big fir grove choked in salal and raspberry bushes. The way then bends west, crossing a small section of an extensive wetland that includes a bulrush marsh. Resuming its course north, the trail skirts old orchard and pasture. The near-level path then passes through a mixed forest of pine, fir, and madrona. Look for aspens too— easy to spot in autumn with their golden foliage. A large stand of them grows in the preserve.

Eventually the trail reaches an old skid road, which leads to a northern trailhead (elev. 60 ft/18 m) on the Mount Baker Road (an alternative starting point). Turn around and enjoy the trip back to the beach.

EXTENDING YOUR TRIP

From the northern trailhead, you can walk east along the Mount Baker Road and then north on Terrill Beach Road, alongside the Stonebridge-Terrill Preserve, to an access

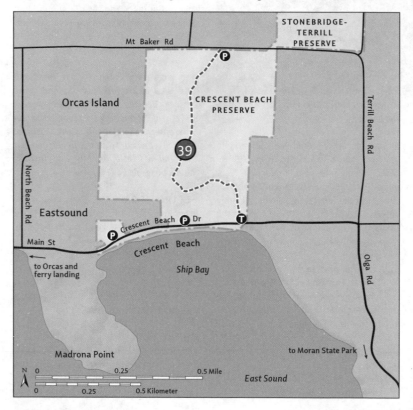

Tranquil woods can be found away from Crescent Beach.

point into an old farm. And by all means, walk the more than 2000 feet (600 m) of Crescent Beach, admiring the view of East Sound. Respect private property (leased oyster-farm beds) on the beach's east end.

40 Cascade Lake

RATING/DIFFICULTY	LOOP	ELEV GAIN/HIGH POINT
***/2	2.9 miles (4.7 km)	200 feet (61 m)/480 feet (146 m)

Maps: USGS Mount Constitution, park map online; **Contact:** Washington State Parks, Moran State Park; **Notes:** Discover Pass required. Partly open to bicycles. Dogs permitted on-leash; **GPS:** N 48 39.374, W 122 51.288

With its three campgrounds,

shaded picnic area, paddle-boat concession, and inviting beaches, Cascade Lake is a hub of outdoor activity in sprawling Moran State Park. An attractive trail circles this body of water, tying together the busy campgrounds, quiet coves, and pretty lakeside bluffs. An excellent evening hike if you're camping at the park, this loop is one children will love no matter the time of day.

GETTING THERE

From Anacortes, take a Washington State ferry to Orcas Island. Head north on Orcas Road (Horseshoe Highway) for 8.1 miles (13 km), turning right onto Main Street (alternatively, follow the truck route that bypasses the village). Proceed through Eastsound on Main Street (which becomes Crescent Beach Drive), driving 1.2 miles (1.9 km) to Olga Road. Turn right and drive 3.6 miles (5.8 km), passing through the Moran State Park entrance gate, to the Cascade Lake day-use area and trailhead (elev. 360 ft/110 m). Privy available.

ON THE TRAIL

Start near the rustic picnic shelter, a legacy of the 1930s Civilian Conservation Corps. Head counterclockwise, crossing Morgan Creek in a stand of big ol' cedars. Hugging the lakeshore, the delightful trail passes through marshy areas and over ledges, teetering on the water's edge. Ignore a right-hand trail that leads to the ranger station at 0.3 mile (0.5 km). At 0.5 mile (0.8 km), a trail leads downhill to the right, to the Rosario Resort, former home of Robert Moran (see "Shipbuilder's Legacy" sidebar) and now on the National Register of Historic Places.

Continue left across ledges that offer excellent views over the lake and its sloping green surroundings. Be sure to stop at a well-photographed "bonsai" Douglas fir. At

0.9 mile (1.4 km), the Lagoon Trail veers right, circling Rosario Lagoon on a 0.75-mile (1.2-km) brushy and muddy route. Head straight instead, crossing an attractive bridge. Meet back up with the Lagoon Trail and carry on left, on an up-and-down course through tall timber.

At 1.6 miles (2.6 km), come to a junction with the Sunrise Rock Trail (Hike 41), and shortly afterward reach the South End Campground. Walk the road 0.2 mile (0.3 km), picking up trail again near campsite number 1. Hug the lakeshore once more and then start climbing away from it, following a paved path to the camp access road. Cross it and shortly afterward cross Olga Road (use caution), and come to a junction (elev. 480 ft/146 m) at 2.2 miles (3.5 km).

The trail right leads to Cascade Falls (Hike 42). Head left to close the loop, following the waterline and then steeply descending to a service road. Skirting the Midway Campground, climb a small rise. Then meander through big firs and cedars, taking in window

The loop hike around Cascade Lake includes plenty of bluffs for viewing.

SHIPBUILDER'S LEGACY: MORAN STATE PARK

In 1875, Robert Moran arrived in Seattle from New York City without a dollar to his name. But the enterprising Moran would go on to become the city's mayor, a prominent shipbuilder, and quite wealthy to boot. He acquired a significant amount of land on Orcas Island and built his Rosario mansion there, where he would retire. Through encounters and writings with John Muir, Moran became a conservationist, prompting him to donate 2700 acres (1092 ha) of his land to form a new state park.

In 1921, Moran State Park opened and through purchases has since grown to more than 5250 acres (2125 ha,) making it the second-largest tract of public land in the San Juans. The park protects old-growth forest, several lakes, and the San Juan Islands' highest summit, 2409-foot (734-m) Mount Constitution. Moran State Park contains more than 30 miles (50 km) of trails, several campgrounds, shelters, and other structures, including a stone tower on Mount Constitution—most of these built in the 1930s by the Civilian Conservation Corps. In 1905, Robert Moran was given a grim prognosis and told he had a year to live. He died in 1943 after living an industrious and charitable life. His gift of Moran State Park is an incredible legacy.

views of the lake. Cross Cold Creek and arrive back at your start at 2.9 miles (4.7 km).

EXTENDING YOUR TRIP

Combine with hikes to Rosario Lagoon, Sunrise Rock (Hike 41), and/or Cascade Falls (Hike 42).

41 Sunrise Rock

RATING/ DIFFICULTY	ROUNDTRIP	ELEV GAIN/HIGH POINT
**/2	1.4 miles (2.3 km)	280 feet (85 m)/ 660 feet (201 m)

Maps: USGS Mount Constitution, park map online; **Contact:** Washington State Parks, Moran State Park; **Notes:** Discover Pass required. Dogs permitted on-leash; **GPS:** N 48 38.881, W 122 50.761

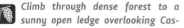 *Climb through dense forest to a sunny open ledge overlooking Cas-*

cade Lake. A nice hike for sunrise, time it so you sit and savor the morning light twinkling on the lake below and kissing the meadows on Little Summit above. Sunsets are also rewarding from this spot, whence you can watch creeping shadows on the placid waters below.

GETTING THERE

From Anacortes, take a Washington State ferry to Orcas Island. Head north on Orcas Road (Horseshoe Highway) for 8.1 miles (13 km), turning right onto Main Street (alternatively, follow the truck route that bypasses the village). Proceed through Eastsound on Main Street (which becomes Crescent Beach Drive), driving 1.2 miles (1.9 km) to Olga Road. Turn right and drive 4.2 miles (6.8 km), passing through the Moran State Park entrance gate, and turn right onto the South End Campground access road. Proceed 0.1 mile (0.15 km) to the day-use parking area (elev. 380 ft/116 m). Privy available.

via a couple of tight switchbacks. The way becomes rocky and rooty, but not for long. At 0.7 mile (1.1 km), emerge atop the mossy open Sunrise Rock (elev. 660 ft/201 m) and behold Cascade Lake glistening below. Break out the thermos of coffee and let the day begin!

EXTENDING YOUR TRIP
Combine with a walk around Cascade Lake (Hike 40) or a trip to Cascade Falls (Hike 42).

Cascade Falls tumbles in a ravine shaded by old growth giants.

ON THE TRAIL
The trail begins from the end of the campground road, but limited trailhead parking necessitates that you start at the day-use lot. Walk the road 0.3 mile (0.5 km) to the trailhead, located near a restroom building. Into old forest you go, in just steps coming to a junction marked by one of Moran's signature rustic yet eloquent signposts. Right leads around Cascade Lake (Hike 40). Instead, head left uphill and reach another junction at 0.4 mile (0.6 km). The trail left journeys to Cascade Falls (Hike 42). Sunrise Rock is to the right.

Through a forest of towering cedars and firs bearing scars from fires long past, begin a short and steep climb. Switchback beneath big rocky ledges, and then continue climbing

42 Cascade Falls

RATING/ DIFFICULTY	LOOP	ELEV GAIN/HIGH POINT
**/2	3.1 miles (5 km)	420 feet (128 m)/ 690 feet (210 m)

Maps: USGS Mount Constitution, state park map online; **Contact:** Washington State Parks, Moran State Park; **Notes:** Discover Pass required. Partly open to bicycles. Dogs permitted on-leash; **GPS:** N 48 38.881, W 122 50.761

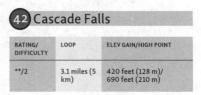 *Tumbling 40 feet (12 m) into a small ravine shaded by old-growth giants, Cascade Falls is a pretty sight. The largest falls in the San Juan Islands, it's also surrounded by some of the archipelago's largest trees. This hike takes you along Cascade Creek through primeval forest to not only Cascade Falls but two other waterfalls as well.*

GETTING THERE
From Anacortes, take a Washington State ferry to Orcas Island. Head north on Orcas Road (Horseshoe Highway) for 8.1 miles (13 km), turning right onto Main Street (alternatively, follow the truck route that bypasses the

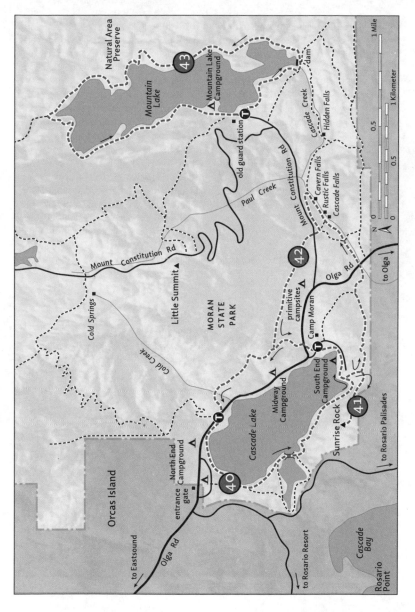

village). Proceed through Eastsound on Main Street (which becomes Crescent Beach Drive), driving 1.2 miles (1.9 km) to Olga Road. Turn right and drive 4.2 miles (6.8 km), passing through the Moran State Park entrance gate, and turn right onto the South End Campground access road. Proceed 0.1 mile (0.15 km) to the day-use parking area (elev. 650 ft/ 198 m). Privy available.

Alternately, for shorter access to the falls, stay on Olga Road another 0.3 mile (0.5 km) and turn left onto Mount Constitution Road. Drive 0.4 mile (0.6 km) to the falls trailhead and day-use parking area (elev. 650 ft/ 198 m). Privy available.

ON THE TRAIL

Cascades Falls can easily be reached from the Mount Constitution Road on a 0.2-mile (0.3-km) trail. But if you're interested in a half-day hike incorporating three cascades and magnificent primeval forest, then you'll love this longer approach via the South End Campground.

Walk the campground road 0.3 mile (0.5 km) to its end and the trailhead (no parking). Within a few steps, come to a junction. Head left to reach another junction at 0.4 mile (0.6 km). The trail right leads to Sunrise Rock (Hike 41). Head left instead, climbing over a small bald (elev. 500 ft/152 m) before steeply dropping to cross a creek (elev. 390 ft/119 m). Soon afterward cross an old water-diversion ditch and continue on a fairly level course through magnificent ancient forest. Admire gargantuan Douglas firs and monstrous Sitka spruces, some of the largest trees in the San Juans.

Find an excellent view of Cascade Lake from Sunrise Rock.

At 1 mile (1.6 km), stay right at a junction (left leads to Camp Moran), soon coming to Olga Road near the west arch (elev. 460 ft/140 m). Cross the road and follow a wide trail through big timber alongside Cascade Creek. At 1.3 miles (2.1 km), reach a major junction (elev. 545 ft/166 m). The wide trail veering left continues 0.2 mile (0.3 km) to the Mount Constitution Road trailhead. The single-track trail straight ahead is your route—but only after you take in good views of fanning Cascade Falls plummeting into a small ravine cloaked in old growth. To do that follow the trail right (which connects to the Southeast Boundary Trail), dropping 40 feet (12 m) in 100 yards (90 m) to a small bridge over Cascade Creek. Look for river otters and dippers while you're there.

Backtrack to the creekside trail and resume hiking, passing the lip of the falls and coming to another junction at 1.5 miles (2.4 km) at small but pretty Rustic Falls. The trail left leads to the Mount Constitution Road. Keep hiking straight along the creek, coming to Cavern Falls gushing through a tight chasm. Shortly afterward, at 1.8 miles (2.9 km), reach a junction (elev. 690 feet/210 m).

Unless you want to first make a 0.3-mile (0.5-km) side trip to Hidden Falls, to the right at a bridged creek crossing, head left here to reach the Mount Constitution Road trailhead (elev. 650 ft/198 m) at 2.1 miles (3.4 km). Cross the road and follow a quiet rose-lined trail through big open timber, skirting a primitive campground and reaching a junction (elev. 460 ft/140 m) at 2.8 miles (4.5 km). Turn left to cross Olga Road and close the loop at 3.1 miles (5 km).

EXTENDING YOUR TRIP
Combine with the Cascade Lake loop (Hike 40) for a 5-mile (8-km) roundtrip.

43 Mountain Lake

RATING/DIFFICULTY	LOOP	ELEV GAIN/HIGH POINT
***/2	3.9 miles (6.3 km)	165 feet (50 m)/1035 feet (315 m)

Maps: USGS Mount Constitution, state park map online; **Contact:** Washington State Parks, Moran State Park; **Notes:** Discover Pass required. Partly open to bicycles Sept 15–May 15. Dogs permitted on-leash; **GPS:** N 48 39.275, W 122 49.133

Enjoy an easy, near-level journey around one of the largest lakes in the San Juans. Free from outboard motors, the waters are peaceful, except perhaps for the cackling geese and shrilling eagles. Along the way, admire old-growth giants and impressive views of Mount Constitution's sheer and stony eastern face.

GETTING THERE
From Anacortes, take a Washington State ferry to Orcas Island. Head north on Orcas Road (Horseshoe Highway) for 8.1 miles (13 km), turning right onto Main Street (alternatively, follow the truck route that bypasses the village). Proceed through Eastsound on Main Street (which becomes Crescent Beach Drive), driving 1.2 miles (1.9 km) to Olga Road. Turn right and drive 4.5 miles (7.2 km), passing through the Moran State Park entrance gate, and turn left onto Mount Constitution Road. Continue 1 mile (1.6 km) and turn right. Drive 0.3 mile (0.5 km) to the trailhead (elev. 925 ft/282 m) near the old guard station. Privy available.

ON THE TRAIL
Hike this loop counterclockwise to face views of Mount Constitution and bask in its

bulky and cliffy presence. Start by heading southeast along a wooded bluff above the large lake. Pass the bicycle-access trail and shortly afterward cross the lake's outlet (elev. 900 ft/274 m) below a dam, reaching a junction at 0.5 mile (0.8 km). Right heads 1.3 miles (2.1 km) to Cascade Falls (Hike 42). Head left and then left again at another junction, lest you venture up Mount Pickett (Hike 44)

Catch your first glimpses of Mount Constitution across a quiet cove. The mountain's well-worn rocky façade above the deeply forested lake looks like a scene out of the Appalachian Mountains. After bypassing a small peninsula, the trail hugs the lake's eastern shoreline on a rolling course through groves of big trees. Look for eagles in those towering giants, particularly in the shoreline snags. Enjoy good views of Constitution too, with its signature stone tower now in view.

Pass monster Douglas firs and gradually ascend, cresting a 1035-foot (315-m) bluff at about 1.7 miles (2.7 km). Then pass through a "fir arch" and descend via switchbacks into a cool ravine, crossing a creek (elev. 935 ft/285 m) and rounding a point graced with pines. Cross a couple more creeks and reach a junction (elev. 965 ft/294 m) at 2.5 miles (4 km).

Right heads to the Twin Lakes (Hike 44). Your way is left, back to the trailhead at the Mountain Lake landing. Drop back to lake level, passing through alder flats and groves of big firs. A small island comes into view before the trail cuts across a big-timbered peninsula. Skirt the placid shoreline once again, keeping eyes open and ears tuned for woodpeckers, eagles, ducks, and osprey.

Pass a memorial for Bonnie Sliger, a popular Youth Conservation Corps supervisor, before reaching the boat launch at 3.7 miles (6 km). Turn right and walk the dirt road 0.2 mile (0.3 km) back to your vehicle.

Mount Constitution provides an impressive backdrop to Mountain Lake.

EXTENDING YOUR TRIP

Combine with a trip up Mount Constitution (Hike 45) or to Mount Pickett and the Twin Lakes (Hike 44).

44 Twin Lakes and Mount Pickett

RATING/ DIFFICULTY	LOOP	ELEV GAIN/HIGH POINT
***/3	7.6 miles (12.2 km)	915 feet (279 m)/ 1749 feet (533 m)

Maps: USGS Mount Constitution, state park map online; **Contact:** Washington State Parks, Moran State Park; **Notes:** Discover Pass required. Open to bicycles Sept 15–May 15. Dogs permitted on-leash; **GPS:** N 48 39.302, W 122 49.130

Hike to a pair of small lakes tucked beneath the cliffs of Mount Constitution on a ridge high above the sea. Then charge up Mount Pickett through one of the largest tracts of ancient forest in the Puget Trough—there are no views, but you'll find solitude, a nice alternative to busy Mount Constitution.

GETTING THERE

See directions to Hike 43.

ON THE TRAIL

Start by hiking north 0.3 mile (0.5 km) on the gravel road leading to a handful of campsites on a small peninsula jutting into Mountain Lake. Pick up trail near the boat launch and hug the 200-acre (80-ha) lake's western shoreline on a near-level journey. Eventually round a 40-foot (12 m) rise at the lake's north end, where at 1.4 miles (2.3 km), beside a creek, you'll find a junction (elev. 925 feet/282 m).

Continue left on the Twin Lakes Trail, up a lush draw that harbors impressive cedars and hemlocks. Upon crossing a creek, notice some Sitka spruce, trees better adapted to the foggy and mist-shrouded Pacific coastline. At 2.3 miles (3.7 km), reach a junction (elev. 1100 ft/335 m). Left goes to Mount Constitution and the North Trail (Hikes 45 and 46). Right leads to Mount Pickett. But you want to head straight to circle the Twin Lakes first.

Follow this less-trodden path 0.5 mile (0.8 km) around the larger lake, passing big cedars and small feeder creeks and entering the YMCA's Camp Orkila. Don't be surprised if there are some happy campers by the lakeshore. The trail gets rougher, climbing about 50 feet (15 m) up and over steep ledges (be careful), with excellent views across the lake to Mount Constitution.

Reenter the park, coming to a junction at a creek connecting the two lakes at 2.8 miles (4.5 km). Right heads back to the main trail. If you've had enough, the trip to this point is satisfying on its own. Or to continue, head left to circle the smaller lake. Cross its outlet stream and peer through trees out to the Salish Sea. Wander through pines and spruce and reach the Mount Pickett Trail at 3.1 miles (5 km). Now turn left, gradually ascending a ridge carpeted in moss. At 3.6 miles (5.8 km), the trail becomes an old fire road.

Wander through groves of stately firs and by wetland pools humming with insect, bird, and amphibian activity. At 4.7 miles (7.6 km), crest Mount Pickett's 1749-foot (533-m) summit. The peak is named for General George Pickett, who garrisoned troops at American Camp on San Juan Island during the Pig War. He is best known for his futile charge for

Mount Constitution and its tower can be seen from the Twin Lakes' shoreline.

the Confederacy in the Battle of Gettysburg during the American Civil War.

Shortly afterward, reach a junction with the Southeast Boundary Trail (Hike 47). Bear right, staying on the old fire road that snakes along the ridge. At 5.5 miles (8.9 km), stay straight at a junction (left drops steeply to the Southeast Boundary Trail), passing a big wetland pool. Gradually descend through impressive ancient forest, bearing right at another junction at 6.4 miles (10.3 km).

In an impressive old-growth Douglas fir grove, bear right at yet another Southeast Boundary Trail connector. Soon afterward come to another junction (elev. 1000 ft/305 m)

at 6.8 miles (10.9 km). The Mount Pickett Trail continues straight for 1 mile (1.6 km) to the Cascade Falls trailhead. You want to head right on another old fire road, dropping to the Mountain Lake loop at 7 miles (11.3 km). Bear left and then right, crossing the outlet stream and returning to the trailhead at the Mountain Lake landing at 7.6 miles (12.2 km).

EXTENDING YOUR TRIP

Combine with the Southeast Boundary Trail (Hike 47) for a quiet all-day journey. Or make it a lake day, combining a trip to Twin Lakes with a hike around Mountain Lake (Hike 43).

45 Mount Constitution

RATING/ DIFFICULTY	LOOP	ELEV GAIN/HIGH POINT
*****/4	7.1 miles (11.4 km)	1640 feet (500 m)/ 2409 feet (734 m)

Maps: USGS Mount Constitution, state park map online; **Contact:** Washington State Parks, Moran State Park; **Notes:** Discover Pass required. Open to bicycles Sept 15–May 15. dogs permitted on-leash; **GPS:** N 48 39.309, W 122 49.150

Why drive to the highest summit in the San Juan Islands when you can hike to it instead? Trek through windblown pines along precipitous ledges to Mount Constitution's open summit. Then climb its stone tower, savoring stunning views of emerald islands sparkling in the Salish Sea, all against a backdrop of snowcapped peaks from Garibaldi to Rainier. You'll hike past three lakes too, on this invigorating loop.

GETTING THERE
See directions to Hike 43.

Sweeping views of the Salish Sea from the "rooftop of the San Juans"

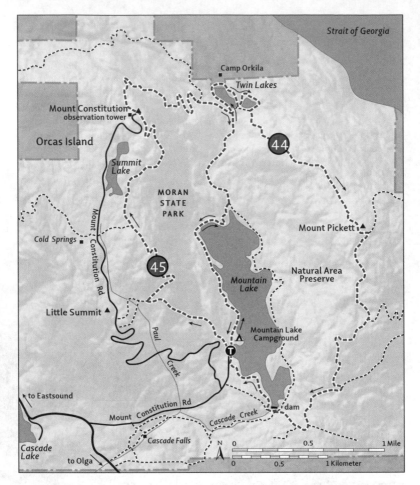

ON THE TRAIL

Locate the Little Summit Trail near a Civilian Conservation Corps (CCC) shelter by the group camp entrance. Then prepare to break a sweat, climbing steeply and with a purpose. Briefly skirt the Mount Constitution Road and continue relentlessly upward. After crossing a creek, pass by big old trees brandishing fire scars and younger trees replacing the old ones that went up in flames. At 1.3 miles (2.1 km), reach a junction (elev. 1925 ft/587 m).

The trail to the left follows an old road 0.3 mile (0.5 km) to Little Summit (elev. 2035 ft/620 m) with its sweeping views to Cypress, Fidalgo, Blakely, and Lopez islands and Orcas's Entrance Mountain.

COLD SPRINGS AND NORTH TRAIL LOOP **131**

The way to Constitution continues north along a lofty ridge. Soon reach the first of many east-facing view-granting ledges. Then traverse a forest of windblown, stunted lodgepole pine, cresting a 2250-foot (686-m) knoll before coming to a junction at 2.1 miles (3.4 km).

The trail left heads 0.3 mile (0.5 km) through big trees to the Cold Springs trailhead (Hike 46). Continue straight instead, soon crossing a creek (elev. 2150 ft/655 m) below an old rock dam that impounds Summit Lake. Then travel along the edge of the ridge, undulating between pine groves and sheer clifftops (use caution) before reaching Mount Constitution's 2409-foot (734-m) broad summit at 3.2 miles (5.2 km).

Join the throngs who drove to the summit and head up Constitution's unique stone tower. Constructed in 1936 from locally quarried sandstone by CCC crews, it's a facsimile of a twelfth-century Caucasus Mountains military fortification. From this rooftop of the San Juans, enjoy an unobstructed view of islands, mountains, sounds, and straits. Look out over Mountain Lake and Mount Pickett. Pick out the prominent Mount Baker and British Columbia's Golden Ears—and Patos, Sucia, Matia, Clark, Barnes, Lummi, Vendovi, and Cypress islands. Be sure to read the historical displays in the tower.

Walk 0.1 mile (0.15 km) to the summit parking lot and pick up the Twin Lakes Trail. Prep your knees for a steep 1300-foot (396-m) descent. Via short switchbacks, weave downward in deep timber beneath a series of ledges. Pass an abandoned trail that veers right. Soon afterward reach a junction with the North Trail at 4.5 miles (7.2 km). Continue straight in old growth, reaching a junction at the Twin Lakes (elev. 1100 ft/335 m) at 4.8 miles (7.7 km).

Complete your loop (or visit the Twin Lakes first, Hike 44) by hiking right 0.9 mile (1.4 km) to the Mountain Lake Trail. Then turn right and hike another 1.4 miles (2.3 km) back to the trailhead.

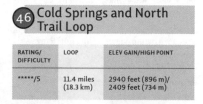

46 Cold Springs and North Trail Loop

RATING/ DIFFICULTY	LOOP	ELEV GAIN/HIGH POINT
*****/5	11.4 miles (18.3 km)	2940 feet (896 m)/ 2409 feet (734 m)

Maps: USGS Mount Constitution, state park map online; **Contact:** Washington State Parks, Moran State Park; **Notes:** Discover

Ancient forest along the North Trail

Pass required. Open to bicycles Sept 15–May 15. Dogs permitted on-leash; **GPS:** N 48 39.367, W 122 51.311

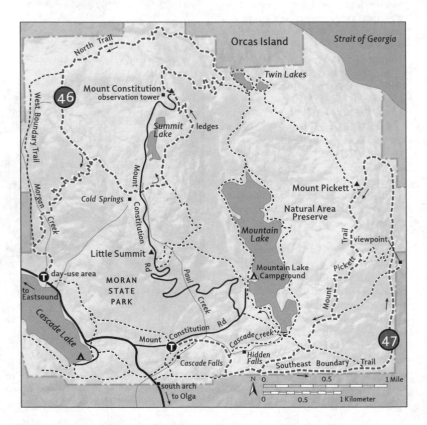

Looking for a challenging hike to Mount Constitution? Do you delight in going where few hikers have gone before? Want some big trees with your views? Then you'll love this loop that ascends the San Juan Islands' highest summit and travels through some of the park's loneliest reaches.

GETTING THERE
See directions to Hike 40.

ON THE TRAIL
This is a lollipop loop and a strenuous one. The hike can be shortened and made considerably easier by just doing the loop part from the Cold Springs trailhead on Mount Constitution Road, 3.7 miles (6 km) from the Olga Road turnoff.

For the full experience from Cascade Lake, follow the Cold Springs Trail up a deep ravine. Pass a trail leading left to North End Campground. Pass a monstrous cedar too. Cross the creek and begin climbing in earnest. At 0.6 mile (1 km), bear right. The trail left, the West Boundary Trail, is 2.5 miles (4 km) of lightly used, difficult, steep tread leading to the North Trail. Consider it as a possible return variation.

Upward, bound through old growth and cross Morgan Creek once more. Start switch-backing, crossing many creek tributaries before traversing an open grassy, ledgy area. Look for an old mine in the hillside. Stop too for teaser views through the trees out to the sea. At 2.6 miles (4.2 km), the relentless climbing stops as you reach a junction (elev. 2090 feet/637 m) with the North Trail on Hidden Ridge.

You'll be returning from the left, so head right on a fairly level path through old-growth forest and by large grassy wetlands. At 3.2 miles (5.1 km), just after passing the old gazebo at Cold Springs and a picnic shelter, reach the Mount Constitution Road trailhead (elev. 2090 feet/637 m). This is the alternative start if you're interested in just doing the loop.

Cross the road and a creek and come to a junction (elev. 2250 ft/686 m) at 3.5 miles (5.6 km.) Turn left, dropping 100 feet (30 m) before gradually ascending Mount Constitution's broad pine-covered and ledge-dotted south ridge. Views are sweeping and the hike is exhilarating. At 4.6 miles (7.4 km), crest Mount Constitution's 2409-foot (734-m) summit. Take time to scale its tower to savor far-reaching views, from British Columbia's Coast Range to the Olympic Mountains and scores of emerald islands in between.

Then walk 0.1 mile (0.15 km) to the summit parking lot and pick up the Twin Lakes Trail. Steeply descend, reaching a junction

(elev. 1300 ft/396 m) with the North Trail at 5.9 miles (9.5 km). Now prepare for a lonesome journey through Moran's hinterlands, home to some of the most impressive trees on the islands.

Wind upward through groves of magnificent old growth, crossing trickling creeks and listening to serenading birdsong. Under a thick canopy high above the Salish Sea, gradually angle around Mount Constitution's northern slopes. Notice the nice stonework in places along the tread. Cross a service road that accesses communication towers on the mountain. Shortly afterward, come to a junction (elev. 2000/610 m) at 8 miles (12.9 km) with the West Boundary Trail (follow it for a shorter, albeit less interesting and more difficult, return).

Continue straight, skirting a small pond before commencing a short steep climb. Pass a boundary marker and return to a familiar junction with the Cold Springs Trail (elev. 2090 ft/637 m) at 8.8 miles (14.2 km). Turn right for a familiar 2.6-mile (4.2-km) trip to the trailhead—except this time it's all downhill!

EXTENDING YOUR TRIP
Combine with the Mount Pickett Trail (Hikes 44 and 47) for a grand loop of Moran's high country.

47 Southeast Boundary Trail

RATING/ DIFFICULTY	LOOP	ELEV GAIN/HIGH POINT
***/4	8.7 miles (14 km)	1665 feet (507 m)/ 1730 feet (527 m)

Maps: USGS Mount Constitution, state park map online; **Contact:** Washington State Parks, Moran State Park; **Notes:** Discover

Pass required. Partly open to horses. Open to bicycles Sept 15–May 15. Dogs permitted on-leash; **GPS:** N 48 38.904, W 122 49.960

Seekers of solitude will enjoy this challenging trail along the southeast periphery of Moran State Park. Although mountain bikers and equestrians play here at times, it's often just you and the deer. Most of the way is through luxurious old-growth forest, but there is a secret viewpoint—and it's a good one.

GETTING THERE

From Anacortes, take a Washington State ferry to Orcas Island. Head north on Orcas Road (Horseshoe Highway) for 8.1 miles (13 km), turning right onto Main Street (alternatively, follow the truck route that bypasses the village). Proceed through Eastsound on Main Street (which becomes Crescent Beach Drive), driving 1.2 miles (1.9 km) to Olga Road. Turn right and drive 4.5 miles (7.2 km), passing through the Moran State Park entrance gate, and turn left onto Mount Constitution Road. Drive 0.4 mile (0.6 km) to the Cascade Falls trailhead (elev. 650 ft/198 m).

ON THE TRAIL

The Southeast Boundary Trail actually begins on Olga Road by the park's south arch. However, a lack of parking there warrants beginning from either the Cascade Falls or Mountain Lake trailhead. You'll bypass the lower 0.9 mile (1.4 km) of the boundary trail, but you can easily tack that on if you like.

From the Cascade Falls trailhead, start with a warm-up on a gently graded old fire road. At 0.3 mile (0.5 km), pass the Cascade Falls Trail. At 0.5 mile (0.8 km), continue right at a junction. The trail left crosses

Cascade Creek above Hidden Falls (check it out), heading 0.7 mile (1.1 km) to Mountain Lake. Your route takes you through a large field that doubles as a picnic-table and firegrate graveyard.

At 0.8 mile (1.3 km), your route merges with the Southeast Boundary Trail (elev. 770 ft/235 m) coming from Olga Road. Stay left on the fire road another 0.4 mile (0.6 km); it straddles the park boundary and passes wetlands and Sitka spruce. Just after crossing a water pipeline, the trails diverge. You'll be returning from straight ahead, so bear right and follow the lightly traveled Southeast Boundary Trail through dark forest and by wetlands. After crossing a bridge (elev. 985 ft/300 m), steadily and steeply descend through a forest of fire-scarred firs. At 2.2 miles (3.5 km), reach a junction in an alder flat (elev. 720 ft/219 m). The trail left climbs 250 feet (76 m) in 0.5 mile (0.8 km) through old growth to connect with the Mount Pickett Trail. It makes for a shorter loop option.

The Southeast Boundary Trail continues straight, passing a side trail leading to private property before dropping steeply. The way then turns north, straddling the park boundary, brushing by a yurt (respect private property), and coming to a trail (elev. 400 ft/122 m) that leads to Winter Falls Lane (private) at 2.8 miles (4.5 km).

Now steeply climb, reaching an unsigned junction (elev. 920 ft/280 m) at 3.5 miles (5.6 km). The trail left travels 0.7 mile (1.1 km) and climbs 200 feet (61 m), passing some viewpoints on its way to the Mount Pickett Trail—another shorter loop option. Continue straight, crossing a creek and coming to another unsigned junction in 0.1 mile (0.15 km). Take this absolute-must side trip for 300 feet (90 m), leaving forest and the park for a grassy open hillside in the San Juan Preservation

Trust's Hogback Preserve. Stay awhile—the view is stunning out to Cypress, Lummi, Sinclair, and Vendovi islands—Mount Baker, too.

Back on the Southeast Boundary Trail, continue climbing and reach yet another trail junction (elev. 1100 ft/335 m) and another loop option at 3.9 miles (6.3 km).

The trail left steeply climbs 500 feet (152 m), meeting the Mount Pickett Trail in 0.5 mile (0.8 km). The Southeast Boundary Trail, now hiker-only, continues straight and climbs steeply too. Following mossy tread, be sure to veer left (west) at 4.7 miles (7.6 km) (ignoring a track straight).

Open hillside in the San Juan Preservation Trust's Hogback Preserve

Reach the Mount Pickett Trail (elev. 1730 ft/527 m) just below Pickett's thickly forested summit at 5.2 miles (8.4 km).

Now return via the Mount Pickett Trail, an easy grade along an old fire road. Near a big wetland pool, reach a junction (elev. 1625 ft/495 m) at 5.9 miles (9.5 km) with a connector trail to the Southeast Boundary Trail. Continue straight, gradually descending through impressive ancient forest and bearing right at another junction (elev. 1100 ft/335 m) at 6.8 miles (10.9 km). Reach yet another Southeast Boundary Trail connector junction (elev. 1000 ft/305 m) at 7.1 miles (11.4 km). In another 0.1 mile (0.15 km), reach a junction with a trail dropping 0.2 mile (0.3 km) to Mountain Lake. Follow it and the Cascade Creek Trail for a shorter route back to the trailhead.

Otherwise, stay straight and once again reach the Southeast Boundary Trail at 7.5 miles (12.1 km). Now retrace your steps on the Mount Pickett Trail 1.2 miles (1.9 km) to the trailhead.

EXTENDING YOUR TRIP

If you're compelled to hike the entire Southeast Boundary Trail, start by following the Cascade Falls Trail 0.5 mile (0.8k) to Olga Road (elev. 400 ft/122 m). Then cross Cascade Creek, walk through the park's south arch, and pick up the trail there and head north.

48 Obstruction Pass State Park

RATING/ DIFFICULTY	LOOP	ELEV GAIN/HIGH POINT
***/2	1.9 miles (3.1 km)	305 feet (93 m)/ 225 feet (69 m)

Maps: USGS Blakely Island, state park map online; **Contact:** Washington State Parks,

Find a gorgeous beach at trail's end.

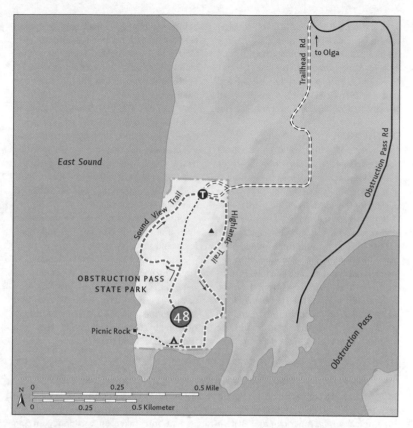

Moran State Park; **Notes:** Discover Pass required. Dogs permitted on-leash; **GPS:** N 48 36.509, W 122 49.584

Consider spending the night at this peaceful park.

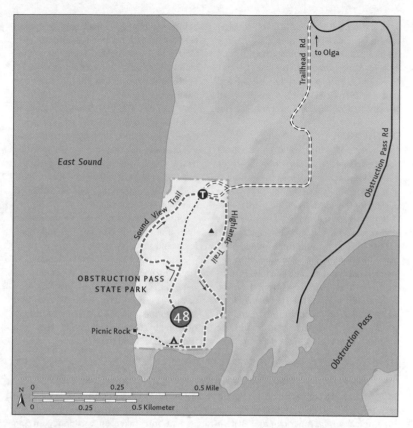 *Wander through an open forest of firs, cedars, and madronas to a secluded sandy beach on Obstruction Pass at the mouth of East Sound. Then while away the time skipping stones, identifying birds, napping on polished driftwood logs, or just staring out at emerald islands and passing ferries.*

GETTING THERE

From Anacortes, take a Washington State ferry to Orcas Island. Head north on Orcas Road (Horseshoe Highway) for 8.1 miles (13 km), turning right onto Main Street (alternatively, follow the truck route that bypasses the village). Proceed through Eastsound on Main Street (which becomes Crescent Beach Drive), driving 1.2 miles (1.9 km) to Olga Road. Turn right and drive 6.6 miles (10.6 km) to Olga, turning left onto Point Lawrence Road. After 0.5 mile (0.8 km), bear right onto Obstruction Pass Road and follow it for 0.9 mile (1.4 km). Turn right onto gravel Trailhead Road and continue 0.9 mile (1.4 km) to the trailhead (elev.125 ft/38 m). Privy and bike rack available.

ON THE TRAIL

Although it's only 80 acres (32 ha), Obstruction Pass State Park packs a lot in—three trails, nine backcountry campsites, and a mile of beautiful shoreline. You can make a beeline for the beach by taking the 0.6-mile (1-km) main trail. For more of a hike take this loop, complete with interpretive signs.

Pass through a stile and immediately come to a junction. The main trail to the beach heads straight, and you'll be returning on the Sound View Trail from the right. So head left now on the fairly new Highlands Trail through open forest, ignoring several side trails that lead to private property. Crest a 225-foot (69-m) knoll

before traversing a small bald and then descending to a madrona- and pine-lined bluff above the beach. Look for white-blotched black-tailed deer along the way. There are a handful of these oddities in the area.

At 1.1 miles (1.8 km), come to a junction with the main trail at the backcountry camping area (privy, no water). By all means take the stairway down to the gorgeous sandy beach. And consider following an unmarked trail 0.15 mile (0.25 km) west to Picnic Rock, which serves delectable views of East Sound and Entrance Mountain.

Once you're ready to return, follow the main trail 0.3 mile (0.5 km) through open forest and along bluffs to a junction (elev. 80 ft/24 m). Then head left on the Sound View Trail, descending to a picnic area along the water with excellent views of Buck Bay. After passing a huge cedar, start climbing and return to the trailhead at 1.9 miles (3.1 km). Head-high stinging nettles will keep you from wandering off the trail.

HOGGING HISTORY: SAN JUAN ISLAND NATIONAL HISTORICAL PARK

San Juan Island National Historical Park commemorates the Pig War, a boundary dispute between the United States and Great Britain in which the only casualty was a Hudson's Bay Company hog. American and British forces had both taken up occupancy on San Juan Island from 1859 until 1872, nearly going to war until the international border was established through arbitration, on Haro Strait, granting American sovereignty over the San Juan Islands.

The 2072-acre (839-ha) park is divided into two sections, American Camp and English Camp. Along with its historical significance, the park protects some important habitat, including one of the few surviving native grasslands along the Strait of Juan de Fuca. In springtime these grasslands burst with lupine, chocolate lily, blue-eyed Mary, and more. Look for the rare island marble butterfly, endemic to a few of the San Juan and Gulf islands and once thought extinct. And of course enjoy miles of some of the best hiking within the San Juans.

San Juan Island

San Juan Island is the most populated of the San Juan archipelago, with about seven thousand people. It's also the second-largest island in area, at 55 square miles (143 sq. km), with the islands' only incorporated town, Friday Harbor, the county seat. Friday Harbor is a bustling place (especially in summer), with many eating and lodging establishments. This town of 2200 has a hospital and a Washington State Ferries terminal, with year-round service to Anacortes and the San Juan islands and seasonal service to Sidney, British Columbia.

The island contains large tracts of national park land (San Juan Island National Historical Park), a state park, and several county parks and land bank properties, as well as a large private preserve open to hiking. Bicyclists will find good roads to these areas and agreeable terrain (much less hilly than Orcas Island, for example). Camping is limited to San Juan County Park's (www.co.san-juan.wa.us/parks/sanjuan.aspx) 20 sites, Lakedale Resort (www.lakedale.com), Sweet Earth Farm (sweetearthfarm.com), and the county fairgrounds (sjcfair.org)

Who says war is hell? Hell, if the Pig War had never happened (see "Hogging History" sidebar), we would not have the longest stretch of public beach in the San Juan Islands. Once the site of an American military encampment, American Camp offers plenty of natural splendors with its historical relics. Wander through the old compound after hiking across native prairie and golden bluffs. And stop frequently to marvel at the snowcapped Olympic Mountains across the glistening Strait of Juan de Fuca.

49 American Camp and South Beach

RATING/DIFFICULTY	LOOP	ELEV GAIN/HIGH POINT
*****/2	2.8 miles (4.5 km)	180 feet (55 m)/ 180 feet (55 m)

Maps: USGS False Bay, park map at visitors center; **Contact:** San Juan Island National Historical Park; **Notes:** Dogs permitted on-leash; **GPS:** N 48 27.874, W 123 01.427

American Camp protects one of the largest stretches of undeveloped coastline in the San Juans.

GETTING THERE

From Anacortes, take a Washington State ferry to Friday Harbor on San Juan Island. Follow Spring Street 0.5 mile (0.8 km) through town. Turn left onto Mullis Street (which becomes Cattle Point Road) and follow it for 5.3 miles (8.5 km). Turn right into American Camp and drive 0.2 mile (0.3 km) to the visitors center and trailhead (elev. 140 ft/43 m). Privy and bike racks available.

ON THE TRAIL

From the main trailhead—the start of several trails—follow the path to Grandmas Cove. You'll be returning via the History Walk, which travels through the American Camp compound. At 0.1 mile (0.15 km), stay left where a trail diverts right to Eagle Cove Drive. Your route bends south to skirt the compound, soon intersecting with the History Walk. Briefly follow it south, and then continue straight where the History Walk angles east.

Now gradually descend, walking across grassy slopes punctuated with snowberry and hawthorn, which provide excellent forage for resident birds. Gone are the more than two thousand sheep that grazed here in the mid-1800s as part of the Hudson's Bay Company's Belle Vue Sheep Farm. At 0.4 mile (0.6 km), come to a junction (elev. 50 ft/15 m). Detour to visit (0.1-mi/0.15-km roundtrip) log-lined, bluff-enclosed Grandmas Cove.

After paying a visit to Grandma, continue hiking east across grassy headlands, enjoying sweeping views of the coastline out to Cattle Point. Ignore side trails leading to headlands. Pass an intriguing stone post (origin unknown) and come to a junction at 0.8 mile (1.3 km). The trail left leads 0.25 mile (0.4 km) back to the History Walk at the redoubt, which will shorten your loop. Other-

wise continue forward on a path that's easy to lose at times, coming to a junction with the wide and fairly new South Beach Trail at the South Beach Picnic Area at 1.3 miles (2.1 km).

Your hike continues via the South Beach Trail. But by all means first walk the more than 1 mile (1.6 km) of sandy beach if you like. Otherwise start hiking westward and upward, reaching a four-way junction at 1.9 miles (3.1 km). The way left heads back to the coast, passing some big glacial erratics. The way right leads a short distance to the redoubt (a small fortified position within the compound). Continue straight 0.1 mile (0.15 km) to the History Walk. Left leads 0.4 mile (0.6 km) to the trailhead. But right is more interesting, following the History Walk interpretive trail for 0.7 mile (1.1 km) back to the trailhead, visiting the redoubt (elev. 180 ft/55 m), officers' quarters, and other historical sites along the way.

EXTENDING YOUR TRIP

Fourth of July Beach on Griffin Bay is accessible via a short trail from Cattle Point Road. Eagle Cove can be reached by hiking from the historical park to Eagle Cove Drive and then picking up trail again after a short road walk.

50 Frazer Homestead Preserve

RATING/ DIFFICULTY	ROUNDTRIP	ELEV GAIN/HIGH POINT
**/1	2.6 miles (4.2 km)	80 feet (24 m)/ 210 feet (64 m)

Maps: USGS False Bay, land bank map online; **Contact:** San Juan Island National Historical Park and San Juan County Land Bank, Frazer Homestead Preserve; **Notes:** Active farming area. Dogs must be on-leash; **GPS:** N 48 27.874, W 123 01.427

The Frazer Homestead trail offers pastoral views.

Explore quiet wood-lands within the San Juan National Historical Park and an old homestead still actively farmed. Enjoy pastoral views of rolling countryside against a backdrop of Griffin Bay and Mount Baker. And wander near the site of the Pig War's only casualty—the pig.

GETTING THERE

See directions to Hike 49.

ON THE TRAIL

Locate the trail on the north side of the national historical park's visitors center. Then begin your journey by traversing meadows, coming to Cattle Point Road in 0.2 mile (0.3 km). Carefully cross the road and resume your hike. Cross a boardwalk and then undulate between evergreen tunnels and field pockets. Contrast the greenness of this trail to the golden slopes of the nearby prairies.

At 0.7 mile (1.1 km), enter the San Juan Land Bank's Frazer Homestead Preserve, which not only preserves a historical landscape but also still allows for the land to be worked by local farmers. Not too far to the east (not accessible by trail) is the site of the Cutlar Farm. It was here on June 15, 1859, that American farmer Lyman Cutlar shot and killed a pig—that belonged to the Hudson's Bay Company—in his potato patch. The incident sparked the so-called Pig War, which nearly brought the United States and Great Britain to blows. The end result was a settled boundary dispute, establishing Haro instead of Rosario Strait as the international border.

The way eventually parallels Cattle Point Road, following alongside a fence line. Catch glimpses of farming activity and good views

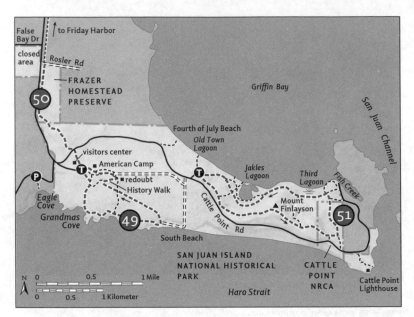

out to Griffin Bay, Lopez Island, Mount Finlayson and Mount Baker. At 1.3 miles (2.1 km), come to Rosler Road (elev. 210 ft/64 m). This is a good spot to turn around.

EXTENDING YOUR TRIP
In 2013, the San Juan Island Trails Committee extended this trail by 6 miles (9.7 km), all the way to Friday Harbor.

51 Mount Finlayson

RATING/ DIFFICULTY	LOOP	ELEV GAIN/HIGH POINT
*****/2	3.5 miles (5.6 km)	350 feet (107 m)/ 290 feet (88 m)

Maps: USGS False Bay, USGS Richardson, park map at visitors center; **Contact:** San Juan Island National Historical Park; **Notes:**

Dogs permitted on-leash; **GPS:** N 48 27.822, W 122 59.947

Unlike British Columbia's Mount Finlayson, this one is gentle and inviting. Stroll across golden lawns lined with windblown firs and marvel at the undeveloped and dramatic coastline spread out below you. Stare out across the Strait of Juan de Fuca to the Olympic Peninsula. Then, on your return, explore a couple of quiet lagoons on Griffin Bay rife with birdlife. This is one of the finest hiking areas within the entire San Juans chain.

GETTING THERE
From Anacortes, take a Washington State ferry to Friday Harbor on San Juan Island. Follow Spring Street 0.5 mile (0.8 km)

through town. Turn left onto Mullis Street (which becomes Cattle Point Road) and follow it for 6.9 miles (11.1 km) to the trailhead (elev. 100 ft/30 m), signed "Jakle's Lagoon."

ON THE TRAIL

Take the Jakles Lagoon Loop to the right—you'll be returning from the left. The wide trail parallels Cattle Point Road and gradually climbs, cutting a swath across golden grasslands lined by wind-blasted, contorted firs. In springtime this rare island prairie environment is awash in beautiful blossoms. Maritime views grow with each step. At 0.3 mile (0.5 km), the Nature Trail loop heads left, offering your first alternative route.

Continue forward through a clump of trees and then begin climbing more steeply, cresting the long ridge of Mount Finlayson.

Roderick Finlayson of the Hudson's Bay Company was a founder of Victoria, British Columbia, and its onetime mayor. You can see his higher and rockier namesake Canadian peak from this trail.

Carry on along the windswept ridge, mouth agape at the astonishing views, from the snowcapped Olympic Mountains to the bluffs of Whidbey Island. Scan the choppy strait for whales and the sky for eagles. After cresting Mount Finlayson's gentle 290-foot (107-m) summit, slightly descend to a junction at 1.3 miles (2.1 km). Here, a 0.4-mile (0.6-km) trail leads left into a cluster of large firs, steeply descending to the Lagoon Loop, offering a shorter loop option. Keep hiking forward, cresting Finlayson's eastern summit and taking in the classic view of Cattle Point

Mount Finlayson's sprawling prairie offers sweeping views.

below against a backdrop of rocky islets and Lopez Island's Iceberg Point.

Now begin steeply descending, entering the Cattle Point Natural Resources Conservation Area and reaching a junction and kiosk at 1.6 miles (2.6 km). The trail right leads a short way to Cattle Point Road. Head left instead, and after 0.1 mile (0.15 km) come to an old road turned trail. Right heads to Cattle Point Road. You want to hike left, entering thick forest, skirting wetlands, ignoring side trails (follow signs), and reaching a junction (elev. 10 ft/3 m) at 2.1 miles (3.4 km).

Trails straight and right can be followed for a 0.4-mile (0.6-km) loop to Fish Creek. The way back to the trailhead is via an old woods road along Third Lagoon and around Jakles Lagoon. Reach the trail that comes down from Finlayson at 2.3 miles (3.7 km). Continue on the old woods road, passing or taking several side trails to Third and Jakles lagoons. At 2.7 miles (4.3 km), the road splits—either way will bring you back to the trailhead at 3.5 miles (5.6 km), after a short drop and climb.

EXTENDING YOUR TRIP

Options abound for shortening or lengthening this hike at various trail junctions. At low tide, it's also possible to walk the beach from Jakles Lagoon to Old Town Lagoon. Views are great of Mount Constitution and Turtleback Mountain across Griffin Bay.

52 Cattle Point

RATING/ DIFFICULTY	ROUNDTRIP	ELEV GAIN/HIGH POINT
***/1	1.4 miles (2.3 km)	Minimal/20 feet (6 m)

Maps: USGS Richardson, DNR map online;
Contact: Washington Department of Natural Resources (DNR), Northwest District; **Notes:** Discover Pass required. Dogs permitted on-leash; **GPS:** N 48 27.263, W 122 57.767

Enjoy this easy and family-friendly hike along the San Juan

Cattle Point Lighthouse

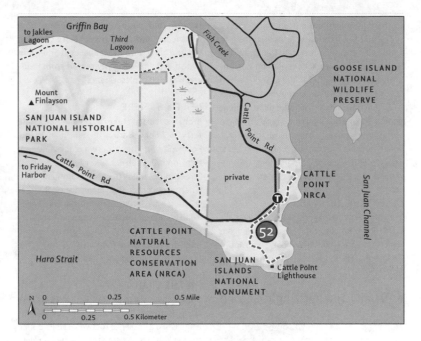

Griffin Bay

to Jakles
Lagoon

Third
Lagoon

Fish Creek

GOOSE ISLAND
NATIONAL
WILDLIFE
PRESERVE

Mount
▲Finlayson

SAN JUAN ISLAND
NATIONAL HISTORICAL
PARK

Cattle Point Rd

← Cattle Point Rd
to Friday
Harbor

private

CATTLE
POINT
NRCA

San Juan Channel

CATTLE POINT
NATURAL
RESOURCES
CONSERVATION
AREA (NRCA)

Haro Strait

SAN JUAN
ISLANDS
NATIONAL
MONUMENT

52

Cattle Point
Lighthouse

N
0   0.25   0.5 Mile
0   0.25   0.5 Kilometer

Channel—a bird and marine mammal hotspot—to a picturesque lighthouse within the new San Juan Islands National Monument. This area was once part of a Hudson's Bay Company ranch, but you won't have any beef hiking this beautiful spot. Gone are the cattle and sheep, but plenty of deer prance around this point._

GETTING THERE

From Anacortes, take a Washington State ferry to Friday Harbor on San Juan Island. Follow Spring Street 0.5 mile (0.8 km) through town. Turn left onto Mullis Street (which will become Cattle Point Road) and follow it for 8.9 mile (14.3 km) to the trailhead at the Cattle Point Interpretive Area. Privy available.

ON THE TRAIL

Start by visiting the interpretive displays housed in a former US Navy Radio Compass Station. The structure is rather ugly—but the natural surroundings aren't! Formed by glaciations, Cattle Point consists of striated ledges and cobbled, sandy, gravelly deposits.

Now walk north on the short 0.2-mile (0.3-km) trail along the grassy bluff overlooking San Juan Channel. Scope the rocky islets (protected as a national wildlife refuge) for pelagic birds, seals, and sea lions.

Retrace your steps and then walk south 0.2 mile (0.3 km) on the lightly traveled Cattle Point Road to the Cattle Point Lighthouse trailhead. Note there is no parking here. Follow the 0.3-mile (0.5-km) interpretive trail through national monument land to the lighthouse and out onto the grassy, rocky point. A lighthouse was built here in 1888 with former American Camp soldier George Jakle its first keeper. The current structure was built in 1935 and gained notoriety in 1984 in an Exxon commercial.

Spend time looking out over the turbulent waters for marine mammals and birds. In springtime, enjoy the prairie blossoms, which include buttercups, chocolate lilies, camas, and lupines. Linger long before returning to the interpretive center.

EXTENDING YOUR TRIP
You can walk 0.2 mile (0.3 km) west on Cattle Point Road to a gated road-trail, from which you can continue hiking to Mount Finlayson, Third Lagoon, and Fish Creek (see Hike 51).

53 Bell Point and English Camp

RATING/ DIFFICULTY	LOOP	ELEV GAIN/HIGH POINT
***/1	1.7 miles (2.7 km)	50 feet (15 m)/ 50 feet (15 m)

Maps: USGS Roche Harbor, park map at English Camp kiosk; **Contact:** San Juan Island National Historical Park; **Notes:** Dogs permitted on-leash; **GPS:** N 48 35.191, W 123 08.874

Stroll along placid bay waters surrounding Bell Point after passing through a former British Royal Marine garrison. The grounds are now peacefully administered by the National Park Service for resource protection and heritage preservation. The United States and Great Britain nearly went to war over the San Juan Islands, but sane heads prevailed. Now Americans and Canadians (Brits too) can enjoy this tranquil corner of San Juan Island, permanently protected from modern world assaults. Cheers.

GETTING THERE
From Anacortes, take a Washington State ferry to Friday Harbor on San Juan Island. Follow Spring Street for two blocks and turn right onto 2nd Street. Bear left onto Guard Street in 0.2 mile (0.3 km), continuing on it when it becomes Beaverton Valley Road at 0.7 mile (1.1 km). Follow Beaverton Valley Road (which eventually becomes West Valley Road) for 7.3 miles (11.7 km), turning left into English Camp. Drive 0.4 mile (0.6 km) to the trailhead. Privy and bike rack available.

ON THE TRAIL
Start by heading to English Camp. It was here along Garrison Bay that the Royal Marines established a presence for twelve years during the Pig War, which ultimately decided on Haro Strait as the international boundary, leaving San Juan Island for the Americans. A restored blockhouse, barracks, hospital, and storehouse remain at the site. During summer a visitors center is operated out of the barracks.

Walk 0.2 mile (0.3 km), passing by a monster maple and formal gardens and through the compound to the Bell Point trailhead, located near the commissary. Now walk along a bluff above Garrison Bay, passing a dock and traveling through a forest of attractive madronas. At 0.8 mile (1.3 km), reach a junction with a 0.1-mile (0.15-km) spur to Bell Point on Westcott Bay. Look for eagles, ravens, kingfishers, and a myriad of other birds in the tranquil water.

Return to the loop and continue 0.5 mile (0.8 km), passing a bayside picnic area before returning to the compound grounds. Then return to the trailhead via the English Camp grounds; or, for a slightly longer return leg, follow a road-trail left, being sure to stay straight at a service road junction in 0.25 mile (0.4 km).

EXTENDING YOUR TRIP

There is a new connector trail from English Camp to the Roche Harbor Trail. Pick up this connector near the hospital and follow it northeast for 0.6 mile (1 km), first on a service road. Then, after crossing West Valley Road, continue on single-track for 0.7 mile (1.1 km) to the main Roche Harbor trailhead parking area. In 2013, 70 acres (28 ha) of shoreline on Westcott Bay, including a historical oyster farm, were added to the national park. A new trail for that area is in the works.

English Camp sits on quiet Garrison Bay.

Young Hill offers excellent viewing over Haro Strait.

54 Young Hill

RATING/ DIFFICULTY	ROUNDTRIP	ELEV GAIN/HIGH POINT
****/3	2.2 miles (3.5 km)	600 feet (183 m)/ 650 feet (198 m)

Maps: USGS Roche Harbor, park map at English Camp kiosk; **Contact:** San Juan Island National Historical Park; **Notes:** Dogs permitted on-leash; **GPS:** N 48 35.197, W 123 08.808

Big oaks, big views, and a historical cemetery await you on this hike to 650-foot (198-m) Young Hill. Wildflowers are dazzling in spring, and the sunsets from the summit are magnificent year-round.

GETTING THERE
See directions to Hike 53.

ON THE TRAIL
Locate the trail for Young Hill at the northeast corner of the large parking lot. Immediately come to a junction. Left heads to Bell Point and the Roche Harbor Trail connector. Bear right and follow a wide path, climbing gently through a forest of Douglas fir and madrona laced with salal and Oregon grape.

At 0.2 mile (0.3 km), carefully cross West Valley Road and resume hiking up the wide trail. At 0.4 mile (0.6 km), reach a junction (elev. 260 ft/79 m) with a connector trail built in 2013 that leads to Mitchell Hill and the historical Sandwith Orchard. Turn left and within a few steps reach another junction. The short spur right leads to the English

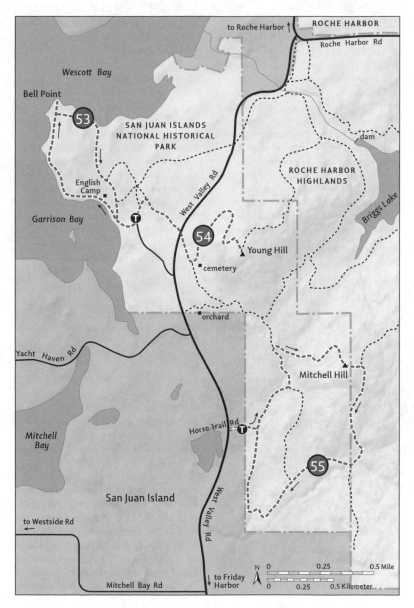

to Roche Harbor ↑

ROCHE HARBOR

Roche Harbor Rd

Wescott Bay

Bell Point

53

SAN JUAN ISLANDS
NATIONAL HISTORICAL
PARK

dam

ROCHE HARBOR
HIGHLANDS

Briggs Lake

English
Camp

West Valley Rd

Garrison Bay

T

54

▲ Young Hill

■ cemetery

■ orchard

Yacht Haven Rd

Mitchell Hill ▲

Mitchell
Bay

Horse Trail Rd T

San Juan Island

55

to Westside Rd
←

West Valley Rd

to Friday
Harbor ↓

Mitchell Bay Rd

N

0   0.25   0.5 Mile

0   0.25   0.5 Kilometer

Camp cemetery, a tranquil final resting spot for six Royal Marines and one British civilian enclosed by a white picket fence and shaded by big, old Garry oaks. Check it out or carry on to Young's summit.

The trail continues left, making a big switchback and emerging at 0.9 mile (1.4 km) at the edge of a grassy ledge (elev. 550 ft/168 m), granting sweeping views west over Garrison, Mitchell, and Westcott bays and out over finger coves and narrow straits to Victoria and the Gulf Islands. Continue another 0.2 mile (0.3 km), climbing and snaking around mossy ledges, and arrive at Young Hill's 650-foot (198-m) summit for more views. Here add

Forested trail on Mitchell Hill

the Olympics and San Juan Island's highest peak, 1015-foot (309-m) Mount Dallas, to the visual menu.

EXTENDING YOUR TRIP

Several unofficial trails traverse Young Hill and park officials hope to create signage that will keep you on the official routes, thus minimizing damage to fragile meadows and balds. Two official trails that make for excellent extended hiking adventures are the 1-mile (1.6-km) path northeast off of Young Hill, connecting to the Briggs Lake loop (Hike 56) in the Roche Harbor Highlands; and the 0.5-mile (0.8-km) connector through old-growth Garry oaks to the Mitchell Hill trail complex (Hike 55). At 0.2 mile (0.3 km) on this second trail, you can follow a right-hand path to a historical orchard, where deer can often be spotted feasting on apples.

55 Mitchell Hill

RATING/ DIFFICULTY	LOOP	ELEV GAIN/HIGH POINT
**/3	2.9 miles (4.7 km)	450 feet (137 m)/ 515 feet (157 m)

Maps: USGS Roche Harbor, park map at trailhead; **Contact:** San Juan Island National Historical Park; **Notes:** Open to mountain bikes and horses. Dogs permitted on-leash; **GPS:** N 48 34.328, W 123 08.262

A former Department of Natural Resources property, the 312-acre (126-ha) Mitchell Hill tract was added to the San Juan National Historical Park in 2010. Consisting primarily of second-growth forest and traversed by old logging roads and user-built trails, it is of primary interest to local equestrians and mountain bikers. But old-growth pockets, remnants of the Old Military Road connecting American and English camps, and the chance to wander aimlessly in the woods will certainly appeal to some hikers. Save it for an overcast day, as the route is nearly entirely beneath forest cover.

GETTING THERE

From Anacortes, take a Washington State ferry to Friday Harbor on San Juan Island. Follow Spring Street for two blocks and turn right onto 2nd Street. Bear left onto Guard Street in 0.2 mile (0.3 km), continuing on it when it becomes Beaverton Valley Road in 0.7 mile (1.1 km). Follow Beaverton Valley Road (which eventually becomes West Valley Road) for 6.6 miles (10.6 km), turning right onto dirt Horse Trail Road (0.7 mi/1.1 km past the Mitchell Bay Road junction). Proceed 0.1 mile (0.15 km) to the trailhead (elev. 120 ft/37 m). Parking is limited.

ON THE TRAIL

Hike past the gate and a huge Douglas fir, immediately coming to a junction. The old logging roads and a tangled web of user-built trails can make for confusion, but the Park Service has been adding signage encouraging you to stick to the official trails. You'll be returning on the road-trail from the right, so continue left here. Ignore side trails and stay on the old road, traversing a grove of big cedars. Bear left where the road-trail splits and cross a small creek, coming to a signed junction at 0.4 mile (0.6 km). Head right, leaving the road for real trail and coming to a junction (elev. 300 ft/91 m) in thick old growth at 0.6 mile (1 km). The delightful trail left heads 0.7 mile (1.1 km) to English Camp, offering an alternative start with better parking facilities.

Your route continues right, slightly descending to cross a creek before climbing through a forest of oak and madrona. Radiating paths may cause confusion, but guideposts should offer some help navigating the way. Pass big wolf Douglas firs and clamber over mossy ledges and grassy balds. At 1.1 miles (1.8 km), crest one of Mitchell Hill's wooded summits (elev. 515 ft/157 m) and begin descending, leaving national park land and reaching a junction at 1.2 miles (1.9 km) with an old fire road.

Go right, gradually descending through attractive forest. At 1.7 miles (2.7 km), follow the road right. At 1.8 miles (2.9 km), after crossing a creek, go right at a pipe gate and reenter national park land. Continue descending, crossing a creek and passing an old logging yard. Ignore side trails and stay right at a road-trail junction. The way eventually makes a sharp turn north. Cross another creek (elev. 100 ft/30 m) and catch a glimpse of Young Hill before closing the loop at 2.9 miles (4.7 km).

EXTENDING YOUR TRIP

From the junction at the pipe gate, you can continue straight on the fire road 0.5 mile (0.8 km) to a limited viewpoint (elev. 550 ft/168 m) on a shoulder of Cady Mountain, looking over nearby farms below and out to Vancouver Island.

56 Briggs Lake

RATING/ DIFFICULTY	LOOP	ELEV GAIN/HIGH POINT
***/2	4 miles (6.4 km)	260 feet (79 m)/ 340 feet (104 m)

Maps: USGS Roche Harbor, trails committee map online; **Contact:** San Juan Island Trails Committee, Roche Harbor

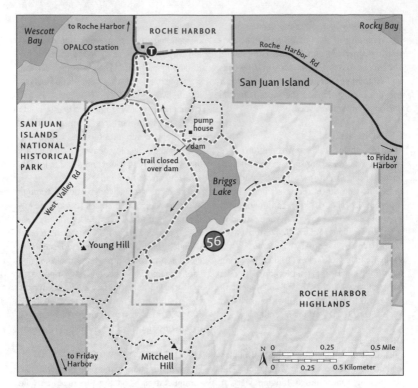

Highlights; **Notes:** Open to mountain bikes and horses. Dogs permitted on-leash; **GPS:** N 48 35.862, W 123 07.900

🧍 🔪 🦆 *Follow gentle fire roads around a pretty reservoir, looking for and listening to bald eagles and a myriad of waterfowl. Centerpiece of the Roche Harbor Highlands, a large privately owned forest open to the public for nonmotorized recreation, Briggs Lake makes for a nice hike yearround. It's especially appealing in winter, however, when the water level and eagle activity are high.*

GETTING THERE

From Anacortes, take a Washington State ferry to Friday Harbor on San Juan Island. Follow Spring Street for two blocks and turn right onto 2nd Street. At 0.3 mile (0.5 km), after bearing left onto Guard Street, turn right onto Tucker Avenue and continue 0.4 mile (0.6 km), bearing left onto Roche Harbor Road. Drive 7.4 miles (11.9 km) to the intersection with West Valley Road and the trailhead (elev. 100 ft/30 m), located on the left.

ON THE TRAIL

Three trails radiate from the trailhead. You'll be returning on the middle one and starting on the one farthest right (west)—the one leading to English Camp. Paralleling West Valley Road through a salal jungle, come to a junction in 0.2 mile (3 km). Continue straight, crossing a creek in a cedar ravine and coming to a signed five-way junction at 0.3 mile (0.5 km). Head left here on a fire road, paralleling the creek-cradling ravine and reaching a junction (elev. 260 ft/79 m) at 0.6 mile (1 km). The way right is a quiet 1 mile (1.6 km) trail to

Grassy shoreline along Biggs Lake invites lounging.

the summit of Young Hill (Hike 54). You want to continue straight on the old fire road, soon reaching the dammed outlet of Briggs Lake (elev. 240 ft/73 m).

The dam is closed to public access—don't even think of walking on it to cut your hike short. Be sure to respect all posted regulations in the Roche Harbor Highlands, and be especially thoughtful around the lakeshore, as Briggs provides water to nearby Roche Harbor village. Continue straight instead, rounding a mossy bald and reaching a spur at 1 mile (1.6 km) to a ledge overlooking the lake. See any eagles or wintering swans? At 1.3 miles (2.1 km), stay left at a junction. The trail right leads to the Mitchell Hill–English Camp connector trail. Now cross an inlet and continue through attractive forest, ignoring an obscure trail right. After crossing a creek, the way pulls away from the lake and reaches a junction (elev. 340 ft/104 m) at 2.5 miles (4 km).

Right leads to Mitchell Hill. Head left instead, coming to another junction at 3.1 miles (5 km). The way straight is the direct way back to the trailhead. The way left is much more interesting, traveling through shore pines to open grassy slopes along Briggs Lake. At 3.3 miles (5.3 km), come to the outlet dam and continue hiking now along the north side of the outlet creek. Bear left at a junction, passing a pump house. Then bear right at another junction, descending to the trailhead at 4 miles (6.4 km).

EXTENDING YOUR TRIP
Long day hikes are possible by combining this hike with Young Hill (Hike 54) or Mitchell Hill (Hike 55). But be sure to have a good map, as all the interconnecting trails can be disorienting.

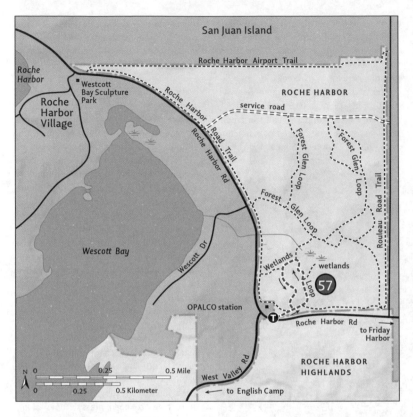

57 Roche Harbor: Wetlands Loop

RATING/ DIFFICULTY	LOOP	ELEV GAIN/HIGH POINT
**/1	0.8 mile (1.3 km)	30 feet (9 m)/ 110 feet (34 m)

Maps: USGS Roche Harbor, trails committee map online; **Contact:** San Juan Island Trails Committee, Roche Harbor Trails; **Notes:** Open to mountain bikes and horses. Dogs permitted on-leash; **GPS:** N 48 35.876, W 123 07.841

This near-level hike to grassy wetlands within the Roche Harbor trail network is perfect for early morning and evening walks if you're staying nearby. Or, combine this easy jaunt with adjoining trails for half- and all-day excursions.

GETTING THERE
See directions to Hike 56.

ON THE TRAIL

The Roche Harbor trail network is privately owned by Roche Harbor Village but open to public use. Please respect all posted regulations.

Start by carefully crossing the road and locating the trailhead near the OPALCO charging station. Begin on a boardwalk and come to a junction at 0.1 mile (0.15 km). Follow the grassy mowed path right, passing a trail on your left—your return. At 0.2 mile (0.3 km), come to a junction with the Rouleau Road Trail, which travels for 1.2 miles (1.9 km), paralleling roads.

Continue left through fir and pine forest, reaching a junction at 0.3 mile (0.5 km). Here a spur leads right a short distance through head-high salal to a wetlands viewpoint. Take it if you care to, or continue straight, soon getting good views of the grassy bird-loving wetlands (elev. 80 ft/24 m). At 0.4 mile (0.6 km), come to a junction. The trail right is a pleasant 0.15-mile (0.25-km) forested path connecting to the 1.75-mile (2.8-km) Forest Glen Loop, which pretty much follows service roads. It makes a better running route than a hike.

Head left and then left again where the wide mowed path splits. At 0.5 mile (0.8 km), leave the path for a more rustic trail left, climbing a small ridge (elev. 110 ft/34 m) and traversing a cedar grove to reach a familiar junction at 0.7 mile (1.1 km). The trailhead is 0.1 mile (0.15 km) to the right.

EXTENDING YOUR TRIP

From the Wetlands Loop you can follow the grassy Roche Harbor Road Trail 1.3 miles

Look for birds and amphibians along the Wetlands Loop.

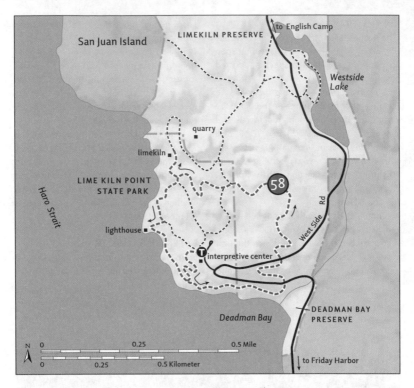

San Juan Island

LIMEKILN PRESERVE

to English Camp

Westside Lake

quarry

limekiln

LIME KILN POINT STATE PARK

Haro Strait

lighthouse

58

West Side Rd

T interpretive center

DEADMAN BAY PRESERVE

Deadman Bay

N

0   0.25   0.5 Mile

0   0.25   0.5 Kilometer

to Friday Harbor

(2.1 km) over rolling terrain and paralleling the road to the Westcott Bay Sculpture Park, which is definitely worth a visit.

58 Lime Kiln Point

RATING/ DIFFICULTY	LOOP	ELEV GAIN/HIGH POINT
****/2	2.2 miles (3.5 km)	265 feet (81 m)/ 280 feet (85 m)

Maps: USGS Roche Harbor, land bank map online; **Contact:** Washington State Parks, Lime Kiln Point State Park, and San Juan County Land Bank, Limekiln Preserve;

Notes: Discover Pass required. Dogs permitted on-leash; **GPS:** N 48 30.925, W 123 08.954

One of the most ecologically and historically fascinating places on San Juan Island, Lime Kiln Point harbors 5 miles (8 km) of interconnecting trails. Protected by a 36-acre (15-ha) state park and more than 170 acres (68 ha) of county preserve, this point once bustled with industry and is now one of the best places in the United States to spot whales from land. A lighthouse, interpretive center, and restored limekiln add to the area's richness.

GETTING THERE

From Anacortes, take a Washington State ferry to Friday Harbor on San Juan Island. Follow Spring Street west through town for 1.6 miles (2.6 km) (the road becomes San Juan Valley Road). Turn left onto Douglas Road and drive 1.8 miles (2.9 km), bearing right onto Bailer Hill Road (which becomes West Side Road) and continuing 5.6 miles (9 km) to Lime Kiln Point State Park. Turn left and drive 0.1 mile (0.15 km) to the trailhead (elev. 60 ft/18 m) . Privy available.

ON THE TRAIL

From the interpretive center follow the wheelchair-accessible interpretive trail 0.2 mile (0.3 km) to the coast and a junction. The lighthouse is to the right. You'll be returning from that direction, so head left along the rocky open coastline and enter the San Juan County Land Bank's Deadman Bay Preserve. Head up and over bluffs and enjoy sweeping views across Haro Strait to Vancouver Island and the Olympic Peninsula. Keep watching for orcas and other whales.

At 0.6 mile (1 km), reach a small parking lot, privy, and a spur leading to a cobbled beach on Deadman Bay. Explore the beach or resume hiking, crossing West Side Road and heading up steps to a view-granting bluff in the Limekiln Preserve. At 0.8 mile (1.3 km), cross the road again, entering madrona groves and passing a big wolf Douglas fir. After reaching an elevation of 280 feet (85 m), begin descending through

Lime Kiln State Park's lighthouse is a great spot to look for whales.

a forest reminiscent of a *Wizard of Oz* scene. Reenter the state park and reach a junction at 1.2 miles (1.9 km).

The trail right leads to old roads and quarries and to 10-acre (4-ha) Westside Lake, if you're looking for a longer hike. Otherwise head left, soon coming to a junction with the state park loop trail. The way left drops steeply through old quarries, reaching the trailhead in 0.2 mile (0.3 km). Go right instead, passing a water tower and reaching a junction at 1.4 miles (2.3 km). Left goes back to the parking lot. Your loop continues straight—but first hike right 0.1 mile (0.15 km) to a restored limekiln and interpretive displays. Industry from 1860 to 1920 denuded much adjacent forest and left big quarry pits behind. The trail continues beyond, passing another limekiln and old quarries.

Double back and continue hiking straight, twisting 0.2 mile (0.3 km) along the rocky coast to the much-photographed lighthouse built in 1919. Linger, or continue hiking along the coast to great whale-viewing spots, reaching the Deadman Bay Trail junction in 0.2 mile (0.3 km). Turn left to reach your vehicle.

EXTENDING YOUR TRIP

The hike to Westside Lake is 0.6 mile (1 km) one-way, and you can then continue on a 0.4-mile (0.6-km) loop along the slender lake's south shore. You can easily spend all day at Lime Kiln Point. Do visit the interpretive center, staffed by the all-volunteer Friends of Lime Kiln Society (FOLKS), who also provide support and educational programs for the park.

POD SQUAD

Spend enough time plying and hiking around the waters of the Salish Sea and you might see some of these waters' most famous residents, its killer whales (*Orcinus orca*). Orcas are widely distributed throughout the world's oceans. Highly social marine mammals, they typically fall into three distinct populations: offshore, transient, and resident.

Here in the Salish Sea we have the Southern Resident population, which consists of three pods: J, K, and L. They're considered a distinct population and are in decline, with just eighty-two individuals in 2013. They were listed in 2005 under the Endangered Species Act, prompting a recovery plan. The biggest threats to these whales include pollution, overfishing, ship collisions, oil spills, noise disturbance from industrial and military activities, and irresponsible whale-watching.

Your best opportunity for spotting one of the three pods in the San Juan and Gulf islands is from May to September, but I have seen orcas off of Cypress Island in February. Many commercial outfitters in the islands offer whale-watching excursions, but some hikes in this book offer excellent land-based viewing, especially East Point on Saturna Island (Hike 89) and Lime Kiln Point on San Juan Island (Hike 58).

Plan a trip to the excellent Whale Museum (www.whalemuseum.org) in Friday Harbor to learn more about these Salish Sea residents, the other cetaceans that ply these waters, and how we can protect them and their habitat.

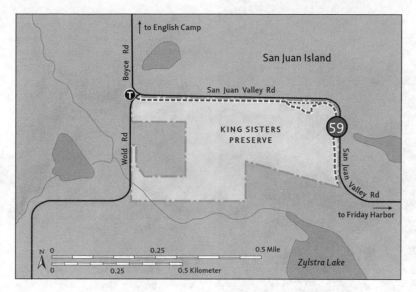

59 King Sisters Preserve

RATING/ DIFFICULTY	ROUNDTRIP	ELEV GAIN/HIGH POINT
**/1	1.4 miles (2.3 km)	75 feet (23 m)/ 150 feet (46 m)

Maps: USGS Roche Harbor, land bank map online; **Contact:** San Juan County Land Bank, King Sisters Preserve; **Notes:** Active farm. Dogs must be on-leash; **GPS:** N 48 31.748, W 123 05.930

Enjoy a pastoral hike in the heart of San Juan Island farm country, in 62-acre (25-ha) King Sisters Preserve. Admire spring flowers, take in views of the island's highest peak and one of its largest lakes, and get a peek at the goings-on of a working farm.

GETTING THERE

From Anacortes, take a Washington State ferry to Friday Harbor on San Juan Island. Follow Spring Street west through town (the road becomes San Juan Valley Road outside the city limits. In 4.2 miles (6.8 km) from the ferry dock, reach the junction of Boyce and Wold roads and the trailhead (elev. 100 ft/30 m). Park at the ride-share pullout on the left shoulder.

ON THE TRAIL

Start in a small thicket and soon emerge in open pasture along a fence line. Keep back from the fence, to avoid an electrifying moment. Gradually ascend on the wide grassy path that parallels San Juan Valley Road, enjoying nice views out to Zylstra Lake and 1080-foot (329-m) Mount Dallas, the highest peak on the island. Depending on the time of your visit, a flock of sheep may be grazing in the adjacent field.

Mount Dallas provides a nice backdrop for the King Sisters Preserve.

At 0.35 mile (0.6 km), the trail splits at a cluster of mature firs. Go right, across a small rocky area (elev. 150 ft/46 m), and rejoin the main trail at 0.5 mile (0.8 km). Now head right, soon bending south to continue along the fence line. Cross a small boardwalk and reach the trail's end (elev. 125 ft/38 m) at 0.7 mile (1.1 km). The San Juan Island Trails Committee hopes the path will someday run all the way to Friday Harbor. Return at your leisure, savoring the bucolic surroundings.

Jones Island

A 188-acre (76-ha) state marine park just 1 mile (1.6 km) off the southwest coast of Orcas Island, Jones Island is popular with boaters, especially kayakers. The park has moorage (7 buoys) and a 24-site campground open year-round (water available May–September).

60 Jones Island

RATING/DIFFICULTY	LOOP	ELEV GAIN/HIGH POINT
****/2	2.4 miles (3.9 km)	200 feet (61 m)/ 140 feet (43 m)

Map: USGS Friday Harbor; **Contact:** Washington State Parks, Sucia Island Marine State Park; **Notes:** Dogs permitted on-leash; **GPS:** N 48 37.080, W 123 02.863

Wander through groves of stately Douglas fir and along grassy shoreline ledges, soaking up exceptional Salish Sea scenery. How many islands can you identify along the way? Admire camas blossoms in spring and bald eagles, seals, oystercatchers, and other wild critters year-round.

GETTING THERE

You need a private boat or to arrange for a watertaxi to access Jones Island. Friday Harbor's San Juan Island Whale and Wildlife Tours (http://sanjuanislandwhales.com) offers reliable service. The trailhead is at the North Bay dock. Privy available.

ON THE TRAIL

From the North Bay dock, follow a wide wheelchair-accessible path to a large lawn flanked by campsites. Campsites are scattered around the lawn at South Bay too, and sites reserved strictly for paddlers can be found along the island's west shore. Jones Island has a few Adirondack lean-tos as well.

At the south end of the lawn, come to a junction. You'll be returning on the wide path straight ahead, so veer right here onto the Northwest Loop. At 0.2 mile (0.3 km), come to a junction. The path left hops over to the Southwest Loop and to paddle-in campsites; take it if you want a shorter loop option.

Otherwise continue right, climbing to a treed knoll (elev. 140 ft/43 m) above North Bay. Then gradually descend back to near sea level, reaching grassy ledges on the island's north shore. Take in great views of Orcas Island's Turtleback Mountain and Waldron Island's Point Disney cliffs. Then follow an up-and-down course that hugs the shoreline, and curve around to head southward.

Pass junipers, big firs, rocky ledges, and grassy bluffs that burst with blossoms in spring. Take in views northwest to Spieden Island, Flattop Island, and Stuart Island's Tiptop Hill. San Juan Island soon comes into view.

At 1.3 miles (2.1 km), reach a junction with the short connector trail. Continue right, passing campsites and now following the Southwest Loop. Enjoy more splendid shoreline serenity, including views out to the Wasp Islands—named not for insects but for the warship commandeered in the War of 1812 by Jacob Jones, namesake of the island you're on. At 2 miles (3.2 km), reach the wide grassy lawn at South Bay. A

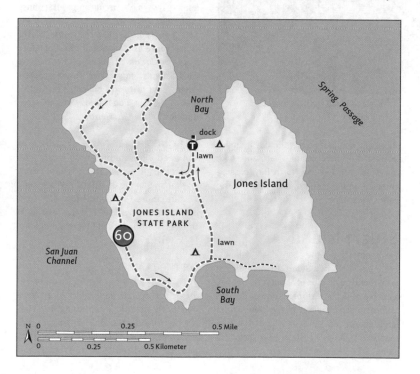

Jones Island's loop trails offer good coastal hiking.

short spur continues along the bay if you're interested—otherwise, turn left and take the wide path back to North Bay, passing en route an old orchard, lean-tos, and the park's water tank.

Stuart Island

Westernmost of the San Juan Islands, 1786-acre (723-ha) Stuart Island hosts a year-round population of about forty people, a couple of public dirt roads, one of the last one-room schoolhouses in the state, and a large unit of the San Juan Islands National Monument. A lovely state park provides camping (18 sites) and moorage.

61 Turn Point

RATING/ DIFFICULTY	ROUNDTRIP	ELEV GAIN/HIGH POINT
****/3	6 miles (9.7 km)	1040 feet (317 m)/ 280 feet (85 m)

Map: USGS Stuart Island; **Contact:** San Juan Islands National Monument and Washington State Parks, Stuart Island; **Notes:** Dogs permitted on-leash; **GPS:** N 48 25.891, W 122 49.714

Hike from a quiet cove along country roads to a stunning lighthouse perched above churning waters busy with boats. The westernmost point in the San Juan Islands, Turn Point sits at the convergence of Haro Strait and Boundary Pass. Unsurpassed views of the nearby Gulf Islands, impressive forest, coastal ledges, and historical buildings make this unit of the San Juan Islands National Monument a beloved destination.

GETTING THERE
You need a private boat or to arrange for a watertaxi to access Stuart Island. Friday Harbor's San Juan Island Whale and Wildlife Tours (sanjuanislandwhales.com) offers reliable service. The trailhead is at the Reid Harbor dock at Stuart Island State Park. Privy available.

ON THE TRAIL
This hike starts from the 85-acre (34-ha) Stuart Island State Park, which straddles a narrow forested ridge separating Reid Harbor from Prevost Harbor. Head up the steep dock ramp to the campground kiosk and trail junction. Then head left on the Prevost Loop,

traversing ledges above Reid Harbor. Ignore a side trail right and reach a junction (elev. 120 ft/37 m) at 0.2 mile (0.3 km).

Continue straight, descending more than a hundred steps through a forest of impressive Douglas firs and madronas to a junction at 0.3 mile (0.5 km). The trail goes right 0.3 mile (0.5 km), circling around a marsh to reach the dirt county road from Reid Harbor. If the tide is low, you can alternatively reach the road by walking the beach.

Follow the road uphill beneath a thick emerald canopy, coming to Stuart's one-room schoolhouse (elev. 260 ft/79 m) at 1.1 miles (1.8 km). The original schoolhouse

is now a museum (visit if school is not in session), next to the newer schoolhouse. Buy a souvenir shirt at the kiosk, payment by honor system.

Continue along the road, reaching a junction at 1.2 miles (1.9 km). Bear right and carry on with pleasant road walking, staying right at two side roads, both leading to the island's cemetery. Pass a wetland and a bucolic farm (respect private property; do not trespass).

At 1.8 miles (2.9 km), come to a T junction. Right leads 0.4 mile (0.6 km) to a public dock (an alternative starting point) on Prevost Harbor and an amazing view of Mount Baker. For

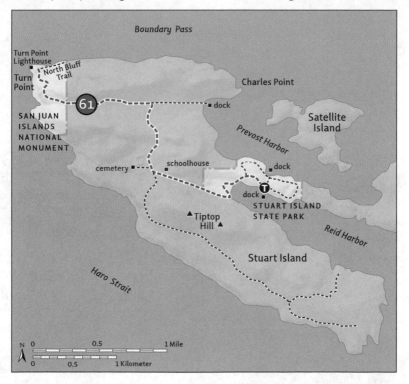

Turn Point, turn left, passing a primitive airstrip and soon afterward entering the national monument. Round ledges (elev. 280 ft/85 m) and steeply descend—passing a short spur leading left to a ledge with good viewing over Haro Strait—before coming to the Turn Point Lighthouse grounds. Pass the keeper's residence first, then a barn serving as a museum and staffed periodically by volunteers, reaching the 1893-built lighthouse at 3 miles (4.8 km).

History aside, this spot is perfect for observing wildflowers, marine traffic, marine life (look for whales and pelagic birds), and a panorama of maritime views: Vancouver Island and Sidney Island are to the left.

Moresby and Salt Spring islands are straight ahead. And Pender and Saturna islands are to the right. Lounge long on this lighthouse lawn, ideal for lunch breaks, and then retrace your steps to the dock.

EXTENDING YOUR TRIP
Near the barn, you can pick up the 0.3-mile (0.5-km) North Bluff Trail leading to a Coast Guard structure and good views north across Boundary Pass. Back at Stuart Island State Park, consider hiking the 0.8-mile (1.3 km) East Loop and 1 mile (1.6 km) Prevost Loop, especially the latter, with its wonderful views across the harbor to Satellite and Saturna islands.

Turn Point provides excellent views of the Gulf Islands across Boundary Pass.

Outer San Juan Islands

Off the north shore of Orcas Island are a series of small idyllic islands, several of which are marine state parks. With their sandstone composition, they are more similar to the Gulf Islands than to the San Juans. Of these islands, Patos, Matia, and Sucia all offer excellent hiking as well as exceptional camping and opportunities to observe wildlife. Access is via private boat or water taxi service.

Patos Island is a unit of the San Juan Islands National Monument, its 207 acres (84 ha) managed by Washington State Parks. Matia Island is one of the eighty-three islands protected in the San Juan Islands National Wildlife Refuge. Matia and Turn are the only sizeable islands within the refuge—and the only ones open to the public. Washington State Parks manages 5 acres (2 ha) around Matia's Rolfe Cove as a marine park. The rest of the 145-acre (59-ha) island is federal wilderness, affording undisturbed habitat for endangered and threatened species.

Many believe Sucia Island to be the most beautiful of the San Juans. The island is a worthy destination for hikers, offering several miles of well-marked and maintained trails. The island is shaped like a horseshoe, with several long slender peninsulas, and it is rich in biological diversity and human history.

Sucia's 564 acres (228 ha) are entirely protected as a state marine park. The island was named by Spanish Captain Francisco de Eliza, after the Spanish word for "foul" or "dirty"—but in this case in a nautical sense, referring to the reefs and rocks surrounding the island. The proper pronunciation is "soo-SEE-uh," but the island is commonly pronounced "SOO-sha." Sucia has 60 campsites, 48 mooring buoys, and seasonal potable water.

62 Patos Island

RATING/ DIFFICULTY	ROUNDTRIP	ELEV GAIN/HIGH POINT
*****/1	2.2 miles (3.5 km)	120 feet (37 m)/ 70 feet (21 m)

Map: USGS Stuart Island; **Contact:** San Juan Islands National Monument and Washington

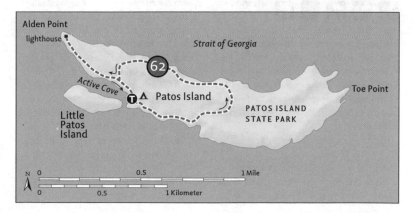

Patos Island Lighthouse

State Parks, Sucia Island State Park; **Notes:** Dogs permitted on-leash; **GPS:** N 48 47.056, W 122 57.848

🚶 🐾 🛶 🌲 🏠 *Situated on Boundary Pass, Patos Island is the northernmost of the San Juans and an excellent destination for watching marine traffic and marine mammals—especially orcas. Enjoy hiking along sandstone-shelved shorelines, through old-growth forests, and to a beautifully restored historical lighthouse.*

GETTING THERE

You need a private boat or to arrange for a water taxi to access Patos Island. Outer Islands Expeditions in Eastsound on Orcas Island, (www.outerislandx.com) offers reliable service. The trailhead is at Active Cove. Moorage (2 buoys), campground (7 sites), and privy available. No water.

ON THE TRAIL

Patos Island was named by Spanish explorer Commander Dionisio Alcalá Galiano in 1792 (*patos* means "ducks" in Spanish). The ducks observed were probably alcids—auks, guillemots, and murrelets, which are common here. Uncommon in the San Juans, oak fern grows only on this island in the archipelago. From Active Cove take the path that veers right from the camping area—you'll be returning from the left on the main path. Walk along the shore, admiring Orcas and Waldron islands. Notice the shelved sandstone—a characteristic shared by the outer San Juan Islands and the Gulf Islands to the north, owing to their younger age than the islands farther south.

The trail eventually turns inland, cresting the island's backbone (elev. 50 ft/15 m) and traversing old-growth forest harboring some giants. Soon reach the island's north shore and turn west. Admire excellent views north to the Gulf Islands, Point Roberts, and British Columbia summits and east to Mount Baker. At low tide, explore the shelved coastline.

The way meanders along the shore through a forest choked in thick understory, owing to the island's dearth of browsers. Climb over a small ridge (elev. 70 ft/21 m) and reach the main path at 1.4 miles (2.3 km). Left goes back to Active Cove—but first you must absolutely go right 0.2 mile (0.3 km), reaching the lighthouse at Alden Point.

Savor the sweeping view of Boundary Pass at one of the most beautiful points in the San Juan Islands, and admire the handsome lighthouse built in 1908. In summer, volunteers with Keepers of the Patos

Light (www.patoslightkeepers.org) staff the lighthouse. Go inside and learn about Helen Glidden, the daughter of a lighthouse keeper who penned the book *The Light on the Island* while living here from 1905 to 1913. When ready to depart, follow the main trail 0.6 mile (1 km) back to Active Cove, passing the old dock site for the lighthouse.

63 Matia Island

RATING/ DIFFICULTY	ROUNDTRIP	ELEV GAIN/HIGH POINT
****/2	1.8 miles (2.9 km)	200 feet (61 m)/ 100 feet (30 m)

Map: USGS Mount Constitution; **Contact:** San Juan Islands National Wildlife Refuge and Washington State Parks, Sucia Island State Park; **Notes:** Dogs prohibited beyond campground; **GPS:** N 48 44.896, W 122 50.509

 Walk among some of the oldest, biggest, and tallest trees in the San Juan Islands. Then *explore a hidden cove and a grassy ledged point with a sweeping view of sea and mountains. One of the least visited of the San Juans, Matia is one of the wildest islands in the archipelago.*

GETTING THERE

You need a private boat or to arrange for a water taxi to access Matia Island. Outer Islands Expeditions in Eastsound on Orcas Island (www.outerislandx.com) offers reliable service. The trailhead is at Rolfe Cove. Dock, moorage (2 buoys), campground (6 sites), and privy available. No water.

ON THE TRAIL

Named Isla de Mata in 1792 by Spanish Captain Eliza for the island's dense shrubbery, the island became Matia in 1854 when the US Coast Guard added an *i*. You'll hear the name pronounced "ma-TEE-a," in keeping with its Spanish origin, and also "MAY-shuh," more anglicized. But no matter how you pronounce it, Matia is worth a visit. Given the island's federal wilderness protection, dogs are not allowed beyond

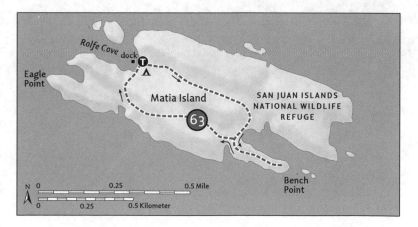

the campground and no off-trail travel is permitted.

From the Rolfe Cove dock, locate the Wilderness Loop next to a humongous Douglas fir. You'll be returning from the right, so hike straight ahead through a tunnel of ancient forest greenery. The trail climbs to about 100 feet (30 m), passing between two tree-shrouded knolls. Pass impressive firs, a huge hollowed-out cedar, and big fern boughs. Then reach a hidden cove wedged between sandstone cliffs.

At 0.6 mile (1 km), come to a junction. Take the spur trail left 0.3 mile (0.5 km) along open sandstone ledges to Bench Point and the tip of a small peninsula. Enjoy excellent views of Orcas, Lummi, and Clark islands as well as Mount Baker. Then retrace your way back to the junction and continue straight on the loop. Pass the site of Civil War veteran Elvin H. Smith's cabin. The famed Hermit of Matia lived all alone here from 1892 until 1921, when he vanished on a supply-seeking rowing trip to Orcas during a storm.

Climb back up to 100 feet (30 m) and then descend through more primeval forest. Pass a tiny cove and wetland before returning to the camping area and dock 0.6 mile (1 km) from the spur junction.

Hikers look out at Orcas Island from Bench Point.

64 Ev Henry Finger and Johnson Point

RATING/ DIFFICULTY	ROUNDTRIP	ELEV GAIN/HIGH POINT
*****/3	4.7 miles (7.6 km)	550 feet (168 m)/ 110 feet (34 m)

Maps: USGS Sucia Island, USGS Eastsound; **Contact:** Washington State Parks, Sucia Island State Park; **Notes:** Dogs permitted on-leash; **GPS:** N 48 45.173, W 122 54.317

🧍🦋🔙🦅🏠 *Hike along the bluffs soaking up spectacular Salish Sea scenery while exploring a couple of Sucia's fingerlike peninsulas. Check out the bays that separate them too, looking for eagles, otters, and harlequin ducks—and possibly a fossil or two.*

GETTING THERE
You need a private boat or to arrange for a water taxi to access Sucia Island. Outer Islands Expeditions in Eastsound on Orcas Island (www.outerislandx.com) offers reliable service. The trailhead is at Fossil Bay dock 2. Privy available.

ON THE TRAIL
This is a two-for-one hike: one trip out and back to Ev Henry Finger and another to Johnson Point.

Ev Henry Finger: From dock 2, head left through a picnic and camping area that occupies the isthmus between Fossil Bay and Fox Cove. Look out into Fox Cove Bay for its famous mushroom rock. At 0.2 mile (0.3 km), turn left onto the Ev Henry Loop and start climbing along steep ledges (elev. 75 ft/23 m) above Fossil Bay. After a few ups and downs, aided by steps, come to the loop junction at 0.5 mile (0.8 km).

Go left (you'll be returning from the right) through a salal jungle, climbing about 75 feet (23 m) and reaching Ev Henry Point at 0.9 mile (1.4 km). From this grassy bluff, the views of Matia, Orcas, Waldron, Pender, and Saturna islands, as well as Mount Baker, are breathtaking. This point was named after yachtsman Everett (Ev) Henry, who led a drive to purchase Sucia from developers who wanted to subdivide it for vacation homes. Henry's campaign was a success, with his purchases later donated to the state for a park.

Continue on the loop, hovering on a high bluff (elev. 100 ft/30 m) above sandstone-shelved beaches (which can be explored at low tide). At 1.4 miles (2.3 km), close the loop. Then retrace your steps 0.5 mile (0.8 km) back to the dock. On your return, consider a 0.6-mile (1-km) roundtrip side trip to 75-foot (23-m) Fox Point for nice views of Ev Henry Finger, Little Sucia Island, and Fox Cove.

Johnson Point: From dock 2, walk north past the dock to a very informative kiosk about the park. Then pass spurs to Fossil Bay dock 1, reaching a service road. Go right and then left, hiking past the park maintenance buildings and skirting Mud Bay. Pass the Mud Bay Trail (hikable only at low tide) and reach a junction with the Johnson Point Trail (elev. 70 ft/21 m) at 0.3 mile (0.5 km).

Head right, walking up and down along a forested ridge (elev. 110 ft/34 m) to a junction at 0.8 mile (1.3 km). The trail right drops to Snoring Bay and camps before continuing to the tip of Wiggins Head, a 0.5-mile (0.8-km) side trip one-way and well worth the effort. For Johnson Point,

Fox Point viewed from Ev Henry Finger

continue straight ahead through madrona and fir forests, going up and over ledges above Snoring Bay.

At 1.4 miles (2.3 km), reach the open point (elev. 15 ft/5 m) with its replica of a historical survey post and sweeping views of Mount Baker; Orcas Island's Mount Pickett, Mount Constitution, and Turtleback Mountain; and Lummi, Matia, and Clark islands. Stay awhile before retracing your steps or considering side trips.

65 Shallow Bay and Lawson Bluff

RATING/ DIFFICULTY	LOOP	ELEV GAIN/HIGH POINT
*****/2	4.1 miles (6.6 km)	350 feet (107 m)/ 160 feet (49 m)

Maps: USGS Sucia Island, USGS Eastsound; **Contact:** Washington State Parks, Sucia Island State Park; **Notes:** Dogs permitted on-leash; **GPS:** N 48 45.173, W 122 54.317

Stroll along Shallow Bay, scanning its serene waters for otters, seals, and guillemots. Check out a sandstone cliff resembling a chunk of Swiss cheese, its façade pockmarked with shallow caves. And walk along a bluff, hovering over crashing surf and soaking up sweeping views of the Gulf and San Juan islands.

GETTING THERE
See directions to Hike 64.

ON THE TRAIL
From Fossil Bay dock 2, head right, passing a kiosk and spur to dock 1 and coming to a service road in 0.1 mile (0.15 km). You'll be returning from the right, so carry on left, following the level service road through thick forest between two ridges. Stay straight at a junction (the trail right leads to Echo Bay), coming to Shallow Bay and a campground at 0.8 mile (1.3 km).

Walk the beautiful sandy beach to the right, enjoying views across the bay to Patos and Little Patos islands and perhaps some *patos* (ducks) in the bay. The beach is hemmed in by a boggy ghost forest, an excellent place for bird-watching. Pick up trail once again and hike up a steep bluff (elev. 30 ft/9 m) adorned with contorted firs and madronas, coming to Echo Bay Camp on a narrow isthmus between Shallow and Echo bays at 1.2 miles (1.9 km).

Follow the China Caves Trail, now traveling over gorgeous wind- and surf-sculpted sandstone ledges (elev. 50 ft/15 m), some of the prettiest and most photographed natural features in the San Juans. The way descends to a junction. Right heads to the Echo Bay North Camp. You want to go left, reaching the shoreline and the China Caves at 1.5 miles (2.4 km). The caves, small depressions in a big sandstone bluff, allegedly hid Chinese laborers smuggled from Canada in the late 1800s. The entire island has a history of smuggling, from illegal immigrants to alcohol during Prohibition to narcotics.

Now walk the sandy beach to the right, to the Shallow Bay North Camp, and pick up the Lawson Bluff Trail at 1.6 miles (2.6 km). Hike along Shallow Bay looking for playful otters and diving kingfishers. Pass big junipers and round an open bluff with sweeping views of the Gulf and San Juan islands. Then continue north, climbing along Lawson Bluff's precipitous cliffs (elev. 75 ft/23 m). There are plenty of sunny spots among clusters of shore

Sculpted sandstone ledges at Shallow Bay

pines, inviting picnicking and lounging. Keep children nearby while enjoying the views.

At 2.3 miles (3.7 km), reach a service road. Right returns to Shallow Bay. You want to go left, climbing a little before descending toward Echo Bay. Ignore a right-hand trail to China Caves and a left turn to Ewing Cove (Hike 66), reaching Echo Bay North Camp at 2.6 miles (4.2 km). Now follow the service road right, along Sucia's largest (and oft windy) bay, admiring Justice and the Finger islands.

At 2.9 miles (4.7 km), come to a junction for trails leading to China Caves and Shallow Bay. Continue on the service road, passing more camps and ignoring a right-hand road shortly afterward. The way, now in forest, marches along the highest ridge (elev. 160 ft/49 m) on the island, coming to a junction just past an old cistern at 3.8 miles (6.1 km). The trail straight goes to Johnson Point (Hike 64). You want to hike right, following the service

road off the ridge, passing park maintenance buildings and a familiar junction and returning to Fossil Bay dock 2 at 4.1 miles (6.6 km).

66 Ewing Cove

RATING/ DIFFICULTY	LOOP	ELEV GAIN/HIGH POINT
*****/2	6 miles (9.7 km)	500 feet (152 m)/ 160 feet (49 m)

Maps: USGS Sucia Island, USGS Eastsound; **Contact:** Washington State Parks, Sucia Island State Park; **Notes:** Dogs permitted on-leash; **GPS:** N 48 45.173, W 122 54.317

Hike to a hidden cove away from Sucia's popular campgrounds and bays. Surrounded by reefs that harbor a plethora of pelagic birds and marine mammals, Ewing Cove is sweet spot to plop down on the beach with binoculars in hand. The trail to the cove, along shoreline bluffs and ledges, grants sweeping views of the sea and islands.

GETTING THERE
See directions to Hike 64.

ON THE TRAIL
From Fossil Bay dock 2, head right, first passing an informative kiosk and spurs to Fossil Bay dock 1 and then reaching a service road. Continue right, skirting Mud Bay and passing park maintenance buildings. Follow the road and ascend a ridge, passing the Johnson Point Trail and soon coming to an old cistern, built by one of the island's early homesteaders. Captain Harnden made a living for his family by farming, barging, shuttling tourists, and remaining friendly with bootleggers who thrived in the San Juans during Prohibition.

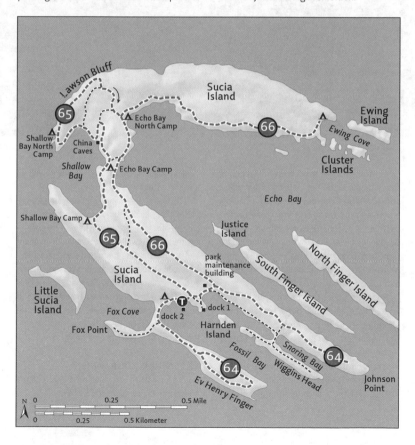

Trail along Echo Bay

Continue on the service road, traversing the island's 160-foot (49-m) high point and reaching Echo Bay Camp on a narrow isthmus at 1.2 miles (1.9 km). Stay on the service road, coming to a junction at Echo Bay North Camp at 1.5 miles (2.4 km). Bear right here onto the Ewing Cove Trail for one of the most scenic shoreline hikes in the San Juans.

Roaming up and over and around bluffs and ledges, the trail hugs the northern shoreline of Echo Bay. Amble past mature firs, gnarled junipers, and contorted madronas. At 2 miles (3.2 km), pause on an emerald blufftop, taking in views of nearby Finger Islands and Justice Island (which was seized from a drug smuggler in the 1980s) and farther out to Lummi, Matia, and Orcas islands.

The trail is pure hiking bliss, cresting grassy bluffs and skirting hidden coves favored by marine life. Look for kingfishers in overhanging trees and swallows nesting in the coastal bluffs. After passing through a stand of aspens (divine in October), reach a small sandy beach and campsites at Ewing Cove at 3 miles (4.8 km). Take a break on a weathered beach log and look out across the cove to Ewing and the Cluster islands, hotbeds for seals and birdlife. Return the way you came when you must.

EXTENDING YOUR HIKE

Combine with a trip around Lawson Bluff and to the China Caves (Hike 65).

tsawwassen and
point roberts

Lily Point Marine Reserve, Point Roberts

Tsawwassen Bluff—encompassing the communities of Tsawwassen (part of Delta, British Columbia) and Point Roberts, Washington (an exclave of the United States)—was once an island and indeed feels like one. This area is the ancestral home to the Tsawwassen First Nation and it is culturally and historically tied to the San Juan and Gulf islands.

Tsawwassen is reached by BC Highway 17, which connects the busy BC 99 corridor (that links Vancouver to the United States) with a major BC Ferries terminal servicing Vancouver Island and the Gulf Islands. The community borders Boundary Bay, one of the best bird-watching locales in the Pacific Northwest. An excellent park and trail system allows exploration of this ecosystem.

Point Roberts (or Point Bob in local parlance) occupies the southern tip of the Tsawwassen Peninsula. In 1846, when American and British diplomats met back east to settle on the 49th parallel as the boundary between the United States and Canada, Point Roberts found itself south of the border. Once the British boundary commission became aware of this situation, it made an offer to the American commission to adjust the boundary, so that dangling Point Roberts would remain in Canada. But, for whatever reason, nothing changed, and the United States wound up with an exclave, the westernmost part of Whatcom County, reachable by land only through British Columbia.

Only about 1300 people call Point Roberts home, but the numbers (mostly Canadian) swell during the summer months. About twenty thousand people live in Tsawwassen, where you'll find a full array of lodging and eating establishments. Thanks to the rainshadow effect, the sun often shines here. In fact, Tsawwassen is the sunniest spot in the larger Vancouver metropolitan area, receiving only a third of Vancouver's annual precipitation. Camping is available seasonally in Port Roberts at Lighthouse Marine Park (30 sites).

67 Monument Park

RATING/ DIFFICULTY	ROUNDTRIP	ELEV GAIN/HIGH POINT
**/2	1.6 miles (2.6 km)	160 feet (49 m)/ 160 feet (49 m)

Map: USGS Point Roberts; **Contact:** Whatcom County Parks and Recreation, Monument Park; **Notes:** Dogs permitted on-leash; **GPS:** N 49 00.125, W 123 05.343

Marvel at an imposing obelisk perched on a bluff, then descend through a lush ravine to a secluded beach on the international boundary. Stroll along the shoreline, admiring perched eagles in big overhanging limbs and watching BC ferries sailing back and forth across the Strait of Georgia.

GETTING THERE
From Blaine, enter Canada at the Peace Arch crossing and follow BC Highway 99 north for 17 miles (27 km) to BC 17. (From Vancouver, follow BC 99 south to BC 17.) Continue on BC 17 toward the Tsawwassen ferry terminal and turn left onto 56th Street after 4.9 miles (7.9 km). Follow it south for 3 miles (4.8 km) to the Point Roberts border crossing. Proceed south on Tyee Drive for 0.2 mile (0.3 km); turn right onto McKenzie Way. After 0.2 mile (0.3 km), turn right onto Delano Way. Proceed 0.2 mile (0.3 km) and turn left onto Roosevelt Road.

The international boundary marker on the beach at Monument Park

Drive 0.7 mile (1.1 km) to Monument Park and the trailhead.

ON THE TRAIL

Pay homage to Johnny Cash and walk the line (in this case the international boundary) on this hike. But before you do, admire the large monument marking the international boundary and commemorating the commis-sion responsible for establishing the 49th parallel as the border. Erected in 1861 while the United States was at war with itself, and six years before the Dominion of Canada was established, this stone monument was the first to be placed along the border.

Now hit the trail, which was upgraded in 2008 from a slick, steep path to a nicely designed switchbacking track. Drop into a

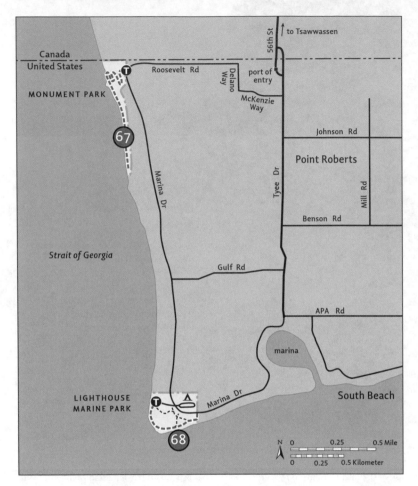

deep ravine cloaked with big maples, cedars, and firs. At 0.3 mile (0.5 km), emerge on a beautiful stretch of beach with views of the Tsawwassen BC Ferries terminal and the Gulf Islands across the Strait of Georgia.

Just to the north, locate a rather unattractive cement border marker: Monument no. 0, since number 1 was taken. Customs won't take kindly to you continuing beyond this monument, so head south along the beach instead. You can easily hike about 0.5 mile (0.8 km) before a big log pileup stymies your way. There are shoreline houses beyond anyhow, making this a good turnaround spot.

68 Lighthouse Marine Park

RATING/DIFFICULTY	ROUNDTRIP	ELEV GAIN/HIGH POINT
**/1	0.8 mile (1.3 km)	None/Sea level

Map: USGS Point Roberts; **Contact:** Whatcom County Parks and Recreation, Lighthouse Marine Park; **Notes:** Dogs permitted on-leash; **GPS:** N 48 58.402, W 123 05.066

Children in particular will delight in exploring along this short hike long on maritime views and marine wildlife. *From May to September, Lighthouse Marine Park is one of the best places in these parts to see a pod of orca whales.*

GETTING THERE

From Blaine, enter Canada at the Peace Arch crossing and follow BC Highway 99 north for 17 miles (27 km) to BC 17. (From Vancouver, follow BC 99 south to BC 17.) Continue on BC 17 toward the Tsawwassen ferry terminal and turn left onto 56th Street after 4.9 miles (7.9 km). Follow it south for 3 miles (4.8 km) to the Point Roberts border crossing. Then proceed south on Tyee Drive 1.3 miles (2.1 km), bearing right onto Marina Drive. Drive 1.1 miles (1.8 km) to Lighthouse Marine Park and the trailhead. Privy available.

Lighthouse Marine Park's inviting beach

ON THE TRAIL

The park is small at 21 acres (8.5 ha), and the trail is a short 0.4 mile (0.6 km), but you can easily spend all day here at the southwestern tip of Point Roberts. Walk a wide trail along the driftwood-littered beach, soaking up scenery and sunshine. You'll be disappointed if you've come to see a lighthouse, however. There is none—it was never built. Instead, there's an uninspiring navigational beacon.

Enjoy good views south of Saturna, Orcas, and Lummi islands and east of Mount Baker hovering above the Salish Sea. Pass the beacon and skirt the campground before reaching the trail's end at Marina Drive. Find a spot to set your scope up for whale-watching, while letting the youngsters splash about. Consider spending the night at this popular park, but note that you'll need to make a reservation.

69 Lily Point

RATING/ DIFFICULTY	ROUNDTRIP	ELEV GAIN/HIGH POINT
***/2	1.6 miles (2.6 km)	220 feet (67 m)/ 220 feet (67 m)

Map: USGS Point Roberts; **Contact:** Whatcom County Parks and Recreation, Lily Point Marine Park; **Notes:** Dogs permitted on-leash. Check tide charts before hiking beach; **GPS:** N 48 58.862, W 123 01.664

Encompassing 247 acres (100 ha) of mature forest, extensive tidal flats, and impressive 200-foot-tall (80-m) bluffs, Lily Point is the crown jewel of Point Roberts. Take in expansive views from blufftop vantages before reaching a wild and secluded beach at the foot of those lofty bluffs.

GETTING THERE

From Blaine, enter Canada at the Peace Arch crossing and follow BC Highway 99 north for 17 miles (27 km) to BC 17. (From Vancouver, follow BC 99 south to BC 17.) Continue on BC 17 toward the Tsawwassen ferry terminal and turn left onto 56th Street after 4.9 miles (7.9 km). Follow it south for 3 miles (4.8 km) to the Point Roberts border crossing. Then proceed south on Tyee Drive for 1.3 miles (2.1 km) and turn left onto APA Road. Drive 1.8 miles (2.9 km) to the road end and trailhead (elev. 220 ft/67 m). Privy available.

ON THE TRAIL

Lily Point Marine Reserve is now the largest natural tract on Point Roberts, but it wasn't always so. From 1884 to 1917 the Alaska Packers Association (APA) operated a large salmon cannery here. All that remains are barnacled

An eagle rests in Boundary Bay under the watchful eye of Mount Baker.

pilings and scattered rusting debris. The area could have become vacation homes, but in 2008 the county acquired it thanks to the tireless efforts of the Nature Conservancy, Whatcom Land Trust, various state agencies, and many concerned locals. The park's trail system received a major overhaul in 2012, with tread rehabilitation, signage, and the closure of habitat-damaging user-built trails (respect closures).

From the trailhead, head east and soon come to a junction. The path forward leads 300 feet (90 m) to an incredible blufftop

view of Lily Point (worth the side trip). Here you can gaze across Boundary Bay to the Cheam Range, Mount Baker, and a slew of North Cascades peaks. Look for eagles (they're ubiquitous here) perched in large maples and firs. Near the viewpoint, a 0.6-mile (1-km) trail travels through big cedars and firs to Cedar Point Avenue. Consider it for more exercise.

For Lily Point, head right on a wide and smooth trail, passing a connector trail and coming to junction at 0.3 mile (0.5 km). The trail right loops back along the park's western border, returning to the trailhead in 0.6 mile (1 km). It makes for a longer return after visiting the point. The trail straight ahead is another worthy side trip: it leads 300 feet (90 m) to a blufftop view south to Lummi, Orcas, and Saturna islands. Lily Point is to the left on excellent trail that switchbacks on a sane grade down into a moist ravine shaded by giant maples. Gone is the dangerous steep, slick path to the beach.

At 0.7 mile (1.1 km), reach a grassy flat and a trail split. Either direction will bring you more or less 0.1 mile (0.15 km) to Lily Point's shoreline, with the rows of pilings to the right. Plop your bum on a driftwood log and embrace the views!

EXTENDING YOUR TRIP
You have other options too: Hike 0.5 mile (0.8 km) west on the beach to the park's western boundary. Or hike north 0.8 mile (1.3 km) along the beach to the park's northern boundary, passing tidal flats, a nice swimming area (with some of the warmest saltwater in Washington), and more impressive bluffs.

70 Boundary Bay Regional Park

RATING/ DIFFICULTY	LOOP	ELEV GAIN/HIGH POINT
***/1	2 miles (3.2 km)	Minimal/10 feet (3 m)

Map: NTS 092G03 Lulu Island; **Contact:** Metro Vancouver Regional Parks, West Area Office, Boundary Bay Regional Park; **Notes:** Partly wheelchair-accessible. The 12th Avenue Dyke Trail is open to bicycles. Dogs permitted on-leash; **GPS:** N 49 00.956, W 123 02.479

 *Walk along Boundary Bay's glistening mudflats and extensive*

A pair of hikers watch for birds from the boardwalk at Boundary Bay Regional Park.

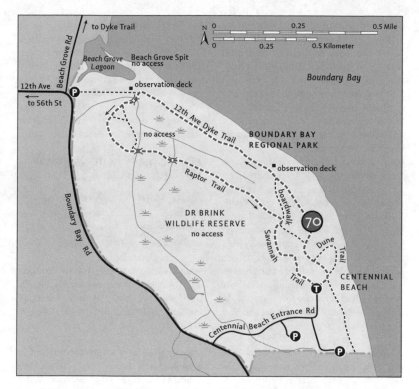

intertidal marshes, beholding birds—
hundreds of thousands of them! A Canadian IBA (important bird area; www.iba
canada.com), Boundary Bay is one of the
best places in the Salish Sea for observing
migratory and residential birds. The
beaches on this hike and views of North
Shore peaks (north of Vancouver) and the
North Cascades aren't too bad either.

GETTING THERE
From Blaine, enter Canada at the Peace
Arch crossing and follow BC 99 north for 17
miles (27 km) to BC 17. (From Vancouver,
follow BC 99 south to BC 17.) Continue on
BC 17 toward the Tsawwassen ferry terminal and left onto 56th Street after 4.9 miles
(7.9 km). Follow it south for 1.2 miles (1.9
km) and turn left onto 12th Avenue. After
0.5 mile (0.8 km), turn right onto Boundary
Bay Road and reach the Boundary Bay Park
entrance in 1 mile (1.6 km). Turn left and
drive 0.5 mile (0.8 km) to a large parking
area and trailhead. Privy available.

ON THE TRAIL
A popular hiking destination just north of
the 49th parallel, Boundary Bay Regional
Park offers a handful of delightful family-
friendly trails. From the trailhead at

Centennial Beach (a popular sunning and wading area in summer), head north on the 12th Avenue Dyke Trail. After bypassing (or taking) the short Dune Trail, reach a junction with the Raptor Trail at 0.2 mile (0.3 km). You'll be returning on it, so keep right.

At 0.4 mile (0.6 km), come to a bird-observation deck at a junction with a boardwalk path that leads south through marsh to the Raptor Trail. From the deck, scan the marsh for songbirds. Then resume hiking on the Dyke Trail, savoring the sights and sounds of Boundary Bay. This area is one of the most important stops along the Pacific Flyway winter migration route, and thousands of sandpipers, dunlins, and plovers pass through here. Look too for snowy owls, short-eared owls, widgeons, teals, brants, snow geese, bald eagles, grebes, and herons.

At 1 mile (1.6 km), reach a junction with the Raptor Trail at an observation deck overlooking the Beach Grove Lagoon and Spit. The Dyke Trail continues west 0.2 mile (0.3 km) to the 12th Avenue trailhead (parking available). Head south on the Raptor Trail, traversing marsh and grasslands. Look for raptors fond of this habitat for its feast of rodents, amphibians, and small birds.

At 1.7 miles (2.7 km), reach a junction. Left leads via boardwalk back to the big observation deck. Right leads 0.3 mile (0.5 km) back to the parking lot via the Savannah Trail. Head that way. Or opt for straight, which will soon reach the familiar 12th Avenue Dyke Trail and then the trailhead.

EXTENDING YOUR TRIP

For an all-day adventure, start at the 12th Avenue Dyke trailhead on 12th Avenue and walk the Beach Grove Road 0.7 mile (1.1 km) to the Dyke Trail. You can take this trail for 9.6 miles (15.5 km)—all the way to Mud

Bay Park in Surrey. The entire way is along Boundary Bay, passing through agricultural lands, wildlife management areas, and parks. The birding and views of the San Juan Islands are outstanding. You can also access this trail from parking areas off of 72nd Street and 104th Street for shorter wanderings. Note that there is no parking at the trail's southern start on 17A Avenue and Beach Grove Road.

71 George C. Reifel Migratory Bird Sanctuary

RATING/ DIFFICULTY	LOOP	ELEV GAIN/HIGH POINT
***/1	1.5 miles (2.4 km)	minimal/10 feet (3 m)

Map: NTS 092G03 Lulu Island; **Contact:** British Columbia Waterfowl Society; **Notes:** Open 9:00 AM–4:00 PM daily. Admission fee. Dogs prohibited; **GPS:** N 49 05.887, W 123 10.715

Located on Westham Island in the Fraser River delta, the nearly 850-acre (344-ha) George C. Reifel Migratory Bird Sanctuary is one of the best bird-watching spots in British Columbia. Each year millions of migratory birds pass through this lowland of tidal flats, sloughs, marshes, and riverbanks. Lesser snow geese and snowy owls are common sights during winter months, while a handful of sandhill cranes are year-round residents. Be sure to pack your binoculars and bird guide.

GETTING THERE

From Blaine, enter Canada at the Peace Arch crossing and follow BC Highway 99 north for 17 miles (27 km) to BC 17. (From Vancouver, follow BC 99 south to BC 17.) Continue on BC 17 south for 1.4 miles (2.3 km) and turn right onto Ladner Trunk Road. Drive 0.9 mile (1.4 km) to 47A Avenue and then 3.5 miles (5.6 km) to River Road. Continue for 2.3 miles (3.7 km) and turn right onto Westham Island Road. After 2.2 miles (3.5 km), turn right onto Robertson Road and proceed 0.4 mile (0.6 km) to Refuge Road. Turn left and drive 0.6 mile (1 km) to the refuge center and trailhead. Privy available.

ON THE TRAIL

Pay your fee at the entrance station and then begin your aviary adventure. The Reifel Sanctuary is pretty compact, but it's not a place to hurry through. Take your time stopping at the bird blinds and the observation deck. You can easily spend all day here.

The land here, like much of Westham Island, was actively farmed throughout the last century. But since the establishment of the sanctuary and the adjacent Alaksen National Wildlife Area in the 1970s, the Canadian Wildlife Service, British Columbia Waterfowl Society, and others have restored some of the lands to their prefarming state. Several of the old dykes remain in place, acting as trails in this saturated landscape.

Start your hike near House Pond, with its warming hut and interpretive signs. Then travel the periphery of the sanctuary, hiking

Sandhill cranes greet a hiker at the Reifel Migratory Bird Sanctuary.

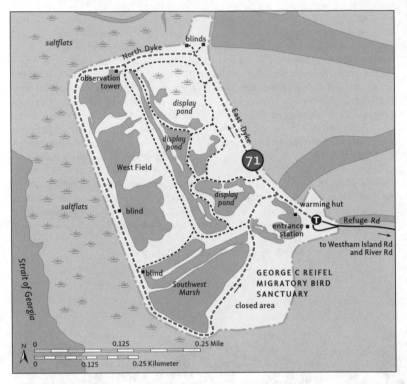

through thick hedgerows and along wildlife-rich sloughs. More than 280 bird species have been recorded here, but you may think that just mallards make up the resident list—they're prolific. Keep looking—there are eagles, mergansers, teals, canvasbacks, owls, hawks, and, in winter, snow geese—thousands of them. Your chances of seeing sandhill cranes are excellent.

As the periphery trail bends westward, peer across the South Fork Fraser River to Stevenson on Lulu Island. Keep walking westward coming to an observation tower that's 32 feet (10 m) tall. The view from it across the sanctuary, with its myriad of fields, ponds,

and sloughs, is not to be missed. The views of Mount Baker, the San Juan and Gulf islands, and Vancouver Island across the Strait of Georgia aren't too bad either.

Continue hiking along the periphery, bending south along the saltflats. All kinds of birds lurk out there among the reeds. Pass more fields and ponds and eventually turn back toward your start, traversing the Southwest Marsh. Return to your start, content with your 1.5-mile (2.4-km) hike and observations—or hike some more, checking out the paths that weave through the inner fields and sloughs. There are more than 4 miles' (7 km) worth to explore.

gulf islands

Sidney Spit, Sidney Island

Galiano Island

Long and slender, Galiano Island is the second-largest of the Gulf Islands, at 23 square miles (60 sq. km). Named after the Spanish explorer Dionisio Alcalá Galiano, who traveled this area in 1792, it has about 1300 residents. Most of the island was owned by timber giant MacMillan Bloedel until the early 1990s. Despite recent subdivisions, Galiano remains a fairly wild and undeveloped place. Its highest summits, biggest lake, and oldest trees, along with miles of its stunning coastline, are protected within several parks and preserves. The Galiano Conservancy (www .galianoconservancy.ca) works to expand the island's preserves and trails.

BC Ferries offers year-round service from Tsawwassen and Swartz Bay to Sturdies Bay, the island's only village and main commercial center. There is a small grocery store near the community hall. Bicyclists will find narrow and hilly roads, but very light traffic. Camping options (open year-round, water, no services in winter) include Montague Harbour Marine Province Park (28 sites and mooring buoys) and Dionisio Point Provincial Park (30 backcountry and paddle-accessible sites).

👫 🦴 ⚙ 🏠 *Good things indeed come in small packages. Although Bellhouse Provincial Park is a mere 5 acres (2 ha), it packs a scenic punch. With its close proximity to the ferry terminal and access via quiet country roads, Bellhouse is an ideal destination if you are visiting Galiano sans car.*

GETTING THERE

From Tsawwassen or Swartz Bay, take a BC ferry to Sturdies Bay on Galiano Island. Drive 0.3 mile (0.5 km) on Sturdies Bay Road and turn left onto Burrill Road. Continue for 0.3 mile (0.5 km) and turn left onto Jack Road. Drive 0.4 mile (0.6 km) to the trailhead. Privy available.

Shoreline at Bellhouse Provincial Park

72 Bellhouse Provincial Park

RATING/ DIFFICULTY	LOOP	ELEV GAIN/HIGH POINT
***/1	0.4 mile (0.6 km)	Minimal/26 feet (8 m)

Map: NTS 092B14 Mayne Island; **Contact:** BC Parks, Bellhouse Provincial Park; **Notes:** Dogs permitted on-leash; **GPS:** N 48 52.363, W 123 18.777

ON THE TRAIL

The former site of Leonard Thorneycroft Bellhouse's Farmhouse Inn, this gorgeous property on Burrill Point was given to the province in 1964 by Mr. Bellhouse. It's now recognized as part of the Active Pass IBA (important bird area) for its wintering Pacific loons and Brandt's cormorants and migrating Bonaparte's gulls. Look for them, along with the resident nesting bald eagles.

This hike is a short loop around Burrill Point over mossy ledges (stay on the trail to protect this fragile ecosystem) and through a patch of fir and arbutus. Plan to spend some time watching the birds and passing ships and ferries in Active Pass, exploring the honeycomb sandstone shelves, and taking in the wonderful views across to the Georgina Point Lighthouse on Mayne Island and to Washington's Point Roberts and Mount Baker.

EXTENDING YOUR TRIP

If you walked here from Sturdies Bay, retrace your steps to Sturdies Bay Road and walk left 0.1 mile (0.15 km) to Sturdies Bay Trail, where you can hike 1.2 miles (2 km) to South Community Hall or take a connecting trail through Bluffs Park (Hike 73).

73 Bluffs Park

RATING/ DIFFICULTY	LOOP	ELEV GAIN/HIGH POINT
***/2	1.4 miles (2.2 km)	190 feet (58 m)/ 470 feet (143 m)

Map: NTS 092B14 Mayne Island; **Contact:** Galiano Island Parks and Recreation and Galiano Club; **Notes:** Smoking prohibited; **GPS:** N 48 52.207, W 123 20.496

Walk along a gentle trail across rolling grassy bluffs that rise more than 400 feet (122 m) above Active Pass. And admire showy spring flowers, majestic eagles perched in towering firs, and an inspiring view of emerald islands parted by sparkling channels. Stay for the sunset and return with an indelible memory.

GETTING THERE

From Tsawwassen or Swartz Bay, take a BC ferry to Sturdies Bay on Galiano Island. Drive 0.3 mile (0.5 km) on Sturdies Bay Road and turn left onto Burrill Road. Continue for 0.9 mile (1.4 km) and turn right onto Bluff Road. Proceed 1.3 miles (2.1 km), passing Bluffs Park viewpoint access road (alternative start), to a sharp bend in the road and the unsigned trailhead (elev. 360 ft/110 m). Parking is on the left.

ON THE TRAIL

Created with an initial gift to the people of Galiano Island in 1948 by residents Max and Marion Enke, Bluffs Park became the island's first nature preserve. Since expanded to 317 acres (128 ha), the popular park contains some of the biggest and oldest trees on the island as well as exceptional views of boat-busy Active Pass. There are several kilometers of trail within the park, allowing for a good day of exploration. This hike takes you along the bluffs' tops.

Four trails radiate from the trailhead. The trail south leads 0.3 mile (0.5 km), steeply dropping to Highland Road. The trail west heads 0.5 mile (0.8 km) through private property to Georgeson Bay Road (where you can continue to Mount Galiano, Hike 74). A trail takes off from across the road, traversing the heart of the park for about 1.5 miles (2.4 km) to

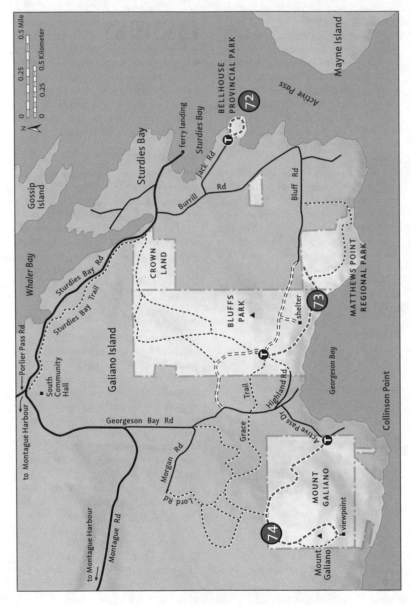

N

0   0.25   0.5 Mile

0   0.25   0.5 Kilometer

Mayne Island

Gossip Island

Whaler Bay

Sturdies Bay

ferry landing

Sturdies Bay

Jack Rd

BELLHOUSE
PROVINCIAL PARK

72

Active Pass

Burrill   Rd

Bluff Rd

to Montague Harbour

Porlier Pass Rd

Sturdies Bay Rd

Sturdies Bay Trail

CROWN
LAND

BLUFFS
PARK

shelter

73

MATTHEWS POINT
REGIONAL PARK

Galiano Island

South
Community
Hall

Trail

Highland Rd

Georgeson Bay

Collinson Point

Georgeson Bay Rd

Morgan Rd

Grace

Active Pass Dr

MOUNT
GALIANO

viewpoint

Lord Rd

74

Mount
Galiano

to Montague Harbour

Montague Rd

Bluffs Park offers good views of Active Pass.

connect with the Sturdies Bay Trail. You want the well-trodden path heading east and uphill.

Hike along the rocky and grassy bluffs through groves of ancient, towering Douglas fir. Scan the canopy for eagles and ravens. As you skirt the ledges and cliffs (use caution), the tree cover eventually thins, revealing good views north to Mount Galiano and west to Mayne Island's Helen Point jutting into shimmering waters. After climbing about 100 feet (30 m), gradually descend to a log shelter and soon afterward, at 0.4 mile (0.6 km), reach the overlook parking lot.

Continue past the lot along the bluff edge, enjoying views and flowers (in season) before coming to an abandoned house at 0.7 mile (1.1 km). Retrace your steps from here.

EXTENDING YOUR TRIP

From the abandoned house, unmarked and often rough trails continue across private property to undeveloped Matthews Point Regional Park. Save Matthews Point for a future trip, after official trails have been built (in the works). For now, consider hiking across the heart of Bluffs Park through mature forest, linking up with the Sturdies Bay Trail. From there, you can hike left 1.2 miles (2 km) to South Community Hall or right 0.5 mile (0.8 km) (mainly on road) to Sturdies Bay.

74 Mount Galiano

RATING/ DIFFICULTY	LOOP	ELEV GAIN/HIGH POINT
*****/3	3.8 miles (6.1 km)	1010 feet (308 m)/ 1020 feet (311 m)

Maps: NTS 092B14 Mayne Island; **Contact:** Galiano Island Parks and Recreation and Galiano Club; **Notes:** Smoking prohibited; **GPS:** N 48 51.903, W 123 21.166

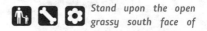 *Stand upon the open grassy south face of*

1119-foot (341-m) Mount Galiano and be dazzled by a maritime mural of islands, bays, passes, and mountains spread before you. Rising precipitously above vessel-plied Active Pass, Mount Galiano is one of the most recognized natural landmarks in the Gulf Islands—and it affords one of the islands' finest views too.

GETTING THERE

From Tsawwassen or Swartz Bay, take a BC ferry to Sturdies Bay on Galiano Island. Drive 1.8 miles (2.9 km) on Sturdies Bay Road and bear left onto Georgeson Bay Road (near South Community Hall). Continue for 1.8 miles (2.9 km), passing first the Park Place trailhead and then Grace trailhead (near Bluff Road), and turn right onto Active Pass Drive. Drive 0.3 mile (0.5 km) to the trailhead (elev. 110 ft/34 m).

ON THE TRAIL

There are four approaches to Galiano Island's highest mountain. Three of them traverse private land (with public easements) and have limited parking access. The trip described here is located entirely within the 200-acre (81-ha) Mount Galiano Nature Conservancy Area, which was targeted for protection in 1991 and is maintained by the Galiano Club, a civil and social service organization founded in 1924.

The trip to the summit is short but steep. On good tread, begin traversing through big firs and cedars and a few big stumps as well. At 0.6 mile (1 km), turn left onto an old skid road. Then immediately turn right, hiking now in much younger forest. At 1 mile (1.6 km), come to a junction (elev. 700 ft/213 m) with an old road turned trail. The way right leads to the trails coming up from Lord Park, Park Place, and the Grace trailhead.

Excellent views south of the Gulf Islands from Mount Galiano

Head left on a pleasant path, passing a wetland and staying left on the main trail at a junction at 1.4 miles (2.2 km). The unmaintained path right also leads toward the summit and can be used as an alternative return route. Gently climbing, crest a 1020-foot (311-m) high point (the trail doesn't directly go over the Galiano summit). Then descend 50 feet (15 m) and bend back around, reaching a junction at 1.8 miles (2.9 km) with the unmaintained trail, at a water tank.

Turn left and reach the trail's end in 0.1 mile (0.15 km), emerging at an oak-ringed grassy open bluff (elev. 1020 feet/ 311 m). Embrace the sun (it shines often here within the rainshadow), and savor the sweeping view—it's a Gulf Islands classic. Look south over Mayne, Saturna, North Pender, Prevost, Salt Spring, Princess Margaret, and Moresby islands, watching battalions of BC ferries and pleasure craft plying Satellite, Trincomali, and Swanson channels.

EXTENDING YOUR TRIP

For a return variation, retrace your steps 0.8 mile (1.3 km) to a junction and continue straight on an old road (now trail). Stay right at two junctions, passing through forest openings being overtaken by Scotch broom (a big problem on Galiano) and coming to another junction at 0.6 mile (1 km) from the prior junction. Either stay straight on the Grace Trail for 0.4 mile (0.6 km) to Georgeson Bay Road, or head left on the Alistair Ross Trail for 0.4 mile (0.6 km) to the Park Place trailhead. Then return to the main trailhead, hiking 0.4 mile (0.6 km) or 0.8 mile (1.3 km), respectively, via the road. Don't miss the short shoreline access trail to Georgeson Bay.

75 Galiano Island Heritage Forest

RATING/ DIFFICULTY	LOOP	ELEV GAIN/HIGH POINT
*/2	1.7 miles (2.8 km)	270 feet (82 m)/ 370 feet (112 m)

Maps: NTS 092B14 Mayne Island; **Contact:** Galiano Club; **Notes:** Dogs permitted on-leash; **GPS:** N 48 54.571, W 123 23.161

Walk some quiet old woods roads through recovering timberlands. Nothing remarkable here—just peaceful wanderings in a 312-acre (126 ha) community forest, newly withdrawn from development and now on its way to being sustainably managed. The resident deer appreciate it—you will too.

GETTING THERE

From Tsawwassen or Swartz Bay, take a BC ferry to Sturdies Bay on Galiano Island. Drive 1.8 miles (2.9 km) on Sturdies Bay Road and bear right onto Porlier Pass Road (near South Community Hall). Continue for 1 mile (1.6 km) and turn right onto Galiano Way. Drive 0.6 mile (1 km) and turn left onto Georgia View Road. Continue for 0.8 mile (1.3 km) to the road's end and trailhead (elev. 100 ft/30 m).

ON THE TRAIL

The community-based Galiano Club acquired this tract of cutover forest in 2005, with the promise of implementing sustainable forestry and recreational opportunities. The property borders the Strait of Georgia and Montague Harbour Marine Provincial Park, which all together create a protected swath across Galiano Island.

Begin by heading to the right on the Georgia View Trail—you'll be retuning from the left on the Mistletoe Main. Cross a creek and pass the Arbutus Main Trail, skirting homes and a lone big fir. At 0.6 mile (1 km), reach a junction.

The trail right leads to a trailhead on Sticks Allison Road and then continues 0.5 mile (0.8 km) to the coast just south of Cook Cove. You want to head left on the Alder Cut Trail, an old grassy skid road. Switchback up a ridge and bear right at a junction (elev. 245 ft/75 m) at 0.8 mile (1.3 km). The Arbutus

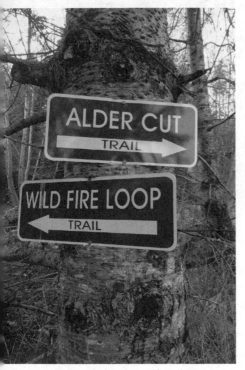

Well-marked junction at the Galiano Community Forest

Main Trail (left) drops back down to the Georgia View Trail.

The grade steepens before the way leaves the skid road to traverse a young alder grove. Continue through cutover lands, catching window views of the Strait of Georgia, Point Roberts, Roberts Banks, and the Coast and Cascade ranges. Reach an elevation of 370 feet (112 m) and start descending. Stay left at an unmarked junction and at 1.2 miles (2 km), reach a junction with the Wildfire Loop just past a big lone fir. Continue straight, descending an open slope and coming to the Wildfire Loop once more in 0.2 mile (0.3 km). The trailhead lies 0.3 mile (0.5 km) straight ahead.

EXTENDING YOUR TRIP
Lengthen your loop by 0.6 mile (1 km) by taking the Wildfire Loop through a burnt and broom-filled landscape back to the Mistletoe Main. Add a trip to the coast by following the Sticks Trail for 0.3 mile (0.5 km) through a wooded corridor.

76 Gray Peninsula

RATING/ DIFFICULTY	LOOP	ELEV GAIN/HIGH POINT
****/1	1.5 miles (2.4 km)	Minimal/20 feet (6 m)

Maps: NTS 092B14 Mayne Island, park map online; **Contact:** BC Parks, Montague Harbour Marine Provincial Park; **Notes:** Dogs permitted on-leash; **GPS:** N 48 54 012, W 123 24.393

 *Amble around a small peninsula that juts into the protected waters of Montague Harbour, and see how many*

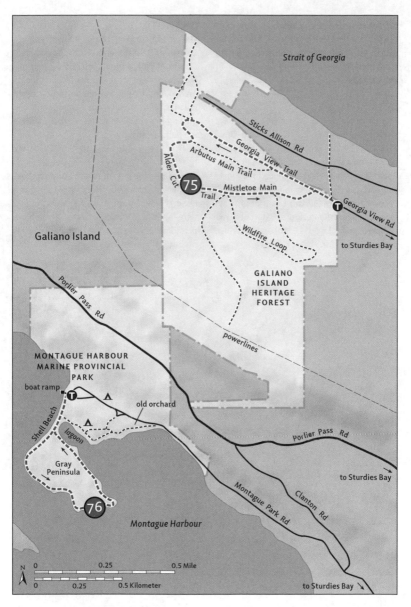

different birds you can identify. Marvel at big firs and gnarled arbutuses. And swoon over a gorgeous snowy-white-shell beach that may have you feeling like you're in the Caribbean.

GETTING THERE

From Tsawwassen or Swartz Bay, take a BC ferry to Sturdies Bay on Galiano Island. Drive 1.8 miles (2.9 km) on Sturdies Bay Road and bear left onto Georgeson Bay Road (near South Community Hall). Continue for 0.8 mile (1.3 km) and turn right onto Montague Road. Follow it for 2 miles (3.2 km), bearing right onto Montague Park Road. Proceed through the campground for 1 mile (1.6 km) to the day-use parking area and trailhead. Privy available.

ON THE TRAIL

One of the crown jewels of the Gulf Islands, 240-acre (97-ha) Montague Harbour Marine Provincial Park protects a lagoon, peninsula, old-growth forest, and several outstanding archeological sites, as well as some rugged uplands. With its spacious campground and inviting beaches, Montague Harbour Marine is a popular park.

Find the trail leading to Gray Peninsula near the boat launch. The peninsula is named not for the American sea merchant captain of Columbia River fame, but for a lesser-known Captain Gray who settled here in the 1890s and cultivated an orchard, providing fruit to Victoria. Remnants of his orchard still remain.

A midden beach on Gray Peninsula

WHAT'S IN A NAME?

The Salish Sea region comprises the traditional lands of the Coast Salish people (encompassing Native American tribes and First Nations bands that share linguistic and cultural origins), but the term Salish Sea wasn't officially recognized until 2009 in the United States and 2010 in Canada. It now refers to the vast network of coastal waterways in southwest British Columbia and northwest Washington, most notably Puget Sound, the Strait of Juan de Fuca, and the Strait of Georgia.

Many of the island names in the Salish Sea, however, reflect very little of the heritage of the Coast Salish peoples and very much of the European and American explorers of the 1700s and 1800s. The name San Juan was bestowed to that group of islands by Spanish explorer Francisco de Eliza in 1791. In 1792, British Captain George Vancouver bestowed the name Gulf of Georgia (later changed to Strait of Georgia) on the waterway separating Vancouver Island from British Columbia's Lower Mainland, mistaking the strait for a gulf—hence the name Gulf Islands.

Vancouver and later US Navy Lieutenant Charles Wilkes both began replacing Spanish names with English names. In 1841, Wilkes renamed scores of features in the San Juans, many after his crew and American heroes of the War of 1812. Some of these names stuck; some slipped away and the places reverted to their Spanish names.

Still another wave of naming in the Salish Sea occurred in 1859–60, when Admiral Richards, a hydrographer of the British Admiralty, set sail on the HMS *Plumper* on a survey mission. Of course, First Nations and Native American names haven't vanished. Many tribal and band members still refer to Salish Sea features by their original names and the now-official name Salish Sea honors this heritage.

Climb a small bluff and then descend a stairway to a narrow berm that separates a muddy lagoon from gleaming white and appropriately named Shell Beach. Native people occupied this spot for more than three thousand years, creating a midden. The white beach is the result of waves crushing and eroding discarded oyster, clam, mussel, and abalone shells. There are several middens in the park.

Continue hiking, coming to a junction in 0.3 mile (0.5 km). Stay right and round the peninsula, traveling beneath a thick canopy, compliments of stately ancient firs and gnarly mature arbutuses. Enjoy good views out to Wise and Parker islands and Mounts Galiano and Sutil across the calm waters of Montague Harbour. Look for ledges carved into rippling patterns by receding glaciers long ago. Pass beneath some unsightly power lines and by some more attractive beaches.

Coming full circle, the trail skirts the lagoon again, offering excellent bird-watching—especially during low tides. At 1.3 miles (2.1 km), reach a familiar junction. Turn right to return to your vehicle or lounge at Shell Beach.

EXTENDING YOUR TRIP

Follow another 0.6 mile (1 km) of trail along the lagoon to a small spit and then through the campground to another midden beach by the old orchard.

77 Pebble Beach Reserve

RATING/ DIFFICULTY	LOOP	ELEV GAIN/HIGH POINT
***/2	2.1 miles (3.4 km)	260 feet (79 m)/ 260 feet (79 m)

Map: NTS 092B14 Mayne Island; **Contact:** Galiano Conservancy Association, Pebble Beach Reserve; **Notes:** Dogs permitted on-leash; **GPS:** N 48 56.575, W 123 29.433

Hike through primeval forest to two beaches tucked along a wild stretch of the Strait of Georgia, offering insights into what Galiano Island looked like before industrial logging and vacation home subdivisions. Warm currents, compliments of the Fraser River, may invite you to stop for a swim. En route, explore the Great Beaver Swamp and contemplate further explorations to Laughlin Lake, Galiano's largest inland body of water.

GETTING THERE

From Tsawwassen or Swartz Bay, take a BC ferry to Sturdies Bay on Galiano Island. Drive 1.8 miles (2.9 km) on Sturdies Bay Road and bear right onto Porlier Pass Road (near South Community Hall). Continue for 7.8 miles (12.5 km) and turn right onto McCoskrie Road (near the firehouse). Proceed 0.3 mile (0.5 km) (bearing left at 0.2 mi/0.3 km) to the trailhead (elev. 260 ft/79 m).

ON THE TRAIL

Consisting of Crown and Galiano Conservancy lands, this 336-acre (135-ha) preserve was saved from clear-cutting and development in 1998. This preserve has historical significance too—this narrowest part of the

island served as a portage from Retreat Cove to Pebble Beach for First Nations peoples on their trips from Vancouver Island to the Fraser River delta.

You'll be returning on the old road-trail that's straight ahead, so start hiking on the old skid-road-turned-trail to the right. Walk the wide path through ancient cedars and Douglas firs, soon coming to a crossing of Beaver Creek, which flows out of the Great Beaver Swamp, one of the largest wetlands on the island. The trail now borders the swamp. Look for mink, otter, and beaver.

At 0.5 mile (0.8 km), come to a junction. The old skid road continues straight, eventually entering private property. Turn left here onto bona fide trail, entering a dark mixed-age forest and slowly descending to the sea. At 1 mile (1.6 km), reach a junction. The short spur right leads to Pebble Beach, with its smooth and pulverized pebbly shore strewn with big driftwood logs—a lovely spot to hang out before continuing the loop.

The trail goes north across mossy openings and through groves of mist-dripping big trees, alongside a wild shoreline of wave-battered sandstone shelves. Look out to sea for pelagic birds and up in the trees for bald eagles. At 1.5 miles (2.4 km), the trail reaches Cable Bay with its inviting beach. The trail resumes at the far end of the beach, near a communication-cable line. An old road leads right, through private property that would make a nice addition to this preserve, protecting the wild coastline north of the bay.

You want to follow the old road-trail that heads west and uphill. At 1.8 miles (2.9 km), cross Beaver Creek and continue uphill, now paralleling the creek. The way soon follows the cable line and passes an interpretive trail, which heads toward Laughlin Lake. At 2.1 miles (3.4 km), return to the trailhead.

Dramatic Strait of Georgia shoreline between Cable Bay and Pebble Beach

EXTENDING YOUR TRIP

Consider extending your hike to Laughlin Lake. From the trailhead, follow the old road-trail north, uphill. At 0.2 mile (0.3 km), pass a junction with the interpretive trail, which winds 0.3 mile (0.5 km) through scrappy forest back to the trail coming up from Cable Bay. Soon afterward, pass a dilapidated cabin and crest a 340-ft (104-m) ridge. Descend 50 feet (15 m) and then start climbing again, passing an old logging road on the left. Reach an old gravel pit and a junction with the Bell Trail (which leads through private land to Porlier Pass Road and public access to Retreat Cove). Continue north, crossing Vineyard Way and entering the Laughlin Lake Preserve. The trail crosses a bridge and ends at 0.9 mile (1.4 km), at a point jutting into the small lake (elev. 320 ft/98 m). Look for mammal and avian activity. Trumpeter swans frequent these waters in the winter months.

78 Bodega Ridge Provincial Park

RATING/ DIFFICULTY	ROUNDTRIP	ELEV GAIN/HIGH POINT
*****/3	2.8 miles (4.6 km)	430 feet (131 m)/ 830 feet (253 m)

Maps: NTS 092B13 Duncan, NTS 092B14 Mayne Island; **Contact:** BC Parks, Bodega Ridge Provincial Park; **Notes:** Dogs permitted on-leash; **GPS:** N 48 56.967, W 123 30.750

The view from Bodega Ridge is simply bodacious. Walk along sandstone

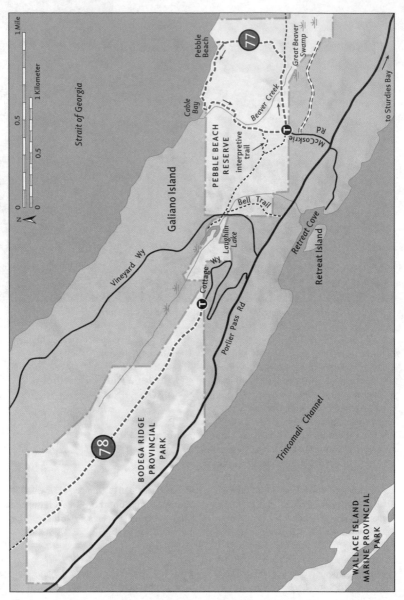

cliffs, taking in breathtaking views of Trincomali Channel, Vancouver Island, Salt Spring Island, and scads of scattered smaller islands. Bodega's vegetation is pretty impressive too—stately Garry oaks, ledge-creeping manzanitas, and wind-blown mature firs.

GETTING THERE

From Tsawwassen or Swartz Bay, take a BC ferry to Sturdies Bay on Galiano Island. Drive 1.8 miles (2.9 km) on Sturdies Bay Road and bear right onto Porlier Pass Road (near South Community Hall). Continue for 8.7 miles (14 km) and turn right onto Cottage Way (just past Vineyard Way), proceeding 1 mile (1.6 km) to the trailhead (elev. 440 ft/134 m).

ON THE TRAIL

Although it sounds like a winery, Bodega Ridge is named for Captain Juan Francisco de le Bodega y Quadra, a Peruvian-born Spanish naval officer and explorer who sailed the Salish Sea in the late 1700s. The captain became friends (despite conflicting interests) with George Vancouver, and British Columbia's largest island shared both of their names at one time.

From the trailhead, immediately enter the 576-acre (233-ha) provincial park, established in the 1990s, saving this ridge from clear-cut logging. The way starts out on wide trail, gradually ascending through open grassy Douglas fir forest. At 0.4 mile (0.6 km), reach an opening and your first view. Invasive broom is a problem here, threatening some of the park's rare native plants.

Continue climbing and crest a small knoll at 0.6 mile (1 km). Lose a few vertical meters and resume upward mobility, once again reaching a clifftop. Using caution, gingerly walk across the open ledge, admiring a stunning view west of Trincomali Channel, long and slender Wallace Island, rolling Salt Spring Island, First Nations Penelakut Island, and a

A turkey vulture catches a thermal above Bodega Ridge.

slew of smaller islands: Secretary, Norway, and Half to name a few. Views are good to the north too, to sparsely populated Valdes Island and countless mountains on Vancouver Island.

Admire the manzanita clutching the ledges. And watch diving peregrine falcons and thermal-riding ravens, turkey vultures, and eagles. Eventually come to an 830-ft (253-m) high point near the park's northern boundary, at 1.4 miles (2.3 km). Beyond, the trail drops, becomes more rugged, and traverses private property. Turn around here.

EXTENDING YOUR TRIP
The Bodega Ridge Trail continues for about another 1.2 miles (2 km) across private property, intersecting Manastee Road and then reaching Cook Road near an ecological preserve in another 0.6 mile (1 km). Request permission to hike this section from the nearby Bodega Ridge Resort.

79 Dionisio Point Provincial Park

RATING/ DIFFICULTY	LOOP	ELEV GAIN/HIGH POINT
****/2	3.3 miles (5.3 km)	180 feet (55 m)/ 180 feet (55 m)

Map: NTS 092G04 Nanaimo; **Contact:** BC Parks, Dionisio Point Provincial Park, and Penelakut First Nation (for overland access); **Notes:** Dogs permitted on-leash. Road to park is closed due to contentious access issues with property owners. Hikers must gain permission from landowners to hike or bike private roads to the park, or ask permission to use the Penelakut First Nation trail. Water access should be attempted by experienced paddlers only due to challenging conditions in Porlier Pass; **GPS:** N 49 00.734, W 123 34.435

Honeycomb ledges, wild *coastline of sculpted sandstone shelves, seals basking on reefs, a bird-rich lagoon, midden beaches, and quiet bays facing the turbulent waters of Porlier Pass—Dionisio Point at the northern tip of Galiano Island is a magical place. And with no auto access, it's a pretty quiet place too. Hike along the Strait of Georgia, sharing the surf with very few human souls but scores of scoters and oystercatchers.*

GETTING THERE
Experienced paddlers can access this hike at Coon Bay. Seek permission for overland access from private landowners or the Penelakut First Nation.

ON THE TRAIL
Assuming you arrived by sea, start your hike from the delightful beach on Coon Bay. Before heading south, make the mandatory 0.2-mile (0.3-km) side trip via a tombolo to Dionisio Point. The point, like the island, is named for Commander Dionisio Alcalá Galiano, a distinguished Spanish explorer who was the first European to circumnavigate Vancouver Island. Galiano died at age forty-five in the Battle of Trafalgar.

From the point, admire big oaks and excellent views north to Valdes Island and east across the Strait of Georgia to snowy mainland mountains. Retrace your steps, pass the beach, and come to a junction. The Porlier Pass Trail (your return) veers right, to Maple Bay. Stay left, skirting Parry Lagoon and its campground equipped with water (in season) and privies.

At 0.2 mile (0.3 km) from Coon Bay, reach a large parking area at the end of a dirt road, which may someday offer vehicle

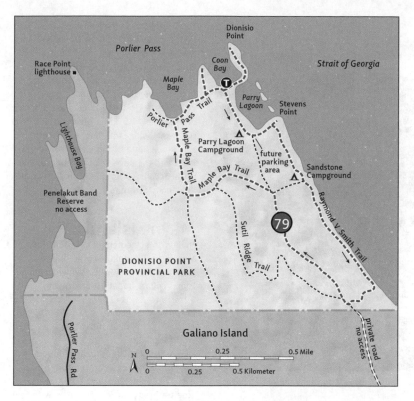

Dionisio
Point

Porlier Pass

Coon
Bay

Strait of Georgia

Race Point
lighthouse ■

Maple
Bay

Porlier Pass Trail

T

Parry
Lagoon

Stevens
Point

Lighthouse Bay

Maple Bay Trail

Parry Lagoon
Campground

future
parking
area

Sandstone
Campground

Maple Bay Trail

Penelakut Band
Reserve
no access

Raymond V. Smith Trail

79

Sutil Ridge Trail

DIONISIO POINT
PROVINCIAL PARK

Galiano Island

Porlier Pass Rd.

private road
no access

N

0   0.25   0.5 Mile

0   0.25   0.5 Kilometer

access to this park. Much of this 351-acre (142-ha) park was given to the province in 1991 by MacMillan Bloedel when it began divesting its timber holdings on the island. The point has had a long human history, from First Nations camps to fishing cottages to hippie commune.

Walk the dirt road a few steps and turn left onto the Stevens Point Trail, reaching a junction in 0.1 mile (0.15 km). First head left 250 feet (80 m) to oak-harboring Stevens Point. Scan Parry Lagoon for birds. Black oystercatchers are among the many species that nest here.

Retrace your steps to the junction and head south on the Raymond V. Smith Trail, named for the former CEO of MacMillan Bloedel who donated this land. In 0.3 mile (0.5 km), reach the Sandstone Campground and a junction with a trail that leads west to the dirt road. Continue south on a trail lined with kinnikinnick through pine and arbutus groves, above sculpted sandstone headlands. Savor the sound of the pounding surf and marvel at the far-reaching view across the strait. The trail ends in 1 mile (1.6 km) at the dirt road (elev. 120 ft/37 m) near the park boundary.

Honeycombed sandstone along Parry Lagoon

in 0.1 mile (0.15 km) reach an old road. Turn right here and pick up the Maple Bay Trail, gradually descending to Maple Bay and the Porlier Pass Trail in 0.3 mile (0.5 km).

After exploring the midden beach, follow Porlier Pass Trail east, passing an interpretive kiosk and coming to a junction in 0.3 mile (0.5 km). Hike the 0.1-mile (0.15-km) side trip left to honeycomb sandstone ledges for views to Dionisio Point and the Race Point lighthouse. Then retrace your steps and turn left at the junction to return to Coon Bay.

Mayne Island

Named for Lieutenant Richard Charles Mayne by Captain George Richards of the Royal Navy HMS *Plumper*, quiet Mayne Island counts about 1100 residents on its 8.1 square miles (21 sq. km). During the Fraser Canyon gold rush of 1858–60, Miners Bay on the island flourished as a supply stop for miners en route from Vancouver Island. Miners Bay continued booming into the late 1800s as a transportation hub. It is still the commercial center of the island, albeit a pretty mellow one, now with few establishments.

The island has a few parks, a small unit of the Gulf Islands National Park Reserve, and many public beach access trails. The Mayne Island Conservancy (www.conservancyon mayne.com) fosters harmony between nature and community and is involved with trail and conservation issues.

BC Ferries offers year-round service from Tsawwassen and Swartz Bay to Village Bay on the island. There are no public camping areas on Mayne, but Mayne Island Eco Camping Tours and Charters (www .mayneislandcamping.com) has nice sites.

Turn right and follow the dirt road. The Sutil Ridge Trail takes off from the other side of the road here and can be used for a loop return, but it's not regularly maintained and can be brushy. Stick with the road and after 0.4 mile (0.6 km), reach a junction. The way straight ahead continues back to Coon Bay. Right leads to the Sandstone Campground. Follow the Maple Bay Trail left.

Through deep forest, gradually ascend, passing the easy-to-miss Sutil Ridge Trail and then shortly afterward reaching another junction in 0.3 mile (0.5 km) from the three-way junction. Bear right, soon cross a creek, and

80 Mount Parke

RATING/ DIFFICULTY	LOOP	ELEV GAIN/HIGH POINT
***/3	2.6 miles (4.2 km)	445 feet (136 m)/ 620 feet (189 m)

Map: NTS 092B14 Mayne Island; **Contact:** Capital Regional District Parks, Mount Parke Regional Park; **Notes:** Dogs permitted on-leash; **GPS:** N 48 50.603, W 123 16.774

Hike a ridge high on Mount Parke, the main peak on Mayne Island. It's one of the best places to see how the Ice Age glaciers shaped the Salish Sea. Look out upon straits and passes and the lumpy bumpy ramped-and-plucked topography of the Gulf Islands. It's a pretty and serene scene.

GETTING THERE

From Tsawwassen or Swartz Bay, take a BC ferry to Village Bay on Mayne Island. Follow Village Bay Road for 1.4 miles (2.3 km) and turn right onto Fernhill Road. After 1 mile (1.6 km), turn right onto Montrose Road. Drive 0.2 mile (0.3 km) to the trailhead (elev. 175 ft/53 m). Bike rack available.

ON THE TRAIL

Three contiguous parks consisting of 160 acres (65 ha) make up what is collectively referred to as Mount Parke. However, the summit remains private property. The way starts on an old road, traversing an impressive old-growth grove of cedars and skirting a small wetland pool. At 0.3 mile (0.5 km), come to a four-way junction, complete with a privy. You'll be returning from straight ahead, part of the Lowland Nature Trail

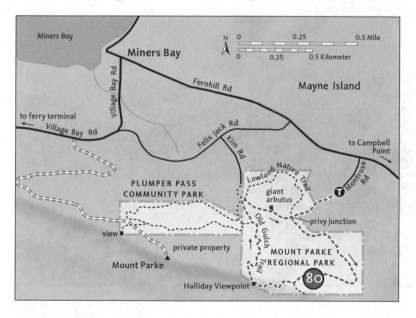

(which continues right). For Mount Parke, head left on well-trodden tread through mossy, dank second growth.

The way eventually steepens, reaching Parke's eastern ridge. At 1.2 miles (1.9 km), come to a junction (elev. 510 ft/155 m). The trail left leads through open forest with some limited views, eventually petering out. Continue right, winding through big Douglas firs to the Halliday Viewpoint (elev. 620 ft/189 m) at 1.4 miles (2.3 km), on a mossy open ledge. Enjoy the views southeast: Vulture Ridge, Saint John Point, Samuel Island, and Mounts Elford and Warburton Pike on Saturna Island. But for the water, the rounded ridges call the Appalachians to mind. There are good views west too of Salt Spring and Pender islands. Watch for eagles and turkey vultures. In spring enjoy pretty floral arrangements. An interpretive sign helps you identify the surrounding landmarks.

Continue your hike, coming to a junction at 1.5 miles (2.4 miles). The trail left soon enters private property, leading to the towered and helipad-draped 863-ft (263-m) summit of Mount Parke. Your way goes right on the Old Gulch Trail, descending steeply into a dark gulch shaded by big, old fire-scarred firs and cedars. At 1.9 miles (3.1 km), reach a junction with a short connecting trail leading left to the Plumper Pass Loop.

Continue straight, coming to a five-way junction (elev. 300 ft/91 m) at 2.1 miles (3.4 km). Left goes to the Plumper Pass Loop. Straight goes 0.1 mile (0.15 km) to the Kim Road trailhead. Right is the beginning of the Lowland Nature Trail. And directly right is your route back to the trailhead. Take it, passing a giant arbutus and returning to "privy junction" at 2.3 miles (3.7 km). Then

Looking south to Plumper Sound

HONORING A LEGACY: MAYNE ISLAND'S JAPANESE CANADIANS

In 1900 Gontaro Kadonaga arrived on Mayne Island and purchased a 160-acre (65-ha) farm. He was the first Japanese settler on the island. Many more Japanese would come, becoming part of the social and economic fabric of the island, particularly in fishing and farming. By 1940 one-third of the island's population was of Japanese ancestry.

But by the end of 1942, all Japanese Canadians on the island were relocated to an internment camp in New Denver, British Columbia, in the Rockies. Their property was expropriated. As in the United States, the Canadian government in the midst of World War II violated the rights of its own citizens and interned a people based on their heritage, one of the most shameful acts for both of these great nations.

The non-Japanese population of Mayne Island appealed the internment but to no avail. Many of the families never returned after the war, but sixty years later at Dinner Bay, on the site of a former Japanese Canadian orchard, a 5-acre (2-ha) Japanese garden to honor the Japanese legacy on Mayne Island was built. It's well worth a visit.

---

continue forward, reaching your starting point at 2.6 miles (4.2 km).

EXTENDING YOUR TRIP

Hike the rest of the Lowland Nature Trail, adding an easy 0.5 mile (0.8 km) to your total. Or get a better workout on the 1.4-mile (2.3-km) Plumper Pass Loop, which climbs more than 250 feet (76 m) along the backside of Mount Parke. A 0.1-mile (0.15-km) spur leads off of it to a limited viewpoint at the park's boundary.

81 Henderson Community Park

RATING/ DIFFICULTY	LOOP	ELEV GAIN/HIGH POINT
**/2	0.8 mile (1.3 km)	300 feet (91 m)/ 480 feet (146 m)

Map: NTS 092B14 Mayne Island; **Contact:** Mayne Island Conservancy Society, Henderson Community Park; **Notes:** Dogs permitted on-leash; **GPS:** N 48 49.608, W 123 15.905

Hoof up a small ridge in this pocket park that protects rare oak habitat and is packed with excellent views of Salt Spring and Pender islands. Watch for raptors and ravens riding thermals, and learn about the species at risk that live in this threatened coastal Douglas fir–Garry oak ecosystem.

GETTING THERE

From Tsawwassen or Swartz Bay, take a BC ferry to Village Bay on Mayne Island. Follow Village Bay Road for 1.4 miles (2.3 km) and turn right onto Fernhill Road. After 1.1 miles (1.8 km), turn right onto Horton Bay Road and continue for 2.1 miles (3.4 km), bearing right onto Beechwood Drive. Proceed 1.4 miles (2.3 km) to the road's end at the trailhead (elev. 180 ft/55 m). Privy available.

ON THE TRAIL

Wedged between subdivisions and occupying recovering cutover lands, this 25-acre (10-ha) park is easy to overlook. However, the Mayne Island Conservancy Society has developed a

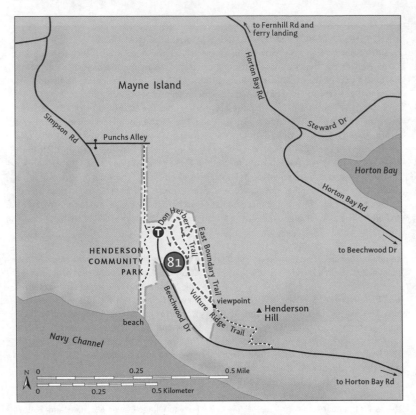

trail network within the park, complete with a glossy interpretive pamphlet. Plus, there's an adjacent trail to Navy Channel allowing for an extended outing.

Grab your interpretive brochure and head right on the Vulture Ridge Trail, immediately coming to the Don Herbert Trail, your return route. Continue straight on narrow steep tread working your way up a sandstone ledge. At 0.15 mile (0.2 km), come to the east end of the Don Herbert Trail. Stay right, hiking along ridgetop through oaks, taking in growing views over Navy Channel.

At 0.3 mile (0.5 km), reach a junction with the East Boundary Trail near a spectacular viewpoint (elev. 480 ft/146 m). Look out over sparkling waters to Pender Island and to Mount Maxwell and Bruce Mountain on Salt Spring Island.

The trail continues for 0.3 mile (0.5 km), steeply dropping (complete with a rope to aid descent) to Beechwood Road, 0.5 mile (0.8 km) from the main trailhead. Better to return on the East Boundary Trail. Pass the misspelled trail sign and hike through an old cut that grants views to Mount Parke and farms in the valley below. At 0.6 mile (1 km), come to the Don Herbert Trail (elev. 300 ft/91 m). The way left climbs 0.1 mile (0.15 km) back to Vulture Ridge. Go right, returning to the trailhead in 0.2 mile (0.3 km).

EXTENDING YOUR TRIP
From the trailhead, head west 300 yards (300 m) to a junction. Right goes 0.3 mile (0.5 km) to Punchs Alley. Left goes 0.3 mile (0.5 km) through a cedar grove, dropping to a small rocky beach. The trail borders a farm with an electric fence—keep dogs and children close to you. Consider the nearby 0.4 mile (0.6 km) trail to Kadonga Bay too; the trailhead is 1.1 miles (1.8 km) east of Henderson Community Park.

82 Campbell Point

RATING/ DIFFICULTY	ROUNDTRIP	ELEV GAIN/HIGH POINT
****/1	1 mile (1.6 km)	Minimal/40 feet (12 m)

Map: NTS 092B14 Mayne Island; **Contact:** Gulf Islands National Park Reserve, Bennett Bay; **Notes:** Dogs permitted on-leash; **GPS:** N 48 50.821, W 123 15.156

Navy Channel from Vulture Ridge

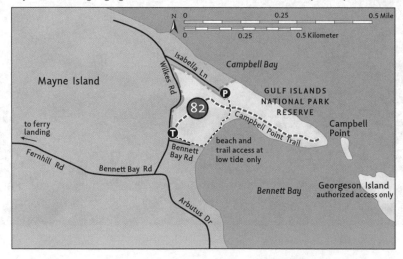

Walk under a canopy of firs and arbutuses on a little sandstone-shelved peninsula, taking in views of the bay and strait. Watch playful otters, preying eagles, and a panoply of pelagic birds plying the sea. Then walk along one of the prettiest beaches in the Gulf Islands.

GETTING THERE

From Tsawwassen or Swartz Bay, take a BC ferry to Village Bay on Mayne Island. Follow Village Bay Road for 1.4 miles (2.3 km) and turn right onto Fernhill Road. Continue for 2 miles (3.2 km), staying straight on Bennett Bay Road. At 0.2 mile (0.3 km), turn left onto Wilkes Road and drive 0.1 mile (0.15 km) to the trailhead.

ON THE TRAIL

The Bennett Bay unit of the Gulf Islands National Park Reserve is a mere 23 acres (9 ha). But you can easily spend half a day here combing a gorgeous beach and watching wildlife and the world go by from Campbell Point.

From the parking area, walk an old road-turned-trail 0.2 mile (0.3 km) through tall timber to a junction complete with privy. Left goes a short distance to an alternative trailhead on Isabella Lane. Right drops to the beach—your return route if the tide is low.

Keep hiking straight on an old woods road through mature firs and arbutuses, reaching Campbell Point at 0.5 mile (0.8 km). Admire junipers and oaks and, in springtime, beautiful flowers. Then cast your eyes across the Strait of Georgia to Point Roberts and the Cascades, across Campbell Bay to Edith Point, and across the waters just in front of you to reefs and the ecologically rich Georgeson Island. Look too across Bennett Bay to Samuel and Saturna islands.

Retrace your steps 0.3 mile (0.5 km) to the junction—and if the tide is low, go left, taking a staircase down to the beach on Bennett Bay. Walk the beach 0.1 mile (0.15 km) to the boat

Saturna was named by Dionisio Alcalá Galiano for the Spanish naval schooner *Santa Saturnina* piloted by José María Narváez, who explored the area in 1791. Nearly half of the island's 12 square miles (31 sq. km) is protected within the Gulf Islands National Park Reserve (GINPR).

Travel amenities are limited to a general store, a pub, café, and a handful of lodging options. There is a small walk-in and boat-in seasonal campground (no water, 7 sites) at Narvaez Bay.

83 Winter Cove

RATING/ DIFFICULTY	LOOP	ELEV GAIN/HIGH POINT
**/1	0.9 mile (1.5 km)	30 feet (9 m)/ 30 feet (9 m)

Map: NTS 092B14 Mayne Island; **Contact:** Gulf Islands National Park Reserve, Winter Cove; **Notes:** Dogs permitted on-leash; **GPS:** N 48 48.574, W 123 11.322

Georgeson Island off Campbell Point

launch. Then turn right and walk a short distance on Bennett Bay Road to a short path back to the parking lot.

Saturna Island

Easternmost of the Gulf Islands, Saturna is surrounded by US waters on three sides. It is mountainous, heavily forested, lightly populated, and one of the wilder of the larger islands. About 350 folks live on Saturna year-round. BC Ferries offers year-round service from Tsawwassen and Swartz Bay to Lyall Harbour. Bicyclists will find the island's narrow and hilly roads challenging, but traffic is extremely light.

This short hike is full of surprises. A well-groomed trail leads through a diverse landscape alongside the protected waters of Winter Cove to the turbulent waters of Boat Pass and the wide-open Strait of Georgia. The views are good across the cove and across the strait. The bird-watching is even better.

GETTING THERE

From Tsawwassen or Swartz Bay, take a BC ferry to Lyall Harbour on Saturna Island. Follow East Point Road for 3 miles (4.8 km) and turn left onto Winter Cove Road. Drive in 0.2 mile (0.3 km) to the trailhead (elev. 20 ft/6 m). Privy available.

Narrow Boat Pass between Saturna and Samuel islands

ON THE TRAIL

A former provincial park and now a unit of the Gulf Islands National Park Reserve, Winter Cove is popular with boaters (there's a good dock) and with local hikers. From the trailhead, follow the wide and near-level trail, soon coming to a junction. You return from the right, so continue left onto a boardwalk across a marshy area rife with avian activity. Notice the plant diversity—cedar, juniper, hawthorn, rose—and unfortunately the invasive Scotch broom. Notice the good views of Winter Cove too.

At 0.2 mile (0.3 km), come to another junction. The trail right connects to your return route and offers a shorter hiking option. Continue straight, coming to another marsh and boardwalk and at 0.4 mile (0.6 km), another junction. The short spur left leads to an overlook above Boat Pass, a tight gap separating Saturna Island from Samuel Island. During outgoing tides, the current can be quite strong here, making this a potentially dangerous gap for boaters, especially paddlers. The rocky outcroppings flanking the pass sport an array of spring

JOINING THE LIKES OF BANFF: GULF ISLANDS NATIONAL PARK RESERVE

On May 9, 2003, the Gulf Islands National Park Reserve (GINPR) became Canada's fortieth national park. Protecting one of the most ecologically at-risk natural regions in the country, the park consists of 9000 acres (3642 ha) of land and marine area scattered over fifteen islands and numerous islets and reefs. The park protects rare Garry oak forests (at its northernmost limit), marine and shorebird habitat, several species at risk (endangered species), and cultural and historical sites. The park also provides exceptional recreation opportunities: boating, hiking, camping, whale- and bird-watching, and educational programs.

Incorporating the transfer of several provincial properties, this new park also acquired many tracts of land through purchase. Park units on Saturna, Pender, and Mayne islands are ferry accessible, while other units can only be reached by private boat or water taxi. Park headquarters as well as a large campground are located in Sidney on the Saanich Peninsula. Most of the park's trails are covered within this book.

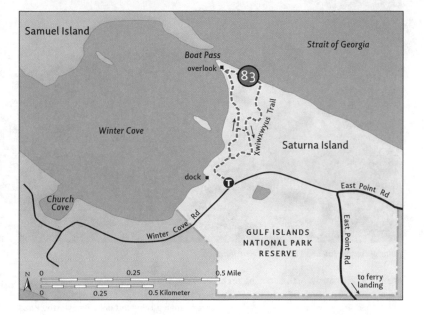

and summer flowers. Bird-watching is good here too—eagles and guillemots galore.

To head back, follow the trail along the Strait of Georgia, stopping to admire views of the mainland and to read interpretive signs. The shoreline here is mostly sandstone shelf and reefs. Binoculars will come in handy for spotting marine life on Anniversary Islet, just offshore. The trail turns back into the forest and comes to the shortcut trail junction at 0.7 mile (1.1 km). Continue straight, soon returning to the first junction—head left and reach the trailhead shortly afterward.

EXTENDING YOUR TRIP
The sandstone, shale, and midden beach at Winter Cove can be walked at low tide, but do not access it by cutting across marsh

from the trail. Reach it from the picnic area near the trailhead instead. An excellent stretch of sandstone shoreline along the Strait of Georgia can be walked at low tide just east of Boat Pass. Find parking and access on East Point Road, 0.6 mile (1 km) east of the junction with Winter Cove Road.

84 Taylor Point

RATING/ DIFFICULTY	ROUNDTRIP	ELEV GAIN/HIGH POINT
****/4	5.6 miles (9 km)	1100 feet (335 m)/ 365 feet (111 m)

Map: NTS 092B14 Mayne Island; **Contact:** Gulf Islands National Park Reserve, Taylor Point; **Notes:** Trail is rough, difficult to follow in spots, can be treacherous. Experienced

Ruins of George Taylor's 1892 sandstone home

off-trail travelers only. Active farming area. Dogs must be on-leash; **GPS:** N 48 46.250, W 123 10.934

![icons] *Hike along a spectacular coastal strip—one of the longest wild stretches in the Gulf Islands— to the ruins of an old stone house, old quarries, and an isolated beach along Plumper Sound. Parks Canada has yet to build an official trail: please exercise extreme caution, respect this fragile environment, and do not trespass onto the adjacent private Campbell Farm.*

GETTING THERE

From Tsawwassen or Swartz Bay, take a BC ferry to Lyall Harbour on Saturna Island. Follow East Point Road for 1 mile (1.6 km) and bear right onto Narvaez Bay Road. Immediately turn right (near the store and recycle center) onto Harris Road. Drive 1.6 miles (2.6 km) on this very steep road, coming to the Saturna Island Family Estate Winery. Proceed, bearing left in 0.1 mile (0.15 km) and then turning left onto Trueworthy Road in another 0.1 mile (0.15 km). Drive this road 0.7 mile (1.1 km) to its end and the trailhead (elev. 180 ft /55 m).

ON THE TRAIL

An unofficial but somewhat defined path traverses this park coastal strip to Taylor Point. The route stumbles up and over and around jumbled sandstone blocks and ledges, gaining and losing considerable elevation with the many ups and downs. It's easy to lose the way and the terrain can be dangerous.

To start, walk past the park kiosk and climb a small bluff before turning right and descending a short way. Then clamber up and over fractured sandstone blocks and cliffs, with occasional views across Plumper Sound to South Pender and Stuart islands. Cross several creeks and pass old-growth

Douglas firs (many with old burn scars), oaks, and arbutuses. Be careful not to follow the paths created by the area's feral goats. And keep alert for them, as they are commonly sighted here.

At 1 mile (1.6 km), pass an old cabin (elev. 365 ft/111 m) and shortly afterward a swinging fence gate. At about 1.4 miles (2.3 km), stay left; be careful not to take a well-defined path dropping to the right to steep cliffs at Murder Point (where a settler father and daughter were murdered by two Natives in 1863). Now traverse jumbled ledges above the point and steeply descend into a creek-cradling ravine (elev. 160 ft/49 m). Climb 80 feet (24 m) out of the ravine and

drop into another one. Bear left in the second ravine, eventually emerging into grassy open forest. Now gradually slope downward and cross through an old wooden fence before reaching, at 2.7 miles (4.3 km), the ruins of George Taylor's 1892-built sandstone home.

Here among old apple trees near Taylor's old quarry, watch for sheep, deer, and feral goats, and enjoy wonderful views up Brown Ridge. Continue a little farther east to Taylor Point and its big firs and gorgeous white midden beach. The views from the point are exceptional out to Sucia, Patos, Orcas, Waldron, San Juan, and Stuart islands. Savor them—you worked hard to get here—before you begin the hike back to your starting point.

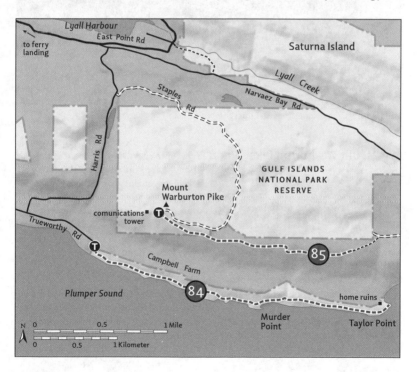

Waldron and Orcas islands from the grassy slopes of Mount Warburton Pike

85 Mount Warburton Pike

RATING/ DIFFICULTY	ROUNDTRIP	ELEV GAIN/HIGH POINT
*****/3	3.4 miles (5.5 km)	515 feet (157 m)/ 1316 feet (401 m)

Map: NTS 092B14 Mayne Island; **Contact:** Gulf Islands National Park Reserve, Mount Warburton Pike; **Notes:** Dogs permitted on-leash; **GPS:** N 48 46.449, W 123 10.285

Walk a lofty, grassy ridge-line, feasting on intoxicating panoramic views of the Salish Sea.

Saturna Island's highest summit grants some of the best views not only of the Gulf Islands but of the San Juan Islands as well. Swaying golden grasses, dazzling wild-flowers, and stoic windblown firs line the trail. Herds of feral goats help to keep this peak's southern face a sprawling meadow—and entertain you as well on this classic island hike.

GETTING THERE

From Tsawwassen or Swartz Bay, take a BC ferry to Lyall Harbour on Saturna Island. Follow East Point Road for 1 mile (1.6 km) and bear right onto Narvaez Bay Road. Immediately turn right (near the store and recycle center) onto Harris Road and proceed for 0.5 mile (0.8 km). Turn left onto Staples Road and follow this steep gravel road 2.5 miles (4 km) to its end at a communications tower and the trailhead (elev. 1316 ft/401 m).

ON THE TRAIL

From just below the parking area near some concrete blocks, locate the trail. It makes a short switchback downward and then heads east along Brown Ridge, through big firs with outstretched limbs. The trail was never formally built, but it's fairly easy to follow. Just stick to the ridgeline and avoid the numerous goat paths radiating down the mountainside (the numerous feral goats here are descendants of domestic herds abandoned more than a century ago). Much of the peak's forested northern slopes are within the Gulf Islands National Park Reserve. Most of its southern face however, remains private—so don't venture south off the trail.

Views are breathtaking from the start and never let up. Stare straight down to Plumper Sound and out to the Pender, Salt Spring, Vancouver, Stuart, and Orcas islands. The views of the Campbell Farm below are quite impressive too. Look for raptors riding the mountain's thermals along the way.

Sticking to the ridgeline, the trail gradually descends, rounding some ledges and small cliffs. Keep children and dogs nearby. Pass a collapsed building and fence line, evidence of past land use. Much of Saturna Island was once owned by Warburton Pike, an adventurous Englishman who came to the island in 1884. He had many business dealings in addition to sheep farming, he spent time in the Arctic, and he authored several books about his time in the Canadian north.

At 0.7 mile (1.1 km), pass beneath a private cabin. Stay on the trail, respecting the owner's privacy. Views continue to grow, with Taylor Point and Java Island now coming into sight. Oaks and maples begin to appear in the forest mix. The mountain, with its terraced slopes compliments of the goats, gives this hike a very Mediterranean feel.

At 1 mile (1.6 km), pass through a forested draw (elev. 950 ft/290 m), where you want to take the path left leading back uphill. At 1.2 miles (1.9 km), come to some impressive cliffs (elev. 990 ft/302 m), where goats can usually be seen, heard, and smelled. Continue hiking, watching Mount Baker come into view. At 1.7 miles (2.7 km), reach an old skid road (elev. 840 ft/256 m), a logical spot to turn around. The path does, however, continue another 0.3 mile (0.5 km), traversing thick timber to reach a dirt road. Parks Canada has plans to acquire an easement and build a trail all the way to Taylor Point (Hike 84). But for now, you'll have to be content returning the scenic way you came.

86 Lyall Creek

RATING/ DIFFICULTY	ROUNDTRIP	ELEV GAIN/HIGH POINT
**/2	1.4 miles (2.3 km)	225 feet (69 m)/ 275 feet (84 m)

Map: NTS 092B14 Mayne Island; **Contact:** Gulf Islands National Park Reserve, Lyall Creek; **Notes:** Dogs permitted on-leash; **GPS:** N 48 47.401, W 123 09.765

Hike along a restored salmon-bearing creek and one of the few protected watersheds within the Gulf Islands. In winter, visit for the spawning chum, cutthroat, and coho, or perhaps to see a small waterfall usually hidden behind a cloak of greenery. One thing you can expect year-round is solitude.

GETTING THERE

From Tsawwassen or Swartz Bay, take a BC ferry to Lyall Harbour on Saturna Island. Follow East Point Road for 1 mile (1.6 km) and bear right onto Narvaez Bay Road. Drive 0.9 mile (1.4 km) to the trailhead (elev. 275 ft/84 m), located on left.

ON THE TRAIL

The rough and at times muddy trail enters a lush second-growth forest, cutting through a dense understory of ferns. Utilizing steps, the trail steeply descends 0.15 mile (0.2 km) to a bench (elev. 160 ft/49 m) overlooking a small waterfall on a tributary creek. Late in the season, the creek trickles while thick greenery obscures it.

Continue the steep descent, passing a huge Douglas fir and some impressive

Bridge over Lyall Creek

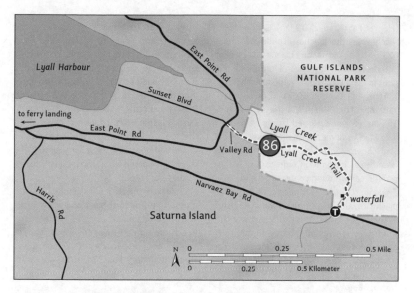

cedars and maples. After crossing the tributary creek on a bridge, the way levels out and follows Lyall Creek. Keep your arms to your side through a patch of head-high nettles. At 0.7 mile (1.1 km), the trail leaves the national park (elev. 50 ft /15 m), a good place to turn around. If you're compelled to keep hiking, the way continues 0.2 mile (0.3 km) on a muddy old road, coming to Valley Road.

87 Narvaez Bay

RATING/ DIFFICULTY	ROUNDTRIP	ELEV GAIN/HIGH POINT
***/2	1.8 miles (2.9 km)	350 feet (107 m)/ 250 feet (76 m)

Map: NTS 092B14 Mayne Island; **Contact:** Gulf Islands National Park Reserve, Narvaez Bay; **Notes:** Dogs permitted on-leash; **GPS:** N 48 46.361, W 123 06.129

Follow an old farm road to two small peninsulas in pristine Narvaez Bay, one of the best spots on Saturna for bird-watching and wildlife observations. Then compare and contrast two smaller bays within the large one. One invites beach explorations and overnight camping; the other, enclosed between rock cliffs and ledges, once offered cover for Prohibition-era bootleggers.

GETTING THERE
From Tsawwassen or Swartz Bay, take a BC ferry to Lyall Harbour on Saturna Island. Follow East Point Road for 1 mile (1.6 km) and bear right onto Narvaez Bay Road. Drive 0.9 mile (1.4 km) to the trailhead, located on the left.

ON THE TRAIL
Follow the gently descending old road to a junction with the Monarch Head Trail

(Hike 88) at 0.2 mile (0.3 km). Continue left, reaching another junction in another 0.2 mile (0.3 km) in an old pasture frequented by deer and raccoons. Left goes to Little Bay. Right goes to Echo Bay. You're going to both.

Head left 0.3 mile (0.5 km) on the Narvaez Bay Trail, passing a grassy wetland. The largely undeveloped bay is named for José María Narváez, captain of the Spanish ship *Santa Saturnina*, whence Saturna Island gets its name. Come to an inviting walk-in campground centered on Little Bay. The campground has picnic tables, tent platforms, and privies but no water. Register at the onsite kiosk. At low tide, explore the sandstone shelves of the bay. In any tide, enjoy the spectacular view of Mount Baker centered between Patos and Sucia islands.

Next, retrace your steps back to the junction and explore Echo Bay. Pass through big shore pines and come to a short spur leading to the bay. The narrow trough is enclosed by steep cliffs and looks remarkably like Lopez Island's Watmough Bay—except the rock here is sandstone. Closely inspect the ledges and caves along the shore for disoriented and momentarily distressed goats. And see for yourself why this bay is named Echo. Kids will enthusiastically figure it out.

Now walk the path left 0.2 mile (0.3 km), on the thin finger of headland (elev. 50 ft/ 15 m) along Echo Bay's north shore. Reach the tip and savor the views. They're magnificent, especially of Orcas Island across Boundary Pass. Scan the waters for

Narvaez Bay

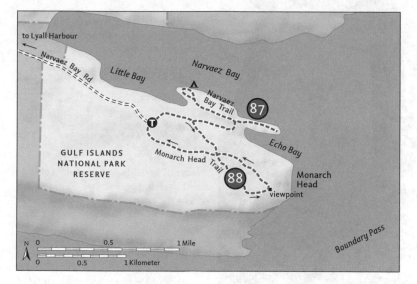

guillemots and seals and the shoreline for oystercatchers. Retrace your steps to the trailhead whenever you tire (doubtful) of the views or must (unfortunately) move on.

88 Monarch Head

RATING/ DIFFICULTY	ROUNDTRIP	ELEV GAIN/HIGH POINT
***/2	1.5 miles (2.4 km)	200 feet (61 m)/ 380 feet (116 m)

Map: NTS 092B14 Mayne Island; **Contact:** Gulf Islands National Park Reserve, Narvaez Bay; **Notes:** Dogs permitted on-leash; **GPS:** N 48 46.361, W 123 06.129

Hike to a high bluff overlooking Boundary Pass and set your sights on the Salish Sea. Peer out across Boundary Pass to Orcas, Patos, Sucia, and Waldron islands and realize just how close

you are to the San Juans—and how arbitrary the international boundary is that bisects this archipelago.

GETTING THERE
See directions to Hike 87.

ON THE TRAIL
This delightful figure-eight hike follows some old roadways transformed into trail. Start by heading toward Narvaez Bay (Hike 87), following a gently descending old road 0.2 mile (0.3 km) to a junction (elev. 180 ft/ 55 m). Turn right on a grassy old road, coming to another junction at 0.4 mile (0.6 km). You'll be returning from the left and exiting stage right—for now, continue straight ahead.

Steadily climb through second-growth cedars, reaching a junction at 0.7 mile (1.1 km). Before continuing left, walk the few steps to the Monarch Head viewpoint (elev.

A feral goat on Monarch Head

reaching the trail's terminus at 1.5 miles (2.4 km), a short distance west of the trailhead parking lot.

89 East Point

RATING/ DIFFICULTY	ROUNDTRIP	ELEV GAIN/HIGH POINT
****/1	0.5 mile (0.8 km)	40 feet (12 m)/ 40 feet (12 m)

Map: NTS 092B14 Mayne Island; **Contact:** Gulf Islands National Park Reserve, East Point; **Notes:** Dogs permitted on-leash; **GPS:** N 48 46.985, W 123 02.795

One of the shortest and easiest hikes in this book, East Point is also one of the most spectacular places in the Gulf Islands. It's an excellent spot to see eagles and killer whales—and the views are killer too, especially of Mount Baker across the strait. Stroll through flowered fields to explore a historical lighthouse, a sculpted sandstone shoreline, and a plethora of marine life here at the Gulf Islands' easternmost point.

GETTING THERE

From Tsawwassen or Swartz Bay, take a BC ferry to Lyall Harbour on Saturna Island. Follow East Point Road (which eventually becomes Tumbo Channel Road) for 9.6 miles (15.4 km) to the trailhead at East Point. Privy and bike rack available.

ON THE TRAIL

Hike east on an old road, passing several interpretive and commemorative signs and a beach access path on your left. The way angles around a steel lighthouse tower,

380 ft/116 m) and interpretive displays straight ahead. It's a precipitous drop, so don't venture too close to the edge, lest you get butterflies in your stomach.

Check out the crashing surf below along Taylor Point (Hike 84) and Java Island. Then cast your attention south across Boundary Pass to Waldron, Orcas, Patos, Sucia, and the rest of the San Juan Islands. So close culturally, historically, naturally, and geographically—yet separated politically by an international boundary. The difference between arbutus and madrona!

Continue your hike by descending along the forested edge of Monarch Head. Watch for feral goats, which frequent the slopes of this kid-friendly bluff. After passing a spring, come to a familiar junction at 1.1 miles (1.8 km). Proceed straight ahead through a cedar-harboring wetland before gradually descending to golden grassy slopes. At 0.1 mile (0.15 km), the trail splits to form a loop. Continue right, coming to the beautifully restored 1938-built former foghorn building. Along with the steel tower, these structures were designated in 2013 as a national heritage lighthouse, the first of two in British Columbia to receive this newly established status.

If the building is open, stop in for a visit. Otherwise, continue walking along the grassy, flower-lined path, skirting above magnificent sandstone ledges sculpted by wind and water and colonized by scads of swallows. Views are absolutely stunning from this small park parcel. Locate the lighthouse across Boundary Pass (one of the Northwest's busiest shipping routes) on Patos Island. Enjoy great views of Orcas and Lummi islands. Locate White Rock and Point Roberts. They're backdropped by a slew of snowy summits, including the easily recognizable Golden Ears. But Mount Baker in its glacial glory steals the show. Look for whales, orcas, and Steller's sea lions here where the Fraser River flushes a bounty of nutrients into the Salish Sea.

Then continue the loop, coming to a gorgeous midden beach and excellent viewing of Tumbo Island and its oak stands, a jewel in the Gulf Islands National Park Reserve. Treacherous currents in the Tumbo Channel make for extremely challenging paddling to reach this island. Here a path leads back

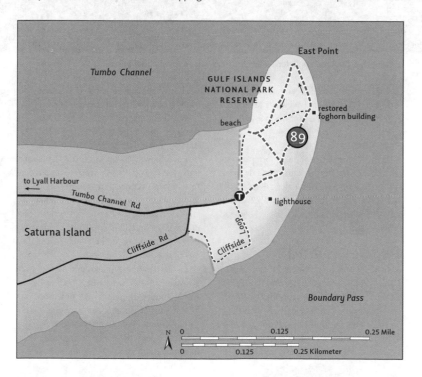

East Point's gorgeous sandstone ledges and historic foghorn building

to the foghorn building and another leads right to close the loop. Follow the latter path, returning to the trailhead at 0.5 mile (0.8 km).

EXTENDING YOUR TRIP

Near the trailhead telephone booth (remember those?), locate the short Cliffside Loop. It leads 0.2 mile (0.3 km) along East Point's south shore to Cliffside Road. Walk the road right 0.1 mile (0.15 km) back to the trailhead.

Pender Island

Named by Captain Richards for Captain Daniel Pender, who surveyed the British Columbia coast in the mid-1800s, Pender Island actually consists of two islands, 14 square miles in total (36 sq. km). In 1903 a narrow canal was dug on the isthmus between Port Browning and Bedwell Harbour, creating North and South Pender islands, now connected by a bridge.

The Penders, with 2200 residents, are some of the more populated of the Gulf Islands. More than a third of South Pender is protected within the Gulf Islands National Park Reserve (GINPR). North Pender contains a large subdivision around Magic Lake and a commercial center as well as many art studios. Overall, the Penders offer numerous parks, large units of the GINPR, a wide array of trails, and more public beach access than any of the other Gulf Islands.

BC Ferries offers year-round service from Tsawwassen and Swartz Bay to Otter Bay on North Pender. Bicyclists will find good but hilly roads. There are two seasonal GINPR campgrounds: Prior Centennial Campground (17 sites), and the walk-in or boat-in only Beaumont Campground (13 sites, no water).

90 George Hill

RATING/ DIFFICULTY	ROUNDTRIP	ELEV GAIN/HIGH POINT
***/3	1.2 miles (2 km)	460 feet (140 m)/ 500 feet (152 m)

Map: NTS 092B14 Mayne Island; **Contact:** Pender Island Parks and Recreation; **Notes:** Dogs permitted on-leash; **GPS:** N 48 49.190, W 123 19.237

This short and steep hike to an open hilltop is long on views of emerald islands and snowy mountaintops, from Vancouver Island to British Columbia's Lower Mainland. Ferries and other boats ply the busy channels below. And majestic eagles perch on wind-blown snags above slopes that come alive with color in spring.

GETTING THERE

From Tsawwassen or Swartz Bay, take a BC ferry to Otter Bay on North Pender Island. Bear right onto MacKinnon Road and at 0.4 mile (0.6 km), turn left onto Otter Bay Road. Drive 1.2 miles (1.9 km) and turn left onto Port Washington Road. After 0.2 mile (0.3 km), turn right onto Bridges Road. Bear left at 0.2 mile (0.3 km) and turn right in 0.1 mile (0.15 km) onto Stanley Point Drive. After 0.3 mile (0.5 km), bear left onto Walden Road. Drive 0.1 mile (0.15 km) to the trailhead (elev. 70 ft /21 m) at the corner of Walden and Ogden roads. Park on the roadside.

ON THE TRAIL

Popular with islanders, the trail at George Hill delivers some nice views. But you'll have to work for them, clambering up ledges on a rocky and rooty route. The trail starts by entering thick forest, cutting through big boughs of ferns. The way is

Salt Spring Island's Mount Bruce forms an inviting backdrop for a BC ferry.

Mayne Island across Navy Channel

steep. A few hand railings offer assistance. Scoot beneath some rocky ledges before surmounting yet another.

The way then traverses a ridgeline of mossy outcroppings and invasive Scotch broom, dipping about 30 feet (9 m) before resuming upward momentum. Then wind through some stately oaks and reach the 500-foot (152-m) open summit at 0.6 mile (1 km). A bench provides your weary body some rest, but the sweeping views may have you wandering around. The view northwest across Port Washington to Salt Spring Island is especially enticing. And the view north of Trincomali Channel, Galiano and Prevost islands isn't too shabby either. Stick around for the sunset if you can—it's breathtaking by George!

91 Clam Bay

RATING/ DIFFICULTY	ROUNDTRIP	ELEV GAIN/HIGH POINT
**/2	1.4 miles (2.3 km)	340 feet (104 m)/ 250 feet (76 m)

Map: NTS 092B14 Mayne Island; **Contact:** Pender Island Parks and Recreation; **Notes:** Dogs permitted on-leash; **GPS:** N 48 48.735, W 123 18.327

Hike through attractive forest and along a working farm to a quiet bay on Navy Channel. The way is short, but it travels through several ecological zones—and the climb back from the bay is sure to give you a little workout.

GETTING THERE

From Tsawwassen or Swartz Bay, take a BC ferry to Otter Bay on North Pender Island. Bear right onto MacKinnon Road and at 0.4 mile (0.6 km), turn left onto Otter Bay Road. Drive 1.2 miles (1.9 km) and turn right onto Port Washington Road. After 0.3 mile (0.5 km), turn left onto Clam Bay Road. Reach

the trailhead (elev. 190 ft/58 m) on the left in 0.3 mile (0.5 km), near a private road.

ON THE TRAIL

North and South Pender contain scores of public beach access trails. Most are short, without much hiking involved. The trail to Clam Bay, through mixed forest and up and over ledges, is one of the longest and most interesting—and one of the more challenging.

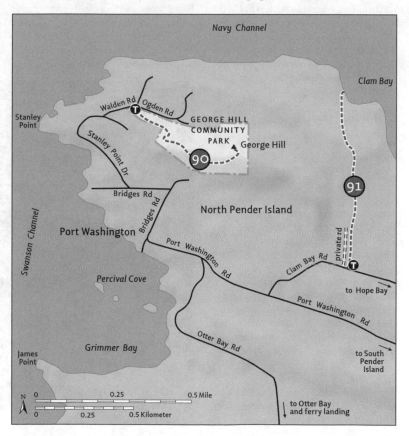

Paralleling a private road and a farm fence line, the way descends through pockets of big cedars and Douglas firs. Soon come to the first of several interpretive signs. At 0.2 mile (0.3 km), cross a wet depression (elev. 100 ft/30 m) via boardwalk, transitioning into open forest. Then start climbing, passing glacial erratics and cresting a 250-foot (76-m) ridge.

The way then abruptly and steeply descends—stairsteps help hasten the plunge. After skirting a private residence, reach the rocky shoreline at Clam Bay at 0.7 mile (1.1 km). Views are limited across the channel to Mayne Island. Watch for marine life and the occasional Saturna-bound ferry. When the tide is low, you can walk the public shoreline to the right, to Bricky Bay. Save energy for the return.

92 Mount Menzies

RATING/ DIFFICULTY	LOOP	ELEV GAIN/HIGH POINT
*/2	0.8 mile (1.3 km)	270 feet (82 m)/ 570 feet (168 m)

Map: NTS 092B14 Mayne Island, park map online; **Contact:** Pender Islands Parks and Recreation; **Notes:** Dogs permitted on-leash; **GPS:** N 48 47.276, W 123 15.437

Wind through a pocket of old growth high on a hill above Plumper Sound. Stroll across mossy carpets and through thickets of salal in this quiet park, part of a patchwork of contiguous protected parcels on North Pender.

GETTING THERE
From Tsawwassen or Swartz Bay, take a BC ferry to Otter Bay on North Pender Island. Bear right onto MacKinnon Road and at 0.4 mile (0.6 km), turn right onto Otter Bay Road. Drive 1.2 miles (1.9 km) and turn left onto Bedwell Harbour Road. Continue 0.6 mile (1 km) (the road makes a sharp right at 0.5 mi/0.8 km) and turn right onto Hooson Road. Reach the trailhead (elev. 300 ft /91 m) at a cul-de-sac in 1.4 miles (2 km).

ON THE TRAIL
Mount Menzies is wedged between the Gulf Islands National Park Reserve's (GINPR) Tyndall Wood and Lorettas Wood tracts and private conservation lands. While the forest here is nice, adjacent Tyndall Wood, with its soaring cliffs above Plumper Sound, is far more interesting. Unfortunately, Parks

Big cedars and clusters of fern line the trail.

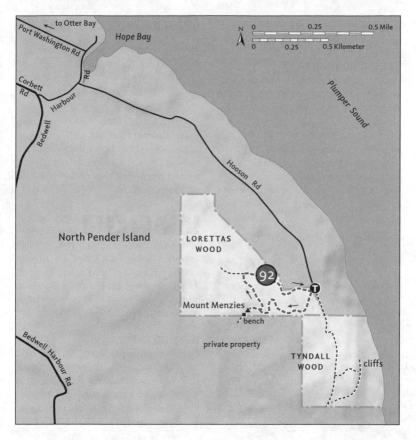

Canada has yet to develop formal trails in that tract, making exploration tricky.

For the Mount Menzies Loop, begin climbing and immediately come to a junction in a grove of big big-leaf maples. You'll be returning from the right, so go left. Climbing, occasionally steeply and with the help of steps, pass through groves of ancient firs and cedars. The way is rocky at times, winding through dark and dank forest. At 0.3 mile (0.5 km), come to a junc-

tion. Take the spur left 0.1 mile (0.15 km) to a mushroom-sprouting bench (elev. 570 ft/ 174 m), with a limited view north through the thick forest canopy.

The path beyond enters private property. Instead, return 0.1 mile (0.15 km) to the junction and continue left, steeply descending and coming to an unmarked trail junction. The trail left leads to the Lorettas Wood unit of the GINPR. Continue right, to an old cedar grove with one lone giant Douglas fir. Then shortly afterward close the loop and return to your start at 0.8 mile (1.3 km).

EXTENDING YOUR TRIP

If you're up for an adventure, from the south end of the cul-de-sac you can follow an old skid road through GINPR's Tyndall Wood for about 0.4 mile (0.6 km) to a trail on the left. Then take this path 0.1 mile (0.15 km) to a series of high ledges (elev. 525 ft/163 m) above Plumper Sound that grant spectacular views of Saturna Island and beyond. It's easy to get lost here. Do not trespass onto adjacent private property and use extreme caution at ledges.

A pretty place to sit along Ella Bay

93 Roe Islet

RATING/ DIFFICULTY	ROUNDTRIP	ELEV GAIN/HIGH POINT
****/1	0.8 mile (1.3 km)	Minimal/40 feet (12 m)

Maps: NTS 092B14 Mayne Island, park map online; **Contact:** Gulf Islands National Park Reserve, Roesland; **Notes:** Dogs permitted on-leash. Islet not accessible at high tide. Respect private inholding; **GPS:** N 48 47.633, W 123 18.418

Stroll back in time to a turn-of-the-twentieth-century "farm-resort." Explore a lovely little island graced with stately trees and offering extensive views. And walk along Ella Bay's sandy shore, watching for otters in appropriately named Otter Bay.

GETTING THERE

From Tsawwassen or Swartz Bay, take a BC ferry to Otter Bay on North Pender Island. Bear right onto MacKinnon Road and at 0.4 mile (0.6 km), turn right onto Otter Bay Road. Drive 0.9 mile (1.4 km) and turn right onto South Otter Bay Road. Follow it for 1 mile (1.6 km), turn right into the Roesland Unit of the Gulf Island National Park Reserve, and find the trailhead. Privy available.

ON THE TRAIL

In 1906, Scottish immigrants Robert and Margaret Roe purchased 640 acres (259-ha) on Pender Island, transforming it into their farm, Roesland. Their son Burt along with his wife, Irene, later developed the property into a farm-resort, which remained in operation until 1991. Parks Canada has restored some

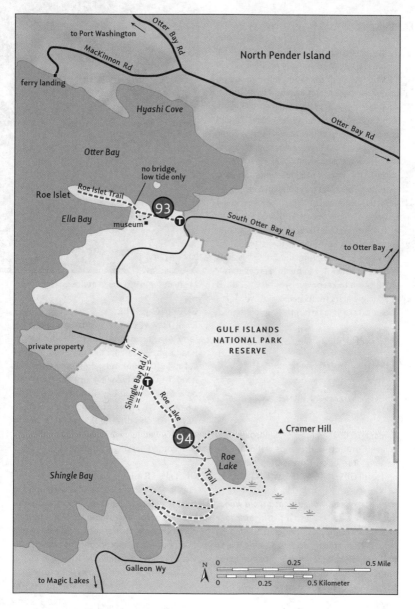

of the original structures, one of which contains a small museum. Check it out—and please be mindful of the structures on the property that are still private residences.

After reading the interpretive displays, follow the path along inviting Ella Bay to a staircase leading to the shoreline. Once a bridge spanned this small pass between Ella and Otter bays to little Roe Islet, but its deteriorating state led to its removal. Visiting the island now requires planning for a low tide.

Once the waters part, hike onto the islet, following a pleasant trail beneath a canopy of attractive arbutuses and firs. The hike is short but one of the loveliest in the Gulf Islands. At 0.4 mile (0.6 km), reach a bench among some junipers at the tip of the island. Savor the views to Salt Spring and Prevost islands and across Otter Bay to the BC Ferries terminal. Be sure to keep your eyes on Otter Bay's sparkling waters for its namesake, which are copious. Take your time retracing your steps.

94 Roe Lake

RATING/ DIFFICULTY	ROUNDTRIP	ELEV GAIN/HIGH POINT
**/2	1.6 miles (2.6 km)	390 feet (119 m)/ 350 feet (107 m)

Maps: NTS 092B14 Mayne Island, park map online; **Contact:** Gulf Islands National Park Reserve, Roe Lake; **Notes:** Dogs permitted on-leash; **GPS:** N 48 47.186, W 123 18.555

Walk a pleasant old woods road to a freshwater lake graced with lily pads and surrounded by ledges. Then steeply drop to Shingle Bay to the site of a once thriving fish-packing plant, now quiet coastline within the Gulf Islands National Park Reserve (GINPR).

Misty autumn afternoon at Roe Lake

GETTING THERE

From Tsawwassen or Swartz Bay, take a BC ferry to Otter Bay on North Pender Island. Bear right onto MacKinnon Road and at 0.4 mile (0.6 km), turn right onto Otter Bay Road. Drive 0.9 mile (1.4 km) and turn right onto South Otter Bay Road. Follow it for 1.6 miles (2.6 km), turn left onto dirt Shingle Bay Road, and drive in 0.2 mile (0.3 km) to the trailhead (elev. 250 ft/76 m) on the left, with limited parking on the right .

ON THE TRAIL

Roe Lake sits in the center of a large wooded tract acquired in 2003 by Parks Canada for the establishment of the GINPR. There is currently only one official trail across this tract, but the property contains miles of old woods roads frequented by islanders.

The official trail follows an old woods road through second-growth forest. In autumn the way is lined with yellow big-leaf maple leaves that may tug at your inner Robert Frost. After gently climbing, reach a woods road junction near a wetland pool at 0.3 mile (0.5 km). The way left hugs the north shore of Roe Lake. Continue right, soon coming to the lily-pad-topped lake (elev. 350 ft/107 m). Look for waterfowl in the coves and eagles in the big shoreline trees. And look for beaver activity.

Then continue hiking, crossing the lake's outlet creek below an active beaver dam. Cross a boardwalk along a small inlet, coming to an unmarked junction at 0.5 mile (0.8 km). The trail to the left is a rough-and-tumble path along the lake's south shore that eventually connects with an old woods road on the north shore. It's about a 0.6-mile (1 km) loop.

The official trail continues straight, following the old woods road. Ignore unmarked trails heading right, and steeply descend to a signed junction at 0.7 mile (1.1 km). The way right runs along a bluff above Shingle Bay, continuing onto private property. Go left, enjoying window views through trees of the tranquil bay. At 0.8 mile (1.3 km), reach the trail's end at Galleon Way (elev. 60 ft/18 m) in the Magic Lakes community. Turn around and hike back up to the lake and down to your start.

95 Mount Norman

RATING/ DIFFICULTY	ROUNDTRIP	ELEV GAIN/HIGH POINT
***/3	1.8 miles (2.9 km)	600 feet (183 m)/ 800 feet (244 m)

Maps: NTS 092B14 Mayne Island, park map online; **Contact:** Gulf Islands National Park Reserve, Mount Norman; **Notes:** Dogs

permitted on-leash; **GPS:** N 48 45.470, W 123 13.722

Climb to the rooftop of the Penders and make like an eagle in an aerie, surveying the spectacular surroundings below. Gaze straight down to the shimmering waters of Bedwell Harbour and out to a flotilla of Gulf and San Juan islands alongside the mother ship, Vancouver Island.

GETTING THERE

From Tsawwassen or Swartz Bay, take a BC ferry to Otter Bay on North Pender Island. Bear right onto MacKinnon Road and at 0.4 mile (0.6 km), turn right onto Otter Bay Road. Drive 1.2 miles (1.9 km) and turn right onto Bedwell Harbour Road. After 1.5 miles (2.4 km), just past the shopping center, the road becomes Canal Road. Continue on Canal for 3.2 miles (5.1 km) (the road makes a sharp left at 1 mi/1.6 km). Turn right onto a gravel road and drive 0.2 mile (0.3 km) to the trailhead (elev. 250 ft/76 m). Privy and bike rack available.

ON THE TRAIL

Follow the Mount Norman Trail, which utilizes an old logging road most of the way. A good section of Mount Norman was logged in the 1980s prior to becoming first a regional park and then in 2003 a unit of the Gulf Islands National Park Reserve.

The alder-lined way soon steepens, traversing a hillside of scrappy cedars and firs. After about 0.5 mile (0.8 km), the way gets a little rockier and makes a few small dips between climbing bouts. Occasionally Saturna Island can be seen through the dense young growth. The way once again steepens as it approaches Norman's 800-foot (244-m) summit.

Bedwell Harbour from Mount Norman summit

After walking through a small patch of uncut forest, come to a junction at about 0.9 mile (1.4 km). You've come for the views, so head left a short distance, down a staircase to the wood-planked observation deck, and start savoring them! Peer straight down to sparkling Bedwell Harbour and out to Moresby, Princess Margaret, Salt Spring, Stuart, San Juan, Isle-de-Lis (Rum), Sidney, and Vancouver islands. Look around at the windblown Douglas firs for bald eagles enjoying the views too.

EXTENDING YOUR TRIP

You can continue along the ridge, dropping steeply 0.6 mile (1 km) to the Beaumont Trail (Hike 96) and then continuing another 0.2 mile (0.3 km) to the Ainslie Point Road trailhead. Or, from the main trailhead, fol-

low the William Walker Trail for a 1.5-mile (2.4-km) rough-and-tumble adventure to Canal Road. Then walk the road 1.1 mile (1.8 km) back—or if the tide is low, you can divert to the shoreline for about 0.5 mile (0.8 km) between two beach access trails along the road.

96 Bedwell Harbour

RATING/ DIFFICULTY	ROUNDTRIP	ELEV GAIN/HIGH POINT
****/3	3 miles (4.8 km)	800 feet (244 m)/ 410 feet (125 m)

Maps: NTS 092B14 Mayne Island, park map online; **Contact:** Gulf Islands National Park Reserve, Beaumont; **Notes:** Dogs permitted on-leash; **GPS:** N 48 45.817, W 123 15.158

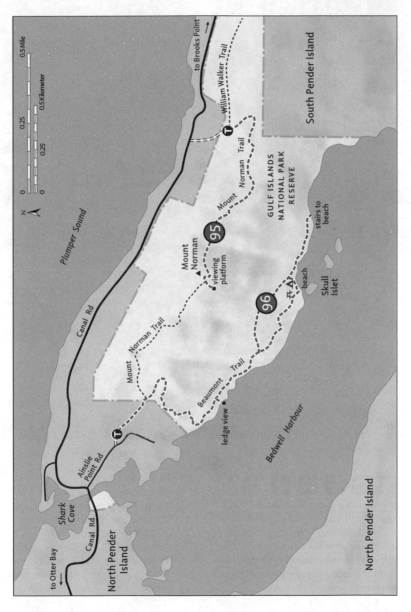

The beach at Bedwell Harbour

🦴 ⚙️ ✳️ 🌲 🍃 Hike to a secluded white-shelled beach on Bedwell Harbour beneath the steep green slopes of Mount Norman. The way is tough, with a steep descent and then climb on the return. But a few views and big arbutuses along the way, plus the anticipation of a beautiful beach, will help keep you motivated.

GETTING THERE

From Tsawwassen or Swartz Bay, take a BC ferry to Otter Bay on North Pender Island. Bear right onto MacKinnon Road and at 0.4 mile (0.6 km), turn right onto Otter Bay Road. Drive 1.2 miles (1.9 km) and turn right onto Bedwell Harbour Road. After 1.5 miles (2.4 km), just past the shopping center, the road becomes Canal Road. Continue on

Canal for 1.8 miles (2.9 km) (the road makes a sharp left at 1 mi/1.6 km). Turn right onto Ainslie Point Road. Drive 0.1 mile (0.15 km) to reach the trailhead (elev. 125 ft/38 m), on a dirt road to the left. Do not block gate. Bike rack available.

ON THE TRAIL

Follow a jeep track steeply up, passing a private residence on the left. At 0.2 mile (0.3 km), come to a junction (elev. 280 ft/85 m). The way left continues 0.6 mile (1 km), steeply climbing to 800-ft (244-m) Mount Norman (Hike 95).

You want to go right on a rocky and rooty path through thick salal, cresting a ridge (elev. 410 ft/125 m) at about 0.4 mile (0.6 km). Then steeply descend, working your way over, around, and beneath a series of ledges. Watch your footing and pause occasionally to admire the surrounding old-growth forest of big arbutuses and Douglas firs.

After leveling off on a bench above Bedwell Harbour, come to a junction at 0.8 mile (1.3 km), where a short spur drops to a lone-oak ledge above the water. The main trail continues up and over a couple of ledges before traversing a grove of big firs and cedars and coming to a junction at 0.9 mile (1.4 km). You'll be returning from the left, so proceed right, passing more ancient cedars and coming to a seasonal campground (13 sites, privy, no water). The camp is popular with boaters (moorage available), and you can certainly backpack here too.

The trail then reaches a picnic area at harbor's edge at 1.2 miles (1.9 km). The setting is breathtaking, near midden beaches and a series of small just-offshore (closed to visitation) islands. The view is agreeable too, extending to Stuart and San Juan islands.

Now walk left along the shore (or on the sandy beach if the tide is low), passing choice campsites. At 1.4 miles (2.3 km), come to a junction. Left is your return route. But first hike right on a nice trail atop gorgeous shoreline bluffs, coming to the trail's end at 1.6 miles (2.6 km) at a stairway (elev. 45 ft/14 m) leading to a beach. Explore the shoreline or start back, retracing your steps 0.2 mile (0.3 km) to the previous junction. Then continue straight 0.3 mile (0.5 km) through ancient forest, coming to another familiar junction. Head straight, preparing for the upcoming steep climb on your way back to the trailhead reached at 3 miles (4.8 km).

97 Greenburn Lake

RATING/ DIFFICULTY	ROUNDTRIP	ELEV GAIN/HIGH POINT
**/1	1.4 miles (2.3 km)	260 feet (79 m)/ 400 feet (122 m)

Maps: NTS 092B14 Mayne Island, NTS 092B11 Sidney; **Contact:** Gulf Islands National Park Reserve, Greenburn Lake; **Notes:** Dogs permitted on-leash; **GPS:** N 48 44.694, W 123 13.241

Mosey up a maple-lined woods road to a large undeveloped lake surrounded by attractive forest. A rarity in the Gulf Islands, this freshwater lake provides excellent habitat for a host of critters and plants. The walk to the lake is easy and is especially delightful with an autumn carpet of yellow leaves.

GETTING THERE

From Tsawwassen or Swartz Bay, take a BC ferry to Otter Bay on North Pender Island. Bear right onto MacKinnon Road and at 0.4 mile (0.6 km), turn right onto Otter Bay Road. Drive

1.2 miles (1.9 km) and turn right onto Bedwell Harbour Road. After 1.5 miles (2.4 km), just past the shopping center, the road becomes Canal Road. Continue on Canal for 5 miles (8 km) (the road makes a sharp left at 1 mi/1.6 km). Turn right onto Spalding Road. Follow it 2 miles (3.2 km) and turn left onto Gowlland Point Road. Drive 0.1 mile (0.15 km) to the trailhead (elev. 160 ft/49 m), on the left just before the fire hall. Do not block gate.

ON THE TRAIL

First acquired by Parks Canada in 2004, the Greenburn Lake tract of the Gulf Islands National Park Reserve was recently expanded to 292 acres (118 ha), making it a considerably larger property. Parks Canada has yet to develop any facilities or trails in the parcel, limiting exploration to an old woods road and several unofficial paths.

Walk past the gate and gently ascend under a thick forest canopy of maple, oak, and fir. Soon emerge from the greenery to skirt a meadow traversed by Greenburn Lake's outlet creek. At 0.5 mile (0.8 km), reach a junction (elev. 400 ft/122 m) near a boulder. The way right crosses the lake's outlet dam and continues to a viewpoint (see Extending Your Hike).

The old road continues straight along the placid, lily-pad-pocked pond. Look for ducks among the reeds and eagles in the trees. At 0.7 mile (1.1 km), the road-trail ends at water's edge (elev. 380 ft/116 m). Sit and savor the sweet serenity.

EXTENDING YOUR HIKE

Rough user-built paths circle the lake. A better plan than following them is to hike the path west across the dam (bearing right at a junction shortly afterward) for 0.3

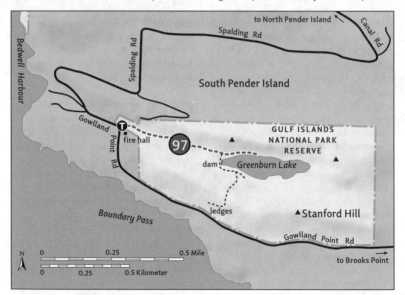

Greenburn Lake is surrounded by thick green drapery.

mile (0.5 km) to a rocky, grassy bluff (use caution). You'll find excellent views across Swanson Channel to Stuart and Moresby islands as well as to Wallace Point on the tip of North Pender.

Salt Spring Island

Compared to the other Gulf Islands, Salt Spring Island is a bustling place. It's the largest of the group, at 70 square miles (180 sq. km), and the most populated, with about eleven thousand residents. In summer, things really get buzzing, especially at the island's two main commercial centers, Fulford Harbour and Ganges. There is a hospital in Ganges.

Salt Spring is named for the salt springs on the island's north shore. The island was one of the first places of European settlement in British Columbia, and folks from all over Canada and the world have been coming here ever since, making it a diverse and vibrant place. Well-known for its art scene, the island also offers excellent hiking opportunities through its large provincial parks, regional parks, Crown lands, community parks and trails, and preserves administered by the Salt Spring Island Conservancy.

Salt Spring Island has three BC Ferries terminals, with interisland service and service to Tsawwassen via Long Harbour; numerous runs to Swartz Bay via Fulford Harbour; and service to Crofton on Vancouver Island. Ruckle Provincial Park offers coastal car and walk-in camping year-round (86 sites, no water November–mid-March). There are also several private campgrounds on the island.

98 Duck Creek

RATING/ DIFFICULTY	LOOP	ELEV GAIN/HIGH POINT
**/1	1.2 miles (1.9 km)	120 feet (37 m)/ 180 feet (55 m)

Maps: NTS 092B13 Duncan, park map online; **Contact:** Salt Spring Island Parks and Recreation, Duck Creek Park; **Notes:** Dogs permitted on-leash; **GPS:** N 48 53.067, W 123 34.165

A popular dog-walking spot for Islanders, Duck Creek makes for a nice evening or early morning leg stretcher. Follow the cascading creek through mossy forest groves, returning through rolling meadows. Visit in late fall for the salmon spawning.

GETTING THERE

From Ganges on Salt Spring Island, follow the Lower Ganges Road west for 2.5 miles (4 km)

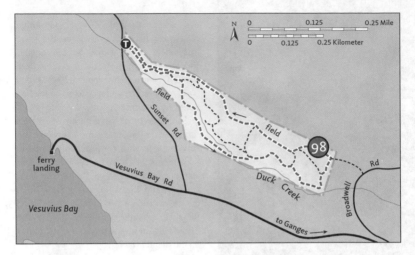

to a four-way stop. Turn left onto Vesuvius Bay Road and drive 1.8 miles (2.9 km), turning right onto Sunset Road, 0.3 mile (0.5 km) before the Vesuvius ferry landing. Drive 0.3 mile (0.5 km) to the trailhead (elev. 60 ft/18 m). Park on the left-hand road shoulder.

ON THE TRAIL

Starting at the edge of a large field, follow the right-hand path to the creek. You'll be returning from the left. Follow the gurgling and tumbling Duck Creek beneath a towering canopy compliments of big and old maples, firs, and cedars. During the winter months the way can get quite muddy—but that's when the creek is at its best.

At 0.2 mile (0.3 km), encounter the first of several paths leading left to the field trail. Always keep right, going with the creek flow. Cross a couple of bridges over the waterway and follow the creek along a field edge and through an emerald ravine.

After passing a sandstone boulder, emerge in a field. Go right, soon connect-

Duck Creek is a great place to watch spawning salmon.

ing with the main park trail at 0.7 mile (1.1 km). Right leads 0.1 mile (0.15 km) to the Broadwell Road trailhead, an alternative starting point.

You want to head left, down the middle of a broad field graced with some big bigleaf maples. Avoid the radiating side trails. After crossing a bridge, reach another big field, weaving along its edge and returning to your starting point at 1.2 miles (1.9 km).

99 Mount Erskine

RATING/ DIFFICULTY	ROUNDTRIP	ELEV GAIN/HIGH POINT
*****/3	3.4 miles (5.5 km)	1325 feet (404 m)/ 1447 feet (441 m)

Maps: NTS 092B13 Duncan, conservancy map online; **Contact:** BC Parks, Mount Erskine Provincial Park, and Salt Spring Island Conservancy, Mount Erskine; **Notes:** Dogs permitted on-leash. Steep drop-offs— keep children and dogs close; **GPS:** N 48 51.380, W 123 33.542

The highest peak on Salt Spring Island sans roads and towers, Mount Erskine contains tracts of old growth, impressive cliffs, and knock-your-sweaty-hiking-socks-off views of the island and mountain parting Stuart Channel. Home to endangered sharp-tailed snakes and forest fairies, Erskine is an enchanting place.

GETTING THERE
From Ganges on Salt Spring Island, follow Rainbow Road west 2.7 miles (4.3 km) and then turn left onto Collins Road. Continue for 0.4 mile (0.6 km) to the trailhead (elev. 200 ft/ 61 m), on the left. Park on the right.

Your dog will appreciate the fancy water bowl on Mount Erskine's summit.

ON THE TRAIL
Until 2005, most of Mount Erskine was privately owned. But thanks to the Salt Spring Island Conservancy, nearly 593 acres (240 ha) have been protected within two reserves and a provincial park.

Start on the Jack Fisher Trail (a.k.a. the Mount Erskine Assault Route), and immediately begin climbing. Stay left at a junction (the trail right passes through private property) and head up a rocky knoll that sports arbutus and manzanita. Descend about 80 feet (24 m) in elevation and meet back up with the trail passed earlier. Veer left and continue upward, following a somewhat rocky route through an area logged a few decades back.

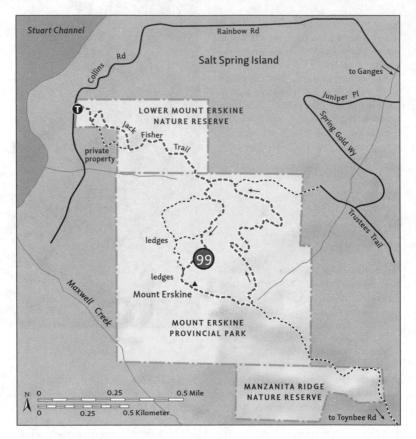

At 0.8 mile (1.3 km), after entering the provincial park in a hollow of big firs, maples, and arbutuses, come to a junction (elev. 930 ft/283 m). You'll be returning from straight ahead, so go right, climbing steeply. Soon a scarcely discernible trail veers right—a not recommended alternative summit route. Continue left instead, soon coming to the first of many intriguing and somewhat mystical fairy doors on rocks and tree trunks. Ask around at the Ganges Saturday Market for their story.

At 1.1 miles (1.8 km), come to a junction (elev. 1225 ft/373 m) at a big fir. The way right loops 0.25 mile (0.4 km) along steep, exposed ledges. The views are grand, but this is no trail for children and those skittish of drops. Plenty of good views are straight ahead too, so keep hiking forward and up, passing more elfin doors. Come to the steep side loop at 1.3 miles (2.1 km) and soon emerge atop Erskine's 1447-foot (441-m) open summit dome of conglomerate rock.

Now, keeping any accompanying children and dogs close, let out a "Wow! What a view!" It's one of the best in the Gulf Islands. Stare down at the tight strait, Sansum Narrows, and Maple Mountain above it. Watch ships and ferries sail to the mill town of Crofton. Scan the Stuart Channel, eyeing Vancouver Island peaks to the left (Hall Mountain, Mount Prevost, and Mount Arrowsmith among them) and islands to the right (Penelakut, Thetis, and Valdes). Admire wind-contorted firs and pines and look for peregrine falcons. They're fond of sharp-tailed snakes. Notice too the memorial bowl for Rosie the Wonder Dog.

After scarfing down lunch and feasting on views, continue on a pleasant path along the summit ridge, traversing mossy conglomerate ledges through attractive forest. Reach a junction (elev. 1325 ft/404 m) at 1.6 miles (2.6 km). The way right (see Extending Your Trip) heads to Manzanita Ridge. Travel left for now, descending steep slopes of open forest to a junction (elev. 940 ft/287 m) at 2.5 miles (4 km).

The way right passes through big cedars to the Trustees Trail trailhead (elev. 750 ft/229 m), an easier, shorter, and less interesting approach than the Jack Fisher Trail. To close your loop and return to your vehicle, turn left and come to a familiar junction in 0.1 mile (0.15 km). From there retrace familiar tread 0.8 mile (1.3 km) back to your start.

EXTENDING YOUR TRIP

A lightly used trail travels along Manzanita Ridge and then down Erskine's southeast slopes for 1.3 miles (2.1 km) to Toynbee Road (elev. 750 ft/229 m). Hike it if you can arrange a pickup—or just travel 0.4 mile (0.6 km) along it to a series of ledges that grant good views north across Ganges to Wallace Island, Galiano Island, and British Columbia's Lower Mainland summits.

Bryant Hill Park and 100 Andreas Vogt Nature Reserve

RATING/ DIFFICULTY	LOOP	ELEV GAIN/HIGH POINT
**/2	2.9 miles (4.7 km)	750 feet (229 m)/ 1075 feet (328 m)

Maps: NTS 092B14 Mayne Island, park map online; **Contact:** Salt Spring Island Parks and Recreation, Bryant Hill Park, and Salt Spring Island Conservancy, Andreas Vogt Nature Reserve; **Notes:** Dogs permitted on-leash; **GPS:** N 48 47.470, W 123 27.938

Hike two loops on a quiet hillside above Fulford Harbour: one mostly forested, the other across meadows and ledges and with pleasant views. Camas and other showy blossoms brighten up Bryant Hill's Garry oak groves, making this peak a delightful destination in the spring.

GETTING THERE

From the Fulford Harbour ferry landing on Salt Spring Island, follow Fulford–Ganges Road 0.2 mile (0.3 km) and bear right onto Beaver Point Road. After 1.5 miles (2.4 km), turn left onto Stewart Road and proceed 1.1 miles (1.8 km). Turn left onto Jasper Road, drive 0.5 mile (0.8 km), and turn left onto Jennifer Way. In 0.4 mile (0.6 km), turn right onto Sarah Way. In 0.6 mile (1 km), turn right onto a gravel road and drive 0.3 mile (0.5 km) to the trailhead (elev. 860 ft/262 m).

ON THE TRAIL

Strata corporation developments and invasive Scotch broom have been creeping up this hill just like elsewhere on this popular Gulf Island. Fortunately, both are being thwarted on Bryant's summit, thanks to an 82-acre (34-ha) park and a 74-acre (30-ha) Salt Spring Island Conservancy reserve. Both have been established to preserve open space and restore native Garry oak habitat, British Columbia's most threatened coastal ecosystem and home to more than a hundred species at risk.

From the trailhead, head to the right past a yellow gate and down an old woods road. You'll be returning from the trail on the left. At 0.15 mile (0.2 km), bear left at a junction. The trail right makes a rough-and-tumble journey along a linear park (trail corridor) to connect with trails in Peter Arnell Park.

Gradually descend through second growth, crossing a creek and reaching a wetland pool. Come to a bridge (elev. 500 ft/152 m) and start climbing, passing window views out to Mount Maxwell before cresting a 775-foot (236-m) knoll. Drop slightly into a cedar grove before reaching a junction (elev. 830 ft/253 m) at 1.4 miles (2.3 km), beside a creek and huge maple.

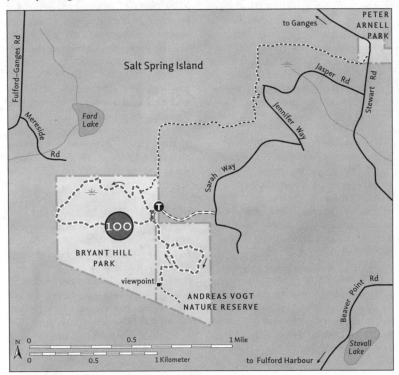

and surrounding peaks. Take it. Then return to the junction and head left 0.1 mile (0.15 km), to close the loop. Turn left again and hike 0.2 mile (0.5 km) back to your vehicle.

EXTENDING YOUR TRIP
Consider hiking the 2 rough, up-and-down miles (3.2 km) to Peter Arnell Park. It's best as a one-way if you can arrange for a pickup.

101 Mount Maxwell

RATING/ DIFFICULTY	LOOP	ELEV GAIN/HIGH POINT
*****/3	4.9 miles (7.9 km)	1600 feet (488 m)/ 1975 feet (602 m)

Map: NTS 092B13 Duncan; **Contact:** BC Parks, Mount Maxwell Provincial Park; **Notes:** Dogs permitted on-leash; **GPS:** N 48 48.314, W 123 29.692

With its snub-nosed summit and cliffy fearsome south face, *Mount Maxwell is one of the most distinctive landmarks in the Salish Sea. It also offers some of the most stunning views. Stand atop sheer cliffs and stare straight down to sparkling Burgoyne Bay and fjord-like Sansum Narrows. Then scan the emerald, bucolic Burgoyne Valley out to Fulford Harbour and a flotilla of islands receding to the horizon.*

GETTING THERE
From the Fulford Harbour ferry landing on Salt Spring Island, follow Fulford–Ganges Road north 5 miles (8 km) and turn left onto Dukes Road. (From Ganges, follow Fulford–Ganges Road south 3.7 mi/6 km and turn right onto Dukes Road.) Drive 1.2 miles (1.9 km) and turn left onto Seymour Heights

You'll find a hummingbird motif trail sign at Andreas Vogt Nature Reserve.

Left returns to the parking lot in a few steps. Head right for the second loop, climbing through thick forest understory. You'll soon reach the Andreas Vogt Nature Reserve and an informative kiosk. At 1.6 miles (2.6 km), come to the loop junction (elev. 965 ft/294 m). Head left on the well-marked trail across balds and ledges that grant good views to nearby Mount Bruce and Reginald Hill.

Crest a 1075-foot (328-m) high point and soon turn sharply right, steeply descending through an oak restoration area (elev. 925 ft/ 282 m). Then traverse a beautiful grassy hillside to a junction at 2.1 miles (3.4 km). The way left is a 0.25-mile (0.4 km) up-and-down spur to an excellent viewpoint (elev. 950 ft/290 m) over a wetland and out to Fulford Harbour

Dramatic view of Burgoyne Bay and Mount Bruce from Mount Maxwell

Road. After 0.4 mile (0.6 km), turn left onto Armand Way and proceed 0.7 mile (1.1 km) to the trailhead (elev. 600 ft/183 m), on the left. Park on the right.

ON THE TRAIL

Most folks drive a narrow gravel road to Maxwell's summit for its sweeping views. Not you—you want to earn those views. And aside from the exercise and challenge,

you'll get to experience this 487-acre (197-ha) park's old-growth forests too. Away from the summit viewpoints, there's a good chance you'll have the trail to yourself.

After starting in scrappy forest, you'll soon transition into beautiful old growth upon crossing the provincial park boundary. At 0.4 mile (0.6 km), keep right at a junction. The trail left is a lightly traveled route that loops back to the main path.

Soon descend slightly to a small pool surrounded by ancient giant conifers.

Next, come to a spectacular cedar grove by a creek. On one giant cedar there's a duck-shaped sign on an overhanging limb, suggesting that you—duck. Stay right at a junction and head through a nettle patch. Then steeply climb to another junction. The trail right goes to Seymour Heights Road. Continue left, soon coming to yet another junction. Stay right and within a few steps, at 1.2 miles (1.9 km), reach one more junction (elev. 1550 ft/472 m). You'll be returning from the right, so continue straight, reentering ancient forest and soon afterward, traversing a grassy bald.

The way now weaves along cliff edges. Avoid dangerous spur paths leading left. Your trail steepens as it heads through open forest and around mossy boulders, coming to a four-way junction. Right heads back down the mountain. Straight goes to the summit parking lot and privy. You want to go left through the picnic area, soon coming to the clifftop summit of Mount Maxwell known as Baynes Peak (elev. 1975 ft/602 m) at 1.9 miles (3.1 km).

Hold on to your breath. The sweeping views are determined to take it away. They're stunning—especially straight down to Burgoyne Bay and the Sansum Narrows. The view out over the patchwork of farms of the Burgoyne Valley to Fulford Harbour and the islands beyond is pretty mesmerizing too. A sturdy fence runs along the summit cliffs, affording some comfort for those scared of heights and a little security for overanxious children. Feel free to roam along the viewing area before continuing your hike.

Now follow the rim trail west along more impressive cliffs that grant more stunning views. When the fence line ends, bear left and soon after that bear right, gradually descending through open fir forest. At 2.5 miles (4 km), come to the park road. Turn left and follow it a short distance, leaving the road and picking up the trail (elev. 1580 ft/ 482 m) again on the north side of the road at 2.7 miles (4.3 km).

Immediately come to a junction. Head right, traveling through old-growth forest and cresting a 1730-foot (527-m) broad ridge. Then gradually descend, coming to a junction (elev. 1590 ft/485 m) at 3.5 miles (5.6 km). Go right 0.1 mile (0.15 km) to another junction, graced with some moss-enveloped signs. Right goes back to the summit. You want to go left, steeply dropping to a familiar trail junction in 0.1 mile (0.15 km). Turn left and retrace your steps (taking care not to make a wrong turn) 1.2 miles (1.9 km) to your vehicle.

102 Burgoyne Bay

RATING/ DIFFICULTY	ROUNDTRIP	ELEV GAIN/HIGH POINT
***/1	1.6 miles (2.6 km)	400 feet (122 m)/ 225 feet (69 m)

Map: NTS 092B13 Duncan; **Contact:** BC Parks, Burgoyne Bay Provincial Park; **Notes:** Dogs permitted on leash. Off-trail travel discouraged; **GPS:** N 48 47.659, W 123 31.272

Hike the north shore of the largest undeveloped bay and estuary in the Gulf Islands. Recently protected within 825-acre (334-ha) Burgoyne Bay Provincial Park, this hike to a grassy bluff beneath the formidable south face of Mount Maxwell is a great introduction to this ecologically and culturally rich new park.

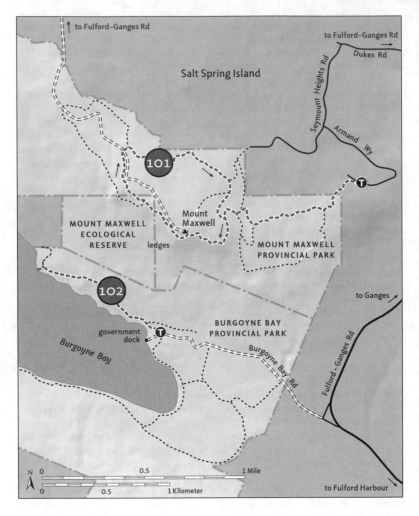

GETTING THERE

From Fulford Harbour ferry landing on Salt Spring Island, follow Fulford–Ganges Road north 2.8 miles (4.5 km) and bear left onto Burgoyne Bay Road. (From Ganges, follow Fulford–Ganges Road south 5.7 mi/9.2 km and bear right onto Burgoyne Bay Road.) Continue 1 mile (1.6 km) on good dirt road to the trailhead (elev. 25 ft/8 m) at the road's end, north of the government dock.

ON THE TRAIL

Though relatively undeveloped, Burgoyne Bay has a long human history, from its importance to several Coast Salish tribes to being one of British Columbia's first interracial settlements. The bay and its surroundings were the focus of a large preservation effort by a consortium of conservation groups, among them the Nature Trust of British Columbia, the Salt Spring Island Conservancy, and the Land Conservancy. They were successful in establishing a near-contiguous belt of protected habitats from Maxwell Lake to Mount Sullivan. Visitor facilities, including trails, have yet to be developed in this park, but its numerous old woods roads invite exploration.

From the north end of the parking area near an old quarry, follow an old road north,

The rocky coastline of Burgoyne Bay

soon bearing left at a junction. Gradually climbing, traverse thickly forested slopes dotted with mossy boulders. After reaching an elevation of 225 feet (69 m), begin descending toward the shoreline, passing through attractive arbutus groves interspersed with big Douglas firs.

Soon reach a junction on a grassy, rocky bluff graced with mature Garry oaks. Here, at about 0.8 mile (1.3 km), beneath the intimidating cliffs of Mount Maxwell, are some of the island's finest oak stands. The old road right peters out at an old farm site. Head left instead, dropping down to coastal ledges that provide sweeping views of the bay, Mount Bruce, Sansum Narrows, and Maple Mountain. Stay for a while watching for eagles, waterfowl, and marine mammals before returning the way you came.

EXTENDING YOUR TRIP

Snoop around some of the park's old farm buildings and perhaps explore the old woods road that hugs the bay's south shore. Old roads radiate toward Mount Sullivan, but navigating them can be very tricky.

103 Mill Farm and Mount Bruce

RATING/ DIFFICULTY	ROUNDTRIP	ELEV GAIN/HIGH POINT
***/4	7.6 miles (12.2 km)	1420 feet (433 m)/ 2310 feet (704 m)

Maps: NTS 092B11 Sydney, NTS 092B13 Duncan; **Contact:** Capital Regional District Parks, Mill Farm Regional Park Preserve; **Notes:** Access road requires high-clearance vehicle. Some trails open to motorized use. Dogs permitted on-leash; **GPS:** N 48 45.368, W 123 31.700

A column of old-growth giants in the Mill Farm Regional Park Preserve

Hike through this early twentieth-century homestead and some of the oldest trees on the island to the highest point in the Gulf Islands. The summit of Mount Bruce is marred with modern communications towers, but the views are as clear as can be. The old Mill Farm is wild and peaceful and full of surprises.

GETTING THERE

From Fulford Harbour ferry landing on Salt Spring Island, follow Fulford–Ganges Road north 0.8 mile (1.3 km) and bear left onto Isabella Point Road. After 0.3 mile (0.5 km), turn right onto Musgrave Road. Follow this gravel (pavement ends in 1.4 mi/2.3 km), rough at times, steep at times, slow-going road 6.3 miles (10.1 km) to the trailhead (elev. 890 ft/271 m), on the right. Parking is limited—there is more space 0.1 mile (0.15 km) farther along the road.

ON THE TRAIL

Much of the hike to Mount Bruce is on old logging roads that are poorly marked

MULTICULTURAL ARCHIPELAGO

The Gulf Islands are remarkably diverse, not only in their ecological makeup, but also in their ethnic and cultural composition. These are traditional lands of several Salish peoples, and under British and Canadian dominion the region saw waves of settlers and immigrants. Workers of the Hudson's Bay Company who settled the islands were Australian, British, Scottish, Irish, French, Portuguese, Cree, and Hawaiian (Kanakas). American blacks escaping slavery came to Salt Spring Island in the 1850s and '60s. Chinese and Japanese people began emigrating to the region in the late 1850s and '60s as well. In the 1960s, American draft dodgers and hippies made their way to the Gulf Islands. Today, folks from all over North America, Asia, Europe, and other parts of the world continue to settle in the Gulf Islands, integrating and adding to the cultural fabric of the region. Admire, reflect upon, and celebrate the rich cultures of the islands as you explore them.

and open to motorbikes. Route-finding can be difficult and much of the route is unappealing. Why go then? The views are grand, and you'll be able to lay claim to hiking the Gulf Islands' highest summit. The Mill Farm Preserve, in contrast, is quite pleasant and will appeal to you if Mount Bruce doesn't.

Start at a gated old woods road and enter the 783-acre (317-ha) Mill Farm Regional Park Preserve. Homesteaded in 1919 by Englishman Arnold Smith and later transformed into a communal farm, this site, with its old growth, was threatened by logging in the 1990s, prompting the Salt Spring Island Conservancy campaign for its preservation. The effort succeeded in 1996.

From the gate, a lightly traveled path branches left through big trees to an old farm pond. The main way heads right, steadily climbing alongside a creek. At 0.3 mile (0.5 km), the trail switchbacks left (ignore the path right) and continues climbing. Ignore secondary paths (unless you want to explore)—they lead to the communal home sites and rock gardens, including one with some dying palm trees.

Pass a small containment pond and at 0.7 mile (1.1 km) come to a gate (elev. 1300 ft/396 m) marking the park's boundary in an old-growth grove. Continue hiking on the now-open-to-dirt-bikes old road, passing beneath some grassy cliffs and traversing open forest that harbors healthy herds of

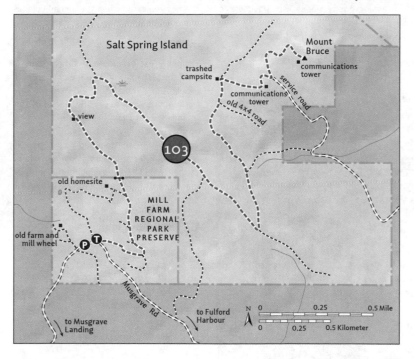

deer. Round a grassy shoulder that grants good views of the Saanich Inlet, and come to a junction (elev. 1520 ft/463 m) at 1.3 miles (2.1 km) that's marked with a "2." The number (along with others) was placed by Salt Spring Island hiking guidebook author Charles Kahn to help hikers find their way in this maze of old roads.

Turn right for some fairly level walking through thick forest, coming to a junction marked "3" at 2 miles (3.2 km). Continue straight, passing big stumps and a wetland pool and reaching a junction (elev. 1,650 ft/503 m) marked "4" at 2.4 miles (3.9 km). Switchback left and steeply climb on rocky tread, ignoring radiating paths. At 2.6 miles (4.2 km), bear left at a Y intersection, soon traversing grassy slopes with good views.

Snout-nosed Mount Maxwell and Fulford Harbour from Reginald Hill

At 3.1 miles (5 km), reach junction "5" at a trashed campsite (elev. 2050 ft/625 m).

Continue up the road a few steps, looking for a lightly traveled trail that branches right. Take it, reaching a helipad and some communications towers at 3.3 miles (5.3 km). You're not on Bruce's summit yet. Walk the service road left 0.2 mile (0.3 km), coming to the summit service road (closed to private vehicles). Turn left and walk 0.3 mile (0.5 km) up this road to the multitowered high point of Mount Bruce.

Look beyond the "communications forest" to sweeping views below of Burgoyne Bay, Vancouver Island, Mount Baker, the Olympic Mountains, and scores of San Juan and Gulf islands. Hopefully the views make up for the less-than-appealing route. Return the way you came when you've had your fill of the Salish Sea scenery before you.

EXTENDING YOUR TRIP

Definitely explore the old farm grounds. Walk the path leaving from the gate 0.3 mile (0.5 km) to a farm pond and barn foundations. About 0.1 mile (0.15 km) west of the trailhead, locate another old road heading north. Follow this path 0.2 mile (0.3 km) to an old pasture and foundations by the mill creek. Look for remnants of the mill wheel by the creek. There are a lot of other intriguing remnants here too. Please leave them for others to enjoy.

104 Reginald Hill

RATING/ DIFFICULTY	ROUNDTRIP	ELEV GAIN/HIGH POINT
****/3	1.8 miles (2.9 km)	670 feet (204 m)/ 800 feet (244 m)

Maps: NTS 092B14 Mayne Island, park map online; **Contact:** Salt Spring Island

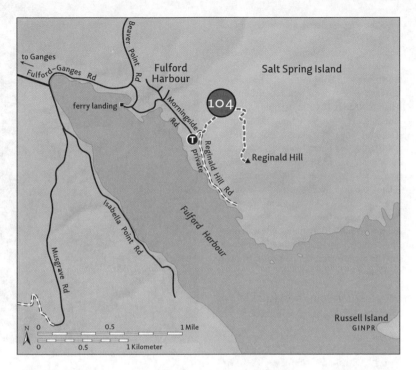

Parks and Recreation, Reginald Hill Trail; **Notes:** No parking on Reginald Hill Road. Dogs permitted on-leash; **GPS:** N 48 45.968, W 123 26.405

This little peak above Fulford Harbour affords one of the finest views on Salt Spring Island of prominent snout-nosed Mount Maxwell. Enjoy excellent views too of Hope Hill, Mount Tuam, and Mount Bruce, the rooftops of Salt Spring.

GETTING THERE

From the Fulford Harbour ferry landing on Salt Spring Island, immediately turn right onto Morningside Road and drive 0.6 mile (1 km) to the junction with Reginald Hill Road. Park here in the cul-de-sac (elev. 130 ft/40 m). Don't even think about parking on Reginald Hill Road.

ON THE TRAIL

This short, sweet, and at times a little steep hike is a local favorite—especially for morning or evening jaunts. The trail travels through private property via an easement, so please stay on the path.

From the parking area, walk up Reginald Hill Road 0.1 mile (0.15 km), coming to the well-signed trailhead. Follow the trail, which at first utilizes an old road bed, on a fairly level course. All that changes at 0.3 mile (0.5 km), where the way bends right to become a bona fide trail—and a steep one at that.

Steeply climb up forested slopes interspersed with ledges, and reach Reginald Hill's 800-foot (244-m) arbutus-framed, open, grassy, ledgy summit at 0.9 mile (1.4 km). Savor the views! Look south to Swartz Bay, watching ferries running back and forth. Look straight across Fulford Harbour to Hope Hill and Mount Tuam. Then face northwest and embrace one of the island's best views: Mount Bruce and Mount Maxwell framing the glacier-carved Burgoyne Valley. Stay for a while and enjoy the sublime setting. Then prep your knees for the steep descent, and return the way you came.

105 Beaver Point and Ruckle Farm

RATING/ DIFFICULTY	LOOP	ELEV GAIN/HIGH POINT
****/1	1.8 miles (2.9 km)	150 feet (46 m)/ 120 feet (37 m)

Maps: NTS 092B14 Mayne Island, park map online; **Contact:** BC Parks, Ruckle Provincial Park; **Notes:** Dogs permitted on-leash, but several trails near active farm are closed to dogs; **GPS:** N 48 46.407, W 123 22.606

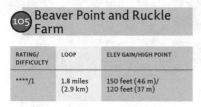 *Visit the oldest continuously operating farm in British Columbia. Then hike along oak- and arbutus-adorned coastal bluffs to Beaver Point, taking in stunning coastal views and watching for ferries, seals, otters, eagles, and oystercatchers.*

The historic Ruckle Farm Homestead

GETTING THERE

From Fulford Harbour ferry landing on Salt Spring Island, follow Fulford–Ganges Road 0.2 mile (0.3 km) and bear right onto Beaver Point Road. Drive 5.6 miles (9 km) to the trailhead (elev. 120 ft/37 m), on the right 0.2 mile (0.3 km) past the handicapped access to the historical farm. Privy and bike racks available.

ON THE TRAIL

Walk 0.2 mile (0.3 km) to the historical orchard, farm, and home of Henry Ruckle, who emigrated here from Ireland in 1872. He and his wife, Ella Anna, raised their family here, and their descendants still own and tend to the active farm within the 1307-acre (529-ha) provincial park they established in 1974 through donation. Spend a little time reading the interpretive panels, checking out the old structures and equipment, and keeping an eye on the large rafter of turkeys (yep, that's what a group of these birds is called).

Then head along the split-rail fence and big-maple-lined trail, coming to a junction at 0.4 mile (0.6 km). The spur to the right drops down to Grandmas Bay, a nice side trip when the tide is low. Your loop, however, continues left through a grassy open forest of arbutus, oak, and Douglas fir, coming to Ruckle's very inviting campground. Follow the camp road right. At 0.7 mile (1.1 km), bear right at a road junction and skirt a quarantine area for the invasive carpet burweed, which threatens Ruckle's native plants, including the endangered Macoun's meadowfoam and Nuttall's quillwort.

At 0.9 mile (1.4 km), pick up the trail again and stay right at a junction, emerging on an open rocky area that screams with wildflowers in spring. A bench located here allows you to sit and soak up the scenery, which includes views of Pender and Moresby islands. Continue hiking, coming to a spur at 1.2 miles (1.9 km). Take it right 0.1 mile (0.15 km) to small and rocky Beaver Point, with its excellent views across Swanson Channel.

Retrace your steps and turn right, descending on sandstone steps to a picnic area at the old Beaver Point ferry landing. Turn left and follow an old road, passing the trailhead for the coastal trail (Hike 106) and then walking a short distance up the road back to your vehicle.

EXTENDING YOUR TRIP
Combine with the hike to Yeo Point (Hike 106).

106 Ruckle Provincial Park: Yeo Point

RATING/ DIFFICULTY	LOOP	ELEV GAIN/HIGH POINT
*****/3	5.7 miles (9.2 km)	600 feet (183 m)/ 150 feet (46 m)

Maps: NTS 092B14 Mayne Island, park map online; **Contact:** BC Parks, Ruckle Provincial Park; **Notes:** Dogs permitted on-leash, but several trails near active farm are closed to dogs; **GPS:** N 48 46.429, W 123 22.329

Meander along coves rich with wildlife and cliffy shelved headlands that seem straight out of the Acadian Coast of Maine and New Brunswick. Marvel at towering ancient trees holding up the sky and delicate blossoms carpeting grassy ledges that drop straight to the sea. One of the longest shoreline hikes in the Gulf Islands, the trail to Yeo Point is full of scenic, historical, and natural surprises.

GETTING THERE
From Fulford Harbour ferry landing on Salt Spring Island, follow Fulford–Ganges Road 0.2 mile (0.3 km) and bear right onto Beaver Point Road. Continue for 5.8 miles (9.3 km) into Ruckle Provincial Park and reach the trailhead (elev. 40 ft/12 m) at the road's end. Privy available.

ON THE TRAIL
The spectacular 1307-acre (529-ha) Ruckle Provincial Park protects more than 4 miles (7 km) of Salt Spring Island shoreline and the oldest continuously operating farm in British Columbia. The topography can be tough along the coast, with rough terrain

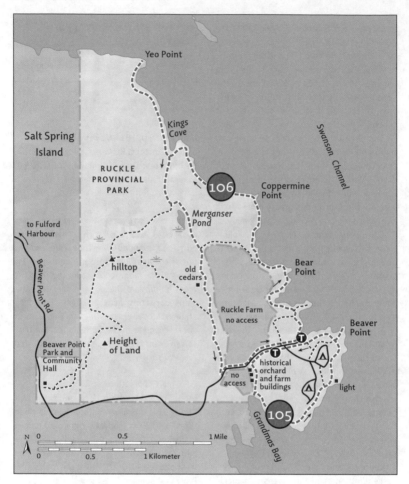

and a lot of ups and downs. But the return on an old woods road is easier, a reprieve for tired souls.

From a picnic area, head north on the Shoreline Trail, passing a stairway leading to a cove. At 0.2 mile (0.3 km), bear right at a junction, passing another cove access stairway and soon coming to another junction.

The spur right leads 0.1 mile (0.15 km) to a flowered headland with excellent views of Beaver Point, Galiano, and Pender islands as well as the rocky coastline north you are about to explore.

The main way continues left through thick forest and over rocky and rooty terrain. Round a cove, cross a creek, and skirt the active farm within the park. Then walk along a scenic coastal stretch, passing a midden beach. Look for otters. Round Bear Point, with its big arbutuses, and cross an old farm road that leads to a big cove.

At 1 mile (1.6 km), near a grove of big firs, come to a junction. The trail left (dogs prohibited) leads 0.6 mile (1 km) along the active farm, connecting with this loop's return trail and offering a shorter loop option or easier route to Yeo Point. The coast trail bears right on a rough and tumble route. After reaching a rocky coastal bluff, the way steeply climbs 100 feet (30 m) and then gradually descends along a mossy ledge, coming to Coppermine Point and its midden beaches at 1.6 miles (2.6 km).

Now hiking westward, traverse a thickly forested and salal-carpeted coastline, passing big cedars and firs along the way. After making a couple of bridged creek crossings, come to a junction at 2.3 miles (3.7 km). You'll be returning via the trail left, after first hiking out and back to Yeo Point. Go right, crossing a creek and soon coming to Kings Cove with its great view of Galiano and Prevost islands.

Then keep hiking north, passing another midden beach and traversing grassy, mossy

Ruckle's shoreline looks remarkably like the Acadian Coast.

ledges that display brilliant blossoms in spring. Pass shelved coastal ledges and pocket coves that look strikingly Acadian. Watch ferries as they busily ply Swanson Channel. Pass an unmarked trail leading to Meyer Road, coming to a grove of big cedars and a beautiful gravelly beach. At 3 miles (4.8 km), reach the trail's end at Yeo Point. Enjoy the views of islands large and small, near and far.

When you're ready to start up again, retrace your steps 0.7 mile (1.1 km) to the Shoreline Trail junction and continue straight, enjoying pleasant walking on an old woods road. At 4 miles (6.4 km), reach a junction. The trail right leads to the Hilltop and to Beaver Point Community Park. You want to continue left, soon coming to Merganser Pond (elev. 150 ft/46 m) and its active beaver colony.

At 4.3 miles (6.9 km), reach a junction with the Active Farm Trail coming from the Shoreline Trail (shortcut route). Continue right, through a gorgeous grove of ancient giant cedars, before crossing over a fence line (via steps) and reaching a junction (elev. 110 ft/34 m) with the Hilltop Trail at 4.7 miles (7.6 km). Keep hiking straight, skirting meadows dotted with cattle and sheep. Climb 50 feet (15 m) and descend, crossing another fence line before reaching the trail's end (no parking) on Beaver Point Road (elev. 110 ft/34 m) at 5.1 miles (8.2 km). Then turn left and walk the road 0.6 mile (1 km) back to your vehicle, passing the historical orchard and farm and adding another 80 feet (24 m) to your cumulative elevation gain.

EXTENDING YOUR TRIP
From the junction near Merganser Pond, hike west 0.6 mile (1 km) through some of the oldest and biggest trees in the park. Turn left at a junction and climb over the Hilltop (elev. 450 ft/137 m), passing deer-loving open groves of big cedars and arbutuses and reaching the old farm road trail in 0.9 mile (1.4 km). If you can arrange for a pickup, from the junction near the Hilltop, continue west 1.6 miles (2.6 km) up and over a 460-ft (140-m) bald called Height of Land to Beaver Point Park and Community Hall (elev. 225 ft/69 m).

Wallace Island

Located in the Trincomali Channel between Salt Spring and Galiano islands, this sliver of an island is packed with scenic and historical delights. Most of Wallace Island is protected within a provincial marine park.

107 Chivers Point

RATING/ DIFFICULTY	ROUNDTRIP	ELEV GAIN/HIGH POINT
****/2	4 miles (6.4 km)	350 feet (107 m)/ 80 feet (24 m)

Map: NTS092 B13 Duncan; **Contact:** BC Parks, Wallace Island Marine Provincial Park; **Notes:** Dogs permitted on-leash. Pack water or treat island water; **GPS:** N 48 56.208, W 123 32.596

Traverse Wallace Island on good trails to sandstone-shelved beaches, hidden coves, and arbutus groves and through a funky old resort. Deer and eagles are profuse; otters and seals are common too. And so are summer visitors, so plan your hike for the off-season.

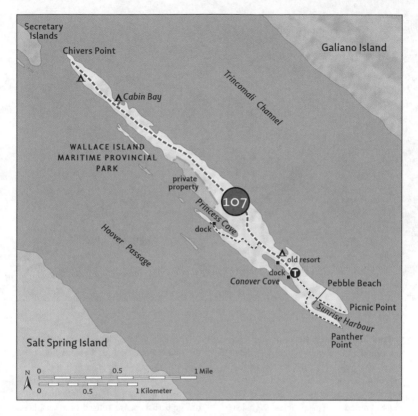

Secretary Islands

Chivers Point

Galiano Island

Cabin Bay

Trincomali Channel

WALLACE ISLAND
MARITIME PROVINCIAL
PARK

private property

107

Princess Cove

dock

Hoover Passage

old resort

dock

Conover Cove

Pebble Beach

Picnic Point

Sunrise Harbour

Panther Point

Salt Spring Island

N
0   0.5   1 Mile
0   0.5   1 Kilometer

GETTING THERE

You need a private boat or to arrange for a water taxi to access Wallace Island. Salt Spring Reel Action (www.ssireelaction.ca) offers year-round water taxi service from Ganges on Salt Spring Island. The trailhead is at the Conover Cove dock. No potable water.

ON THE TRAIL

From the Conover Cove dock, walk to a park kiosk and vintage sign pointing out your options. Definitely head left to the old resort established by American David Conover after

he purchased the island in 1946. A successful author and documentary photographer noted for discovering Marilyn Monroe, Conover ran the resort with his wife, Jeanne, until the 1960s. He sold the island to a group of teachers from Seattle, but legal wrangling resulted in a court-order sale leading to the establishment of a park in 1990. Two private parcels remain, while the park occupies 178 acres (72 ha) of this beautiful island.

Snoop around the remaining old buildings, especially the cabin that hosts thousands of driftwood engravings of island

Have fun reading all of the driftwood plaques on this old resort cabin.

visitors' boat names. Here too find one of the island's three walk-in campgrounds (18 sites, open year-round). Then continue hiking, first past an old quarry and water tower and then coming to an abandoned old truck in a wet meadow at a junction at 0.3 mile (0.5 km). Left leads 0.5 mile (0.8 km) to a small dock on a narrow peninsula along Princess Cove. You want to go right, following a wide track on a gently rolling course that passes through wetland depressions and periodically crests small sandstone ridges.

At 1.6 miles (2.6 km), reach a junction. The trail right leads 100 yards (100 m), dropping to gorgeous, snug Cabin Bay and its 2 campsites. Peer across the channel to Galiano Island's coastal cliffs. Visit the bay or keep hiking forward, passing a cabin of some sort choked in greenery.

Through a fold cloaked in salal, come to Chivers Point and its 9 campsites at the northern tip of the island, at 2 miles (3.2 km). The point is named for Jeremiah Chivers, a Scotsman who came to British Columbia for the gold rushes. He retired here and lived alone on the island until 1927. Spend time admiring junipers, big arbutuses, tide pools, and a great view to the nearby Secretary Islands. Hall, Reid, and Valdes islands are in the distance. Retrace your steps to Conover Bay and consider more hiking options.

EXTENDING YOUR TRIP

Consider hiking to the island's southeastern tip too. From the dock, follow good trail right 0.1 mile (0.15 km) to a junction. The trail left travels 0.4 mile (0.6 km) to Pebble Beach and Picnic Point. The trail right travels

0.5 mile (0.8 km) to Sunrise Harbour and Panther Point, the latter named not for a big cat but for a big ship that ran aground here in 1874. Both points offer spectacular viewing of Galiano and Salt Spring islands as well as offshore reefs rife with marine life.

Princess Margaret (Portland) Island

At 560 acres (227 ha), Princess Margaret Island, also known as Portland Island, is the largest island protected entirely within the Gulf Islands National Park Reserve. It was settled and farmed in the 1880s by Kanakas (Hawaiian Islanders) who came to British Columbia to work for the Hudson's Bay Company, and it was nearly developed into a major resort in the 1920s by an ambitious businessman. Today the island is as wild as ever. Given to Princess Margaret (hence the dual name) by the provincial government in 1958, the royal deeded the island back to the BC people in 1967 during Canada's centennial, for preservation as a park. The island has three excellent camping areas (24 sites, no water, open May 15–September 30).

108 Princess Margaret (Portland) Island

RATING/ DIFFICULTY	LOOP	ELEV GAIN/HIGH POINT
*****/2	4.3 miles (6.9 km)	600 feet (183 m)/ 50 feet (15 m)

Maps: NTS 092B11 Sidney, Parks Canada Gulf Islands brochure; **Contact:** Gulf Islands National Park Reserve, Portland Island; **Notes:** Dogs permitted on-leash. Pack water or treat island water; **GPS:** N 48 43.144, W 123 22.279

Roam a pristine island entirely protected as national park land. Explore First Nations middens and old orchards cultivated by Kanakas who homesteaded here in the 1880s. Visit quiet coves and gentle headlands, savoring views of the Salish Sea and her cornucopia of islands. Watch for whales, otters, eagles, and oystercatchers on this royal island indeed.

GETTING THERE

You need a private boat or to arrange for a water taxi to access Princess Margaret Island. Eco Cruising Tours and Charters (www.ecocruising.com) at the Canoe Cove

Gorgeous view of Salt Spring Island's Mount Maxwell from Kanaka Bluff

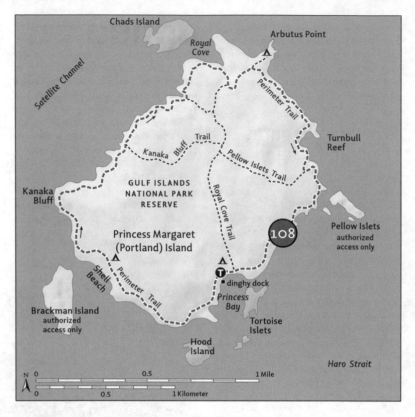

Marina, located near the BC Ferry terminal at Swartz Bay on Vancouver Island, offers reliable service. This hike starts from Princess Bay's dinghy dock (removed October 1–May 14). Privy available. No potable water.

ON THE TRAIL

At Princess Bay find privies, campsites, and interpretive signs around a former orchard. The Royal Cove Trail makes a 0.9-mile (1.4-km) beeline across the island to its namesake cove on the north shore. We'll get there eventually by circumnavigating the island.

From the dock, head left on the Perimeter Trail, enjoying excellent views of nearby islets as well as of Moresby, Pender, Saturna, Sydney, and Stuart. The way stays close to the shoreline, rolling up and over small rises (that add some cumulative elevation gain) and traversing groves of cedars, firs, and arbutuses.

As you round the western shore, archeologically important (and restricted) Brackman Island comes into view. So too does BC Ferries' flotilla of boats plying the busy Shute Passage and Satellite Channel.

At 0.8 mile (1.3 km), reach gorgeous Shell Beach, its white midden shoreline tempting you to linger (there's a campground here). Walk a short distance along the beach, picking up trail once more. The way is a little rough and brushy here. Announcements for ferries from Swartz Bay can be heard along with the gull, eagle, and crow chatter. Reach Kanaka Bluff, with its small beacon, and marvel at an exceptional view across the channel of Salt Spring Island's snout-nosed Mount Maxwell rising behind Fulford Harbour.

Continue through arbutuses, oaks, junipers, and cedars, traveling up and over bluffs and grassy ledges. At about 1.7 miles (2.7 km), come to the easy-to-miss junction with the Kanaka Bluff Trail which leads 0.5 mile (0.8 km) inland to the Royal Cove Trail. Continue straight, encountering another rough stretch and reaching a shortcut to the Royal Cove Trail at 2.1 miles (3.4 km).

Continue straight, rounding a point to enter Royal Cove, protected by Chads Island. Pass the dinghy dock and reach a junction at 2.4 miles (3.9 km). Right, the Royal Cove Trail, is the direct way back to Princess Bay. You want to head left, crossing a creek on a boardwalk and coming to a junction at 2.6 miles (4.2 km). The spur left leads a short distance to Arbutus Point, with its beautiful beach and nice camping area.

Your loop veers right. Walk along the northern shore, enjoying views out to Pender and Galiano islands. Scan coastal shelves at low tide for rummaging raccoons. Notice the abundance of kingfishers here too. At 3 miles (4.8 km), a spur leads left to a point overlooking busy-with-marine-life Turnbull Reef.

The Perimeter Trail skirts a nice cove and beach before climbing over a 50-foot (15-m) bluff, coming to a junction with the Pellow Islets Trail at 3.3 miles (5.3 km). It leads 0.5 brushy, boggy miles (0.8 km) inland to the Royal Cove Trail. Head left over another 50-foot (15-m) bluff, catching views of the Pellow Islets (no public access) just offshore. Then enjoy a gorgeous stretch of trail that heads up and over steep bluffs, through thick forest groves, and across grassy bluffs that burst with spring wildflowers. Views are divine of Moresby, Stuart, and San Juan islands; Mount Baker and the Olympics; and the Saanich Peninsula. At 4.1 miles (6.6 km), return to Princess Bay. The dinghy dock is another 0.2 mile (0.3 km) away.

Sidney Island

One of the southernmost of the Gulf Islands, 2200-acre (890-ha) Sidney Island is known for its wide sandy beaches. It was once a private hunting preserve. In 1981 a 440-acre (178 ha) provincial marine park was established on the island's northern tip, encompassing its large sandspits. The remainder of the island was purchased by the Sallas Forest Strata corporation for a 111-lot private development. Sydney Spit became a unit of the Gulf Islands National Park Reserve in 2003. Popular with boaters, campers (28 seasonal sites), and local sun and surf worshipers, Sidney Island offers great hiking too.

109 Sidney Spit

RATING/ DIFFICULTY	ROUNDTRIP	ELEV GAIN/HIGH POINT
*****/1	3.9 miles (6.3 km)	120 feet (37 m)/ 90 feet (27 m)

Map: NTS 092B11 Sidney, Parks Canada Gulf Islands brochure; **Contact:** Gulf Islands National Park Reserve, Sidney Spit; **Notes:**

Dogs permitted on-leash. Pack water or treat island water. Water taxi runs summer only; **GPS:** N 48 38.509, W 123 19.847

 *Wander along a long slender sandy spit, one of the finest beach walks in the Gulf Islands. Watch ferries ply the waters and plovers comb the shore. Then roam through stately forest, sprawling fields, and back through history to an old brick-making operation. If you desire more exploring, a wildlife-rich lagoon and another sandy spit awaits.*

GETTING THERE

From the Port of Sidney marina on the Saanich Peninsula, take the Alpine Sidney Spit water taxi (www.alpinegroup.ca/comp anies/alpine-sidney-spit-ferry; mid-May–Labor Day) to the Parks Canada dock on Sidney Island. Privy and seasonal water available (must be treated).

ON THE TRAIL

From the long park dock, notice the purple martin boxes before setting out. Thirty years ago there were only five nesting pairs of this bird in the entire province. Today there are hundreds thanks to nesting boxes placed here and in other areas.

Start exploring by first walking the 1.1 miles (1.8 km) to the tip of the long spit, graced with a small beacon. Be sure to stay out of the dunes, where nesting birds and rare plants struggle to survive—keep your walking to the inviting shoreline. Enjoy excellent views of Mount Newton and Salt Spring Island's Mount Tuam as well Isle-de-Lis, Moresby Island, Stuart Island, and scores of other islands. Sidney and nearby James Island are unique in that they are composed of cakes of glacial sand, clay, and gravel covered with a thin layer of soil. The bluffs here easily erode, causing the spit to constantly reshape, making each hike here a little bit different.

Saunter along the surf, then return to the dock area and the loop trail starting at the end of the boardwalk. Head up a bluff 0.1 mile (0.15 km) to a junction. You'll be returning from the left, so veer right toward the campground on nice trail through an open forest of big trees. Notice how dry the

Sidney Spit contains one of the finest beaches within the Gulf Islands.

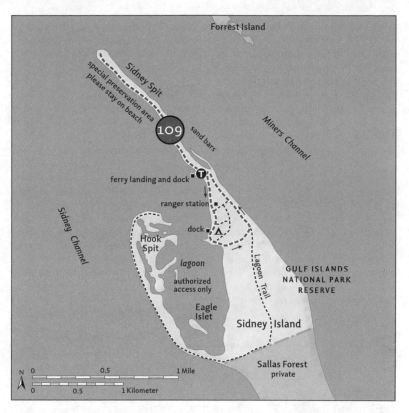

Forrest Island

Sidney Spit

special preservation area
please stay on beach

109

sand bars

Miners Channel

ferry landing and dock ■ **T**

ranger station ■

dock ■ △

Hook
Spit

lagoon

authorized
access only

Sidney Channel

Eagle
Islet

Lagoon Trail

GULF ISLANDS
NATIONAL PARK
RESERVE

Sidney Island

Sallas Forest
private

N 0   0.5   1 Mile

0   0.5   1 Kilometer

landscape is—this is one of the driest islands in the chain. Look for European fallow deer, descendants of a herd introduced in 1902 when the island was a private hunting preserve. Their presence has greatly altered the island's ecosystems.

At 0.3 mile (0.5 km), stay right at a junction near the ranger station. Soon emerge from forest to a large open area pocked with large depressions. A clay brick mining and milling operation was here from 1906 to 1925. A path here leads through the fields, offering a shorter loop option. Continue

right, passing inviting campsites and coming to a dock at 0.6 mile (1 km). Here, thanks to Hook Spit across the way, a large lagoon has formed. It's rich in wildlife, and so entry into it is prohibited—but with binoculars you can get some good views from this spot.

Now continue hiking, passing more campsites before reentering forest and coming to another junction at 0.8 mile (1.3 km), on a bluff. The Lagoon Trail right (see Extending Your Trip) makes an excellent option for an all-day adventure. Otherwise, turn left and continue hiking, passing through a grove of big cedars.

After topping out at an elevation of 90 feet (27 m), peek through trees from the bluff out to the San Juan Islands. At 1.2 miles (1.9 km), stay straight at a junction. The way left goes to the ranger station. The right-hand path to the beach is closed due to erosion. Pass another junction that leads to privies and continue straight, reaching a good viewpoint of the spit at 1.5 miles (2.4 km). Then head left 0.2 mile (0.3 km), returning to the dock to catch the water taxi back to Sidney.

EXTENDING YOUR TRIP

For a quiet and extended hike, follow the Lagoon Trail 1.1 miles (1.8 km), passing through deer study plots and dropping 150 feet (46 m) from a ridge to a beautiful and deserted shoreline. Catch a glimpse of

Smooth sandstone ledge at Pilkey Point

Eagle Islet in the lagoon and then walk 1.5 miles (2.4 km) to the end of Hook Spit. Don't forget to bring water and sunscreen.

Thetis Island

Named after the HMS *Thetis*, a Royal Navy frigate, Thetis Island is the least populated of the ferry-accessible Gulf Islands. Home to about four hundred residents and three Christian camps, the 2560-acre (1036-ha) island is a peaceful place with few commercial establishments. BC Ferries provides year-round service to Thetis from Chemainus on Vancouver Island. Unfortunately for hikers, Thetis is almost entirely privately owned, with no public trails and very little public beach access. But its lightly traveled roads make for some fine walking, and the island is just too pretty to ignore.

110 Pilkey Point

RATING/ DIFFICULTY	ROUNDTRIP	ELEV GAIN/HIGH POINT
***/3	9.4 miles (15.1 km)	700 feet (213 m)/ 440 feet (134 m)

Maps: NTS 092B13 Duncan, NTS 092G04 Nanaimo; **Contact:** Thetis Island Community Association; **Notes:** Road hike, also good for bicycles; **GPS:** N 48 58.842, W 123 40.706

Walk quiet country roads on this small island, up and over Moore Hill to pretty Pilkey Point, where you can sit and stare at a serene seaside scene.

GETTING THERE

From Victoria or Nanaimo, take Trans-Canada Highway 1 to Henry Road and follow

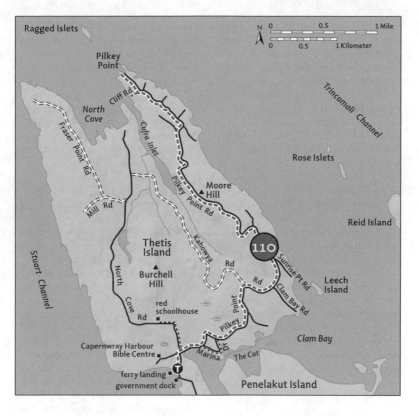

Thetis Island Ferry signs approximately 2 miles (3.2 km) to the Chemainus ferry landing. Park along Croft Street and walk on the ferry. The hike begins from the Thetis Island ferry landing.

ON THE TRAIL

From the ferry landing, walk 300 feet (90 m) to Foster Point Road. To the right 0.1 mile (0.15 km) is the government dock, if you choose to arrive via your own watercraft. The hike goes left along the lovely grounds of the Capernwray Harbour Bible Centre. Share the

wonderful (dare I say heavenly) views across Stuart Channel to Vancouver Island peaks with the center's geese and cows. Sign in at the reception desk if you want to walk the grounds.

At 0.2 mile (0.3 km), the road bends right upon cresting a small hill (elev. 50 ft/15 m), coming to a junction. Keep right, now following Pilkey Point Road, which drops to hug oak- and arbutus-lined Telegraph Harbour. At 0.4 mile (0.6 km), come to a junction with Marina Drive near the Pot o' Gold Coffee Roasting Company. An alternative route, Marina Drive loops back to Pilkey Point Road in 0.4 mile (0.6 km), passing a marina and beach access at the narrow channel separating Thetis from Penelakut Island (formerly known as Kuper and closed to non–First Nations peoples).

Your way heads left, passing a sheep farm and small pond, reaching Marina Drive once again at 0.7 mile (1.1 km). Continue straight along a tidal lagoon before taking to a series of rolling hills. Stay on Pilkey Point Road, ignoring all side roads, and eventually start a prolonged climb. Just after passing Sunrise Point Road, catch a limited but good view to Reid and Galiano islands.

The way then steeply climbs up a hillside of arbutuses, cresting a shoulder (elev. 440 ft/134 m) high on Moore Hill at 2.7 miles (4.3 km). Catch window views west before steeply descending through attractive forest. At 4.7 miles (7.6 km), reach the road's end at Pilkey Point, where a bench invites you to relax and recharge. Walk around the juniper-graced, sandstone-shelved point (minding private property), watching for seals and oystercatchers. Enjoy excellent views, too, out to Yellow Point, Gabriola Island, Valdes Island, De Courcy Island, and a handful of islets. Prepare for the grunt back over Moore Hill on the return, retracing the route you took to get here.

EXTENDING YOUR TRIP
At the end of short Cliff Road (0.25 mi/0.4 km south of Pilkey Point), you can catch a glimpse of the narrow and deeply cut Cufra Inlet. Near the bible center, walk North Cove Road 0.3 mile (0.5 km), passing a huge arbutus, to the island's little red schoolhouse, one of the last one-room schoolhouses in the region.

Gabriola Island

Owing to its proximity to Nanaimo, Gabriola Island is the second-most populated of the Gulf Islands. And unlike the islands farther south, which are part of the Capital Regional District, Gabriola is part of the Nanaimo Regional District. About 4400 folks call this 22.2-square-mile (57-sq.-km) island home. Known for its arts community, Gabriola has many studios and sports a small village with commercial establishments. Much of the island is rural, however, with large tracts of Crown land and parks.

The island also has several public beach access points, and at low tide a good portion of Gabriola's sandstone-shelved shore can be hiked. The Gabriola Land and Trails Trust has been developing an extensive trail system throughout the island, offering many extended walks and loop options.

BC Ferries offers year-round service from Nanaimo, making the island a convenient day trip from southern Vancouver Island. Folks coming from British Columbia's Lower Mainland can get to Nanaimo (Departure Bay or Duke Point) via BC Ferries from either Horseshoe Bay (north of Vancouver) or Tsawwassen. Camping options include Descanso Bay Regional Park (seasonal, 32 sites) and year-round Page's Resort and Marina (www.pagesresort.com). Page's also offers moped rentals.

111 Malaspina Galleries

RATING/ DIFFICULTY	ROUNDTRIP	ELEV GAIN/HIGH POINT
****/2	1.6 miles (2.6 km)	Minimal/20 feet (6 m)

Maps: NTS 092G04 Nanaimo, land trust map online; **Contact:** Gabriola Land and Trails Trust, Malaspina Galleries; **Notes:** Dogs permitted on-leash. Shoreline hike only

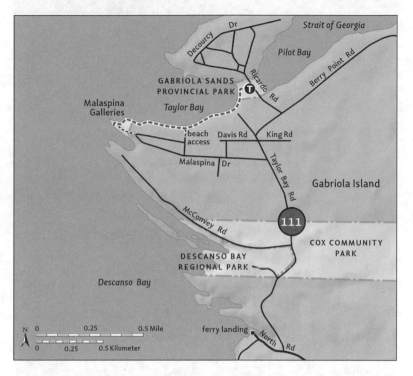

Strait of Georgia

Decourcy Dr

Pilot Bay

Berry Point Rd

GABRIOLA SANDS PROVINCIAL PARK

Ricardo Rd

Malaspina Galleries

Taylor Bay

beach access

Davis Rd   King Rd

Malaspina Dr

Taylor Bay Rd

Gabriola Island

111

McConvey Rd

COX COMMUNITY PARK

DESCANSO BAY REGIONAL PARK

Descanso Bay

N 0   0.25   0.5 Mile
   0   0.25   0.5 Kilometer

ferry landing

North Rd

possible at low tide. Respect adjacent private property; **GPS:** N 49 11.653, W 123 51.522

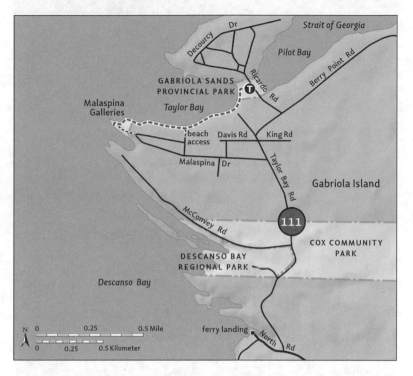 *Hike from a gorgeous bayside beach along a shoreline of honeycombed sandstone shelves to one of the Gulf Islands' most famous landmarks—the Malaspina Galleries. A large wind- and surf-sculpted overhanging wave of sandstone at the edge of the sea, the galleries have been intriguing visitors for hundreds of years.*

GETTING THERE

From Nanaimo, take a BC ferry to Gabriola Island. Drive 0.2 mile (0.3 km) and turn left onto Taylor Bay Road. Follow it for 1.1 miles (1.8 km), turning right onto Berry Point Road. After 0.2 mile (0.3 km), turn left onto Ricardo Road and proceed 0.2 mile (0.3 km) to Gabriola Sands Provincial Park. Park on the right—the hike begins across the road. Privy available.

ON THE TRAIL

From the small isthmus separating Pilot and Taylor bays, walk west across an inviting lawn to the wide sandy beach of Taylor Bay. If the tide is high, sit down and enjoy the view. Otherwise, begin walking left along the sandstone-shelved tidelands. Property above the high tide line is private, so stay below.

Malaspina Galleries' honeycombed and surf-sculpted overhanging sandstone ledges

The walking is easy—like on a hard surfaced road. Stroll up and over ribs of rock and along salty honeycombed outcroppings. Admire interesting sculptures and cannonball rocks. The view across Taylor Bay to Mount Benson, and to Newcastle, Quadra, and Lasqueti islands, is sublime.

Check out tidal pools for big purple starfish and other intriguing critters. Watch plovers, eagles, ravens, and other birds dine at these open markets.

Pass by the totem pole of the Haven (a residential learning center) and shortly afterward, the Lloyd Crescent Beach

Access. Keep walking along the shoreline, approaching a finger peninsula topped with Douglas firs and arbutuses. At about 0.8 mile (1.3 km), round the small peninsula and behold the Malaspina Galleries. One of the Gulf Islands' most notable natural landmarks, the galleries consist of waves of hooded sandstone ledges above a honeycombed shelf that teeters above the surf. Stay off of them; they are fragile. They are best viewed from the water if you have access to a kayak. The galleries were named for Alessandro Malaspina, an Italian nobleman who sailed as a Spanish naval officer and explorer. He spent much of 1791–92 in the Pacific Northwest, and his name can be found on many features along the British Columbia coast.

Return the way you came. You probably noticed that there's a trail at the galleries. It's the 0.1-mile (0.15-km) short way here from Malaspina Drive. It's far more interesting getting here via Taylor Bay.

112 Sandwell Provincial Park

RATING/ DIFFICULTY	ROUNDTRIP	ELEV GAIN/HIGH POINT
***/2	1.4 miles (2.3 km)	185 feet (56 m)/ 90 feet (27 m)

Maps: NTS 092G04 Nanaimo, land trust map online; **Contact:** BC Parks and Gabriola Land and Trails Trust, Sandwell Provincial Park; **Notes:** Dogs permitted on-leash; **GPS:** N 49 11.005, W 123 48.710

Walk along one of the finest strands of sand on Gabriola Island, a gorgeous stretch of beach with views of the Sunshine Coast and little Entrance Island. And when the tide is low, have fun locating a prehistoric petroglyph.

GETTING THERE

From Nanaimo, take a BC ferry to Gabriola Island. Follow North Road 2 miles (3.2 km), turning left onto Barrett Road. After 0.7 mile (1.1 km), turn left onto Bluewater Road and then immediately turn left onto Bond Street. After 0.2 mile (0.3 km), turn left onto The Strand Road and drive 0.5 mile (0.8 km) to the trailhead, on the left.

Enjoy the sandy beach at Sandwell Provincial Park.

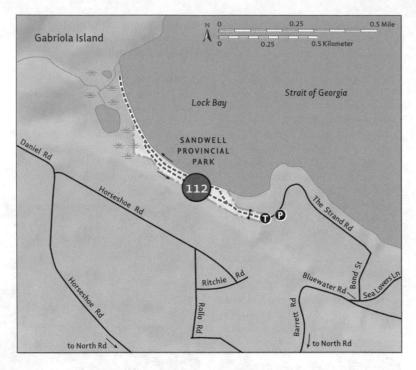

ON THE TRAIL

Begin on an old dirt road through a tunnel of alders. Pass a gate and some big Douglas firs, burly maples, and cedar stumps, coming to a junction at 0.15 mile (0.2 km). If the tide is low, head right. Drop steeply (with the aid of steps) to the beach at 0.2 mile (0.3 km) after passing through a grove of big cedars.

Now start walking left along the long sandy beach—one of the island's best. Look for a petroglyph in one of the sandstone rocks along the surf. Enjoy views out to little Entrance Island, with its lighthouse, and Bowen Island, along with the impressive peaks surrounding Howe

Sound in the background. Mosey along the old-growth-flanked shoreline. At 0.4 mile (0.6 km), come to where the old road that you started on ends. This is your return (and high-tide) route. But first continue another 0.3 mile (0.5 km) on the beach along Lock Bay. The smooth sand transitions to cobblestones before you reach private property. Look for killdeer in the cobbled rocks.

Turn around and return to the old road access. Pass a privy and steeply climb under a cool canopy provided by towering ancient trees. After about 90 feet (27 m) of climbing, drop a little and climb a little, scooting along sandstone ledges. Then gradually descend to the trailhead at 1.4 miles (2.3 km).

113 707-Acre Community Park

RATING/ DIFFICULTY	LOOP	ELEV GAIN/HIGH POINT
**/2	4.8 miles (7.7 km)	250 feet (76 m)/ 485 feet (148 m)

Maps: NTS 092G04 Nanaimo, land trust map online; **Contact:** Gabriola Land and Trails Trust, 707-Acre Community Park; **Notes:** Some trails open to bicycles and horses. Dogs permitted on-leash; **GPS:** N 49 09.900, W 123 47.540

Stroll miles of old logging roads and trails in Gabriola Island's largest park, a large swath of public land in the center of the island. Explore meadows, wetlands, regenerating forests, and hillsides that grant a few views out to Vancouver Island's mountains.

GETTING THERE
From Nanaimo, take a BC ferry to Gabriola Island. Follow North Road 2.9 miles (4.7 km) to the Stumps trailhead (elev. 400 ft/122 m), on the right.

ON THE TRAIL
Established in 2005, Gabriola Island's 707-Acre Community Park shows great recreational promise. It consists primarily of recently logged-over lands and a myriad of old roads and trails. Hiking here once meant assured disorientation, but that changed in 2013 with the installation of new and excellent signage throughout the park.

Starting from the Stumps trailhead (where a new parking lot and trailheads are planned), follow the North Road Trail south, staying left at an unmarked junction and coming to a signed one at 0.2 mile (0.3 km).

You'll be returning from the right on the Old Centre Road Trail, so keep hiking straight, traversing a grassy cutover area flourishing with daisies in early summer.

At 0.6 mile (1 km), come to a junction with the Coats Drive Trail. Left leads to a road of the same name. You want to go right, hiking fairly easy terrain, passing alder and arbutus groves and cutting across a small wetland. At 1.3 miles (2.1 km), once again reach the Old Centre Road Trail (elev. 460 ft/140 m). For a short loop, turn right and return to the trailhead in 1.2 miles (1.9 km). Otherwise, continue straight on the Old Centre Road Trail, staying left at several junctions, signed and unsigned.

At 2.2 miles (3.5 km), turn right onto the Erratic Trail, passing a few junctions and reaching the Tin Can Alley Trail (elev. 360 ft/110 m) at 2.5 miles (4 km). Bear right, soon

At least the Trail to Nowhere is well marked.

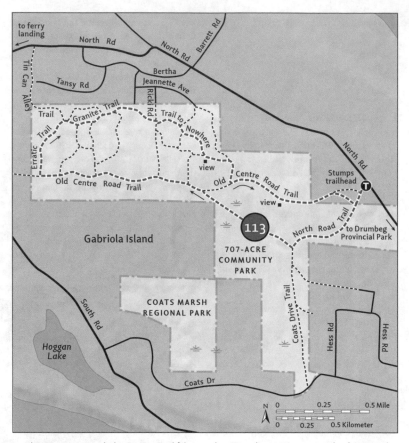

reaching a junction with the Granite Trail (elev. 380 ft/116 m) at 2.6 miles (4.2 km). Head left here, following the rolling Granite Trail and ignoring radiating trails left and right, reaching the Ricki Road Trail (elev. 400 ft/122 m) at 3.1 miles (5 km).

Walk right a few steps and then head left on the Trail to Nowhere (a bit of a misnomer), staying on this trail and ignoring radiating side trails. At 3.5 miles (5.6 km), crest a small ridge (elev. 485 ft/148 m), where limited views can

be enjoyed out to Vancouver Island. At 3.8 miles (6.1 km), once again come to the Old Centre Road Trail (elev. 435 ft/133 m).

Turn left and follow this wide, grassy, and enjoyable-to-walk path through wetlands and forest openings and over a small ridge (elev. 450 ft/137 m) that grants window views. At 4.4 miles (7.1 km), bear right at a junction in a field, reaching the North Road Trail at 4.6 miles (7.4 km). Turn left on familiar tread, coming to your starting point in 0.2 mile (0.3 km).

114 Elder Cedar Nature Reserve

RATING/ DIFFICULTY	LOOP	ELEV GAIN/HIGH POINT
***/2	1.1 miles (1.8 km)	Minimal/240 feet (73 m)

Map: NTS 092G04 Nanaimo; **Contact:** Islands Trust Fund and Gabriola Land and Trails Trust, Elder Cedar Nature Reserve; **Notes:** Dogs permitted on-leash; **GPS:** N 49 09.366, W 123 45.427

Walk among the biggest and oldest trees remaining on Gabriola Island. Permanently saved from the chainsaw in 2006 after a fifteen-year campaign, this grove of cedars sacred to the Snuneymuxw First Nation is a testament to the grand forests that once cloaked the islands of the Salish Sea.

GETTING THERE

From Nanaimo, take a BC ferry to Gabriola Island. Follow North Road 5.2 miles (8.4 km) to a small dirt drive on the left. The turnoff is easy to miss—it's 0.1 mile (0.15 km) west of Degnen Road—and the trailhead is just off the road.

ON THE TRAIL

Former Crown land, this 160-acre (65-ha) tract was spared from the logging frenzy of the 1980s and '90s through the diligence of the Snuneymuxw First Nation, Gabriola Land Conservancy, Islands Trust Fund, and local

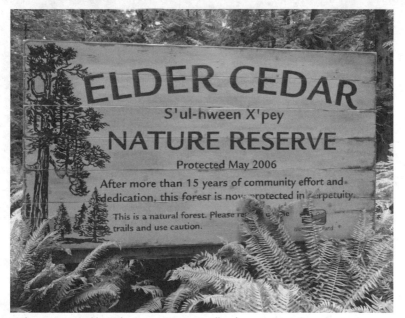

Dedication sign at Elder Cedar Nature Preserve trailhead

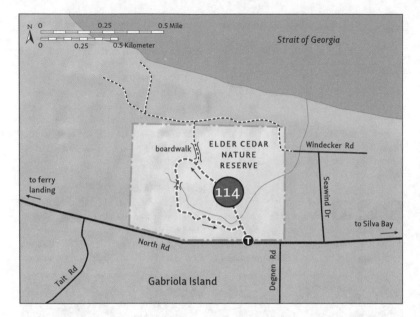

citizens. This place is revered by the Snuney-muxw people as home to ancient spirits. Walk in awe among the giant trees and let the forest's little yet equally important denizens—frogs, owls, bats, thrushes—garner your reverence as well.

From the commemorative reserve sign, walk about 150 feet (50 m) to a junction. You'll be returning from the left, so carry on right, soon hopping on rocks across either a creek (in winter) or dry stream bed (in summer). Hike deeper into the reserve on a fairly level path, through a dark forest of cedars and firs and lined with ferns and salal. At 0.2 mile (0.3 km), you will reach a massive lone cedar.

At 0.4 mile (0.6 km), come to a junction. Your loop heads left, remaining on a somewhat level course through mature second-growth timber interspersed with some

big giants. After a bridged creek crossing, come to a marshy area and follow alongside a small creek. At 1.1 miles (1.8 km), return to the first junction, closing the loop. Your vehicle is just a few steps to the right.

EXTENDING YOUR TRIP

From the second junction, a good trail heads to the right through attractive forest and across a boardwalk, coming to an old woods road in 0.25 mile (0.4 km). You can then follow that road to the right 0.5 mile (0.8 km) to Windecker Road; or, explore several kilometers of old woods roads and trails to the left through adjacent Crown lands that extend from the 707-Acre Community Park to the Joyce Lockwood Community Park on the coast. Be sure to have the Gabriola Land and Trails Trust map with you.

115 Drumbeg Provincial Park

RATING/ DIFFICULTY	ROUNDTRIP	ELEV GAIN/HIGH POINT
****/1	1.2 miles (1.9 km)	100 feet (30 m)/ 60 feet (18 m)

Maps: NTS 092G04 Nanaimo, land trust map online; **Contact:** BC Parks and Gabriola Land and Trails Trust, Drumbeg Provincial Park; **Notes:** Dogs permitted on-leash; **GPS:** N 49 08.034, W 123 41.754

Drumbeg Provincial Park packs quite a bit of beauty within its mere 49 acres (20 ha). Walk through flowering meadows and oak groves above a sandstone-shelved shoreline along Gabriola Passage's turbulent waters. Admire eagles, seals, oyster-catchers, and a score of nearby islands.

GETTING THERE
From Nanaimo, take a BC ferry to Gabriola Island. Follow North Road 0.5 mile (0.8 km), bearing right onto South Road. Continue for 8 miles (12.9 km) and turn right onto Coast Road. In 0.1 mile (0.15 km), turn right onto Stalker Road and continue for 0.5 mile (0.8 km) (the road becomes gravel), turning left onto the Drumbeg Park access road. Proceed 0.3 mile (0.5 km) to the road's end and trailhead. Privy available.

ON THE TRAIL
The trails here are short but the scenery is quite satisfying, inviting you to lounge. Walk on the wide path toward the shoreline, immediately coming to a picnic area and junction. Both ways are worthy of exploration. Go left first, coming to a kiosk. Learn that this park received its name from the Scottish town that former owner Neil Stalker emigrated from. And learn about the dreaded Scotch broom, an invasive plant from Scotland that threatens native species in this park and throughout the Gulf Islands and is a challenge to eradicate. Be aware too of another invasive in the park—giant hogweed—and avoid contacting it, as it can cause severe blistering and blindness.

Now pass oak groves and come to a beautiful meadow above a sandstone-shelved shoreline. Continue hiking, rounding a small bluff and coming to the trail's end at the park boundary at 0.3 mile (0.5 km). Look out at nearby Rogers Reef, Breakwater Island, and a handful of other small islands—some uninhabited. Scan their shoreline snags for bald eagles.

Valdes Island across Gabriola Passage

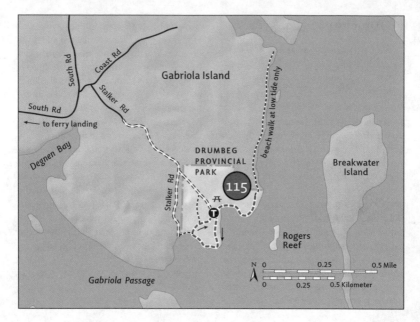

Then retrace your steps to the picnic area and continue hiking straight, rounding a small beach. Here, along narrow Gabriola Passage, which separates Gabriola Island from Valdes Island, the currents run strong. Admire long and slender and sparsely populated Valdes Island. It's a popular destination for boaters, and about one-third of the island is owned by the Lyackson First Nation.

Continue on this short but scenic forested coastal walk, complete with arbutuses and honeycombed rocks. Catch a nice view all the way to Saturna and Orcas islands. At 0.3 mile (0.5 km) from the picnic area, come to a junction. The trail left leads a couple of hundred meters to Stalker Road. Turn right instead and follow a quiet path through attractive open forest over a small bluff. Bear right at another junction

to soon return to the trailhead, at 0.3 mile (0.5 km) from your turnaround spot.

EXTENDING YOUR TRIP
At low tide, you can walk north on sandstone shelves for about 0.6 mile (1 km) to a pass separating Gabriola from little Sear Island. Take note: above the high-water mark is private property.

Newcastle Island
Sitting directly in Nanaimo Harbour, 756-acre (306-ha) Newcastle Island is one of the finest provincial parks in British Columbia. Popular and well-loved, Newcastle has a colorful history. It was first settled by Coast Salish peoples. Then coal was mined on the island from 1853 until 1883 and sandstone

quarried from 1869 until 1932. Japanese immigrants operated a saltery and shipyard until 1941, when they were interned during World War II. In 1931 the Canadian Pacific Steamship Company bought Newcastle and built a resort that included a dance pavilion, tea house, wading pool, and playfields. It was extremely popular until operations were curtailed and finally ceased during World War II. At last, in 1961, Newcastle became a provincial park and is now managed by the Snuneymuxw First Nation. The park (www.newcastleisland.ca) has mooring buoys and 18 year-round campsites (seasonal reduced services).

116 Newcastle Island

RATING/ DIFFICULTY	LOOP	ELEV GAIN/HIGH POINT
*****/2	6.4 miles (10.3 km)	400 feet (122 m)/ 170 feet (52 m)

Map: NTS 092G04 Nanaimo; **Contact:** Snuneymuxw First Nation and BC Parks, Newcastle Island Marine Provincial Park **Notes:** Some trails open to mountain bikes. Dogs permitted on-leash. Water taxi runs late Mar–mid-Oct; **GPS:** N 49 10.826, W 123 55.718

Wander on manicured trails along towering sandstone cliffs and through arbutus groves as you hike back in time on this fascinating island in Nanaimo Harbour. Explore midden bays, old quarries, and beautifully restored buildings from an early twentieth-century resort. Now a marine provincial park, it is a prime spot to spend a few hours, the night, or several days.

GETTING THERE

From Nanaimo, at Maffeo Sutton Park on Comox Road which is one block east of Trans-Canada Highway 1, take the Nanaimo Harbour Ferry (nanaimoharbourferry.com; late March–mid-October) to the docks at the south end of Newcastle Island.

ON THE TRAIL

From the park docks, walk past purple martin boxes to a well-groomed path that cuts across manicured lawns. The many interpretive displays and signs on the island help you appreciate this culturally rich place. In 0.1 mile (0.15 km), come to the restored dance pavilion now serving as a concession (think ice cream on your return).

You'll be returning from the left on the Date Point Trail, so head to the right on the Shoreline Trail—a double-track lined with mature firs, maples, and oaks. Pass camp and picnic sites, coming to sandstone-shelved beaches. Enjoy excellent views of nearby Protection Island (with its floating pub, the only one in North America), Gabriola Island, and North Shore peaks north of Vancouver, across the Strait of Georgia. At 0.4 mile (0.6 km), bear right at a well-marked (like most in the park) junction. Left leads to sports fields and the Kanaka Bay Trail, popular with mountain bikers.

After passing the last of the campsites, cross a bridge over a lagoon outlet at Brownie Bay. Then head north along a bluff through oak groves and old-growth firs, savoring sweeping coastal views. At 1.3 miles (2.1 km), reach a junction with the Kanaka Bay Trail. Continue right, along Kanaka Bay, watching for the golden (albino) raccoons of the island. At low tide, the bay begs for exploration.

At 1.4 miles (2.3 km), bear right at a junction. Left leads 0.9 mile (1.4 km) to the

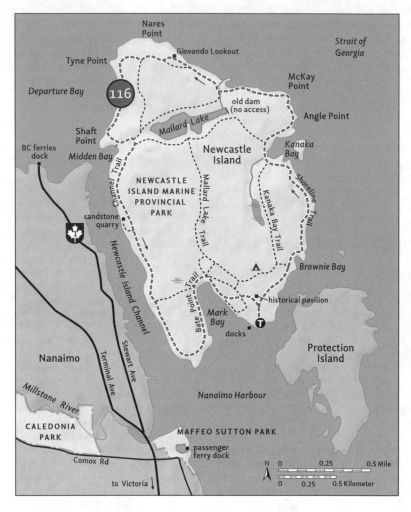

Nares Point

Giovando Lookout

Strait of Georgia

Tyne Point

McKay Point

Departure Bay

116

old dam (no access)

Angle Point

Shaft Point

Mallard Lake

Kanaka Bay

BC ferries dock   *Midden Bay*

Newcastle Island

NEWCASTLE ISLAND MARINE PROVINCIAL PARK

sandstone quarry

Brownie Bay

historical pavilion

Mark Bay

docks

Nanaimo

Protection Island

Millstone River

Nanaimo Harbour

CALEDONIA PARK

MAFFEO SUTTON PARK

passenger ferry dock

Comox Rd

to Victoria ↓

N   0   0.25   0.5 Mile

0   0.25   0.5 Kilometer

Channel Trail, passing Mallard Pond en route and making for a nice shorter loop trip. Your route now becomes a rougher single-track, soon coming to Angle Point, with its spectacular 270-degree coastal view. The trail then rounds salal-choked McKay Point before traversing a cedar grove. Shortly after a bridged creek crossing, come to a junction at 2.2 miles (3.5 km).

Left leads 0.7 mile (1.1 km) along the north shore of Mallard Lake to Midden Bay, offering another loop option (note: the trail over the old dam is closed). Continue right, through ancient forest to the Giovando Lookout loop at 2.8 miles (4.5 km). Take it, coming to the lookout pavilion (elev. 170 ft/52 m) located on a towering pine-cloaked bluff above Fairway Channel. Enjoy views to the Sunshine Coast before returning to the main trail and continuing right.

Pass a privy and descend to a junction in a grove of old cedars at 3.1 miles (5 km). Go right, on a rugged up-and-down path along sandstone cliffs above Departure Bay. Watch seaplanes and ferries arriving and departing in the busy bay and catch good views of Mount Benson in the background.

Descend to the shoreline, passing good beaches before crossing a creek near the ruins of an old mining operation. Continue rounding Shaft Point, with its blooming Nootka roses (in season), coming to a junction at Midden Bay at 3.8 miles (6.1 km). Right leads to the bay. Stay left, soon coming to another junction. Left leads to Mallard Lake. Bear right, soon coming to yet another junction (elev. 100 ft/30 m) at 4 miles (6.4 km). Left leads to the south shore of Mallard Lake. Hike right instead on the Channel Trail, traversing a bluff above Newcastle Island Channel. At 4.5 miles (7.2 km), come to a short spur that leads right into an old quarry, which provided sandstone for the construction of such buildings as the San Francisco Mint. The side trip is worth the diversion.

The main way continues along the noisy channel, coming to a junction at 5.2 miles (8.4 km). Left is the direct way back to the dock. If you have the time and energy, continue straight on the Bate Point Trail, looping around Bate Point, traveling through oaks and arbutuses, and enjoying excellent views of Nanaimo Harbour.

Monstrous overhanging arbutuses line Newcastle Island's Shoreline Trail.

At 6 miles (9.7 km), bear right at a junction, and soon afterward bear right again where a trail left leads to Mallard Lake. Rounding Mark Bay, climb back up on the bluff, following a wide double-track trail to the pavilion at 6.3 miles (10.1 km). Linger to check out a nearby old quarry, or directly return 0.1 mile (0.15 km) to the dock, content after exploring this fascinating island.

EXTENDING YOUR TRIP

Spend the night on the island and/or explore the interior trails to Mallard Lake. Explore some of the excellent trails and parks in and around Nanaimo, including Westwood Lake, Mount Benson, and Bowen parks.

victoria and saanich peninsula

Finlayson Arm from Jocelyn Peak

Occupying the southeast corner of Vancouver Island, the Saanich Peninsula and Victoria—British Columbia's capital city—are not only gateways to the Salish Sea and Gulf Islands; they are historically, culturally, and naturally linked to them as well. The entire region is also politically linked within the Capital Regional District, encompassing the southern Vancouver Island coast and Gulf Islands. Home to more than 360,000 people, the area is well known for its outdoor recreation lifestyle and its environmental consciousness.

BC Ferries offers year-round service to Swartz Bay, on the northern tip of the Saanich Peninsula, from Tsawwassen on the province's Lower Mainland. From the United States, Washington State Ferries serves the region with its seasonal Anacortes-to-Sidney run; and the Black Ball Ferry Line runs (almost) year-round from Port Angeles to Victoria Harbour.

Victoria and the Saanich Peninsula are blessed with scores of parks, many of them regional parks with well-developed trail systems, offering some of the best hiking in the region. The Gulf Islands National Park Reserve operates seasonal McDonald Campground (49 campsites) on Saanich Peninsula. Goldstream Provincial Park (167 campsites) is north of Victoria.

117 John Dean Provincial Park

RATING/ DIFFICULTY	LOOP	ELEV GAIN/HIGH POINT
***/3	2.9 miles (4.7 km)	500 feet (152 m)/ 1000 feet (305 m)

Maps: NTS 092B11 Sidney, park map online; **Contact:** BC Parks, John Dean Provincial Park; **Notes:** Dogs permitted on-leash. Park

road closed to vehicles Nov–Mar. Walk road to trailhead or access park from trailheads at Alec Road and Carmanah Terrace; **GPS:** N 48 52.363, W 123 18.777

Occupying Mount Newton, a locally prominent peak topped with a giant golf ball (radar installation), 430-acre (174-ha) John Dean Provincial Park offers kilometers of excellent hiking trails. The park protects one of the largest tracts of old-growth Douglas fir and Garry oak on the Saanich Peninsula, as well as rare and copious wildflowers.

Views abound from Pickles' Bluff.

GETTING THERE

From the BC Ferry terminal at Swartz Bay or the Washington State Ferry terminal at Sidney, follow BC Highway 17 (Patricia Bay Highway) south to the McTavish Road exit near the airport. (From Victoria, head north on BC 17.) Follow McTavish Road for 0.4 mile (0.6 km) and turn left onto East Saanich Road. Continue for 0.9 mile (1.4 km) and turn right onto Dean Park Road. Follow it for 2 miles (3.2 km) to its end and the trailhead (elev. 825 ft/251 m). Privy available.

ON THE TRAIL

Start by following the Valley Mist Trail 0.1 mile (0.15 km) west, dropping into a cool

forested draw and coming to a junction. The Illahie Loop continues left to the Emerald Pool and site of John Dean's cabin. Born in England in 1850, Dean homesteaded here in 1884. In 1921 he donated much of his claim to the province, making it the first donated park in British Columbia. In subsequent years, other families and folks donated adjoining lands and the province added parcels too, enlarging this beloved park to its current size.

Continue right, passing a wetland and soon coming to a junction with the looping Skippers Trail. Stay left, following a creek through gorgeous old-growth forest to lovely little Lily

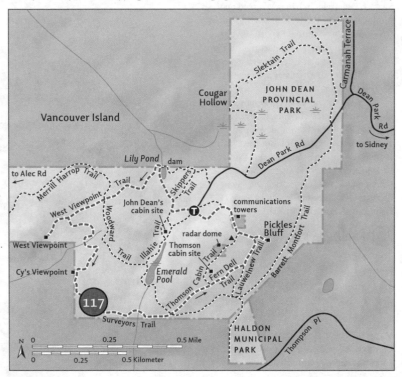

Pond (elev. 740 ft/226 m) and, in 0.3 mile (0.5 km), a junction. Scout out the old dam and gazebo just to your right if you like, before continuing left on the West Viewpoint Trail up a stairway. Pass more old-growth beauties, including a pair of humongous cedars. At 0.6 mile (1 km), come to a four-way junction (elev. 860 ft/262 m). The Merrill Harrop Trail heads right 1.1 miles (1.8 km), dropping 450 feet (137 m) on its way to Alec Road. The Woodward Trail travels left to the Emerald Pool, offering a short loop option back to the trailhead. Continue straight, coming to another junction at 0.7 mile (1.1 km).

You'll be continuing left on the Surveyors Trail—but first continue 0.15 mile (0.2 km) to the West Viewpoint (elev. 770 ft/235 m), located on a grassy, rocky outcropping graced with arbutuses. Take in a view of Finlayson Arm and then return to the last junction, continuing right on the Surveyors Trail. The way winds through gorgeous ancient trees, dropping to cross Owl Creek (elev. 750 ft/229 m) before climbing to Cy's Viewpoint (elev. 800 ft/244 m) at 1.4 miles (2.3 km), with its limited view of the Malahat.

Continue on the Surveyors Trail a short distance to a much better lookout, taking in a sweeping view of Mount Douglas, Mount Work, the Gowlland Range, Saanich Inlet, the Olympics, and more. The way steeply descends into a gully (elev. 750 ft/229 m), crossing Canyon Creek and then steeply climbing to a four-way junction (elev. 840 ft/256 m) at 1.9 miles (3.1 km). Here the Woodward Trail travels left to the Emerald Pool and right to the quiet Barrett Montfort Trail.

Proceed straight ahead through oak forest on the Thomson Cabin Trail, coming to the cabin site and a junction at 2.1 miles (3.4 km). The Thomson Cabin Trail veers left, climbing some stairs and then skirting

the radar installation on Mount Newton's 1000-foot (305-m) summit. Instead, head right on the Fern Dell Trail, reaching the Lauwelnew Trail at 2.2 miles (3.5 km). Head left up grassy ledges, coming to another junction (elev. 940 ft/287 m) at 2.3 miles (3.7 km). The 0.1-mile (0.15-km) side trip to the right, down a long staircase to Pickles Bluff (elev. 860 ft/262 m), is a must. What a view! Out to Saturna, James, Sidney, Stuart, and San Juan islands—Victoria, the Olympics, and Mount Baker, too!

After feasting on the views, retrace your steps (literally) and continue up the Lauwelnew Trail on stone steps, reaching the radar service road (elev. 1000 ft/305 m) on Mount Newton's (viewless) summit at 2.6 miles (4.2 km). Don't bother heading to the nearby Abraham Collins Viewing Platform near the communications towers, as surrounding trees have obscured the views. Instead, turn right and follow the service road back to the trailhead, reaching your start at 2.9 miles (4.7 km).

EXTENDING YOUR TRIP

You can spend all day hiking in this park. For extended hiking, consider starting this loop from the Carmanah Terrace trailhead and hiking into the park 1.6 miles (2.6 km) via the Barrett Montfort and Woodward trails. The 0.9-mile (1.4 km) Slektain Trail is another option, with solitude almost assured.

118 McKenzie Bight

RATING/ DIFFICULTY	ROUNDTRIP	ELEV GAIN/HIGH POINT
***/3	3.2 miles (5.1 km)	585 feet (178 m)/ 475 feet (145 m)

Maps: NTS 092B11 Sidney, park map online; **Contact:** BC Parks, Gowlland Tod Provincial

Park; **Notes:** Dogs permitted on-leash; **GPS:** N 48 33.001, W 123 29.426

Hike to a quiet cove on the Squally Reach at the mouth of the Finlayson Arm, the small but dramatic fjord separating the Saanich Peninsula from the Malahat region. Then walk along the reach's rocky coastline, passing big trees, old quarries, and favorite haunts of local divers.

GETTING THERE
From Victoria or Sidney, follow BC Highway 17 (Patricia Bay Highway) and exit onto Royal Oak Drive. Proceed west 0.3 mile (0.5 km) and turn right (north) onto BC 17A (West Saanich Road). Drive 3.6 miles (5.8 km), bearing left onto Wallace Drive. In 0.3 mile (0.5 km), turn left onto Willis Point Road. After 2.5 miles (4 km), turn left onto Ross–Durrance Road and drive 0.1 mile (0.15 km)

McKenzie Bight on the Saanich Inlet

to the trailhead (elev. 475 ft/145 m), on the left. Privy available.

ON THE TRAIL
At more than 3000 acres (1200 ha), Gowlland Tod Provincial Park encompasses some of the most breathtaking scenery in the Capital Regional District. The park's diverse landscape includes much of the Gowlland Range along the eastern shore of Finlayson Arm and a good portion of the Tod Inlet adjacent to the renowned Butchart Gardens. Wildlife, plant species, and cultural and historical sites are numerous; trails too, more than 15 miles (25 km) within the park. This hike provides access to the park's stunning shoreline.

Locate the trailhead directly across the road from the parking lot. Then follow the wide path through mature second growth steeply down into a moist ravine. Save some energy for the return climb up. Cross a creek and come to a junction with the Cascade Trail at the bight at 0.8 mile (1.3 km). Take time to explore the bight—especially during low tides. Watch for otters.

The trail continues right if you care to keep hiking. Pass a privy and spur trail leading to a small rocky point adorned in arbutus and granting excellent viewing to the Saanich Inlet and Salt Spring Island. The trail then climbs about 70 feet (21 m) up a wooded bluff, passing some big firs. It then bends left and steeply drops, reaching shoreline ledges perfect for resting. Now utilizing an old road continue hiking, reaching trail's end at 1.6 miles (2.6 km) on Mark Lane. Return the way you came.

EXTENDING YOUR TRIP
For a variation on the return, take the Cascade Trail from the bight. Cross a creek and

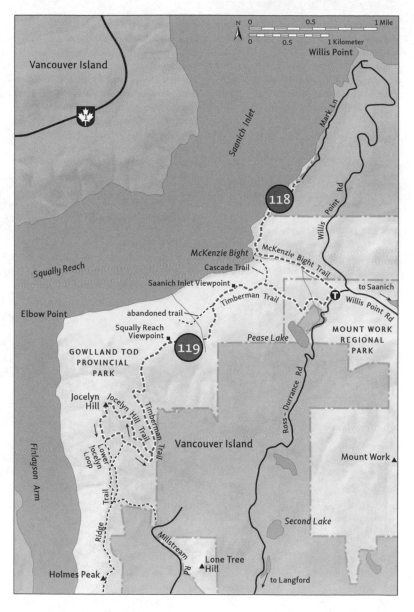

N

0   0.5   1 Mile
0   0.5   1 Kilometer

Willis Point

Vancouver Island

Saanich Inlet

Mark Ln

Willis Point Rd

118

McKenzie Bight

McKenzie Bight Trail

Cascade Trail

Squally Reach

Saanich Inlet Viewpoint

to Saanich

Timberman Trail

Willis Point Rd

Elbow Point

abandoned trail

Squally Reach
Viewpoint

119

Pease Lake

MOUNT WORK
REGIONAL
PARK

GOWLLAND TOD
PROVINCIAL
PARK

Ross – Durrance Rd

Jocelyn Hill

Jocelyn Hill Trail

Timberman Trail

Vancouver Island

Lower
Jocelyn
Loop

Mount Work

Finlayson Arm

Ridge Trail

Second Lake

Millstream Rd

Lone Tree
Hill

Holmes Peak

to Langford

steeply climb, utilizing steps at times, along the edge of a ravine. Pass a small cascade tumbling into the ravine before reaching the Timberman Trail (Hike 119) at 0.5 mile (0.8 km). Follow this trail left 0.7 mile (1.1 km) to Ross–Durrance Road. Walk the road left 0.15 mile (0.2 km) back to the parking lot.

119 Jocelyn Hill

RATING/ DIFFICULTY	ROUNDTRIP	ELEV GAIN/HIGH POINT
*****/4	8.3 miles (13.4 km)	1600 feet (488 m)/ 1400 feet (427 m)

Maps: NTS 092B11 Sidney, NTS 092B12 Shawnigan Lake, park map online; **Contact:** BC Parks, Gowlland Tod Provincial Park; **Notes:** Dogs permitted on-leash; **GPS:** N 48 32.929, W 123 29.527

From this open summit in the Gowlland Range, enjoy stupendous views overlooking the Saanich Inlet fjord. Stand upon grass-lined striated ledges, staring at the Finlayson Arm sparkling straight below. One of the finest ridge walks on the Saanich Peninsula, the traverse to Jocelyn is rife with jaw-dropping views, dazzling wildflowers, and impressive groves of arbutus and oak. It's a challenging hike too, with copious ups and downs and ledgy terrain.

GETTING THERE
See directions to Hike 118.

ON THE TRAIL
Walk left (south) on Ross–Durrance Road 0.15 mile (0.2 km) to reach the trailhead for the Timberman Trail. Then start your jour-

Rounded Mount "Finney" (left) and the dramatic Finlayson Arm

ney along the Gowlland Range, which flanks the eastern slopes of the Saanich Inlet. The trail starts out easy enough as a wide woods road. Soon enter the more than 3000-acre (1200-ha) Gowlland Tod Provincial Park, which protects a large swath of rugged terrain along Finlayson Arm and Tod Inlet.

At 0.8 mile (1.3 km), after crossing a creek, bear left at a junction with the Cascade Trail, which drops steeply to McKenzie Bight. Continue on good trail, occasionally encountering some rocky sections. Ignore bootleg trails radiating left and right. Don't bother following the old Malahat View Trail either, as it's no longer maintained. The Timberman Trail is well trodden and marked, however, so you shouldn't be led astray.

Pass a window view of the Saanich Inlet and steadily climb. Round a knoll (elev. 980 ft/299 m) after passing some big cedars and descend to a creek crossing (elev. 940 ft/287 m). At 2 miles (3.2 km) come to a junction (elev. 1000 ft/305 m). Absolutely go right on the 0.1-mile (0.15-km) roundtrip to the Squally Reach Viewpoint atop a 1050-ft (320-m) flowered bald with sweeping views of the Saanich Inlet out to the Gulf Islands.

Then continue hiking on the Timberman Trail, cresting another flowered bald (elev. 1200 ft/366 m) and proceeding on a rocky, ledgy route lined with arbutus and shore pine. Pass wetland pools and undulate between short, steep ups and downs. Eventually traverse grassy southern slopes that radiate with flowers in summer and provide good views of Mount Work and the Olympics year-round.

Steeply descend once more before reaching a junction (elev. 1075 ft/328 m) at 3.3 miles (5.3 km). You'll be returning from the left. So continue right on the Jocelyn Hill Trail, through groves of big arbutus to grassy slopes streaked with striated ledges. At 3.8 miles (6.1 km),

emerge atop Jocelyn's 1400-foot (427-m) summit and bask in splendid views out over Victoria to the Olympics and west over rounded Mount Finlayson and the jumbled Sooke Hills.

The best is yet to come, so keep hiking, traversing open ledges that teeter on the edge of the Saanich Inlet. Revel in the beauty of the shimmering waters of Finlayson Arm straight below. Carry on, each ledge offering new angles and perspectives—and in summer scads of flowers. Watch for scads of raptors, too, riding the thermals.

At 4.5 miles (7.2 km), reach a junction (elev. 1200 ft/366 m). The Ridge Trail continues south to Holmes Peak. Take the trail left to begin your return. Ignore a trail right and continue straight, descending on an old road to a bridged creek crossing (elev. 1000 ft/305 m) before steeply climbing. At 5 miles (8 km), reach a familiar junction. Turn right and retrace your steps for 3.3 miles (5.3 km) of beautiful and challenging Gowlland Range terrain back to your vehicle.

EXTENDING YOUR TRIP

You can also access Jocelyn Hill from the south via the 2.4-mile (3.9-km) Ridge Trail over Holmes Peak (also with excellent views), from the Caleb Pike access. The start is much higher (elev. 700 ft/213 m) and can be reached from Millstream Road (see directions to Lone Tree Hill, Hike 127).

120 Mount Work

RATING/ DIFFICULTY	ROUNDTRIP	ELEV GAIN/HIGH POINT
****/4	4 miles (6.4 km)	1020 feet (311 m)/ 1473 feet (449 m)

Maps: NTS 092B11 Sidney, park map online; **Contact:** Capital Regional District

Parks, Mount Work Regional Park; **Notes:** Dogs permitted on-leash; **GPS:** N 48 32.992, W 123 29.401

Hike to the highest summit on the Saanich Peninsula, named for a chief factor of the Hudson's Bay Company, for nice views and gneiss outcroppings. You'll have your work cut out for you clambering over Mount Work's ledges. But the views—from Victoria to Mount Baker—are divine and all in a day's work.

GETTING THERE
See directions to Hike 118.

ON THE TRAIL
There are two ways to summit Mount Work. The southern approach is a little shorter, with less elevation gain but a steeper ascent. The northern approach described here tends to see less use. Starting on a wide old woods road, begin hiking in a deep lush forest of cedars and firs. At 0.15 mile (0.2 km), veer right at a junction, continuing on single-track. The grade soon steepens, the tread now more difficult due to roots and rocks. At 0.7 mile (1.1 km), encounter big rocky outcroppings—glacially striated ledges of gneiss.

The grade eventually eases as the trail works its way up a ridge. Pass wetland pools and big trees and several bootleg paths. Your route is marked with yellow blazes, so keep an eye out for them. The way once again steepens, switchbacking through some ledges, where manzanita, arbutus, and shore pine begin to dominate.

At about 1.4 miles (2.3 km), after passing a viewpoint east, the trail drops to wiggle through some small ledges. Because of its age and rocky, well-worn demeanor, much

Salt Spring Island's emerald peaks hover in the distance above the Saanich Inlet.

of the mountain feels like it belongs in the Appalachians or Laurentians. Encounter more steep ledges that may have you using your hands, and emerge on an open slab that grants exceptionally fine views of Pease Lake, Saanich Inlet, Malahat, and Salt Spring Island.

Continue hiking a short distance, cresting the nondescript 1473-foot (449-m) summit at 2 miles (3.2 km), where you'll find southwestern-exposed ledges and excellent viewing of the greater Victoria area. Pick out Esquimalt Harbour, Sooke Hills, and Mount Finlayson. Enjoy scanning the Strait of Juan de Fuca, too, and its

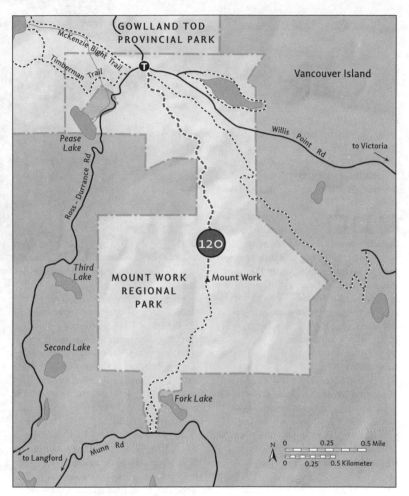

snowy backdrop of the Olympic Mountains. Wander a little way down the other side of the mountain for better vantages before the trail returns to the trees and steeply descends to its southern trailhead. Then work your way back over the summit and return the way you came.

EXTENDING YOUR TRIP

Arrange for a pickup on Munn Road and continue hiking the trail 1.7 miles (2.7 km) down the mountain's south side. It's a steeper descent, with some nice cedar forest along Fork Lake near its terminus (elev. 740 ft/226 m) on Munn Road.

121 Elk/Beaver Lake

RATING/ DIFFICULTY	LOOP	ELEV GAIN/HIGH POINT
**/2	6.7 miles (10.8 km)	Minimal/220 feet (67 m)

Maps: NTS 092B06 Victoria, park map online; **Contact:** Capital Regional District Parks, Elk/Beaver Lake Regional Park; **Notes:** Partly wheelchair-accessible. Open to bicycles and horses. Dogs permitted on-leash; **GPS:** N 48 30.557, W 123 23.416

Once two separate lakes and the water supply for Victoria, the now adjoined Elk/Beaver Lake is one of the Capital Regional District's most popular parks. Paddlers, cyclists, equestrians, swimmers, fishers, runners, and hikers in large numbers descend upon this 1095-acre (443-ha) regional park year-round. The hike around the lake(s) makes for a nice calorie burner any time.

GETTING THERE

From Victoria or Sidney, follow BC Highway 17 (Patricia Bay Highway) and exit onto Elk Lake Drive (the turnoff is 1 mi/1.6 km north of the Royal Oak Drive exit). Proceed 0.3 mile (0.5 km), turning right into the park entrance. Continue 0.3 mile (0.5 km) to the trailhead at Beaver Beach. Privy available.

ON THE TRAIL

Bordering the Patricia Bay Highway and on the radar screen of so many recreationists, this is not a wilderness hike. However, there are quiet coves and tranquil forest groves along the way—and if you visit in the rain or on a dark winter day, you just may have a stretch of trail to yourself.

Trail approaching Hamsterly Beach on Elk Lake

From Beaver Beach head right on the 10K loop, a route designed and maintained by the Peninsula Runners of Victoria. You'll be following this mostly level route the entire way—with a few deviations to continuously hug the shoreline of Elk/Beaver Lake. At 0.6 mile (1 km), head left on a shore-hugging trail, reuniting with the 10K route at 1.4 miles (2.3 km) after passing the "strait" that connects the two lakes.

Now turn left, passing Eagle Beach and the Elk Lake Rowing Centre. Enjoy views of Bear Mountain and Observatory Hill across the lake. For a short distance, the trail is wedged between the lake and the Patricia Bay Highway, before a row of cottonwoods greet you at Hamsterly Beach.

Continue through a nice forest grove and enjoy views of the Olympic Mountains across the lake, far to the south. Skirt a few private residences before coming to a junction at 3 miles (4.8 km) with the Bear Hill Trail. Next pass through a boat launch area and cross O'Donnel Creek at the lake's northern tip and begin hugging Elk's western shore. Traverse a grove of big timber and the horse beach before intersecting Bear Hill Road at 3.7 miles (6 km).

Go left on the road, coming to trail once again at a fishing pier at 3.9 miles (6.3 km).

The trail utilizes the old rail bed of the Victoria and Sidney Railway, which operated from 1894 to 1919. Under a canopy of greenery, pass by marshes and over small creeks, coming to a junction at 5.5 miles (8.6 km). Go left here on the lake trail through gorgeous old growth and along lakeshore ledges perfect for lounging. Ignore trails leading to

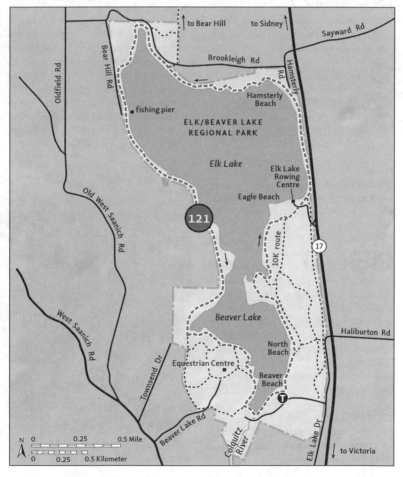

the right, to the equestrian center, and soon return to the 10K route at 6.3 miles (10.1 km).

Hike left, passing the small Colquitz River dam responsible for amalgamating the lakes. Cross a bridge by some filtering pools, returning to Beaver Beach and your start at 6.7 miles (10.8 km).

EXTENDING YOUR TRIP

Consider the short climb up adjacent 722-ft (220-m) Bear Hill for spring wildflowers and nice Saanich Peninsula views.

122 Mount Douglas

RATING/ DIFFICULTY	ROUNDTRIP	ELEV GAIN/HIGH POINT
****/3	2.6 miles (4.2 km)	695 feet (212 m)/ 745 feet (227 m)

Maps: NTS 092B06 Victoria, park map online; **Contact:** District of Saanich Parks and Recreation, Mount Douglas Park; **Notes:** Dogs permitted on-leash; **GPS:** N 48 29.774, W 123 20.079

Affectionately referred to as Mount Doug by the locals, this prominent Saanich Peninsula peak is one of the area's most popular recreation spots. Protected within a 449-acre (181.5-ha) park that includes Cordova Bay coastline, Mount Doug is traversed by quite a network of trails. Follow them to flower fields, old-growth groves, and some of the best views in the Capital Regional District.

GETTING THERE

From Victoria or Sidney, follow BC Highway 17 (Patricia Bay Highway) and exit onto Royal Oak Drive. Head east for 1.6 miles (2.6 km) to an intersection and continue straight, now on Cordova Bay Road. Turn left into the park at 1.2 miles (1.9 km) (just before the junction with Ash Road). Drive 0.1 mile (0.15 km) to the trailhead (elev. 50 ft/15 m) at the day-use area. Privy available.

ON THE TRAIL

Mount Douglas, like so many places throughout the province, was named for Guyana-born Sir James Douglas, second governor of the colony of Vancouver Island and first governor of the colony of British Columbia. Of Scottish, Creole, and African descent, Douglas lived a fascinating life in the fur trade, including as chief factor for the Hudson's Bay Company. He spent nineteen years at Fort Vancouver in Washington

Mount "Doug" offers great views over Haro Strait to the San Juan Islands.

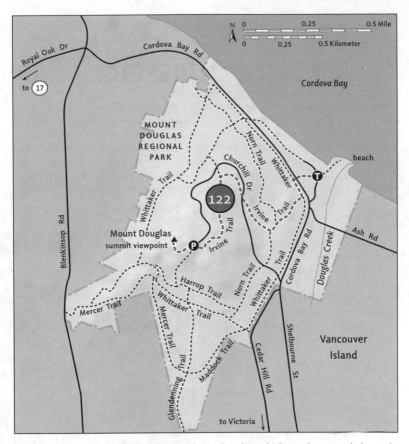

before founding Fort Victoria. This peak was originally known as Cedar Hill. When its name was changed to honor Sir James Douglas, *Hill* was also changed to *Mount* to honor the governor's status.

The park includes miles of trails—many unofficial, making navigation confusing. The Irvine Trail described here is well marked and should pose few problems. The easiest and least confusing route is via Churchill Drive, the park's summit road, which is closed to vehicles until noon each day, making it very popular with cyclists and runners.

Locate the Irvine Trail and begin hiking north. Carefully cross Cordova Bay Road and reach a junction in 0.1 mile (0.15 km) with the Whittaker Trail, in gorgeous old growth. Veer left and at 0.2 mile (0.3 km) veer right, ignoring side trails. At 0.4 mile (0.6 km), the Norn Trail merges with Irvine. The two trails diverge shortly afterward, where you go right.

Pass a swamp and begin climbing through impressive, towering Douglas firs. At 0.6 mile (1 km), cross Churchill Drive, traversing ledge outcroppings and transitioning into an oak-arbutus forest. Following arrows and signs, the way climbs more steeply now, skirting and negotiating open ledges. Pass many good viewing spots.

At 1.2 miles (1.9 km), emerge at a parking lot (elev. 650 ft/198 m) at Churchill Drive's terminus. Here join other hikers and runners on a 0.1-mile (0.15-km) paved path through rocky flower gardens to Douglas's open 745-ft (227-m) summit and its stunning 360-degree viewing. A large locater plaque will help you identify all of the sites in sight: the Gulf Islands, San Juan Islands, Mount Erie on Fidalgo Island, Mount Baker, Three Fingers, the Olympics, Sooke Hills, Gowlland Range, Malahat, Mount Work—the list goes on. The views of Victoria, Oak Bay, and the farms of the Blenkinsop Valley just below are wonderful too. Stay long or until it gets a tad bit crowded for comfort, then return to your vehicle.

EXTENDING YOUR TRIP
From the summit parking lot, consider descending on the Glendenning Trail and then taking the mountain-encircling Whittaker Trail back to your start. Carry a map and be prepared for a wrong turn or two. Take the short path down to the beach at Cordova Bay too.

123 Rithet's Bog

RATING/ DIFFICULTY	LOOP	ELEV GAIN/HIGH POINT
**/1	1.9 miles (3 km)	50 feet (15 m)/ 80 feet (24 m)

Maps: NTS 092B11 Sidney, conservation society map online; **Contact:** Rithet's Bog

Conservation Society; **Notes:** Dogs permitted on-leash; **GPS:** N 48 29.612, W 123 23.014

The last of seven bogs once found on the Saanich Peninsula, Rithet's Bog is a plant and wildlife oasis minutes from downtown Victoria. A domed (raised) bog, it was once drained and used for various agricultural practices. In 1994 it became a conservation area managed by the City of Saanich and restored and cared for by an active conservation society.

A lone Canada goose wades in Rithit's Bog.

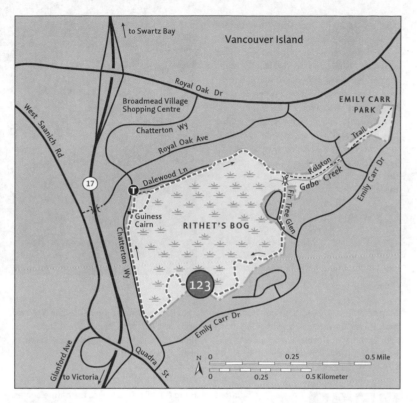

GETTING THERE

From Victoria or Sidney, follow BC Highway 17 (Patricia Bay Highway) and exit onto Royal Oak Drive. Proceed east 0.3 mile (0.5 km), passing the Broadmead Village Shopping Centre, and turn right (south) onto Chatterton Way. Drive 0.5 mile (0.8 km) and turn left onto Dalewood Lane at the trailhead. Park on the road. Bike rack available.

ON THE TRAIL

With its well-manicured, nearly level trail encircling its 94 acres (38 ha), Rithet's Bog can be enjoyed by hikers of all ages and abilities. It's a popular place with locals for evening walks and bird-watching forays.

Starting from the kiosk, head south and immediately come to a junction, interpretive sign, and memorial to the Guinness family, who donated this property to the city. Turn left and begin circling the bog, passing through thickets of willow, cottonwood, and spirea. Briefly walk on a sidewalk before returning to trail and traveling through fir and oak groves. At 0.6 mile (1 km), veer right at a junction; the trail straight heads to the small Emily Carr Park. Now cross Gabo Creek and briefly walk on Fir Tree Glen Road before resuming your trip on trail.

Skirt the cattail-rich bog and keep your eyes and ears open for birds and small mammals. Plenty of benches and interpretive signs along the way invite lingering. Red-winged blackbirds try their darnedest to drown out distant highway noise. As the trail bends back north, good views of wetland pools, usually teeming with ducks and geese, can be had. Mount Douglas rises in the background. At 1.9 miles (3 km), close the loop.

124 Swan Lake

RATING/ DIFFICULTY	LOOP	ELEV GAIN/HIGH POINT
**/1	1.7 miles (2.7 km)	Minimal/50 feet (15 m)

Swan Lake's floating bridge

Maps: NTS 092B06 Victoria, sanctuary map online; **Contact:** Swan Lake Christmas Hill Sanctuary; **Notes:** Partly wheelchair-accessible. Dogs prohibited; **GPS:** N 48 27.940, W 123 22.452

Once a foul, polluted body of water, Swan Lake is now a lovely urban nature sanctuary boasting a healthy avian population. Located in Saanich just minutes from downtown Victoria, the restored lake and surrounding marsh are graced with a nature center and family-friendly trails, which include a floating bridge.

GETTING THERE

From Victoria or Sidney, follow BC Highway 17 (Patricia Bay Highway) and exit onto McKenzie Avenue. Proceed east, turning right upon passing a pedestrian overpass onto Rainbow Street. Drive 0.2 mile (0.3 km) and turn left onto Ralph Street. After one block, turn right and immediately come to the trailhead, on the left.

ON THE TRAIL

Head 0.1 mile (0.15 km) to the nature center. Open year-round, it is full of displays, exhibits, live critters, and friendly staff. Kids will love it. You will too. Then head to the dock at the Lake Loop Trail. Scan the lake for ducks, geese, and in winter the occasional swan, and then set out for your hike around the lake, heading clockwise.

Pass the Aspen Loop Trail and a few paths leading back to the parking lot before coming to a major junction at 0.2 mile (0.3 km). The trail left leads to Christmas Hill, a noncontiguous part of the sanctuary. The now 148-acre (60-ha) sanctuary began in 1975 with help from the Nature Trust of British

Columbia, which has protected more than 170,000 acres (70,000 ha) in the province since its inception in 1971.

Continue right on a good and near-level trail, traveling through an emerald jungle before reaching open fields. Cross Blenkinsop Creek, a spur to another dock, and a couple of spurs that lead to the Lochside Regional Trail—an 18-mile (29-km) paved rail trail leading from Swartz Bay to Victoria and intersecting with the 34-mile (55-km) Galloping Goose Trail (see the "Take a Gander at the Galloping Goose Trail" sidebar).

Undulate between field and thickets and the occasional boardwalk. Round the lake's southern shores and enjoy views of Christmas Hill in the background. Pass spurs leading to Saanich's municipal offices, and traverse a nice grove of cottonwoods before crossing Swan Creek. Pass yet another spur before coming to the hike's highlight—a

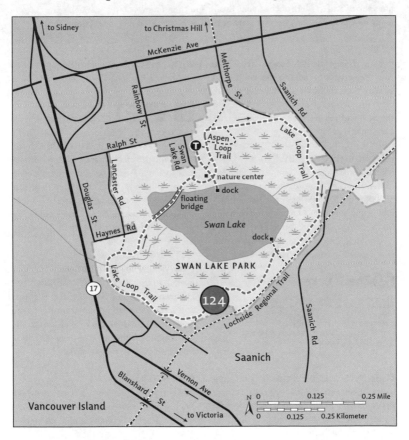

TAKE A GANDER AT THE GALLOPING GOOSE TRAIL

British Columbia's lovely capital city is traversed by kilometers of excellent and scenic urban trails. One of its finest and most famous is the Galloping Goose Trail (www .gallopinggoosetrail.com), where flocks of runners, walkers, hikers, and cyclists can be spotted year-round. Named after a 1920s gasoline-powered passenger car, the Galloping Goose Trail consists of both paved and gravel sections of a former rail line.

Beginning at the city's Upper Harbour, the trail spans the Gorge Waterway via the 985-foot (300-m) wooden Selkirk Trestle. Then it makes its way northwest, skirting Portage Inlet and Esquimalt Harbour, before traversing western suburbs on its way to wilder country. The trail traverses Matheson Lake and Roche Cove regional parks (Hikes 135 and 136), hugs the northern shore of the Sooke Basin, and then follows along the Sooke River to terminate 34 miles (55 km) from its start at the site of an old mining town, Leechtown.

floating bridge across Swan Lake. Take your time crossing, counting blackbirds and swallows en route. At 1.6 miles (2.6 km), close the loop at the nature center. Return to the trailhead, or consider a merry side trip up Christmas Hill.

EXTENDING YOUR TRIP

Follow the 0.5-mile (0.8-km) Corridor Trail to the 0.4-mile (0.6-km) Summit Loop Trail on 358-feet (109-m) Christmas Hill. A great hike any time of year, Christmas Hill contains Garry oak groves and camas fields, offers nice views, and is home to endangered sharp-tailed snakes. Much to celebrate!

125 Thetis Lakes

RATING/ DIFFICULTY	LOOP	ELEV GAIN/HIGH POINT
***/2	3.2 miles (5.1 km)	500 feet (152 m)/ 250 feet (76 m)

Maps: NTS 092B06 Victoria, park map online; **Contact:** Capital Regional District Parks, Thetis Lake Regional Park; **Notes:** Parking fee May 1–Sept 30 (Can$2.25 in

2013, credit cards accepted). Dogs permitted on-leash; **GPS:** N 48 27.789, W 123 28.046

Established in 1958 as Canada's first nature sanctuary, the 2060-acre (834-ha) Thetis Lake Regional Park is one of the Capital Regional District's most popular outdoor recreation areas. The park offers swimming, paddling, and miles of multiuse trails—you won't be alone here. This loop around the two adjoined Thetis Lakes is a great introduction to this park.

GETTING THERE

From Victoria, follow Trans-Canada Highway 1 north to exit 10 (Burnside Road/Old Island Highway). Bear left on Old Island Highway and after 0.9 mile (1.4 km), turn right onto Six Mile Road. Drive 0.6 mile (1 km) to the parking area and trailhead (elev. 170 ft/52 m). Privy and bike racks available.

ON THE TRAIL

While throngs of hikers and runners take to this loop year-round, during the winter months it can be considerably quieter. In spring the forest floor and mossy surrounding ledges sport a wide array of showy flowers.

From the massive parking area, follow the Beach Trail 0.1 mile (0.15 km) to the sandy beach on Lower Thetis Lake, veering right to the Lower Thetis Lake Trail. Many official (signed) and unofficial (unsigned) trails radiate from this loop. You'll be sticking mostly to the lakeshore, with little chance of going astray.

With the Lower Lake on your left and impressive ledges and groves of firs and oaks on your right, begin your circumnavigation of the lakes. Watch for eagles, beavers, and otters. Pass several trails that head up to Seymour Hill (Hike 126) as you hike along on this wide and smooth, but up and down, trail that sneaks in some elevation gain. At

0.5 mile (0.8 km), reach some ledges (elev. 250 ft/76 m) that grant excellent lake views.

At 0.7 mile (1.1 km), after crossing a creek, climb ledges again and bear left at a junction. Soon afterward bear left once more, cross a bridge over a spillway, and walk across an earthen dam. Bear left at junctions again, reaching the Trillium Trail at a bridge over the narrow inlet that separates the lower and upper lakes at 1.2 miles (1.9 km). Left offers a shorter loop option. Continue right to circle Upper Thetis, immediately rounding a sunny ledge that overlooks the narrower and more cove-filled Upper Lake.

Cross another earthen dam and bear left at the Seaborn Trail junction, immediately coming to another junction at 1.5 miles (2.4 km). Left heads over a ledgy knob and right is easier walking—either way will work,

Shore hugging trail along the Lower Thetis Lake

as the two paths soon meet up again. At 1.8 miles (2.9 km), pass a trail to the right (north), soon crossing a creek in a quiet cove. The way passes a couple of trails that lead to Phelps Avenue, traveling along a narrow lake arm through big firs.

At 2.8 miles (4.5 km), after passing a quiet cove, reach the Trillium Trail once again. Pass a small beach and parking lot and spur trails leading to a peninsula, returning to the main beach where you started your loop at 3.1 miles (5 km). Return to the parking lot in another 0.1 mile (0.15 km).

EXTENDING YOUR TRIP

There are miles of trails and old fire roads in the park, as well as trails that connect to Francis/King and Mill Hill regional parks. Navigation can be tricky or fun, depending on your mind-set. There are good views from Mill Hill and Stewart Mountain and exceptional old growth at Francis/King. The

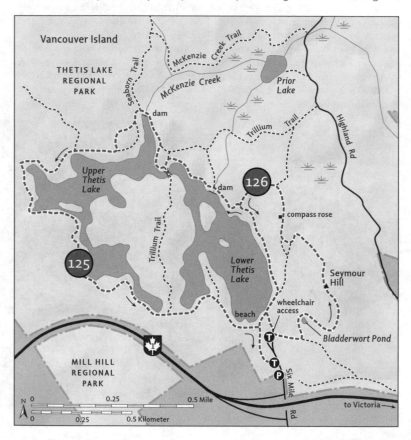

McKenzie Creek Trail along Prior Lake offers solitude and some impressive old-growth forest as well.

126 Seymour Hill

RATING/ DIFFICULTY	LOOP	ELEV GAIN/HIGH POINT
***/3	2 miles (3.2 km)	420 feet (128 m)/ 463 feet (141 m)

Maps: NTS 092B06 Victoria, park map online; **Contact:** Capital Regional District Parks, Thetis Lake Regional Park; **Notes:** Parking fee May 1–Sept 30 (Can$2.25 in 2013, credit cards accepted). Dogs permitted on-leash; **GPS:** N 48 27.789, W 123 28.046

Seymour Hill's compass rose

You can see a lot more from Seymour Hill than what you can see from the Thetis Lakes below. Amble through open forest across mossy ledges that transform into exquisite rock gardens in spring, and find a cairn sporting a compass rose that will help you identify the panorama of peaks before you. This short hike in Thetis Lake Regional Park offers a quiet reprieve from the busy lakeshore trails.

GETTING THERE

See directions to Hike 125. The trailhead for Seymour Hill is near the wheelchair access at the end of Six Mile Road (no parking).

ON THE TRAIL

From the parking lot, walk 0.1 mile (0.15 km) toward the beach, veering to the right to the wheelchair lake access, where you'll find a kiosk with trail and flower information. Then set off on the Dr. Lewis Clark Trail for a little discovery. Travel through an open forest of oak, fir, and arbutus, staying left at a junction at 0.2 mile (0.3 km). Soon afterward cross a cement dam that impounds Bladderwort Pond, and begin climbing in earnest.

Transition from parkland forest to open balds. Invasive Scotch broom is prevalent on these slopes, crowding out native flowering plants. The floral show here is still good—it could just use some broom eradication to make it even better and healthier. At about 0.7 mile (1.1 km), crest Seymour's 463-ft (141-m) summit for excellent views. Gaze below at the Thetis Lakes and out to Esquimalt Harbour, the Olympic Mountains, Sooke Hills, the Gowlland Range, and more.

Keep hiking, entering forest and descending, eventually reaching a junction (elev. 370 ft/113 m) in a gully at 0.9 mile (1.4 km). The trail left descends over some open ledges, returning to Lower Thetis Lake in 0.4 mile (0.6 km). Go right instead, steeply climbing, ignoring a path left. Soon come to the Seymour Hill cairn and compass rose (elev. 440 ft/134 m) at 1 mile (1.6 km). The views from this open knoll are excellent, and the cairn will help you identify what you're looking at—Mount Finlayson, Lone Tree Hill, Mount Work, Scafe Hill, and more!

After soaking up the scenery, continue hiking north, dropping steeply to a junction (elev. 230 ft/70 m) at 1.2 miles (1.9 km). The path right reaches the Trillium Trail in 0.2 mile (0.4 km), offering a longer loop option. Otherwise, turn left to reach the Lower Thetis Lake Trail in 0.2 mile (0.3 km). Then reach your vehicle by following this trail 0.7 mile (1.1 km) up and over ledges along the busy lake.

EXTENDING YOUR TRIP
Extend your loop by hiking 0.4 mile (0.6 km) to the Highland Road, and then walk the road 0.4 mile (0.6 km) to the McKenzie Creek Trail. Follow this pretty trail 0.9 mile (1.4 km) to the Seaborn Trail. Then turn left, heading up and over some ledges, and return to the Thetis Lakes loop after 0.4 mile (0.6 km). Continue left or right to return to the trailhead.

127 Lone Tree Hill

RATING/ DIFFICULTY	ROUNDTRIP	ELEV GAIN/HIGH POINT
****/3	1.5 miles (2.4 km)	475 feet (145 m)/ 1194 feet (364 m)

Maps: NTS 092B11, park map online; **Contact:** Capital Regional District Parks, Lone Tree Hill Regional Park; **Notes:** Dogs permitted on-leash; **GPS:** N 48 31.122, W 123 31.009

The lone fir tree that graced this peak in the Highlands for two centuries has been gone for a couple of decades now, but the sweeping views and

A lone snag is all that is left of the lone tree on Lone Tree Hill.

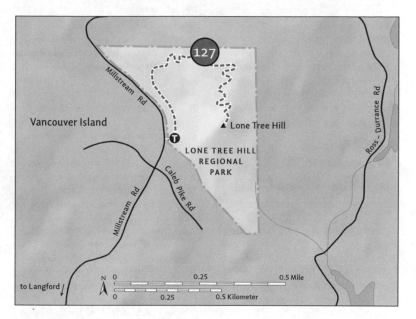

brilliant wildflower displays are as good as ever. This is a short hike with a big payoff.

GETTING THERE

From Victoria, follow Trans-Canada Highway 1 to exit 14 in Langford and turn right onto Millstream Road. At 3.4 miles (5.5 km), bear left at a Y intersection and then continue on Millstream Road for 1.6 miles (2.6 km) to the trailhead (elev. 720 ft/219 m), on the right. Privy available.

ON THE TRAIL

Under a thick forest canopy, begin on a wide and well-built trail. The way steepens after an easy start, slowing your pace. The surrounding forest is grand with a lot of big Douglas firs and arbutuses. In spring the forest floor is carpeted with enough shooting stars you'd swear you were witnessing a floral meteor shower.

Ledges soon punctuate the forest. At 0.75 mile (1.2 km), reach the open summit. Grassy patches tucked between worn ledges display showy blossoms—camas, shooting stars, and lilies in spring and early summer. The heritage lone fir that gave this peak its name is all but a mere gnarled stump now. A few lonely arbutus trees, however, tenaciously cling to life on this dry rocky peak.

The views are wonderful, especially of nearby Mount Finlayson, Mount Work, and the Gowlland Range. Views are good outward, too, to the Malahat, Olympic Mountains, and San Juan Islands. When you're tired of looking out, look up. Lone Tree Hill is a good place for watching raptors, ravens, and vultures ride the thermals. Next, look back the way you came as you retrace your steps to your vehicle.

EXTENDING YOUR HIKE

Just 0.7 mile (1.1 km) south of the Lone Tree Hill trailhead is the southern trailhead for the Ridge Trail in the Gowlland Tod Provincial Park, located 0.4 mile (0.6 km) off of Caleb Pike Road. The scenic Ridge Trail crosses over Holmes Peak to Jocelyn Hill (Hike 119) along the Finlayson Inlet.

128 Goldstream Provincial Park: Grand Loop

RATING/ DIFFICULTY	LOOP	ELEV GAIN/HIGH POINT
***/3	5.6 miles (9 km)	1110 feet (338 m)/ 510 feet (155 m)

Maps: NTS 092B05 Sooke, park map online; **Contact:** BC Parks, Goldstream Provincial Park; **Notes:** Dogs permitted on-leash. Loop not possible when Goldstream River level is high; **GPS:** N 48 28.793, W 123 32.899

A beautiful 1179-acre (477-ha) provincial park on the edge of metropolitan Victoria, Goldstream contains a salmon-bearing river, six-hundred-year-old forest, breathtaking waterfall (named Niagara no less), historical goldmine, campground, nature center, and miles of excellent hiking trails. This grand loop ties all of it together, making for an excellent all-day exploration.

GETTING THERE

From Victoria, drive 12.4 miles (20 km) on Trans-Canada Highway 1 to Goldstream Provincial Park, exiting onto Finlayson Arm Road. Immediately turn left into the park's day-use area and find the trailhead (elev. 30 ft/9 m). Privy available.

ON THE TRAIL

By far the most popular trails within this park are the short Visitor Center Trail and the arduous Mount Finlayson Trail (Hike 129). But Goldstream contains several other trails often ignored by visitors. Part of the problem is access. The park is bisected by busy Trans-Canada Highway 1, with barriers and unsafe crossings that limit approaches to trailheads and loop combinations. However, when Niagara Creek and the Goldstream River are running low, a grand loop can be made by safely crossing under the highway.

Begin by following the wide, graveled Visitor Center Trail along lush river bottomlands graced with towering cottonwoods and cedars. At 0.2 mile (0.3 km), the short Lower Goldstream Trail veers to the Goldstream River, offering opportunities for observing resident otters. At 0.3 mile (0.5 km), cross

The not as famous (but still pretty) Niagara Falls of Goldstream Provincial Park

Niagara Creek on a bridge. If the excellent kid-friendly Goldstream Nature House (www.naturehouse.ca) is open, consider heading straight 0.1 mile (0.15 km) for a visit.

For the loop hike, head left to a large culvert below Trans-Canada Highway 1. If the culvert is dry (Niagara Creek often takes a subterranean route here), walk through it and come to a trailhead (no northbound highway access). Here find a short path leading 0.1 mile (0.15 km) into a dank ravine to the base of impressive 156-foot (47.5-m) Niagara Falls. It's well worth the side trip.

For the loop, locate a path along the road barrier and follow it north, soon coming to the Gold Mine Trail. Start steeply climbing, crossing Niagara Creek on a bridge above the falls, where there is no falls view—but it's plenty audible. Fencing helps persuade the foolhardy not to risk getting a view.

The trail climbs steeply out of a narrow chasm, reaching a junction at 0.8 mile (1.3 km). The path right climbs to an impressive rail trestle over Niagara Creek (active rail line—stay off). You want to continue left through open forest. Reach a ledge (elev. 420 ft/128 m) with a growing-in view of Finlayson Arm, and then descend to an 1863-dug gold mine at 1.5 miles (2.4 km).

Traverse a steep slope (ignore a side trail left to a spring) before descending through attractive old growth, reaching a junction with the Arbutus Ridge Trail (elev. 90 ft/27 m) at 2.2 miles (3.5 km). Left leads a short distance to a trailhead and the unmaintained spur to little Hidden Spring Falls. Go right, ascending through a grove of big Douglas firs. Bear left at an unmarked junction and cross a creek. At 2.8 miles (4.5 km), come to a junction with the Arbutus Trail.

The going is easier right, so head that direction, cresting a 420-foot (128-m) ridge before

again reaching a junction with the Arbutus Trail at 3 miles (4.8 km). Go right again, reaching a campground spur at 3.2 miles (5.2 km). Bear left, skirting a wetland pool and entering a thick stand of arbutus (hence the ridge and trail name). At 3.5 miles (5.6 km), reunite once again with the Arbutus Trail (elev. 380 ft/116 m). Bear right, passing a historical survey cairn and steeply descending to a junction at 3.6 miles (5.8 km). Right leads to the campground. Go left, soon reaching the Prospectors Trail.

Continue left, paralleling the Goldstream River and steeply descending through luxuriant old-growth forest. At 4 miles (6.4 km), reach a bridge that spans the beautiful waterway just before a trailhead (elev. 120 ft/37 m) on busy Trans-Canada Highway 1. The trail continues on the east side of the highway. If the river is low, walk next to it below a highway bridge—otherwise, you'll need to cross the highway, which is extremely dangerous. Proceed rapidly and only if the highway is absolutely clear.

Resume hiking on trail, following concrete steps up a steep slope. Reach a junction at 4.2 miles (6.8 km) with a trail coming from park headquarters. Bear left, reaching another junction at 4.4 miles (7.1 km). Take the view loop right, climbing steeply through oaks, arbutuses, and flower gardens to a small ledge (elev. 510 ft/155 m) with limited views of the valley and Mount McDonald.

Then descend. returning to the Prospectors Trail at 4.6 miles (7.4 km). Now gradually descend, passing an old mine bore and entering an ancient forest with some massive firs. At 5.2 miles (8.4 km), stay left at a junction with a trail that leads to the Mount Finlayson Trail. Reach your trail's end on the Finlayson Arm Road at 5.4 miles (8.7 km). Turn left and walk the road 0.2 mile (0.3 km) back to your vehicle.

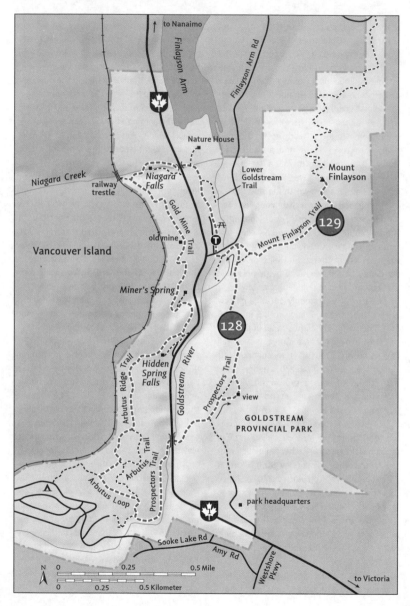

to Nanaimo

Finlayson Arm

Finlayson Arm Rd

Nature House

Lower
Goldstream
Trail

Mount
Finlayson

Niagara Creek

railway
trestle

Niagara
Falls

Mount Finlayson Trail

129

Gold Mine Trail

old mine

Vancouver Island

Miner's Spring

128

Arbutus Ridge Trail

Hidden
Spring
Falls

Goldstream River

Prospectors Trail

view

**GOLDSTREAM
PROVINCIAL PARK**

Arbutus
Trail

Prospectors Trail

Arbutus Loop

park headquarters

Sooke Lake Rd

Amy Rd

Westshore Pkwy

to Victoria

N

0   0.25   0.5 Mile

0   0.25   0.5 Kilometer

129 Mount Finlayson

RATING/ DIFFICULTY	ROUNDTRIP	ELEV GAIN/HIGH POINT
*****/5	2.6 miles (4.2 km)	1395 feet (425 m)/ 1375 feet (419 m)

Maps: NTS 092B05 Sooke, park map online; **Contact:** BC Parks, Goldstream Provincial Park; **Notes:** Trail requires scrambling on open ledges with steep drop-offs, potentially dangerous for inexperienced hikers and in wet weather. Dogs permitted on-leash, but not advised; **GPS:** N 48 28.732, W 123 32.770

A well-known Victoria-area landmark and one of the most climbed peaks on Vancouver Island, Mount Finney, as the locals like to call Finlayson, is no walk in the park. Rocky, brutally steep, and with most of the trail a mere route up at-times exposed ledges, this hike should only be attempted by strong hikers comfortable with scrambling. The payoff for those who reach the top, however, is grand: sweeping views of the Malahat, Saanich Peninsula, Victoria, and a whole lot more—plus dazzling wildflowers from spring through summer.

GETTING THERE
See directions to Hike 128.

ON THE TRAIL
From the parking area, walk a short distance east on the Finlayson Arm Road through a magnificent grove of ancient cedars. Cross salmon-bearing Goldstream River and pass the Bridge Trail, coming to the Mount Finlayson trailhead at 0.2 mile (0.3 km) (note: there's no parking here).

Read the warning sign (there'll be more along the way) and begin your ascent. Immediately bear left at a junction with the Prospectors Trail and steadily ascend a ravine cloaked in old-growth timber. At 0.4 mile (0.6 km), bear left at a junction with a connector trail that leads back to the Prospectors Trail.

Steeply climbing on a wide and well-used path, crest a gully lip and drop steeply 50 feet (15 m) to a bridged crossing of a creek (elev. 425 ft/130 m). Then head straight up a steep slope entangled in gnarled and potentially ankle-twisting roots. Next the trail resembles a steep, rocky, dry (or not) creekbed.

At 0.8 mile (1.1 km), the trail bears left, leaving the old rocky creekbed to begin an even steeper ascent as it approaches bulky,

Much of the trail up Mount Finlayson is on smooth, steep ledge.

ledgy, and domed Mount Finlayson. Follow the blue arrows and orange markers to stay on course as you scramble up jumbled rocky sections, and up and along polished (slippery when wet) steep-at-times ledges.

Clusters of oaks cling to pockets of soil between rocks and beneath cliffs. In spring, camas, satinflower, monkey flower, and other brilliant blossoms brighten the mountain's gray façade. Views increase as you slowly and gingerly work your way up this hulk of a peak. However, you'll be too busy watching your footing to fully admire them.

After negotiating a narrow, steep crevasse, you're granted a reprieve from arduous ascending with some real tread on a sane grade. Pass through a cluster of arbutus and pine and make one final grunt up a fairly easy ledge (at least by comparison). At 1.3 miles (2.1 km), but feeling like twice that distance, reach the 1375-foot (419-m) rounded summit. Now enjoy the views!

Look over the adjacent Bear Mountain mega–golf development to Victoria, Mount Douglas, Mount Wells, Mount McDonald, and the Sooke Hills. You can also see Mount Baker, the Olympics, and on a clear day—even Mount Rainier. Many of the San Juan Islands are also visible, including San Juan Island's Mount Finlayson—named for the same Hudson's Bay Company employee and Victoria founding father, Roderick Finlayson, that this peak is named for. But the US version is a much easier and gentler peak! Walk along the summit a little way west to spot the impressive rail trestle over Niagara Creek in the valley below. And prepare your knees and nerves for the arduous descent.

EXTENDING YOUR TRIP

A slightly longer and easier ascent of the mountain can be made from the north. From the main parking area, follow steep and narrow Finlayson Arm Road 1.9 miles (3.1 km) to this trailhead. Consider making a loop by walking the road.

130 Mount Wells

RATING/ DIFFICULTY	ROUNDTRIP	ELEV GAIN/HIGH POINT
*****/4	2 miles (3.2 km)	865 feet (264 m)/ 1155 feet (352 m)

Maps: NTS 092B05 Sooke, park map online; **Contact:** Capital Regional District Parks, Mount Wells Regional Park; **Notes:** Dogs permitted on-leash. Stay on trail to protect rare plants; **GPS:** N 48 26.855, W 123 33.292

A challenging hike up steep open ledges, Mount Wells gushes with gorgeous wildflowers and exceptional views. Stare down at the Humpback Reservoir below—and bulky Mount Finlayson rising behind it. Then cast your gaze east and south to Victoria and the Olympics, across the Strait of Juan de Fuca.

GETTING THERE

From Victoria, follow Trans-Canada Highway 1 for 10.5 miles (17 km), exiting onto the West Shore Parkway. In 0.2 mile (0.3 km), turn right at a roundabout onto Amy Road. After 0.5 mile (8 km), turn left onto Sooke Lake Road. In 0.2 mile (0.3 km), turn left onto Humpback Road and continue for 0.9 mile (1.4 km) to the trailhead (elev. 340 ft/ 104 m), on the right. Privy available.

ON THE TRAIL

Start hiking from the base of the Humpback Reservoir, which supplied Victoria with its

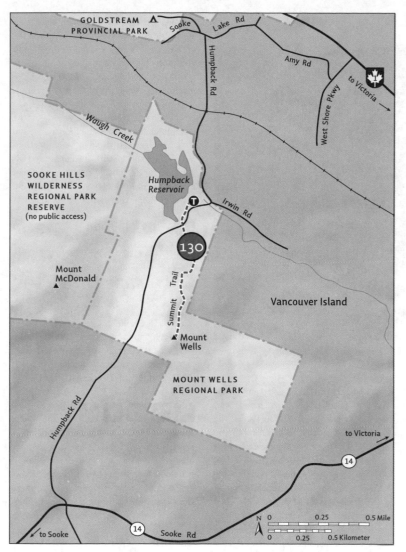

GOLDSTREAM
PROVINCIAL PARK

Sooke   Lake Rd

Humpback Rd

Amy Rd

West Shore Pkwy

to Victoria →

Waugh Creek

SOOKE HILLS
WILDERNESS
REGIONAL PARK
RESERVE
(no public access)

Humpback
Reservoir

Irwin Rd

130

Summit Trail

Mount
McDonald

Mount
Wells

Vancouver Island

MOUNT WELLS
REGIONAL PARK

Humpback Rd

to Victoria →

14

N

0   0.25   0.5 Mile

0   0.25   0.5 Kilometer

14   Sooke Rd

← to Sooke

drinking water from 1915 until the 1990s. Parallel the Humpback Road and climb stairs across the old water pipeline. Then carefully cross the road and the pipeline once again, and begin ascending steep slopes of open Douglas fir and arbutus forest.

Humpback Reservoir and Mount Finlayson from Mount Wells

At 0.6 mile (1 km), after passing an old trail, bend right, heading up very steep and rocky ledges that'll have you using your hands. The old, worn, and striated rock will make you think you're hiking in the Maritimes. Emerge onto polished open ledges lined with lodgepole pines, manzanita, oaks—and flowers! The blossoms are brilliant, especially in May. Camas, shooting star, and elegant satinflower transform Mount Wells into purple mountain majesty. Look for prairie lupine—found nowhere else in Canada. And watch the skies for vultures and raptors.

Railings protect you from cliff edges while also protecting the delicate flowers. At

0.8 mile (1.3 km), crest an open knoll (elev. 1000 ft/305 m) with excellent views over the greater Victoria area and out to the islands. Embrace them and continue, dropping into a small saddle (elev. 950 ft/290 m) before making the final climb to Well's 1155-ft (352-m) summit at 1.1 mile (1.8 km).

Savor more sensational views—to the Humpback Reservoir, Mount Finlayson, and Finlayson Arm north, and to Mount McDonald west in the closed-to-hiking Sooke Hills Wilderness Regional Park Reserve that encompasses Victoria's water supply. Delight in the blossoms that carpet the summit.

131 Witty's Lagoon

RATING/ DIFFICULTY	ROUNDTRIP	ELEV GAIN/HIGH POINT
***/2	1.6 miles (2.6 km)	150 feet (46 m)/ 140 feet (43 m)

Maps: NTS 092B05 Sooke, park map online; **Contact:** Capital Regional District Parks, Witty's Lagoon Regional Park; **Notes:** Dogs permitted on-leash but prohibited on beach June 1–Sept 15; **GPS:** N 48 23.346, W 123 31.479

Containing one of the finest beaches in the Capital Regional District, 143-acre (58-ha) Witty's Lagoon Regional Park also encompasses a gorgeous waterfall, a headland that bursts with spring wildflowers, and of course a lagoon—where more than 160 species of birds have been sighted. And did I mention the hiking trails too?

GETTING THERE
From Victoria, follow Trans-Canada Highway 1 to exit 14 and turn left onto BC Highway 14 (Veterans Memorial Parkway).

After 3.5 miles (5.6 km), turn left onto Latoria Road and continue 1.1 miles (1.8 km), turning right onto Metchosin Road. Drive 2.2 miles (3.5 km) to the park and trailhead. Privy available.

ON THE TRAIL

Stop by the nature center if it's open. Then start hiking along Bilston Creek, coming to a junction in 0.1 mile (0.15 km). You're taking the Beach Trail right, but the Lagoon Trail left is an excellent choice too (see Extending Your Trip).

Cross the cascading creek on a good bridge, soon coming to the railed edges of a large amphitheater bowl where Sitting Lady Falls plummets into the lagoon below. Via steps, steeply descend, passing big firs and old apple trees and coming to salt marsh traversed by a boardwalk. Now hike along Witty's Lagoon, noting its amazing diversity of birds—herons, oystercatchers, eagles, kingfishers, the list goes on.

The trail splits—go either way, rolling up and over some mounds that harbor gnarled firs and arbutuses. At 0.8 mile (1.3 km), reach the beach. Here on Parry Bay, views are excellent across the strait to the Olympics. At low tide, the flats are quite extensive, inviting walking and exploring. When you're ready, retrace your steps to your vehicle.

EXTENDING YOUR TRIP

You can easily walk north 0.25 mile (0.4 km) to the tip of the sand spit at the

Witty's Lagoon contains extensive tidal flats that can be explored during low tides.

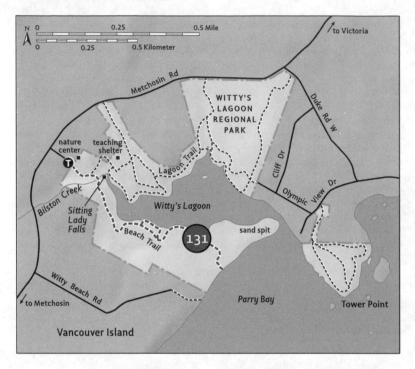

mouth of the lagoon, or south more than 1 mile (2 km) to Devonian Regional Park. At low tide, and if you don't mind getting your feet a little wet, you can make a great loop by first crossing Bilston Creek on tidal flats at the mouth of the lagoon. Then head 0.3 mile (0.5 km) to Tower Point, a flower-bursting headland also within the regional park. Walk back to your start first on the Tower Point Trail to Olympic View Drive, then along the road, and finally via the Lagoon Trail back to the trailhead. It's 1.3 miles (2.1 km) from Tower Point, with exceptional lagoon views and a great overlook of Sitting Lady Falls.

132 Pike Point and Iron Mine Bay

RATING/ DIFFICULTY	ROUNDTRIP	ELEV GAIN/HIGH POINT
***/1	2.8 miles (4.5 km)	80 feet (24 m)/ 120 feet (37 m)

Maps: NTS 092B05 Sooke, park map online; **Contact:** Capital Regional District Parks, East Sooke Regional Park; **Notes:** Open to horses. Dogs permitted on-leash; **GPS:** N 48 21.204, W 123 42.120

 *Follow an old logging road for an easy walk through thick timber to a*

pretty bay and a rocky headland. Come for the autumn hawk migration or year-round for stunning views across the Strait of Juan de Fuca to the Olympic Peninsula.

GETTING THERE

From Victoria, follow Trans-Canada Highway 1 to exit 14 and turn left onto BC Highway 14 (Veterans Memorial Parkway). After 2 miles (3.2 km), turn right, remaining on BC 14 (now Sooke Road), and follow it for 8.2 miles (13.2 km). Turn left onto Gillespie Road and continue for 3.4 miles (5.5 km), turning right onto East Sooke Road. Proceed 5 miles (8 km) and turn left onto unpaved Pike Road. Drive 0.1 mile (0.15 km) to the trailhead. Privy available.

ON THE TRAIL

The Capital Regional District's largest park, the 3543-acre (1434-ha) East Sooke Regional Park, protects one of the wildest stretches of coastline along the Strait of Juan de Fuca. It is ruggedly beautiful, home to bears, cougars, seals, and sea lions, and First Nations peoples and settlers have a long history with this land. There are more than 30 miles (50 km) of trails within the park, many of them demanding. This hike to Pike Point is one of the easier options.

Follow the old Pike Road Trail along a small creek through some big cedars and Sitka spruces. There are some big stumps too, attesting to the area's logging history. Shortly after crossing Pike Creek, come to the Anderson Cove Trail (Hike 133) at 0.6 mile (1 km). Continue straight, coming to another junction (elev. 100 ft/30 m) at 0.8 mile (1.3 km). The main road-trail continues straight for 0.2 mile (0.3 km) to a privy, beach access trail, and junction with the Coast Trail at an overlook of Iron Mine Bay.

Take the trail right instead, crossing Pike Creek. Soon pass a spur that drops to Iron Mine Bay, a wonderful place to explore when the tide is out. The main path continues on a rocky tread, climbing a little up and over ledges to Pike Point and its shore pines at 1.4 miles (2.3 km). The view is breathtaking, sweeping from Donaldson Island just offshore, to East Sooke Regional Park's rugged shoreline, to Washington's majestic Olympic Mountains and Juan de Fuca coastline. Return the way you came.

Looking east over Iron Mine Bay to Beechey Head

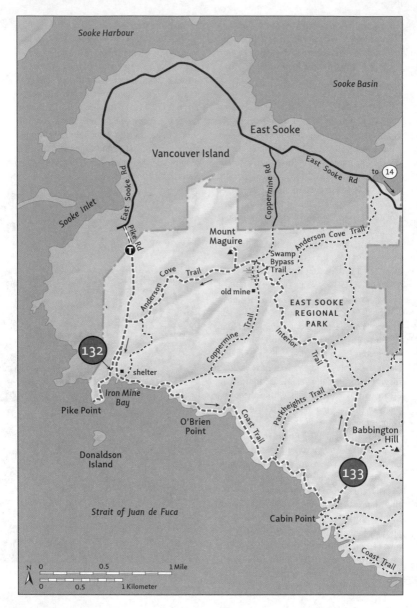

133 Coast Trail: Mount Maguire Loop

RATING/ DIFFICULTY	LOOP	ELEV GAIN/HIGH POINT
****/5	10.2 miles (16.4 km)	2600 feet (792 m)/ 879 feet (268 m)

Maps: NTS 092B05 Sooke, park map online; **Contact:** Capital Regional District Parks, East Sooke Regional Park; **Notes:** Some trails open to horses. Dogs permitted on-leash. Coast Trail can be dangerous in wet and foggy weather; **GPS:** N 48 21.204, W 123 42.120

🔰 🎿 🏠 *Hike a portion of the challenging Coast Trail, exploring hidden coves, rocky headlands, steep bluffs, and shoreline ledges. Watch for whales, including orcas, and an offshore pelagic cormorant roost. Then head inland for an equally challenging rolling ridge romp to Mount Maguire, highest summit in the sprawling East Sooke Regional Park— from where you can survey the rugged country you just conquered with your hiking boots.*

GETTING THERE
See directions to Hike 132.

ON THE TRAIL
The 6.2-mile (10-km) Coast Trail (which is actually closer to 7.2 miles/11.6 km) is one of the most beautiful and challenging trails in the Victoria area. If you can arrange a pickup, the entire trail makes for a great one-way journey. If not, it is far too taxing for most hikers as an out-and-back. This hike explores the western half of the trail, combining it with a climb over Mount

Maguire for an excellent all-day loop and cardiac workout.

Follow the old Pike Road Trail, passing the Anderson Cove Trail at 0.6 mile (1 km)—your return route. Continue straight, passing another junction. Reach a privy at an overlook of Iron Mine Bay and the start of the Coast Trail (elev. 75 ft/23 m) at 1 mile (1.6 km). Head left on the Coast Trail and kiss easy walking goodbye.

Pass a shelter, an interpretive display on past mining activity, and a trail leading to Mount Maguire. Your route hugs the coast, clambering over rocks and ledges that will slow your gait and allow for scenery savoring. The cumulative elevation gain on this hike is significant and hand usage frequent. The trail is well defined but easy to lose in foggy weather, especially on the rocky sections. Watch for yellow blazes.

Watch for eagles and kingfishers too, as you grunt up and over ledges, dropping to hidden coves and climbing to stunning headlands. Pass a small island just offshore and great views of the Olympic Mountains. At about 1.7 miles (2.7 km), after crossing a creek on a bridge, reach a junction with the Coppermine Trail, a road-trail offering a bailout from the Coast Trail if you need it. Otherwise, carry on forward, traversing impressive ledges over O'Brien Point and enjoying views back to Pike Point. Pass some big trees before coming to the eastern extension of the Coppermine Trail at 2.5 miles (4.2 km).

Drop into a couple of ravines before beginning a steep climb up some ledges (elev. 230 ft/70 m). Note a deep coastal chasm as Cabin Point now comes into view. At 3.4 miles (5.5 km), reach another bailout option—the Parkheights Trail (elev. 90 ft/27 m). Continue on the Coast Trail, exercising caution as you traverse exposed ledges above the shore. Begin a steep and difficult climb over a 180-foot (55-m) rib. Then steeply drop 100 ft (30 m) and steeply climb 100 feet (30 m)—repeat. A steeper climb warranting the use of your hands greets you next as you begin working your way up a 225-ft (69-m) coastal headland. Survey the wild coast with its myriad of rocky fingers and deep inlets. It bears a remarkable resemblance to Maine's Acadian coast.

Now moving inland and descending, come to the Babbington Hill Trail (elev. 130 ft/40 m) at 4.3 miles (6.9 km). Head left to begin circling back, first climbing a rocky route and then an old road to reach a junction (elev. 410 ft/125 m) at 4.8 miles (7.7 km). Go left on the Interior Trail, climbing up

The Coast Trail travels over a ruggedly beautiful wild coastline.

a grassy bald before descending slightly into a cedar grove. Then crest a notch in a ridge (elev. 560 ft/171 m), following an old road. At 5.5 miles (8.9 km), turn left at a junction (elev. 450 ft/137 m). Soon afterward, turn right at another junction lest you return to the Coast Trail.

Crest a 620-ft (189-m) knoll and then steeply descend to an alder flat (elev. 470 ft/143 m) before steadily ascending to a 700-foot (213-m) bald with limited views. Drop 150 feet (46 m), then climb 50 feet (15 m), drop 40 feet (12 m), climb 60 feet (18 m)—the terrain is a rough-and-tumble roller coaster. At 7.2 miles (11.6 km), reach the Anderson Cove Trail (elev. 550 ft/168 m). Right heads to East Sooke Road. Head left, cresting a 625-foot (191-m) ledgy knoll. Then drop to the Swamp Bypass Trail (elev. 550 ft/168 m) and shortly afterward reach the Coppermine Trail at 7.6 miles (12.2 km).

Continue straight on the Anderson Cove Trail, reaching another junction (elev. 610 ft/186 m) at 7.8 miles (12.6 km). If you have any energy remaining, go right 0.3 mile (0.5 km), up the steep Mount Maguire Trail, skirting the 869-foot (268-m) pine-cloaked summit to a (much appreciated) bench at a viewpoint of the Olympics across the strait.

Retrace your steps to the previous junction and follow the Anderson Cove Trail right, dropping 60 feet (18 m), then climbing 90 feet (27 m), and finally beginning a last descent. Follow the trail across grassy ledges and through thick understory before reaching an old road bed. After passing a lone giant fir and crossing Pike Creek, reach a junction at 9.5 miles (15.3 km). Go right, following the creek through big timber, reaching the Pike Road Trail (elev. 120 ft/37 m) at 9.6 miles (15.4 km). Your vehicle is an easy 0.6 mile (1 km) to the right.

Petroglyphs at Aldridge Point

134 Coast Trail: Babbington Hill Loop

RATING/ DIFFICULTY	LOOP	ELEV GAIN/HIGH POINT
*****/5	7 miles (11.3 km)	1800 feet (549 m)/ 755 feet/230 m

Maps: NTS 092B05 Sooke, park map online; **Contact:** Capital Regional District Parks, East Sooke Regional Park; **Notes:** Dogs permitted on-leash. Coast Trail can be dangerous in wet and foggy weather; **GPS:** N 48 19.595, W 123 38.296

Hike the eastern half of the challenging Coast Trail, exploring hidden coves, rocky headlands, historical sites, petroglyphs, and shoreline ledges. Watch for whales, including orcas. Then head inland to climb Babbington Hill for sweeping views of the Strait of Juan de Fuca and Olympic Moun-

tains. Shorter and easier than the western park loop, it's still plenty challenging—but packed with even more surprises.

GETTING THERE
From Victoria, follow Trans-Canada Highway 1 to exit 14 and turn left onto BC Highway 14 (Veterans Memorial Parkway). After 2 miles (3.2 km), turn right, remaining on BC 14 (now Sooke Road), and follow it for 8.2 miles (13.2 km). Turn left onto Gillespie Road and continue for 3.4 miles (5.5 km), turning left onto East Sooke Road. Proceed 1.2 miles (1.9 km) and turn right onto Becher Bay Road. Reach the trailhead (elev. 80 ft/24 m) at the road's end in 1.1 miles (1.8 km). Privy available.

ON THE TRAIL
While this loop is challenging, the hike just to Creyke and Aldridge points can be enjoyed by most hikers. Follow a gravel path through pastures and apple orchards of the old Aylard Farm. At 0.1 mile (0.15 km), come to a junction

with the 6.2-mile (10-km) Coast Trail (actually closer to 7.2 mi/11.6 km). A demanding path with many ups and downs and ledges requiring handholds, it is best done as a one-way hike (if a pickup can be arranged) or in sections as recommended here.

Wander down to Campbell Cove, passing big arbutuses and coming to a junction at 0.4 mile (0.6 km). The spur left leads 0.1 mile (0.15 km) to Creyke Point, providing exceptional views of Becher Bay as well as Christopher Point and Beechey Head, the southernmost points in western Canada. The Coast Trail turns westward here, passing inviting beaches along Becher Bay. At 0.6 mile (1 km), pass a trail leading to a picnic area and back to the parking lot.

Now walk either along the shore or on an easier parallel path in the old pasture—they eventually link up. Enjoy beautiful shoreline hiking. Stay left at a junction (the trail right returns to the trailhead), soon coming to Aldridge Point at 1.3 miles (2.1 km). On the shoreline ledges, look for two petroglyphs. One—a seal—is easy to spot. The other—a mystery—is more difficult to locate. Beyond this point, the Coast Trail gets more difficult, going up and down ledges that often have you using your hands to negotiate them. Be sure to follow yellow blazes, as routefinding is sometimes difficult, especially in fog. This trail is not at all advisable in bad weather.

At 2.1 miles (3.4 km), stay left at a junction and soon come to the 0.1-mile (0.15-km) spur to Beechey Head. It's worth the scramble, as views are excellent of the East Sooke coastline. The boundary reference monument may look familiar—it's similar to the ones at Iceberg Point (Lopez Island) and Turn Point (Stuart Island) (Hikes 31 and 61).

Now through windblown pines and dew-laden Sitka spruce, work your way up, over, and around ledges, headlands, and chasms. The going is slow and rough, requiring concentration and occasional handholds. At 2.3 miles (3.7 km), come to a shelter and a trail leading back to Aylard Farm. The Coast Trail continues left, traversing a bluff backed by towering cliffs. Look for seals and birds on the islands just offshore. Encounter more tough climbs around headlands and over ledges, while waves thunder in chasms below.

At about 3.4 miles (5.5 km), climb around a big chasm and formidable cliffs (elev. 120 ft/37 m). Drop to a junction with a trail leading to the Interior Trail at 3.6 miles (5.8 km). Stay left, skirting a hidden cove and coming to another junction with a link to the Interior Trail. Stay left again, soon coming to Cabin Point, with its restored historical cabin at 3.8 miles (6.1 km). The cabin—a trap shack—is representative of the many that were once found along this coastline, used by watchmen attending adjacent fish traps. The cabin has an interpretive display and will be welcome on a rainy day (no overnight use).

Now start climbing through thick salal and towering spruces. At 4 miles (6.4 km), say *arrivederci* to the Coast Trail, continuing straight on the Babbington Hill Trail. Climbing, reach a junction (elev. 410 ft/125 m) at 4.5 miles (7.2 km) with the Interior Trail. Go right, immediately veering right at another junction with the Endurance Ridge Trail, and continue climbing. At 4.6 miles (7.4 km), come to another junction (elev. 500 ft/152 m) and a must-do 0.6-mile (1-km) roundtrip side trip. Head left up ledges, veering right at a junction in a notch to reach Babbington Hill's 755-ft (230-m) summit. Walk around for the views, which include the nearby coastline and out to the Olympics and North Cascades.

Then return to the Interior Trail and continue hiking east, up and down and over ledges

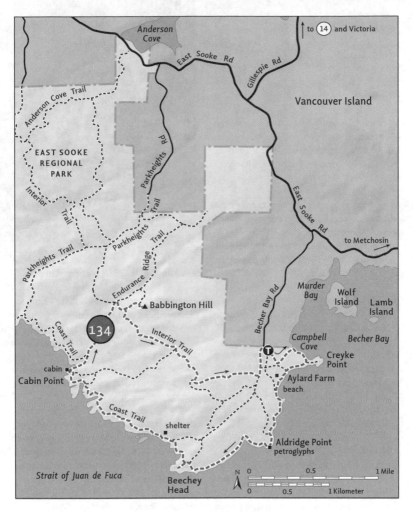

and through thick forest. At 5.8 miles (9.3 km), come to a junction (elev. 410 ft/125 m) with a road-trail. Right returns to Cabin Point. You proceed left, cresting a 500-foot (152-m) ridge and coming to another junction at 6.2 miles (10 km). Go left, steadily descend-

ing through impressive groves of big trees to a park service road near Aylard Farm at 6.8 miles (10.9 km). Go left, following this service road in trees, or take a path that veers to the right through pasture, returning to the trailhead at 7 miles (11.3 km).

135 Cedar Grove

RATING/ DIFFICULTY	LOOP	ELEV GAIN/HIGH POINT
**/2	2.9 miles (4.7 km)	150 feet (46 m)/ 225 feet (69 m)

Maps: NTS 092B05 Sooke, park map online; **Contact:** Capital Regional District Parks, Roche Cove Regional Park; **Notes:** Open to horses. Dogs permitted on-leash; **GPS:** N 48 22.452, W 123 38.007

Wander through an impressive grove of cedars sporting trees that are five centuries old. Then gallivant along the famous Galloping Goose Trail, gazing out upon Roche Cove and its dabbling ducks.

GETTING THERE

From Victoria, follow Trans-Canada Highway 1 to exit 14 and turn left onto BC Highway 14 (Veterans Memorial Parkway). After 2 miles (3.2 km), turn right, remaining on BC 14 (now Sooke Road), and follow it for 8.2 miles (13.2 km). Turn left onto Gillespie Road and continue for 1.7 miles (2.7 km) to the trailhead (elev. 75 ft/23 m), on the left. Privy and bike rack available.

ON THE TRAIL

Start by hiking the fern-lined Cedar Grove Trail, gradually ascending through patches of big firs and Sitka spruce. At 0.2 mile (0.3 km), bear left at a junction and then left again at another junction. The trails right lead, respectively, to the Galloping Goose and a nearly viewless viewpoint.

Now skirt a seasonal wetland, passing beneath some grassy ledges. At 0.5 mile (0.8 km), bear right onto an old road and climb

Galloping Goose Trail along Roche Cove

to another junction (elev. 225 ft/69 m) for the viewpoint at 0.7 mile (1.1 km). Continue forward and finally begin encountering cedars—soon many, growing in boggy draws between grassy balds. Some of these trees are quite impressive—and old too, exceeding five hundred years. There are some big old firs mixed in too.

The trail eventually bends south, descending beneath cliffs to the Galloping Goose Trail (elev. 100 ft/30 m) at 2 miles (3.2 km). Turn right and walk along this beloved rail-trail that travels for 34 miles (55 km) from downtown Victoria to the Sooke Hills. At 2.3 miles (3.7 km), pass a trail heading down to Roche Cove. The cove, like Roche Harbor on San Juan Island, is named for Richard Roche, third lieutenant on the British naval vessel HMS *Satellite*. The cove thrives with marine activity and birdlife, including migratory waterfowl in autumn. At 2.7 miles (4.3 km), pass a trail that leads back to the Cedar Grove Trail. Then pass good cove views, returning to the trailhead in 0.2 mile (0.3 km).

EXTENDING YOUR TRIP
Although the view is all but gone, the 0.4-mile (0.6 km) hike to the viewpoint is still pleasant. Better is the short spur from the trailhead west to Sooke Basin or the 0.7-mile (1.1-km) Matheson Creek Trail (flooded in winter) from Roche Cove to Matheson Lake.

136 Matheson Lake

RATING/ DIFFICULTY	LOOP	ELEV GAIN/HIGH POINT
***/2	2.4 miles (3.9 km)	200 feet (61 m)/ 210 feet (64 m)

Maps: NTS 092B05 Sooke, park map online; **Contact:** Capital Regional District Parks, Matheson Lake Regional Park; **Notes:** Dogs permitted on-leash; **GPS:** N 48 21.644, W 123 35.668

Hike around a pretty lake tucked between knolls of evergreens, maples, and oaks. Encounter too a lot of kingfishers and eagles—and fellow hikers, especially during the warmer months when Matheson Lake's inviting waters call for a postworkout swim.

GETTING THERE
From Victoria follow Trans-Canada Highway 1 to exit 14 and turn left onto BC Highway 14 (Veterans Memorial Parkway). After 2 miles (3.2 km), turn right, remaining on BC 14 (now Sooke Road), and follow it for 1.1 miles (1.8 km), turning left onto Happy Valley Road. After 4.3 miles (6.9 km), turn right onto Rocky Point Road and proceed 3.1 miles (5 km). Turn right onto Matheson Lake Park Road and reach the trailhead (elev. 170 ft/52 m) at the road's end in 0.9 mile (1.4 km). Privy and bike rack available.

ON THE TRAIL
A popular spot for swimmers, runners, and hikers, 388-acre (157-ha) Matheson Lake Regional Park and the abutting 402-acre (162.5-ha) Roche Cove Regional Park also serve as a glorious greenbelt for more than 2.5 miles (4 km) of the multiuse Galloping Goose Trail.

Follow the trail down to the beach and veer right, soon passing some sunny ledges with excellent views of the lake

Matheson Lake's waters invite a post-hike swim.

and its little island. Cross a creek on a long boardwalk through thick vegetation. Then continue through forest interspersed with lakeside ledges. At 1 mile (1.6 km), come to the Galloping Goose Trail. Go left on it, walking through a railroad cut on a bluff above the lake. At 1.2 miles (1.9 km), leave the Goose and resume walking on the Matheson Lake Trail.

Pass some big trees and stay left at a junction, soon coming to another junction at 1.4 miles (2.3 km), at the lake's outlet creek. The trail right (flooded in winter) follows Matheson Creek for 0.7 mile (1.1 km) to Roche Cove.

You want to continue left, crossing the creek and soon climbing steeply to a ledge (elev. 210 ft/64 m) that overlooks the lake. Descend on rough tread, passing a nice beach and several spurs to lakeshore ledges. Then continue along the south shore, going up and down and finishing the loop with a short, steep section, returning to the trailhead at 2.4 miles (3.9 km).

EXTENDING YOUR TRIP

Combine with Roche Cove by walking the Galloping Goose or Matheson Creek trails (see Hike 135).

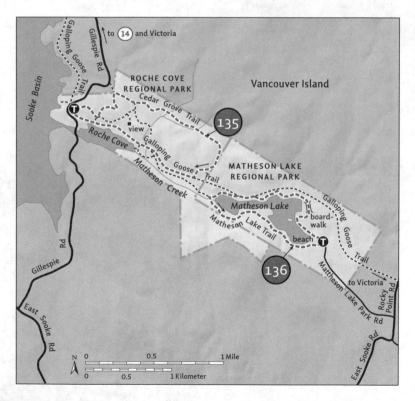

Contact Information

Anacortes Parks Foundation
(360) 293-1918
www.anacortesparksfoundation.org
and www.guemeschanneltrail.com
BC Parks
(250) 539-2115
www.env.gov.bc.ca/bcparks
British Columbia Waterfowl Society
(604) 946-6980
www.reifelbirdsanctuary.com
Capital Regional District Parks
(250) 478-3344
www.crd.bc.ca/parks
City of Anacortes Parks and Recreation
(360) 293-1918
www.cityofanacortes.org/parks.asp
District of Saanich Parks and Recreation
(250) 475-1775
www.saanich.ca/parkrec/parks
Friends of Lopez Hill
www.lopezhill.org
Gabriola Land and Trails Trust
www.galtt.ca
Galiano Club
(250) 539-2175
http://galianoclub.org
Galiano Conservancy Association
(250) 539-2424
www.galianoconservancy.ca
Galiano Island Parks and Recreation
http://crd.bc.ca/galianoparks/trails.htm
Gulf Islands National Park Reserve
(250) 654-4000
www.parkscanada.gc.ca/gulf

Islands Trust Fund
(250) 405-5186
www.islandstrustfund.bc.ca
Lummi Island Heritage Trust
(360) 758-7997
www.liht.org
Mayne Island Conservancy Society
(250) 539-5168
www.conservancyonmayne.com
Metro Vancouver Regional Parks
West Area Office, (604) 224-5739
www.metrovancouver.org/services
/parks_lscr/regionalparks
Pender Island Parks and Recreation
www.crd.bc.ca/penderparks
Penelakut First Nations
(250) 246-2321
www.penelakut.ca
Rithet's Bog Conservation Society
www.rithetsbog.org
Salt Spring Island Conservancy
(250) 538-0318
www.saltspringconservancy.ca
Salt Spring Island Parks and Recreation
(250) 547-4448
www.crd.bc.ca/ssiparc/parks
San Juan County Land Bank
(360) 378-4402
www.sjclandbank.org
San Juan County Parks
(360) 378-8420
www.co.san-juan.wa.us/parks
San Juan Island National Historical Park
(360) 378-2240
www.nps.gov/sajh

San Juan Islands National Monument
Bureau of Land Management Spokane
District Office
(509) 536-1200
www.blm.gov/or/resources
/recreation/sanjuans

San Juan Islands National Wildlife Refuge
(360) 457-8451
www.fws.gov/washingtonmaritime
/sanjuanis

San Juan Island Trails Committee
(360) 378-4953
http://sanjuanislandtrails.org

San Juan Preservation Trust
(360) 468-3202
www.sjpt.org

Skagit County Parks and Recreation
(360) 336-9414
http://skagitcounty.net

Skagit Land Trust
(360) 428-7878
www.skagitlandtrust.org

Snuneymuxw First Nation
(250) 754-7893
www.newcastleisland.ca

Swan Lake Christmas Hill Sanctuary
(250) 479-0211
www.swanlake.bc.ca

Thetis Island Community Association
www.thetisisland.net

Washington Department of Fish and Wildlife
(360) 445-4441
http://wdfw.wa.gov

Washington Department of Natural Resources
Northwest District
(360) 856-3500
www.dnr.wa.gov

Washington State Parks
(360) 902-8844
www.parks.wa.gov

Whatcom County Parks and Recreation
(360) 733-2900
www.co.whatcom.wa.us/parks

Conservation and Trail Organizations

Anacortes Parks Foundation
www.anacortesparksfoundation.org
www.guemeschanneltrail.com
Deception Pass State Park Foundation
www.deceptionpassfoundation.org
Friends of Lime Kiln Society
http://friendsoflimekilnsociety.org
Friends of Lopez Hill
www.lopezhill.org
Friends of Moran State Park
http://friendsofmoran.com
Friends of the Forest
www.friendsoftheacfl.org
Gabriola Land and Trails Trust
www.galtt.ca
Galiano Conservancy Association
http://galianoconservancy.ca
Habitat Acquisition Trust (Victoria)
www.hat.bc.ca
Islands Trust
www.islandstrust.bc.ca
Keepers of the Patos Light
www.patoslightkeepers.org
Lummi Island Heritage Trust
www.liht.org
Mayne Island Conservancy Society
www.conservancyonmayne.com

The Mountaineers
www.mountaineers.org
The Nature Conservancy
www.nature.org
Nature Trust of BC
www.naturetrust.bc.ca
Pender Islands Conservancy Association
www.penderconservancy.org
Rithet's Bog Conservation Society
www.rithetsbog.org
Salt Spring Island Conservancy
www.saltspringconservancy.ca
San Juan Preservation Trust
www.sjpt.org
Skagit Land Trust
www.skagitlandtrust.org
Spring Trust for Trails
http://springtrailtrust.org
Swan Lake Christmas Hill Nature Sanctuary
www.swanlake.bc.ca
SWITMO (Skagit-Whatcom-Island Trail Maintaining Organization)
www.switmo.org
Washington Trails Association
www.wta.org

Recommended Reading

Casey, Rob. *Kayaking Puget Sound and the San Juan Islands*. 3rd ed. Seattle: Mountaineers Books, 2012.

Conover, David. *Once Upon an Island*. Woodinville, WA: San Juan Publishing, 2003.

Glidden, Helene, and Michael McCloskey. *The Light on the Island*. 50th anniversary ed. Woodinville, WA: San Juan Publishing, 2001.

Kahn, Charles. *Salt Spring: Story of an Island*. Madeira Park, BC: Harbour Publishing, 2001.

Mueller, Marge, and Ted Mueller. *British Columbia's Gulf Islands Afoot and Afloat*. Seattle: Mountaineers Books, 2000.

———. *San Juan Islands Afoot and Afloat*. 4th ed. Seattle: Mountaineers Books, 2004.

———. *Washington State Parks: A Complete Recreation Guide*. 3rd ed. Seattle: Mountaineers Books, 2004.

Vouri, Mike. *The Pig War: Standoff at Griffin Bay*. Seattle: Discover Your Northwest, 2013.

1% for Trails & Washington Trails Association

Your favorite Washington hikes, such as those in this book, are made possible by the efforts of thousands of volunteers keeping our trails in great shape, and by hikers like you advocating for the protection of trails and wild lands. As budget cuts reduce funding for trail maintenance, Washington Trails Association's volunteer trail maintenance program fills this void and is ever more important for the future of Washington's hiking. Our mountains and forests can provide us with a lifetime of adventure and exploration—but we need trails to get us there. One percent of the sales of this guidebook goes to support WTA's efforts.

Spend a day on the trail with Washington Trails Association, and give back to the trails you love. WTA hosts over 750 work parties throughout Washington's Cascades and Olympics each year. Volunteers remove downed logs after spring snowmelt, cut away brush, retread worn stretches of trail, and build bridges and turnpikes. Find the volunteer schedule, check current conditions of the trails in this guidebook, and become a member of WTA at www.wta.org or 206-625-1367.

Index

About the Author

Since relocating from New Hampshire to Washington State in 1989, award-winning guidebook author Craig Romano has thoroughly hiked the Evergreen State. He has logged more than 16,000 miles on the trail, from the San Juan Islands to the Salmo-Priest Wilderness. And he has put in a fair amount of time on British Columbia trails too, from Pacific Rim National Park Reserve to Kootenay National Park.

An avid hiker, Craig counts running, paddling, cycling, and protecting natural areas among his passions. Content provider for Hikeoftheweek .com, Craig has also written for more than two dozen publications, including *Adventures NW*, *Northwest Runner*, *Northwest Travel*, *Outdoors NW*, and *Seattle Met*. Craig is author of nine books and coauthor of three others, and he is is currently working on *Day Hiking: Mount Saint Helens* (Mountaineers Books) with Aaron Theisen. His *Columbia Highlands: Exploring Washington's Last Frontier* was recognized in 2010 as a Washington Reads book for its contribution to the state's cultural heritage.

Craig lives with his wife, Heather, and cats, Giuseppe and Mazie, in Skagit County, close to the San Juan Islands. Visit him at CraigRomano.com and on Facebook at "Craig Romano Guidebook Author."

MOUNTAINEERS BOOKS

SKIPSTONE   BRAIDED RIVER

recreation • lifestyle • conservation

MOUNTAINEERS BOOKS is a leading publisher of mountaineering literature and guides—including our flagship title, *Mountaineering: The Freedom of the Hills*—as well as adventure narratives, natural history, and general outdoor recreation. Through our two imprints, Skipstone and Braided River, we also publish titles on sustainability and conservation. We are committed to supporting the environmental and educational goals of our organization by providing expert information on human-powered adventure, sustainable practices at home and on the trail, and preservation of wilderness.

The Mountaineers, founded in 1906, is a 501(c)(3) nonprofit outdoor activity and conservation organization whose mission is "to explore, study, preserve, and enjoy the natural beauty of the outdoors." One of the largest such organizations in the United States, it sponsors classes and year-round outdoor activities throughout the Pacific Northwest, including climbing, hiking, backcountry skiing, snowshoeing, bicycling, camping, paddling, and more. The Mountaineers also supports its mission through its publishing division, Mountaineers Books, and promotes environmental education and citizen engagement. For more information, visit The Mountaineers Program Center, 7700 Sand Point Way NE, Seattle, WA 98115-3996; phone 206-521-6001; www.mountaineers.org; or email info@mountaineers.org.

Our publications are made possible through the generosity of donors and through sales of more than 500 titles on outdoor recreation, sustainable lifestyle, and conservation. To donate, purchase books, or learn more, visit us online:

MOUNTAINEERS BOOKS
1001 SW Klickitat Way, Suite 201 • Seattle, WA 98134
800-553-4453 • mbooks@mountaineersbooks.org • www.mountaineersbooks.org

 Mountaineers Books is proud to be a corporate sponsor of The Leave No Trace Center for Outdoor Ethics, whose mission is to promote and inspire responsible outdoor recreation through education, research, and partnerships • The Leave No Trace program is focused specifically on human-powered (nonmotorized) recreation • Leave No Trace strives to educate visitors about the nature of their recreational impacts and offers techniques to prevent and minimize such impacts • Leave No Trace is best understood as an educational and ethical program, not as a set of rules and regulations • For more information, visit www.lnt.org, or call 800-332-4100.

OTHER TITLES YOU MIGHT ENJOY FROM MOUNTAINEERS BOOKS

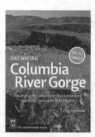

Day Hiking Columbia River Gorge
Craig Romano
100+ fabulous hikes in and around the
Columbia River Gorge Scenic Area—
plus the Portland region

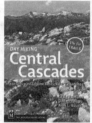

Day Hiking Central Cascades
Craig Romano and Alan Bauer
125 great hikes in the heart of
Washington State—including Lake Chelan

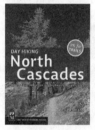

Day Hiking North Cascades
Craig Romano
125 glorious hikes in the North Cascades...
and the San Juans too!

Backpacking Washington
Craig Romano
70 overnight and multiday
routes throughout Washington State

Day Hiking Snoqualmie Region, 2nd edition
Dan Nelson and Alan Bauer
125 gorgeous hikes close to the Puget
Sound region—includes the Alpine Lakes

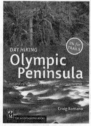

Day Hiking Olympic Peninsula
Craig Romano
125 excellent hikes on the rugged, wild,
and beautiful Olympic Peninsula—
coast included!